FUTURE HUMANS TRILOGY

Book 2—The Cosmic Architect Tools of Our Future Becoming

Return of the Avatars

Anneloes Smitsman Ph.D. **& Jean Houston** Ph.D.

Future Humans Trilogy
Book 2—Return of the Avatars: The Cosmic Architect Tools of Our Future Becoming
Copyright © 2022 by Anneloes Smitsman Ph.D. and Jean Houston Ph.D.

1st Edition, 2022
Editor: Diane Nichols
Cover Artwork: Sam Brown, "Dragonfly Spiral"
Cover Design: Anneloes Smitsman, and Steve Walters, Oxygen Publishing
Interior Design: Steve Walters, Oxygen Publishing
Illustrators: Anneloes Smitsman and Patrice Offman

Independently Published by
Oxygen Publishing Inc.
Montreal, QC, Canada
www.oxygenpublishing.com

ISBN:978-1-990093-40-1
Imprint: Independently published

Dedication

To the Future Self in each of us

PRAISE FOR
RETURN OF THE AVATARS

"As we awaken to our true reality, dormant supernatural powers and potential will become the norm. This book is prophetic."

~ **Deepak Chopra**, M.D. Author, *Total Meditation*,
Founder of the Chopra Foundation

"In the second installment of this ingenious trilogy, an allegory with all the revelations of a *New Age Game of Thrones*, heroine Rose uncovers many timeless truths in her quest to learn the mysteries of higher human potential. A mix of frontier science and ancient wisdom, *Return of the Avatars* also offers a practical set of tools for its readers to 'upgrade' into an evolved realm of being—which is more necessary than ever during these tumultuous times. Follow Rose into the heart of transformation and discover for yourself how to 'play better' at the game of life."

~ **Lynne McTaggart**, Author, *The Power of Eight*,
Architect of the Intention Experiment

"Science acknowledges that human behavior has undermined the web of life and that today's global chaos is a symptom of our own imminent extinction. A primary principle of both quantum physics and the new science of epigenetics is that consciousness creates our life experiences. Consequently, civilization's survival is predicated upon a radical change in our collective consciousness. Unfortunately, the innate conscious creative potential for most of the population has been disempowered before age seven by limiting, and self-sabotaging developmental programs. To survive through evolutionary chaos, we must first recover our creative powers. In *Return of the Avatars*, book 2 of the *Future Humans Trilogy*, distinguished visionaries Anneloes Smitsman and Jean Houston offer vital tools for accessing, activating, and empowering innate creative consciousness. *Return of the Avatars* is a profoundly important science-based guide for future humans to become Cosmic architects of a sustainable and thrivable world. Thankfully, Smitsman and Houston have transformed what would be a heady topic into an informative and entertaining parable, spiritual lessons as edutainment. I highly recommend this readable book as a valuable and empowering contribution in nurturing our evolving civilization."

~ **Dr. Bruce H. Lipton**, Ph.D. Author, *The Biology of Belief & The Honeymoon Effect,* stem cell Biologist, Pioneer in Epigenetic Science

"*Return of the Avatars* is a masterpiece that works on multiple levels to facilitate awakening in the most pleasurable and profound of ways. Interweaving story with sacred practices, this brilliant book is less a book than a portal, activating us to become conscious future creators. Thank you Anneloes Smitsman and Jean Houston for this roadmap. Your collaboration is a work of genius and a great gift."

~ **Dr. Sasha Siem**, Ph.D. Sound Alchemist, Singer, Composer

"This extraordinarily powerful sequel in the *Future Humans Trilogy* continues to share profound insights and way-showers for our cosmic destiny. Beyond reading, this is a book to be experienced and essentially embodied. Compassionately facing the shadow and trauma of our evolutionary journey thus far, the authors offer wise and practical tools for their and so our re-soulution. Empowering us at the inner depths of our being, they inspirationally support our hearing and aligning with the emergent impulse of the entire Universe and our planetary home Gaia; to arise to become their co-evolutionary partners and actualize our future human potential."

~ **Dr. Jude Currivan**, Ph.D. Cosmologist, Author, *The Story of Gaia: The Big Breath and the Evolutionary Journey of Our Conscious Planet,* Co-Founder of WholeWorld-View

"Few authors have the courage and skill to discuss the impossibilities of the human factor from the perspective of consciousness evolution, and to give hope at a time of crisis. Anneloes Smitsman and Jean Houston have that courage because they know that as we evolve, we can make the impossible of the previous stage of evolution possible in the next stage by using the exponentially growing complexity of consciousness evolution to our advantage. This genre-defying book captures this new potentiality and paints a powerful future with stunning insights and beautiful imagination."

~ **Dr. Mariana Bozesan**, Ph.D. Author, Integral Investing: From Profit to Prosperity, Full member Club of Rome, Co-founder & General Manager of AQAL Capital GmbH

"*Return of the Avatars* catapults us at quantum pace into a mytho-poetic journey of exploration and expansion of our fathomless inner capacities and of unfathomed cosmic realities. I found myself torn between devouring the pages at high speed in breathless fascination, and lingering to savor each word of this portable masterpiece. I have no doubt that this book will remain ensconced at my bedside table for years to come, so I can plunge into it over and over again to contemplate, apply, and integrate the incandescent wisdom and scintillating scientific innovations woven seamlessly into every chapter. Building on the wonder of *The Quest of Rose*, this book offers us an illuminating adventure into our possible future, and I wholeheartedly recommend it to questers of all ages."

~ **Dr. Rama Mani**, Ph.D. Co-Founder of Home for Humanity, Convenor, Enacting Global Transformation, Centre for International Studies, University of Oxford

"This much-anticipated book 2, *Return of the Avatars*, of the *Future Humans Trilogy* does not disappoint! The deep wisdom of scientist co-authors Anneloes Smitsman and Jean Houston illuminates and continues the engaging story of book 1, *The Quest of Rose*, following this young woman's exploration of her latent evolutionary potentials. As Rose deepens her self-knowledge and widens her planetary, solar system, and cosmological awareness, we follow her on this evolutionary path available to humans. Rose creates an evolutionary 'Cosmic Compass Game' with new roles for our Avatars, far beyond earlier models. These returning Avatars link humans' full range of experiences and potentiate our past, present, and future possibilities. They foster our long-held visions of our oneness, and with all other species and life, on a peaceful abundant planet, powered by the daily free photons from our mother star, the Sun. I loved this book and eagerly await the additional spiritual nourishment of book 3 of this powerful trilogy."

~ **Hazel Henderson**, Futurist, Evolutionary Economist, Author, *The Politics of the Solar Age: Alternatives to Economics*, Founder & President of Ethical Markets Media

"*Return of the Avatars* is a profound guidebook for exploring the deep societal transition that humanity is right now entering into. It helps us to experience and re-member who we are from our eternal bonds of life, as children of the evolutionary process and ancestors of the future. Nordic myths and indigenous wisdom are masterfully woven together with the latest scientific discoveries about the nature of consciousness and the systemic architecture of life. *Return of the Avatars* also gives you tools to decode and transform the harmful systems of dominance, beginning with ourselves, and change the ways we relate, and the why and how we play the game of life on planet Earth."

~ **Tomas Björkman**, Author, *The World We Create: From God to Market*, Founder of Ekskäret Foundation

"*Return of the Avatars* is like a guide book to imagining our fullest potential— except that the genius of these authors is their ability to inspire you to want to reach that potential. In this era of transformation and chaotic change, sometimes our most essential guidance comes through fiction. This book is a wondrous experience."

~ **Dr. Caroline Myss**, Ph.D. *Author, Intimate Conversations with the Divine*

"I am celebrating this evolutionary masterpiece! *Return of the Avatars*, book 2 in the *Future Humans Trilogy*, exudes creative genius, visionary insight, and archetypal pathways to navigate these liminal, evolutionary times of whole-systems transformation. The relatable, relevant, and real-time storytelling is brilliant. Grounded in new science and ancient spiritual wisdom, it leaves the reader with a peculiar sense of comfort and hope. The adventure and intrigue catalyze our innate capacities and quicken our gestating evolutionary potentials. From the Cosmic Compass to the Cosmic Mirror, we are invited into layers upon layers of teachings and tools that will induce higher states of consciousness, access the imaginal realm, and activate new codes and patterns. Bravo, Drs. Jean Houston and Anneloes Smitsman! *Return of the Avatars* is a magnificent, inspiring guide to consciously evolve ourselves and our world. With the turning of each page, we become equipped Cosmic architects of the future human we know is possible."

~ **Dr. Julie Krull**, Ph.D. Author, *Fractured Grace: How to Create Beauty, Peace and Healing for Yourself and the World*, Founder & President of GOOD of the WHOLE

Table of Contents

Introduction

Welcome to *Return of the Avatars*, the second book of the *Future Humans Trilogy*. The journey of the future humans continues and deepens as we are called to explore with them many essential lessons about power, unity, ego, shadow, hope, courage, and love. Whole new choices and possibilities open up by embarking on the next stage of the Future Humans Quest for the co-creation of a thriving world and planetary home for all.

The codes of the higher heart of humanity are called to awaken. Humans are gathering to change how the game of life is played on planet Earth. These codes are also awakening in Rose and her friends. The Cosmic Dragon returns to teach us essential lessons of the alchemy fire through the unifying wisdom of the higher heart. The wake-up call from Mother Earth is hitting home as the giants of domination and their archetypes start to feel the trembles that shake their guarded castles and ivory towers. And yet, many are resisting the call to evolve. Instead, they are spreading fear, confusion, and chaos. We have a choice. We can stop the programs of self-destruction and the harmful operating systems if we face the shadow within, and unite our powers through the higher heart of humanity.

The cry of our planet is loud and clear, but many still ignore her while under the hypnotic influence of the giants of domination and their weapons of disunity. Many people fight to regain their autonomy from the systems and cultures they want no part of, not realizing how the gamers of deception are so seductive that if we are not vigilant, we could fall into the arms of yet another giant.

Is Rose ready to take on these immense tasks and resist the seductive influence of her shadow? How will she prevent being overtaken by the powers that are awakening within and through her? Empowered with the discoveries of the Cosmic architecture of life and the knowledge of a unified universe, Rose now embarks on a journey to decode the systems, algorithms, and agendas of the economics of domination and the governance of disunity.

She calls us to join her, together with her friends. They are preparing to gather the teams of the future humans of the new era, as they discover how to co-create a thriving world that works for all, and evolve how humans play the game of life on planet Earth. But first she wants to share her story of what she discovered in confronting the giants, facing her shadow, and getting to know her ego, and how she came to befriend the Cosmic Dragon of the higher heart.

Will you join her now on this spell-breaking journey through *Return of the Avatars*, and answer the call of your higher heart? Once you do, know that a profound alchemical transformation will start to happen within you, which is why we've included seven Cosmic Architect Tools to support you through that process.

Explore and discover the whole new teachings, practices, and tools that this book offers. We have designed it to activate our personal and collective awakening through the further actualization of our future human potentials of the emerging new era. Times of trouble call for a deeper stimulation of reality from both sides of the veil, and this is precisely what happens through this next stage of the Future Humans Quest.

As you read, you'll be guided in ways you can develop your future human potentials and powers through the wisdom of the higher heart, the Cosmic heart. You'll receive the masterful support of our Cosmic friends, the Avatars from the Cosmic side of the veil who represent the higher orders of being of our innate Cosmic potentials. And when it may seem as if all is becoming too much, just ask Rose's young nephew Olaf to show you the Cosmic reset button that's hidden within for awakening from the hypnotic influence of the sleeping giants and radically evolving the ways the game of life has been played on planet Earth.

As with our first book, the future humans of this trilogy are presented with fictional first names. They are archetypal characters we can all relate to. During their quest, they meet real-life people who are nonfictional characters, like the futurist and cosmologist Dr. Jude Currivan in *The Quest of Rose* and the futurist and evolutionary economist Hazel Henderson and integral investor Dr. Mariana Bozesan in the final chapter of this second book of the trilogy. The future human characters are again encountering real-life world events and places that are nonfictional. We chose this unique hybrid genre of allegory to express how this journey of the future humans belongs to all of us, and is thus not unique to us as the authors.

After *The Quest of Rose*, several readers asked us: "Is Jean the character Verdandi, and is Anneloes the character Rose?" The short answer is *no*. Verdandi and Rose are fictional characters with their own identities who each reveal and share aspects of the awakening future humans that live in us as the seeds of a new beginning—a new mythos for who we can become.

How to Work with This Book

We understand how challenging this transition time can be, especially when faced with growing uncertainties about our future and the state of our planet. That's why we've written this book to give you real-life support that can make a vital difference by reminding and guiding you how to bring forth the inner powers of your Cosmic potential. This book supports you to rise to the challenges of this time, and not be squashed by them. Especially as people become more stressed and reactive, thus increasing the potential for escalation, polarization, and violence. Uncertainty has a way of triggering deep-seated fears and survival patterns, which is precisely when the connective future humans patterning can provide essential life support.

Many of the old paradigm giants and world icons are trying to maintain their influence rather than evolve. They are resisting the ending of their empires and influence. The archetypes of domination have become the status quo in so many human affairs. Yet within all this, you hold access to powers that have never before been united in the collective human heart and have the potential for becoming a new kind of covenant for our species. Together we are weaving a new and unstoppable pattern of change and transformation, as long as we stand united in our care for the whole of life on the principle of our Cosmic driven Bond of Unity.

Read this book from your heart. Read it with your friends and family. Don't worry about trying to understand it all with your local mind; let the understanding emerge from a deeper place within you. Put on your favorite music while reading or listening, cook the lovely recipes that form part of the stories, and invite the wisdom that's behind these words to enter your life and kindle your heart. Notice what starts shifting within and around you as you work with the practices in this book. Observe how new and deeper synchronicities may start to manifest. And please remember to laugh, laugh, and laugh again. Especially when feeling triggered and annoyed with the authors, or when what you're reading is not as you'd expected or wanted it to be! Humor is one of the best medicines for dispelling tensions and opening our minds. Allow nurturing, healing time for the feelings that may emerge, including tears. Know that while you are reading or listening, you are not alone. We are always together in the fields of life, and now also in this story that is about all of us and the shifting roles we each play in the new story that is being born.

Thank your ego and shadow for their roles in *the story of you*, and for revealing the powers they seek to cultivate and claim. Before we begin, a little message in support of some of our dear old Cosmic friends. Whenever you encounter the Cosmic Dragon, please be kind to him. He is tired of being the scapegoat of our egos portrayed as a monstrous beast who needs to be fought and slain. He has witnessed for way too long the predictable human game of our obsession with power and our persistent desire to conquer the fire of life. Whenever the Cosmic Serpent slithers into your dreams, don't panic. She is simply reminding you of your own creative power. She can become a powerful teacher, when invited. Let's not bore the Dragon or blame the Serpent, or any of the other archetypes who are reminders of our greater Cosmic selves. Instead, rise to the occasion and become the future human you were born to be through the far more exciting possibilities that this book invites and opens the reader to.

For those of you who like to skip steps and read from the endings first, this trilogy unfolds sequentially. We thus recommend that you begin the journey with *The Quest of Rose*, if you have not already done so. If, however, you truly feel in your heart of hearts that *Return of the Avatars* is calling you first, or you are simply impatient and want to read this book now, then please do read the brief synopsis of *The Quest of Rose* below.

Synopsis from *The Quest of Rose*

The following synopsis serves as a refresher or introduction for those who haven't read *The Quest of Rose*. The main character of the trilogy is Rose, a courageous and bright, multicultural woman in her mid-twenties who was born in the Netherlands, after which she lived and traveled all over the world with her parents, including Southern Africa, Australia, the United States, and Iceland, where her grandparents are living. Rose studied evolutionary biology in New York with a keen interest in quantum physics, cosmology, and systems sciences. She loves to play her violin and had been working in a bookshop in Amsterdam until she became ill. True to her name, she represents a universal symbol of beauty, mystery, grace, and strength—a symbol of hope for our own transformation during times of chaos, death, and breakdown.

The Quest of Rose begins when she is admitted to the hospital with a very serious case of COVID-19. Doctors try desperately to save her life, and she realizes that she may not be able to make it. She reaches out to the Cosmic Mother who returns her to the Cosmic womb of life. The Cosmic Mother offers her the possibility of rebirth through a new cycle of time and consciousness. Her acceptance of this choice catalyzes a metamorphic transformation through which she discovers the Cosmic Keys of consciousness and a rebirth of herself and our world. When she passes beyond the veil, she discovers the Cosmic architecture of the Universe and the immortal digital alphabet of the Cosmic hologram of consciousness. Her view and understanding of reality and the nature of the physical world alter radically.

To integrate her profound awakening, Rose receives essential support from the wise magus Verdandi, her grandmother from her mother's side of the family. Verdandi is of Nordic and indigenous Sami descent. She comes from a long line of seers, wizards, alchemists, and shamans from the far north of Europe. She has been guiding Rose since she was a little girl, noticing the unusual abilities of the child and her Cosmic potentials for the architecture of a whole new world. Verdandi has the gift of deep insight in what is to come, and how to get ready for it. She instructs Rose in the teachings of the nine Cosmic Keys that her granddaughter discovered during her near-death experience. These are the Cosmic Keys of Conscious Choice, Imaginal Power, Cosmic Communication, Trinity, Paradox, Darkness, Self Awareness, Becoming, and Unity. Each key offers a vital perspective on the Cosmic architecture of life that is essential for the co-creation of the world of the future humans of this emerging new era.

Rose is also joined and supported by one of her closest friends, Sophia, who is a highly intuitive and committed young woman in her late twenties who's studying to become a medical doctor in the Netherlands. Sophia is of mixed Aboriginal Australian and Dutch descent. She is able to draw from her indigenous ancestral roots to join Rose in her Cosmic explorations of the new era of the future humans.

Then there's Olaf, Rose's delightful young nephew who is the son of her older brother Lucas living in Norway. Olaf carries the creative genius of the future human coders of the new world. He understands intuitively how to unfold the Cosmic Compass game that Rose discovered as a means to change the way humans play the game of life on planet Earth. Olaf's creative mind and purity of heart help us to pierce through all the complexity so we may discover the ways out of the labyrinth. In this second book, Rose, Verdandi, Sophia, and Olaf are joined by entirely new characters, Li and Diego, as the plot thickens and new dangers loom on the horizon.

In *The Quest of Rose*, we shared essential insights from the new paradigm sciences about the nature of reality, consciousness, and our universe. This forms the scientific foundation for the whole trilogy, which we summarized at the end of the first book. These vital new insights are essential for the co-creation of a world that is able to thrive, and for transforming the unsustainable systems, cultures, and mechanisms that are bringing us to the brink of collapse. Below is a brief synthesis of seven of these ground-breaking insights:

1. *The Universe exists and evolves as a single, unified entity, an undividable wholeness*—Life is a unified reality, whereby energy-matter and space-time are complementary informational expressions of consciousness that originate from deeper, implicate, and more subtle nonlocal orders of reality.

2. *Consciousness exists, creates, and evolves as a unified holographic field of life*—This field acts like a womb of life and is sentient, responsive, and communicative.

3. *The Cosmic architecture of the Universe is coded as a Cosmic hologram*—This Cosmic architecture in-forms as well as potentiates the process and evolution of creation through an "alphabet" of digits that fractal out into all levels of existence and interdependent relationships.

4. *The imaginal realm forms part of the Cosmic architecture of life*—The imaginal realm is cosmologically present in all living systems as the space to dream into the higher dream, and the means for evolving, transforming, and growing into our future becoming of higher and more integral orders of consciousness.

5. *Futures exist now as nonlocal information within the imaginal realm of consciousness attracting life to evolve and renew*—The future is enfolded in the present as nonlocal information in the superposition quantum state of simultaneous possibilities, which can be activated imaginally or through the transformative dynamics of present conditions of change.

6. *We can imaginally activate and attract our futures into being*—The imaginal state is essentially a future state of consciousness. We can consciously evolve by imaginally activating and attracting the future potentials of higher orders of reality into the embodied states of our local contexts.

7. *The Cosmic architecture of life is evolutionarily coherent and precisely tuned to actualize the potentials of consciousness*—By architecting with the Cosmic architecture of life, we can co-create evolution-arily coherent systems, cultures, and worlds that enable global consciousness to self-actualize and become self aware in the human experience.

Guidelines for Working with the Cosmic Architect Tools and Practices

Like its predecessor, this second book offers powerful real-life practices and systems for developing your future human potentials and powers. If you would like to go further and learn more, please check out our *Future Humans* courses, quests, intensives, and coaching sessions via our website.

Through this book you'll receive seven Cosmic Architect Tools that serve as universal archetypal wisdoms for developing your future human potentials and powers. As Cosmic Tools of consciousness, they belong to the realms of the beyond, and transcend any particular spiritual tradition. We've included ten transformative practices to support your process. Seven of these practices specifically focus on working with each of the seven Tools. Please read the guidelines below for how to work with these practices. Each chapter also contains an integration section at the end.

The practices have been designed to safely guide you through the activation and development of your future human potentials and powers. You can benefit from these practices by simply reading the story, and you may also choose to go deeper by applying these practices to your life. You can benefit by going through the material with others who are reading or listening to *Return of the Avatars* as well.

The practices range between 15 and 30 minutes, and can be repeated whenever required. There is no fixed order for these practices; you can create your own sequence. However, we recommend that you read the book in sequence, since each chapter is designed for specific activations and realizations. The following guidelines are recommended for receiving the full value from these practices:

1. As mentioned, you may go through these practices by yourself or together with others. When practicing with others, please respect each other's privacy and do not counsel each other. Allow for new insights and realizations to emerge naturally and as a consequence of the practice itself.

2. Create a quiet and safe place for going through the practices without interruptions. Give yourself the time and space to integrate your inner changes and to support yourself during times of transformation and healing. It is recommended that you drink a glass of clean water after each practice to support your body's integration.

3. Don't force or push your process. Allow it to unfold and emerge naturally. The deep work happens from the roots, which is often invisible. Honor and trust in the natural cycles of your inner growth, and lovingly acknowledge each step along the way.

4. Remember to ease expectations and tensions with laughter and humor. This is one of the most effective ways to achieve healing and transformation.

5. Audio recordings of some of the practices are available via www.futurehumans.world. You can also record your own voice by reading the practices out loud and then listening to your voice (with your eyes closed). Furthermore, you can ask a friend, partner, or family member to read the practices to you and you can enjoy the experience together. Please make sure that your voice (or the voice of the person reading this to you) is calm and soothing, and allows time between the words and sentences for you to experience what is shared.

6. Write down (or record) your experience in a personal journal for keeping track of the inner shifts and changes while going through the trilogy. This may include dreams, visions, ideas, feelings, thoughts, and new realizations that may emerge.

7. The practices have been designed to safely explore the higher consciousness states of your developing future human powers and capacities. If, however, you need additional medical or personal healing support, please consult a professional therapist, coach, or physician.

Now before you jump into the first chapter, take in a deep breath, hold it for a few seconds, then breathe out and relax. Bring your awareness to yourself, here and now. Wiggle your toes, gently shake your head, smile from your heart, and soften your mind. You are about to embark on a mythic, soul-stirring journey, which goes even deeper and further than *The Quest of Rose.*

Pause now for a brief moment to consciously and intentionally enter this next stage of the Future Humans Quest, knowing that many new discoveries and experiences await you. Become available to the mysteries that are woven through this book, including knowledge of ceremonies and initiations that have rarely been shared to this depth with the greater public before.

Take another deep breath in and out. Release any tension you may be holding. Relax yourself even further. Open, and now turn the page—of this book and of your life.

Anneloes Smitsman & Jean Houston

CHAPTER 1

Signs and Omens

The Cosmic Dragon

"It's 'code red,' Grandma! That's what the climate scientists are saying. Humanity has entered *code red*! How can I plan for my future if we're heading for collapse? How can anyone?" Rose's voice rises in despair.

Verdandi listens quietly to her granddaughter on the computer screen.

"What can we do to stop this insanity?" Rose brushes a stray curl from her forehead and snatches a tissue from the box beside her. "I want to take action! To do something! But I feel so helpless. The problems are overwhelming, and I'm only one person. How can I make a positive difference?"

"Your future is not lost, my darling. There's a lot you can do," Verdandi says. "Do you think you went through your death and rebirth for nothing? It's been almost eighteen months since that happened, and you continue to grow and shift in new ways every day. You're gaining wisdom; you're becoming stronger. And Gaia is strong, too. But you're right, the situation is grave."

"I know this information isn't new to you. You showed me early signs of this in nature when I was just a little girl. Still, it hit me like I'd fallen through thin ice when I heard it announced like that. All of my friends are upset and scared. A few of them have even threatened to take their own lives if our political and economic leaders are not willing to make the necessary changes. They don't see the point of continuing if life is nothing but chaos and catastrophe."

"Keep those friends close to you, love. Help them."

"How can I help them when they feel like their world is dying?" Rose wipes tears from her eyes and blows her nose.

Verdandi looks at her intensely and answers, "By reminding them that it's always in the times of trouble that new paths and possibilities open up.

Show them how they can connect with Gaia. Let them know that our ancient Mother of Life is there for them in their darkest hours. Show them the power of standing united in our care for all of life, and *not* the ending of their own lives. We've had enough martyrs already. It's time to create a new pattern of change."

"I can do that, but I still don't see how this will stop the people who are stealing our future. What's happening is wrong. The widening gap between the rich and the poor…the exploitation and plunder of our planet, and the manipulation of our lives. Our economic and political systems are rotten to the core. Why aren't the billionaires investing in the regeneration of our planet and the complete stop of fossil fuels? Why do we continue to invest in war and weapons, rather than world peace? Why does big pharma thrive on people getting sick and dependent on medicines? Why does democracy renew itself by creating winners and losers, always rejecting parts of itself? How can we stop the economic predators? And why have we given our democratic powers to economic politicians who act like puppets for big business?"

"Rant on, my love!" Verdandi exclaims. "Ride that dragon! Express yourself wildly! Let it all out. Do you think I haven't asked myself these same questions every day? And sometimes every minute?"

"I know you have," Rose says, "but were you aware that the biggest corporations also have a seat at the United Nations now? It's called 'public-private partnerships' or the 'new stakeholder capitalism.' That means that even the World Economic Forum—"

"The WEF?"

"Yes. The WEF, who represents many of these companies, has a say in global decision making, including what happens with our food."

"That's very troubling." Verdandi shakes her head. "So these companies are now driving what gets decided at the level of the United Nations."

"To some extent, yes. But worse, these companies sit beside representatives of our governments, but they haven't been elected by any of us. We have no democratic control over them. This privatization of global interests severely undermines our democratic rights. How am I supposed to stop people from destroying our future if I have no democratic means to do so?"

"Democratic rights and responsibilities? Since when do you take such an interest in politics?" Verdandi smiles at her granddaughter's passion.

"Since I started to understand what's behind 'code red' and our climate emergency. And the virus pandemic, the growing violence and divisions, the new forms of slavery, the killing of more than fifty percent of our biodiversity, the loss of fertility of so many life-forms, and the growing despair among my generation," Rose replies with a shaking voice. She grabs another tissue and wipes the tears of rage streaming from her eyes.

"Sit down and breathe," Verdandi urges. "You know a lot, and you've become razor sharp."

Rose becomes quiet for a moment. She tugs another tissue from the box. When she finally speaks, her tone is deliberate, her words crisp.

"Nature is regulated by checks and balances for what grows and who dies. Yet in our human systems, these balancing feedback loops are completely lacking. We decide what grows and who dies. And soon, the artificial intelligence programs will make the decisions for what grows and who dies. Furthermore, in classical economics, when growth goes exponentially, we call it 'progress.' Nothing in nature grows exponentially, other than viruses and bacteria, and then only until their host dies. If democracy cannot serve as a 'check and balance' for what gets decided, then who or what does? Do I need to travel around the world giving speeches like Greta Thunberg? Do I need to go on a hunger strike? What are my options?"

"Interesting," Verdandi says, deep in thought.

"That's all you've got to say about this? 'Interesting?' Don't you care? Doesn't this keep you up at night?" Rose is still fired up.

"Of course I care," Verdandi tells her. "And no, I don't let them steal my night's rest. These people have caused enough harm already, I won't let them take my precious time for sleep and dreaming. My mind belongs to me and the great Oneness. I said 'interesting' because I recently had a dream about you becoming a political leader for a new civilization. Who knows what the future has in store for you?"

"Me, in politics? No way. I hate politics. In any case, who'd listen to me? People will think I'm a crazy woman with unrealistic ideas who believes she can speak with the Cosmos."

Rose wants to discard Verdandi's suggestion, but she can't deny a strange attraction to the possibility. She also notices the presence of something deep and ancient awakening within her. It feels as if the presence is listening to

Verdandi through her. And it seems to know exactly what this dream is about. Rose ponders. *What if Grandma is right?*

"Do you really think we can stop the collapse of our world?" she asks aloud.

"That's the wrong question, my girl. Don't focus on whether or not we'll succeed; focus on the tasks at hand." Verdandi gets up from her chair. "Have I ever told you that I was almost called to be on the stage?"

Rose knows what's coming. Ever since she was a child, her grandma has done this routine with her from time to time to shift stressful energy. "What? I never knew that," the young woman responds, feigning surprise.

"Oh yes, indeed. I could have been a famous actress." Verdandi clears her throat dramatically, and starts to sing as if she's the lead character in a theater musical. "The world that is collapsing now was never made to last! The world that is collapsing now was never made to last! It was never made to last! It was never…maaaade…to laaaast." She pauses. "Oops, I woke the dog." Verdandi shrugs and continues. "It was formed long ago by those who wished to rule this Earth. They wanted to become like gods. But they lived on borrowed time, they lived on borrowed tiiiime!"

Rose joins in the song. "No, they lived on *stolen* time! They lived on *stolen* time."

Verdandi stops singing, turns, and opens her arms. She speaks in a commanding theater voice. "This world was stripped of life from its beginning. Death and disease spread to all who came under the influence of these humans and their voracious desire to dominate. Growing like a parasitic vine, they strangled the earth; sucked the life support right out of the planet. Don't try to avoid the collapse of *that* world. No! Let it be revealed fully. Expose this false promise for what it is: empty! Devoid of substance!" Verdandi is on a roll. She raises her arms to the ceiling and makes a sweeping gesture. "Gaia, release us from the clutches of falseness and deceit! Release us now!"

Verdandi lowers her arms, turns back to Rose, and says matter-of-factly, "Oh, and talk to my dear friend Hazel; she'll have a lot to tell you about this topic."

"Hazel Henderson? The famous futurist and evolutionary economist who's been exposing all of the economic lies?"

"Yes, of course, dear. Who else?"

"I had no idea you two were friends. I would love to talk with her. Could you please introduce me?"

"It would be my pleasure. I'm sure she'd love to talk with you as well, and she'll be able to teach you a great deal about the issues you feel so passionate about."

"Thanks, Grandma." Rose's mood perks up. Another thought occurs to her. "Have you heard from my mom lately?"

"No."

"I'm worried about her and my dad with all that's happening in the United States right now. I'm so glad I went to see them earlier this year. I wish I could've stayed longer. I'm exploring Dad's suggestion to start a Ph.D. program in the Netherlands."

"Aha, so you've finally made up your mind?"

"Not completely. I had a few talks with potential universities. I've given myself another month to make my decision because I also want to explore a business idea that I've been working on with my friend Li."

"Your dad must be happy that you're at least considering it."

"He is. But none of that really matters if nature is so out of balance. We're at the start of many dangerous escalation events caused by runaway climate change. People don't realize how the new 'normals' will be unlivable for so many." Rose's throat gets tight again as her anger rises. "Meanwhile, our so-called 'elected' leaders claim they're 'doing what they can.' Ha! They need to try harder!"

"Breathe, love, breathe." Verdandi speaks gently. "Go back to that night in the hospital when you slipped beyond the veil. Remember how you saw the earth cocooned?"

"Yes. I saw a huge cocoon enveloping the earth and each of us." Rose makes a figure eight infinity sign with her hands, then puts her arms together as if hugging the earth. She continues, "Around the cocoon, I saw beautiful butterfly wings of light, like Cosmic wings."

"Good, keep giving whatever needs to die and dissolve to that cocoon so it can become composted nutrients for the creation of new life." Verdandi pauses. "Could you hold on just a moment, love? I need to check on Dagaz out in the garden."

"Check on him? Why? Is he alright?" Rose asks.

Verdandi opens the window and spies her husband kneeling in the dirt with his back to her, peacefully weeding between the carrot and cabbage beds. Verdandi closes the window and returns to the computer screen.

"He's fine now, but he got himself into trouble recently," she explains to Rose. "The neighbor offered to prune the scraggly parts of the trees in the back by the fence, but Dagaz wouldn't hear of it. He had to prove to himself that he's still as fit as your brother, so off he went to get the ladder. Honestly, I don't know who's more stubborn, teenagers or men in their seventies. Maybe he's living out his second teenage phase."

"What happened?"

"I warned him! I reminded him that a good-sized raven and her partner have a nest up there. 'Do not disturb that nest!' I told him. 'I haven't seen the ravens up there in a while,' he insisted, and up the ladder he climbed. Whoosh! Out swooped the raven, and down he tumbled, right on his bum."

"Oh no!"

"He was alright. Just a little shaken. Next time I'll invoke Odin; that'll teach him. Odin is a great advocate of ravens, as you know. Or maybe I'll invoke Loki. He's very cunning."

"Invoke Loki. Then Grandpa will think you're just talking to your cat instead of the Norse trickster god." Both women laugh at the thought of that.

"I see that Loki tricked you too, if you think he's just my cat," Verdandi winks.

"Oh, Grandma!"

"Well, Dagaz may be stubborn, but I love him. He's been working hard all morning; he's probably ready for lunch. Hold on, I'll be right back."

Verdandi steps out the door and trots over to her husband.

The Omen of the Carrot Roots

Rose reflects on their previous discussion. She can't let go of her worries about the state of the world. *It's unjust and unfair, and far too big for me to change.* Verdandi returns with a big smile, slightly out of breath from her quick trip to the garden.

"All okay with Grandpa?" Rose asks.

"Oh, yes. This time it was all sweetness. He left the trees alone, which is just as well. Look at what he gave me." Verdandi puts an enormous carrot in front of the computer camera just as Dagaz enters the kitchen. The carrot has grown three roots that look like fingers.

"Hi, Grandpa!" Rose smiles. "That's quite a green thumb you have."

"Hey there, sunshine!" Dagaz beams. "I felt that you and your grandma should see that carrot since you two are always going on about the trinity."

"That reminds me, Rose," Verdandi interjects. "I need to tell you about the triple Goddess at some point, but that's for another conversation."

"Thanks for showing us the carrot, Grandpa. It's amazing," Rose says.

"It's not just amazing; it's the last sign I needed." Verdandi gives Dagaz a light kiss on his cheek. "Go wash up so we can have lunch." She turns back to her granddaughter's image on the screen. "One day soon you'll understand what I mean by that. Now it's time to begin the next phase of your training."

Verdandi's piercing eyes gaze at Rose with such intensity, they could have stirred the gods from their dreaming state. *There's that feeling again!* Rose thinks, meeting her grandmother's gaze. *That "presence," as if something or someone else is listening in on our conversation.*

Dagaz overhears what Verdandi just said and pipes in, "So you're going to teach her about the triple Goddess, huh? Isn't it about time you also teach her about the masculine side of life?" Dagaz turns to his granddaughter. "You'll love the masculine side, Rose. We barbecue a lot, and lift heavy things, and open pickle jars. Maybe a few other things."

"I thought you or her dad could teach Rose about that," Verdandi chuckles.

Dagaz protests, "Why do you always put it back on me when I give you a good suggestion? Like the other day when I suggested that it would be a fabulous idea if somebody did the dishes, and then you put me in charge of it. Don't I do enough already? Who do you think is opening all of those pickle jars?"

"Come here, sweet man." Verdandi gives him a big kiss on his lips. "Have no fear, our Rose is learning about the masculine as well as the feminine, even here right now. Now let me continue with her for a few minutes before lunch."

"Good luck, kiddo," Dagaz whispers to Rose as he starts to move toward the hall.

"Ready for your next training?" Verdandi grins.

"Do I have a choice?" Rose laughs.

"Of course not," Verdandi says teasingly.

Dagaz turns back toward the computer screen. "There you go, Rose. That says it all. Women make you think you have a choice, and yet we all know how they've always ruled the household, and our minds."

"Well..." Verdandi tells him, "we're good at it."

Dagaz shakes his head and leaves the kitchen. Verdandi and Rose give each other a meaningful look and burst out laughing.

"Now back to that carrot," Verdandi says. "Does it evoke any ideas in that creative mind of yours?"

"Actually, it reminds me of the Cosmic dream I had about the organ a little while ago. Remember? The one where I discovered a third keyboard higher up on the organ. I told you about it."

"I remember."

"Do you think it's all connected?" Rose asks.

"I do. You are ready to learn how to play the Avatar Keyboard," Verdandi tells her.

"That sounds interesting."

"Tell me again how you felt in your dream when playing this third keyboard?"

Rose thinks for a moment. "I felt like my entire life was lifted up into a higher order of reality. My consciousness expanded with additional abilities that I had no idea of prior to that. I discovered Cosmic harmonics that activated whole new possibilities."

Rose mimics the dream with her hands as if she's playing the organ while humming the harmonics of a Bach Fugue. When she finishes, she says, "The third keyboard activated the symphony of the spheres. It felt as if the keys of this keyboard had been carefully crafted by the Cosmic composers and architects from the worlds beyond this world. Worlds of much higher consciousness than our human world." Rose has a faraway look, as if she is back in the dream.

"Yes, those are the keys of the Cosmic Avatars."

"What's your definition of an avatar?" Rose asks curiously. "I know the 'avatar' concept in games where you make an icon with a name and image to represent you. But I have a sense that there's a lot more to that mysterious word."

"The word 'avatar' comes from the Sanskrit 'avatāra,' which is a concept in Hinduism that refers to the incarnation of divine qualities that descend into human form."

"Quite different from the avatars used in games then!" Rose laughs.

"Avatars are the main characters of myths, in their roles as guardians, helpers, and Cosmic agents with divine qualities and abilities," Verdandi continues. "In many ways, Avatars represent who we can become as Cosmic humans. That is, if we radically change our educational systems and get rid of the current factory modes of learning."

Rose recalls many heated debates with her grandparents about the role of education, and particularly Dagaz's warning that the present educational "factory learning" is killing the creativity and natural intelligence of children.

"I like the sound of these Avatars. Can I call on them for help?" she asks.

"Please do! And remember: you already have the Cosmic Avatar codes inside of you. We all do. For some, it will manifest and activate in this lifetime. While you're learning to become a human, another part of you is learning to become an Avatar. You feed and grow each other into being. Just like you represent yourself through an avatar icon in the world of games, your Avatar codes represent your Cosmic self in our human affairs."

"Aha! So an Avatar is a Cosmic interface!" Rose exclaims. "Now it makes sense."

"Tell me what you mean by that?"

"If we are Cosmic and physical beings simultaneously, then there must be an interface through which the feedback of one reality becomes the nourishment for the other. You always say that we also grow the gods, which means something in us turns our human experience into food stuff for the gods or Cosmic archetypes. Maybe the avatars of the gaming world reveal a principle that we unconsciously apply. In games and on social media, your avatar gives you a presence in this virtual world, which enables you to interact with others in that world. Yet, the avatar is not who you are; it merely represents you. Can the Cosmic Avatars help us to connect with these divine qualities in ourselves? Can we all develop our Avatar capacities, instead of worshipping a small group of people who we believe have exclusive access to the divine?"

"Yes, my girl," Verdandi confirms. "This collective awakening is often what is referred to as the 'spirit of the Age of Aquarius,' where the Divine no longer descends via just a few humans, but through the collective itself. Your Avatar capacities are your *interface* capacities, as you call them. They allow us to interface with more subtle realms of consciousness that can awaken in us a profound understanding and respect for the unity of life."

"Given that so many people are *not* experiencing this unity, is that what's been missing in our human development? Our Avatar interface?"

"That and more. Talk with your grandfather about it; he'll have many things to tell you. Now, let's thank the carrot before I include it in the stew for dinner later this evening. Enough talking, my girl. Go out and do something to get your thoughts off all of these world problems. You won't be able to solve anything with your mind twisted up with stress like that. Take a breath and step back into your creative self."

"Will do. Tell Grandpa to watch out for ravens."

"I'm pretty certain he will from now on, if he knows what's good for him. I love you and I'll talk with you soon."

"Bye. Love you, too."

Designing the Cosmic Compass Game

The Avatar conversation with Verdandi prompts Rose to get back in touch with her nephew Olaf. She wants to explore some of her new ideas for designing a Cosmic Compass game with him. The Cosmic Compass first came to Rose in a vivid dream many months ago. She saw it rise up from the dark waters of our collective unconscious with a luminous light that was not of this world. She then started to explore this compass further and discovered how it holds the coordinates for guiding us through the dark and difficult times by applying the Cosmic architecture of life.

Since that dream, Rose has been spending a few minutes each day connecting with her inner compass, and exploring the compass coordinates. The more she connects with this compass, the more she starts to realize how the Cosmic architecture of life is truly a navigational system.

After talking with Verdandi, she wants to see how she can include Cosmic Avatars in the game; maybe through special avatar symbols that people gain access to by solving key challenges in the game collaboratively. Rose wonders whether gamifying the hardest challenges of our world is not a more effective way to solve our climate crisis. Her mom had told her that the world-renowned inventor, Buckminster Fuller, had attempted to do something similar with his "World Game." She calls Olaf to get his perspective on a few ideas she's tossing around in her mind.

"Hey, Olaf, how's life?"

"Hi, Rose. Cool. How is it with you?"

"It's going well. Remember that talk we had about a Cosmic Compass game a while back?"

"Yeah."

"I have some new ideas that I'd like to try out with you."

"Sure. I have some ideas, too." Olaf smiles with sparkly eyes. "I'm curious to hear what you've come up with."

Rose starts by giving Olaf a full account of all the Cosmic architecture codes that she has included in the Cosmic Compass game since they last spoke. She also shows him the images she made for this. Olaf is more interested in the gaming elements. After a few minutes of listening, he interrupts her.

"But Rose, what can I *do* in the game? How do I unlock the game's features? Can I earn points to buy new avatars, or can I get a special game pass as a reward or what?"

"It's not quite like that. Yes, there will be rewards and new avatar powers, and a special game pass, but not by shooting or killing enemies in the game. This is not about battling for fortune, glory, or fame."

"Okay, but you're going to make it fun, right?"

"Yes, there'll be lots of fun, mystery, and adventure," Rose assures him.

"I want to hear more about that stuff."

"Well, I haven't coded the game with a game designer yet, so these are only ideas. I'm working on a grant application to get some funding so I can hire a game developer."

"Tell me your ideas, then." Olaf is not sure that Rose's concepts are going to work with his friends.

Rose takes a deep breath and enters deeply into her imaginal self. "Alright. Close your eyes, Olaf, and join me on this adventure. Are they closed?"

"Yes."

"Imagine receiving a mysterious invitation, with the following message: 'Welcome to the Future Humans Quest. You have been chosen to join a special task force of Cosmic agents, and the greatest inventors and artists of our time. News has gone out to all of the nearby galaxies that planet Earth is in great trouble. A team of the finest Cosmic agents has formed to help humanity in this most challenging quest. The regeneration of the entire earth is at stake, as well as the advancement of the human species. If we fail, we will lose the earth and we will be stripped of our human powers. We will fall under the full control of AI protocols for the future management of life on this planet. We must not fail. Earth needs you. Humanity needs you. But you will not be facing these challenges alone. You will be introduced to other volunteers from around the world you do not know yet. If you choose to answer this call, click the blue pearl and you will be given your first task.'"

Rose pauses for a moment to observe Olaf, who has his eyes closed and the biggest smile on his face. "Let me know if you choose to click the blue pearl."

"Yes," Olaf answers enthusiastically. "I accept the call. I'm in!"

"Welcome, Olaf! You have now been added to the task force for the Future Humans Quest. You will now move on to your first task. The compass on your avatar suit will be activated, which will help you navigate through the game. Start by clicking the little black dot at the center of your compass. Just nod your head when you've done this."

Olaf nods his head with vigor.

"Good. Now notice how when this black dot is 'on' you can see a web of interconnections. These look like fibers of light woven all around you and through the landscape. You may also notice how some of these fibers glow with different colors. Like the golden fibers, for example, which are fibers of time. You'll learn about this later in the game when you'll meet the Avatar time masters."

Olaf nods again.

"When your black dot is turned off, you won't be able to see these fibers, and you won't be able to advance through the game. You start the game by declaring your commitment, which then enters you into a small team of five players. When your team solves one of the game's challenges, these fibers of light will create a specific configuration in the form of a symbol that becomes visible on your avatar suit. This symbol connects you to the team of Cosmic Avatars who have come to Earth to help you. There are many different teams and many different symbols. Each symbol also gives you access to different levels, powers, and responsibilities in the game."

"This is so cool, Rose. Keep going." Olaf is enjoying this fully.

"One word of warning: If you abuse the powers of your avatar or stop collaborating, it diminishes the powers of your team, and your avatar symbol will glow less brightly. If you lose all of the powers, this will sever the connection with your Cosmic Avatar team, which then triggers more difficult game challenges for everyone in the game. It is therefore in everyone's best interest to keep helping one another in order to advance in the game."

"Also, when you cause harm to others, the fibers of light will prevent you from moving forward until you have acknowledged the damage and reversed the harm you or your team have caused. These fibers of light also serve as wires of information which let you know who are indigenous to this place and their customs, who are visitors like you, who are residents here from other countries, and the unique wildlife in this place, and their state of health. These fibers of light further tell you about potential dangers in this place, and the problems that need to be solved. Please know that each time you touch one of these fibers, it also becomes aware of you. Your presence and interaction then become part of the collective knowledge and memory of this place. Now get a sense of these fibers of light. Can you see them around you? Just nod your head if you do."

Olaf nods his head with a big smile.

"Now, move to the first fibers of light that are ahead of you. Touch the fibers gently and tell me what information they give you."

Olaf now adds his own imagination to the game and begins to co-create with Rose. This is precisely what she'd hoped for.

"I'm touching them now," he says. "Oh! They make a sound. I feel a little electric buzz moving through my body. There's a river appearing in front of me. The river is crying and speaking to me."

"What is it saying?" Rose asks.

"'I'm hurt. I can't breathe! My fish are dying.'"

"Ask the river to show you the root of the problem and what you could do to help solve it," Rose instructs him.

"It's showing me all these chemicals and soap," Olaf tells her. "This has caused all of these algae to grow. The algae are taking the oxygen from the water that the fish need. It tells me that I need to contact the water regenerators to heal the water." Olaf is seeing the game as if he is fully inside the game world now.

"Check with your team to see if any of them have these skills. If none of you do, touch the fibers again, and this will activate a screen where you can write a message to get the help you need."

"Done," Olaf says. "A regenerator team is on its way. Oh, what's that? The regenerator team says that they'll need access to a special mineral for cleaning the water, which they don't have. They're asking us to find this mineral in the Blue Mountains. How can we find these mountains?"

"Activate the compass on your avatar suit. This will give you compass vision," Rose explains. "You'll see the coordinates of the Blue Mountains."

"It works! Okay, I see the coordinates, but have no idea how to get there."

"Touch the compass rose. This will give you access to the Cosmic Avatars who have been assigned to your challenge. Let me know what happens next."

"Wow! Yeah, that works, too. A portal just appeared in front of me that can bring us directly to the mountains. Cool, I'm now with my team in the Blue Mountains. We're being greeted by a team of scientists who say they've been expecting us and are looking for the algae from our river. They're explaining how they'll need the algae for a technology they're working on to capture the greenhouse gas emissions from the atmosphere. It looks like the next challenge is about helping one another solve each of our challenges. I'm having fun. Can I keep going?"

"I'm really glad you like it, Olaf," Rose laughs. "Your mom is sending me not-so-secret messages on my phone to let me know that she has your dinner ready, but we'll continue the game again soon. Thanks so much for playing! Enjoy your dinner."

Getting Down to Business

A few weeks later, Rose takes the train to a board meeting of the company where she submitted her funding proposal for the Cosmic Compass game. It was her friend Li who gave her the idea to pitch the game to investors, and told her how to go about it. Li studied economics at the same university she attended in New York, and she trusts him, but she still feels nervous. She changed her outfit three times this morning before settling on what she would wear. Untamed curls had to be tugged and clipped into submission, with less than perfect results. Rose remembers her mother shaking her head while braiding her young daughter's hair every morning before school. By mid-morning, stray curls had always managed to free themselves. *Just like today.* Rose sighs. *Ah well. It'll be alright. I look professional.*

She works to calm her mind by focusing on the fast-moving landscape. She goes over and over the main points of her presentation in her mind. It's a lot to remember and she doesn't want to leave anything out.

The train glides quietly through the Dutch farmlands. She's never been in front of a corporate board before. It feels strange to ask people to fund her ideas. She's starting to regret listening to Li. Her thoughts are racing, and so are the butterfly feelings in her stomach.

Next life, I'm coming back as a cow. Graze, graze, and graze some more. Oh, wait. No. After that, the poor, innocent animals get slaughtered and eaten. Let's try another animal. A hawk, maybe? Then I can fly freely with the wind under my wings and glide over the earth safely from above. But what if all the forests disappear and I have no more place to build my nest? Hmm. Fish in the river? No, that won't work either. Good grief, isn't there any place safe from human hands these days? We definitely need a moral compass, and not just a Cosmic Compass! Rose ponders these feelings, which leaves her even more unsettled than she was before.

Since her last call with Olaf, it's become even more clear to her that the Cosmic Compass game should be designed as a quest; an exciting adventure with fun rewards of game tokens and real regenerative currencies, as well as quest bounties and treasures. She hasn't put all of these ideas into her proposal yet. First, she wants to test the water to see if this company is even open to her ideas. Li advised her to make certain that her proposal sounds professional and that her ideas sound business-like. She's not sure she succeeded. She pulls out the introduction she wrote and re-reads it as the train moves along the tracks:

The Cosmic Compass game has been carefully designed to:

1. Playfully guide people to discover collaboratively how we can resolve the multiple crises that are threatening the collapse of our world and planet.

2. Reveal the underlying unity of life and the interdependencies of our worlds, and how to make this work for solving our greatest challenges.

3. Help players think and act regeneratively by focusing on improving the conditions that support life to thrive, with expanding commitments to our future wellbeing.

4. Inspire stewardship for the things we share in common. Discover how we can become the future ancestors of new civilizations that place the wellbeing of life at the center of our intentions and actions, which are ecological by design.

5. Invoke a deeper desire to evolve our species consciously, while becoming wiser humans, through a sense of wonder, joy, and care for one another and the earth, as our common home.

Rose still feels nervous. *Oh, Li, I wish you were here with me right now to pitch these ideas. You'd do a much better job. I'm not an economist. I'm not a business person. I need a pep talk!* She decides to give her friend a quick call before arriving at the station. His voice on the other end of the phone sounds reassuring and calm.

"You've got this, Rose. Don't worry. You've been through far worse situations. If you survived death, you can certainly do this. Just picture these people being interested and helpful."

"What if they don't like my ideas?"

"They're busy people. If they had no interest in what you've come up with, they never would've called you for this interview. Just remember, be succinct. You have to catch them in the first 3 minutes of your pitch. That's when the decisions are made. Watch for their body language. You can do this. Call me when you're finished."

Li has been a close friend for many years. Like Rose, he found a part-time job in Amsterdam after he finished his studies. Li was born and raised in China in a well-established, powerful family, as the oldest son. Traditional values are extremely important to his family, which includes all the etiquettes of what it means to be a "good son" and "doing right by your ancestors." In other words, many moral obligations, and not as much free will as Li would like.

Li studied economics, somewhat unwillingly, yet not wanting to let his parents down. They expect him to follow in his father's footsteps by taking over the family business, and to later settle somewhere near them in Hong Kong with a "nice, Chinese wife." His father runs a big financial wealth management fund and comes from a long line of Asian bankers and financial investors.

Li is groomed to keep the family fortune under Asian control, which is now expanding to Africa by financing major developments there. He feels reluctant about all of these expansions, and doesn't believe in the economics he learned about at the university, nor his family's company. In fact, he feels torn between the old corporate models and these wonderful new ideas he's heard about from Rose.

The train arrives at the station. Now all that's left is a short walk for Rose to arrive just in time for her board meeting. She brushes a loose thread from her skirt and heads toward her destination with determination.

"Coffee or tea?" the secretary asks politely as she enters the expansive lobby.

"Juice would be great, thank you," Rose answers.

"We don't serve juice. Coffee or tea?"

"Just plain water then." Rose tries to calm her nerves while waiting.

After a few minutes, the secretary returns and says, "You may enter now; the board is expecting you."

The Inner Dragon Awakens

Rose takes a deep breath and bounces into the room. The board members, seated around a large, imposing table, look bored. No one makes eye contact with Rose. One middle-aged man in an expensive suit seems preoccupied with his phone.

"Alright, let's hear it." The CEO motions to Rose to begin. She is a slender woman with a high-pitched voice, perfectly coiffed hair, and heavy make-up.

Rose clears her throat, recalls Li's encouraging words, and smiles warmly. No one notices. She shares her vision with passion and enthusiasm, but a few minutes into her presentation, she notices that the CEO's body language is not looking receptive. Rose had hoped that a CEO, who is a woman like herself, would be more supportive of her case, but it seems not.

The CEO sharply taps her manicured fingers on the table and says roughly, "I think we've heard enough of that. Show us where you've outlined the return on our potential investment?"

"What do you mean by a 'return on investment?'" Rose asks her.

"How do you intend to make money with your project?" an attractive young man in an expensive suit and tie inquires. "I'm Mike, the financial director here. We explained to you in the funding criteria that we require a majority of the company shares."

Rose doesn't think along those lines. "Company shares? You want to own my project?"

"Didn't you read the criteria?" the CEO asks. "Majority control is standard practice for investors. I'm surprised that an intelligent young woman like yourself would not have understood this. We like your ideas, and we may choose to help you get this project off the ground by funding the start-up costs, but not without a clear return on our investment."

"Why do you want so much control over my project?" Rose feels herself becoming more anxious.

"Because it's our money." The CEO looks annoyed. "We're not a charity. This is business. We want to minimize our risks."

"What about all of the financial losses that my project will prevent by helping to save our planet from human destruction? Big business is ruining my future and creating havoc for our planet!" Rose exclaims with a growing sense of indignation.

A white-haired board member with a thin mustache furrows his brows and frowns at her. A fleeting thought crosses her mind that she should rein in her feelings in front of these people, but she can no longer control the flood of strong emotions flowing through her.

"What's the return on investment for all the trees who have to sacrifice their lives in the name of 'progress' every day? Or the animals who no longer have a place to live because every acre of land is covered with concrete and high-rise buildings? I don't want you to control what I can do with my ideas. This compass is for all of humanity!"

"You're out of line, young woman," the mustache man grumbles. A few other heads nod in agreement.

But Rose's inner dragon is up in full force. She looks each of them in the eye. "Did any of you even read my proposal?" No one responds. Rose continues,

"Do you realize what's at stake here? Do you? We are 'playing' for the very survival of the human species in the game of life. If we lose this game, we lose our planet. We lose the chance to continue to exist! We've wasted so much time being too arrogant to admit that we've been destroying our planet and each other's future. There's no time for hesitation. We must take appropriate action. *Now!*"

"You've pitched your ideas to the wrong company," the CEO answers sternly. "As I said, we are not a charity, and without financial capital, your nice little ideas won't get far. If you don't like our conditions, then we have finished here."

Rose feels overwhelmed by a deep sense of injustice. She's overcome with a burning desire to expose the lies and manipulations of corporate greed and their abuse of power. She feels close to rage and is ready to spit fire. The intensity of these raw emotions takes her by surprise.

"You are exactly what's wrong with this world," Rose says sharply. "It's because of people like you and companies like yours that our world is in such a mess. Because of your corporate interests, I now have to fight for my future. You're the reason I developed this game: to get people to opt-in to the game of life and opt-out of the game of greed and control. You know what? Never mind. I'm going to develop my game with blockchain technologies." The board members look at her blankly. "I'll bet you don't even know what that means. Blockchain makes it possible to work transparently and in a decentralized way with open-source codes and smart contracts. In my project, I want multiple developers from around the world to be able to work together and be protected through a creative commons license. This 'central control' that you want is a thing of the past. These days everything is done through smart contracts."

"We've heard enough," the white-haired man declares, but the CEO waves her hand at him to be quiet. She leans forward to hear more about this.

"Smart contracts?"

"Yes," Rose says. "Digital agreements based on blockchain protocols that avoid the kind of corruption and control that kills so many new innovations."

"You're very outspoken," the CEO tells her. "How old are you?"

"Twenty-five. You would have known that if you'd actually read my CV," Rose answers sharply.

"No experience and idealistic. That explains why you chose to underdress for this meeting. Next time make the effort to appear more professional before lecturing us on how we should be running our business."

"I didn't come here to be judged about my looks."

"You clearly have no idea how things work in the *real* world." The CEO narrows her eyes at Rose. "You don't want to take my advice? Fine. That's a typical response for young people of your generation. You believe you know how to do everything better than those with more experience."

"There you go, insulting me again." Rose is fuming inside.

The man who'd introduced himself as the financial director cuts in. "Calm down, Rose. Ms. Van Heersen only wants to help you. She started out just like you and made her way to the top through hard-earned experience. Her advice is gold, even if you don't realize it yet."

"Thank you, Mike," the CEO replies coolly. "If only our young friend could come down off her soapbox and realize that." She pauses for a moment, looking at the fiery woman with bright eyes standing before her. "You are inappropriate and outspoken, but there's something about you that interests me." She turns to Mike. "I'll tell you what. Why don't you coach her on how to write a proper proposal?" She turns back to Rose. "And that's the last chance I'm willing to give you."

"That's a very generous offer," Mike says.

Rose still feels triggered. "Frankly, I don't see the point, but thank you for your…kind offer. You might want to consider hiring young, 'naive' people like me. You need a few members of this so-called 'idealistic' generation to bring you up to speed with where the world is going. I come from the future, and not the world that's dying."

The white-haired man and the middle-aged man seated next to him both scowl at Rose as they gather their things and leave the room with the other board members.

"I'll leave you here to wrap up matters with our little activist," the CEO tells Mike before rushing out the door to another meeting without a backward glance.

Rose watches her go. "I put months of work into that project," she says. "I prepared beautiful visual designs and a really strong game plan, none of which I got to present, just because I didn't include a section for a return on investment." She sighs. "I'm beginning to realize that my world of digital currencies, regenerative economics, and decentralized governance sounds like futurism to people like these."

Mike's eyes trace the shape of Rose's body as she speaks. He scans her hair, her neck, and the curve of her mouth. She doesn't notice, as she is still caught up in the energy of what happened in the meeting. He smiles a little too broadly, clears his throat, and straightens his silk tie. He has no idea what trouble he is getting himself into.

"Rose, can you stay for a few more minutes?"

"Okay, but why?"

"You do look like an intelligent woman, and you obviously feel very passionate about this." Mike picks up a folder containing her CV from the table.

"I am."

"I see here that you even have a Master's degree in Biology. Impressive. Oh, and you have a little bit of work experience. Too bad they didn't read this."

"Yeah," Rose agrees.

"Would you be willing to share with me your thoughts regarding a return on investment?"

Rose looks up. "Alright. I've detailed it here. Page ten of my proposal. It's not a return on investment in the traditional sense, since I didn't focus on profit for shareholders." Her voice becomes more enthusiastic as Mike appears to listen. "Instead, my focus is on value creation. I've also indicated the strategies for how we can develop collective leadership capacities and resources for investing in systems change, as well as the conditions for a thrivable future."

Mike nods. "Uh-huh."

"I want my project to create value for everyone, through fair allocation and value distribution that prevents wealth accumulation in the hands of a few. I've also included indicators in the game that help people to become aware of the carrying capacities of our planet, as well as the social and ecological ceilings."

"So you did give it some thought."

"I did! Your website says your company is committed to 'ethical investment' and 'sustainable development,' but apparently, you're not. Or maybe you're into greenwashing by using the disguise of sustainable finance as a cover for business as usual?"

Mike turns away briefly so Rose can't see how annoyed he is by that question and the fact that she appears to be more informed than he'd suspected.

"Right. Well…it's just semantics, isn't it, Rose?" He flashes her another big smile. "I have to go now, but I'll be happy to guide you in the rewriting of your proposal another time. Are you free tomorrow?"

Rose looks at Mike. He is an attractive man. He whips a business card out of his wallet and gives it to her, brushing her hand a little too long.

"Here's my number. Call me. Lunch tomorrow at noon. I'll pay," Mike says with a determined voice.

Rose feels uneasy, but she's also intrigued by what she may discover. "Okay Mike, let's have lunch so you can show me how to 'rewrite' my proposal, but not tomorrow. Meet me in Amsterdam this Saturday. There's a nice coffee shop where they make homemade carrot cake and the best fresh juices. I meet my friends there regularly on Saturdays. Will that work for you?"

"That sounds like a plan, Rose. I'll meet you there at 11am on Saturday. Send me the details later." Mike looks pleased.

Rose watches him leave the room. Her emotions are still churning because of the meeting. She looks at the business card in her hand and wonders if she's made a big mistake by accepting Mike's offer for lunch. As she walks back to the train station, she remembers her promise to call Li, but feels too upset to do that right now.

Special Delivery

Later that afternoon, Verdandi calls Rose to see how her meeting went. She doesn't have a good feeling about that company.

Rose is still burning with anger and feels deeply insulted. She gives Verdandi the full download of what happened. After a few minutes, her grandmother interrupts her. "Oh love, that sounds challenging. I'm sorry you went through all of that. But I do have something to cheer you up. When your doorbell rings, please answer it. I've arranged for a special surprise to be delivered to you."

"What is it?"

"Your favorite cookies! It was quite something to get them to you."

"Your timing is amazing, Grandma. I just heard the doorbell. It's a good thing you told me about the delivery because I wouldn't have answered it otherwise. I'm cautious these days."

"That's wise, my girl, but I'm sure you don't want to miss those cookies. They're being delivered by a trusted source, so you'll be safe. Go ahead and open the door."

"Alright, hold on a second. I'll be right back."

Rose races down the stairs, nearly tripping over her socks. Old Dutch houses are notorious for having impossibly steep and narrow staircases. She unlocks the door and flings it open, expecting to see the delivery man.

"Surprise!"

"GRANDMAAAA!!!! Oh my gosh! How is this even possible? How did you get here?"

"Hello, my love! By plane of course. I thought the boat would take too long." Verdandi chuckles while they give each other the biggest hug. "And here, as promised, are your favorite cookies, all the way from Iceland."

"I can't believe it!" Rose exclaims, taking the box of cookies. "I am soooo happy to see you. I missed you soooo much." She notices a large number of people behind her grandmother, smiling and talking in the street. "Who are all of these people looking at you?"

"You know how I am; I always like to share my joy. So, I may have given them a few cookies as well."

"I hope you didn't give them too many," Rose teases. "I can't believe you're really here in the flesh. Let me pinch you to see if you're real."

"Ach!" Verdandi laughs. "Don't pinch me too hard. I'm really here! Now will you let me in?"

Rose picks up her grandma's suitcase and ushers her into the apartment. While the two women climb the stairs, she says, "Does Mom know you're here? I can't believe she didn't tell me!"

"Only dear old Dagaz knows I'm here. I didn't tell anyone else because I didn't want anyone to try to talk me out of it. Ohh, this is a lovely place, Rose," Verdandi says, admiring Rose's small apartment. "It's light and cozy, and you've added a lot of charming touches. There's even a small balcony for your plants and herbs. And you have a lovely view of the canal. I like it."

"Thank you. I like it, too. I can't believe you're sitting here in my living room. It's the first time you've ever visited me in Amsterdam."

"That's what grandmothers do. I simply had to come. It's been way too long and I didn't know when you'd be able to travel to Iceland. Besides, you're going through so many changes. I was also given quite a few not-so-subtle nudges from the ancestors, but that's for later..." Verdandi says, with a mysterious twinkle in her eye.

"Well, I'm so happy you came. Let me pinch you again, just to make absolutely certain you're truly here."

"Better pinch yourself this time!" Laughing, the two women give each other another big hug.

"You can sleep in my bedroom, Grandma. I'll sleep here in the living room. The couch rolls out to become a comfortable little bed. You must be hungry after your flight. I have some apple pie left in the fridge and I can make you a warm drink. Would you like that? I'll eat your cookies, of course. Tea or coffee?" Rose asks.

"I think I'd like some juice," Verdandi smiles.

Rose quickly forgets about the challenging time she had earlier that morning. She is overjoyed to see her grandmother after more than a year. They spend the rest of the day catching up, laughing, cuddling, sharing stories, and enjoying their precious time together.

A few days later, after finishing a particularly delicious dinner, Verdandi brings up the subject of Rose's corporate meeting. She puts her hand on Rose's arm. "Now, tell me more about what happened in that meeting where you went to pitch your Cosmic Compass game. You never told me the whole story."

Rose shares the full account of all that happened with her grandmother, which only confirms for Verdandi why she felt so concerned.

"How did this meeting make you feel, my darling?" Verdandi asks gently.

"Like a powerful dragon who woke up from the dungeons after a very long time."

"That's the omen I've been waiting for. Have you experienced any further sense of this inner dragon and its energy?" Verdandi asks. "Your powers are growing. New alliances are gathering around you. Have you felt any other awareness of this recently?"

"Not really," Rose answers. "Other than feeling this huge fire burning in my chest and a fierce desire to blow up lies and manipulations. I felt quite triggered at that meeting, but I managed to control myself…somewhat. I feel like this anger in my belly is more than just my own anger. It's as if it also includes the anger of the earth and the ancient guardians. Oh, and I felt that presence again, as if something was witnessing what was happening through me."

"It is." Verdandi nods. "I'm glad I got here in time. Now let me tell you some more about the dragon you've been sensing."

The Cosmic Dragon and the Alchemy of Fire

Verdandi puts her red velvet scarf around her shoulders and takes a slow, full breath. She closes her eyes in deep contemplation, as if she is talking with something or someone. Even though Rose has seen her do this many times, it still intrigues her and rouses her curiosity; however, she has learned not to interrupt her grandmother when she does this.

"Okay, love, you felt your inner dragon rise when you became triggered by all the injustice and corporate greed, correct?"

"Yes."

"The pain of the world is now becoming a catalyst for awakening your mythic powers, although you don't realize this yet. And not just yours; the same is also true for many people around the world, even though they may not realize it either. The crisis of our world, including our climate crisis, boils down to primary lessons of fire, which certain members of humanity have persistently ignored, to the detriment of many. When the power of fire expresses only through the masculine or only through the feminine, and not the *unity* between the masculine and feminine that is within the Cosmic Dragon's heart, our powers become destructive and excessive. Fire itself is neither masculine nor feminine. That lady CEO you spoke of was expressing herself as the unbalanced masculine."

Rose nods. "Yes, she sounded like a harsh man in a woman's body, although saying that isn't really fair to men, as she was much harsher than my male friends."

Verdandi smiles. "The dragon as a mythic creature is androgynous, meaning it is both male and female. Hence, it is said that the dragon renews itself by eating its own tail, which means it can make itself pregnant by putting the male part of itself, its tail, into its feminine part, which is its mouth."

"Like the symbol of the Ouroboros!"

"Yes. The androgynous represents how in the beginning the creative powers had not yet externalized to become outwardly male or female. In those days, the powers were still unified within one body of consciousness. We are at the beginning of another cycle, a new beginning, so we'll see again the rise of the androgynous, and thus, also, the powers of the Cosmic Dragon."

"Is that why so many people say they feel both male and female these days? Or say they want to switch genders? And there are all of these gender variations?" Rose asks.

"Yes Rose, I believe it is. When the powers of the Cosmic Dragon awaken within us as our own dragon powers, it's a clear sign that ancient, inner, psychic forces are stirring up from the depths of the unconscious. These psychic forces are our primordial powers of creation that have not yet been filtered by the human mind. We are all called now to learn the lessons of the alchemical fire, or else we'll burn up our world and destroy our future."

"So that's why my heart has been feeling so hot lately!" Rose exclaims. "Go on, Grandma, please tell me more."

"In many of humanity's mythologies, there are stories that tell how fire came to humans from the world of the gods. Fire, as a creative force, turns destructive when the *power* of fire gets disconnected from the *consciousness* of fire; the classic duality trap for those who believe in the separation between matter and spirit. A mind consumed by fire is a mind consumed by greed, hatred, and domination. However, a mind that expresses the consciousness of fire brings illumination, generosity, compassion, and wisdom."

Rose listens intently as Verdandi continues. "The dragon came to humanity to teach us these lessons about the alchemy of fire. In many Eastern societies, dragons were portrayed and honored as benevolent creatures; omens of good fortune, and Avatars of great wisdom. Dragons were also seen as immortal creatures that teach the lessons of the higher heart, protect the Buddha, and guard the entrances of temples. Unfortunately, in many of the Western societies that became increasingly patriarchal and materialistic, the dragon became a symbol for evil and all that's seen as bad. Especially in the Christian doctrines where the dragon was portrayed as a cunning beast who hoards treasures in its cave, and captures virgins to lure mankind into darkness and sin. Taming and slaying the dragon came to represent taming our primitive, animalistic nature, and slaying our ego. In so many ways, these stories reveal our own tendencies toward violence, as well as our fear of the underworld, and our own unconscious."

"I love dragons, Grandma. I always have," Rose says dreamily.

"I know you do, sweet girl. That's not surprising because you come from a long line of druids, wizards, Gnostic knights, alchemists, and high priestesses and priests. They, like their counterparts in the Eastern traditions, were also initiates of the Cosmic Dragon heart and the alchemical fire, which is the Flame of Love that arises from the awakened higher heart. When we break the trinity that is at the heart of alchemy, the fire we use no longer transmits the powers of love. In our tradition, the Cosmic Dragon is the guardian of these ancient alchemical laws, which were seen as magic by those who didn't understand them. The Dragon as a mythic creature can also fly and mediate between the mythic and human realms, and is thus one of our most powerful allies."

"What about the Cosmic Serpent? Is that the same creature as the Cosmic Dragon? Is the Serpent also our ally?"

"Yes, of course. They both represent the same primordial powers of creation, yet express this through a slightly different process. Whereas the Dragon represents the primordial masculine expression of this power, the Serpent represents the primordial feminine expression of this power. I'll teach you the lessons of the Cosmic Serpent another time, but now, the powers of the Cosmic Dragon are awakening within you. And it's about time you become more conscious of your masculine qualities as well, after all this deep diving into Cosmic wombs and birth canals! Especially if you want to get more outwardly active in the world in order to effect change and deal with the economic powers."

"Oh, that reminds me. I wanted to ask you why you think Mike, that financial director of the company where I made my pitch, wants to meet with me?" Rose asks shyly.

"Isn't it obvious? You won't like what I have to say about this." Verdandi sighs. "I don't think it has anything to do with your game proposal. You're a beautiful, young woman, and he probably thinks you're naive. Mike is your typical male Western Dragon, and would probably love to lure you into his cave."

"Naive? Ha. I'll show you how naive I am. I asked him to meet me on Saturday in the coffee shop where I'm meeting Li. Mike doesn't know that, of course. Li will sort him out. He knows how to deal with guys like him. The two of us already discussed it. Li is really knowledgeable about finance and economics; his relatives have been bankers for many generations."

"Alright, but is Li also knowledgeable about these male Western Dragons who chase young women like you? Be careful. Li may know all about finance and economics, but that's not the game that's being played here. You may not know what you're getting yourself, and Li, into. Please ask the young man to come and see me here for a short visit before you two meet with Mike on Saturday."

"Okay, I'll ask him. I'm sure he'd like to meet you. And don't worry; I'll be careful. The three of us are meeting in a public place, so I'll be safe. And Li can be the Eastern Dragon! Now tell me more about Iceland, and how you and Grandpa are doing."

"We can talk about that, but before we change the subject, let me tell you about a special tool and initiation I need to share with you before you try to confront the dragon of Mike."

Verdandi has piqued Rose's curiosity.

"What is it?" she asks.

"This is no ordinary tool. It has been part of our families for more than a thousand years. You may have seen me wearing this for our ceremonies in the past. I've been the last keeper of this sacred tool since I was about your age. You'll need to keep this on you during your meeting with Mike to make sure you'll have the protection of the Cosmic Dragon so your untrained inner dragon doesn't overtake you."

"That sounds amazing, Grandma. Can you show it to me now?" Rose wonders if this tool is from the mysterious and beautiful velvet pouch embroidered with ancient symbols that is always on Verdandi's altar.

"Not so fast, love. I have to initiate you first, through a special ceremony. This tool contains ancient powers that don't like to be disturbed, just like that dragon you felt. This sacred tool has to get to know you first. I need to introduce you to each other. We'll get started on that in the coming days. For now, let's go get some sleep."

Integration –
The Cosmic Dragon

The powers of Rose's inner dragon are awakening within her as she embarks on the next stage of the Future Humans Quest. This inner stirring has been triggered by her growing sense of injustice and frustration with the state of the world and the abuse of power that she sees all around her. Verdandi has received several signs and omens that this would happen. She knows this will bring a whole new set of lessons to Rose; challenges which require the guidance of the Cosmic Dragon and careful preparation. Rose's powers are growing rapidly, and she doesn't yet realize what this will attract.

> *The Cosmic Dragon represents the sacred masculine expressions of the primordial powers of creation and the lessons of the awakening higher heart; the Cosmic heart. You can call upon the Cosmic Dragon to guide you to develop and direct the powers of your inner dragon through the alchemical Flame of Love and the unifying wisdom of the higher heart.*

The summary and questions below will help you to integrate and apply the essential teachings of this chapter:

◉ The Cosmic Compass game exploration between Rose and Olaf catalyzes the next stage of her Future Humans Quest and her awakening connections with the Cosmic Avatars. *Are you willing to play the game of life for our conscious evolution, and opt-out of the games of harm, dom ination, and division?*

- The dragon as a mythic creature has been part of humanity's stories since the early beginnings. In some cultures, it is represented as wise and benevolent, and in other cultures, as a cunning beast. *What is your relationship with the dragon archetype?*

- In the *Future Humans Trilogy*, we relate with the dragon archetype as the Cosmic Dragon; a Cosmic Avatar who offers essential lessons about the alchemy of fire, the wisdom of the higher heart, and our use and sources of power. *What is your relationship with power and how do you use it in the world and for (your) life?*

- The shadow aspects of the dragon archetype teach us about the shadow aspects of our powers, and the destructive qualities of fire when this becomes disconnected from the alchemy of love and the wisdom of the higher heart. This disconnection can manifest as the fire of greed, weapons of mass destruction, the excessive burning of fossil fuels, the desire for domination and harmful expansion, excessive criticism, unhealthy sexuality, hatred, violence, harmful seductions, and imbalanced masculine expressions. *What lessons are there for you to learn about this?*

- The awakened aspects of the dragon archetype teach us about the consciousness of fire, the alchemical transformations of the awakening higher heart, and the power of love. This can manifest as wisdom, enlightenment, compassion, joy, luminosity, generosity, courage, the use of solar and renewable energy solutions, ecological guardianship, healthy sexuality, and balanced masculine expressions. *What lessons are there for you to learn about this?*

- Rose's encounters with the harsh realities of the corporate world represent how, in certain societies and cultures, the archetypal dragon powers of humanity have become disconnected from the heart of fire and the unity between the feminine and masculine qualities of ourselves. The Cosmic Dragon is teaching Rose about the deeper root causes for our world in crisis. *What is the Cosmic Dragon teaching you about the state of the world and your own life?*

CHAPTER 2

The Avatar Training Begins

The Ring of Unity

R ose wakes early to make breakfast; much earlier than usual, and even before Verdandi, which rarely happens. This is the day of her initiation. Throughout the night, Rose kept waking up to see if it was morning yet. She realizes that Verdandi must have felt something serious was about to happen. Why else would she have come here like this? Not just to bring cookies, that's for sure.

Rose sets the table with a cheerful tablecloth and napkins. She pulls a carton of eggs and several oranges out of the refrigerator, just as Verdandi appears in the doorway in her nightgown and slippers, her hair looking wild. Her grandmother grins. Rose feels a wave of love wash over her.

"Good morning, Grandma! Did you sleep well? Would you like some freshly squeezed orange juice with eggs on toast, and a croissant?"

"That sounds lovely. Thank you for getting all of this prepared, and so early. What's up? You couldn't sleep?"

Verdandi knows very well how Rose's young mind must be jumping up and down with anticipation. She plans on using this energy fully for Rose's initiation, which requires a strong build-up of inner determination.

"Yeah, I couldn't sleep." Rose cracks the eggs into a mixing bowl. "Must have been that coffee I drank after dinner last night, and our talks about Mike and his boss lady."

"Or maybe it's knowing that something really special and mysterious awaits you in the other room? Not at all curious, my girl?" Verdandi laughs.

"Maybe," Rose admits with a smile. "I can't hide anything from you. Please, please tell me more about this initiation! What do I need to do to get ready? Why are you really here? What's this omen about? And the other signs?"

"Always a million questions, my sweet Viking girl. All will become clear soon. Enjoy the discovery. After breakfast, I'll need you to prepare yourself for your ceremony. Take some time to be alone. Go for a walk in the park. Find an old tree to sit with and reflect on what this next stage of your journey means to you. Become present to all that's inside you. Consider whether you are ready to receive new powers."

"You mean, dragon powers?" Rose asks excitedly.

"Well, before powers, there has to be character. You're still a young dragon who has much to learn and discover."

The Willow Embrace and the Dragon's Heart

Rose takes Verdandi's advice and spends the morning in the park with her favorite willow tree. She realizes that this next step signifies another death and rebirth; an even deeper letting go of who she thought she was by embracing who she is being called to become.

Leaning against the willow tree, she reflects on all that happened over the last year: her hospitalization with COVID-19, the night she briefly died and went beyond the veil to return to the Cosmic womb, her future human choice, the death of her beloved cousin Otto, and her deepening friendship with her best friend Sophia. She thinks about all of her training with Verdandi and the nine Cosmic Keys, the precious time with her parents and her brother and his family, her incredible dreams and new discoveries, her conversations with her friends Lillian and Rob, her financial uncertainties as she stopped working at the bookstore, and the beginning of her new life. Yet despite having had all of these remarkable experiences, Rose suddenly feels a deep sadness welling up inside her.

Tears roll down her cheeks as she once more grieves the loss of Otto. They were so close, and she still misses him so much. She also cries for the death of one of her classmates who recently committed suicide, and wonders how hopeless and desperate this young woman must have felt to kill herself. She wishes she could have done more to prevent this. Images flash in her mind of the many people who died in the COVID-19 pandemic, and how many died alone, as nobody was allowed near them.

The willow tree embraces her tenderly with its energy, supporting Rose to cry deeply for all of this suffering and loss. Image upon image rises up in her inner vision. Rose sees the destruction of our planet; the many fertile fields that have been turned into barren wastelands. She feels herself standing in the fields that have been ravaged by war, terror, death, and destruction.

Next, she feels herself inside the ocean. She sees continents of waste in which helpless turtles, dolphins, sharks, fish, and many other sea creatures are trapped. They are suffering; waiting for death to release them from the clutches of suffocating nets, plastic in their bellies, and the tightening snares of carelessly tossed trash around their necks and fins.

She then watches the remains of the thousands of animals and insects who could not escape the wildfires around the world. She sees the birds who suffocated to death. Wherever she turns her mind, she sees death and destruction and the footprints of human recklessness.

"NOOOO!" Rose exclaims aloud. "This is wrong! So wrong! Humanity, please, wake up. This is not who we are! We are so much more than cold-blooded killers and terminators of nature! We can do better. We *must* do better! I did not renew my vows of life for this version of humanity."

Rose cries out to the space around her, hoping that something or someone hears her. She feels the roots of the willow beneath her, drawing her plea into the depths beneath the soil, then spreading it out in all directions.

"Dear willow friend, thank you for always being here," Rose whispers to the tree. "You were here for me when I returned from the hospital, and when I felt overcome with grief from the death of my cousin. You were here when I cried because I missed my parents so much. You're always here for me. But what will happen to you? Will you be cut into pieces and sold to the highest bidder someday?"

Rose puts her arms around the trunk of the old willow as she continues to grieve, engulfed by all the sadness and pain that has filled her heart. She doesn't know that her plea has been heard and received. A circle of light from the Cosmic Avatars surrounds and supports her. She has a sense that something has landed beside her. *Could it be the Cosmic Dragon?* she wonders, and feels that it is. Her connection with the ancient laws is awakening. The Cosmic Dragon will become her teacher to initiate her into the mysteries of the alchemical fire and the wisdom of the higher heart. The Dragon gently lends its fire to hers, quietly purifying her tears, anguish, and anger with the alchemical Flame of Love.

Thoughts and images dissolve into the great emptiness as the last tears roll down her cheeks. Her heart feels purged. Silence enters her mind. Even nature has become totally quiet. She's never experienced such a vast and profound silence. She realizes that when all has been said, thought, felt, and done, this silence remains as the eternal ground of being. In her mind, she hears the words, "Return yourself to this silence and surrender into the arms of eternity where you will be reunited with all that is and will forever be."

After some moments in this timeless silence, Rose puts her hands on the soil and kneels down. She then lowers herself completely until her body lies flat on the ground. She feels her heart connect with the heartbeat of Mother Earth, while her outstretched arms embrace the earth.

Into the earth and the roots of the willow tree, she whispers, "Mama Earth, I love you so much. I'm so sorry for all the hurt and harm we've caused you. Please forgive us. We are your children. Help us, and hear my plea. Guide, direct, and teach us the ancient and future ways of life that we've forgotten. I will do whatever I can to stop this violence and help humanity return to life. I love you."

As she lies there, Rose becomes aware of the qualities of herself that she doesn't like: her impatience, quick temper, judgmental tendencies, and her own arrogance when she stubbornly tries to defend her position and convince others that she is right. She also becomes aware of her own insecurities and immaturity, and understands in that moment how she needs to forgive herself.

She puts her arms around her body and curls up into the fetal position. She sobs as she learns to forgive herself for her own hurtfulness and her judgments of perceived mistakes and shortcomings. She sends her love to all these feelings and insecurities and the pressures of so many expectations. She feels her inner being soften and relax to the point that she falls asleep while still in the fetal position, lovingly held within the womb of the earth and the willow's embrace. Above her, a hawk flies in lazy circles. A little frog hops across a stretch of grass on its way to the nearby pond. A butterfly lands softly on Rose's shoulder as she enters into a vivid dream.

She journeys to an inner realm of Earth where the dragons, unicorns, Pegasus, phoenixes, winged serpents, and other mythical animals have retreated after the humans severed their connections with the lands of magic. Rose is greeted here by the Cosmic Dragon. She recognizes how this Dragon is of the same energy as the presence she has felt within and around her these past few weeks. The Dragon's heart glows like an emerald jewel. Rose wonders if this is the Grail stone of eternal life that her grandmother has spoken of. The ancient laws of the multi-worlds and universal orders have taken the shape of this Dragon in order to teach Rose what she needs to know and understand to fulfill her purpose for this time.

Rose bows before the Dragon and declares her willingness to be trained and become an apprentice of the ancient laws of life. The Dragon blows its mighty fire on the ground in front of her, producing a circle of flames. Rose understands that she is to step into this circle. As she does, she feels an enormous unity with all that is, will be, and has been since the beginning of time.

She knows that inside this circle is the Bond of Unity that is to be restored through new covenants for the healing of our worlds. As the fire turns to ash, she discovers a ring with an emerald stone shaped like an egg; the same emerald color that she saw in the Dragon's heart. The egg is held by the head of a dragon and the head of a serpent. Just as she is about to reach for the ring, a buzzing bee wakes her from her dream, and she finds herself back in the park.

She realizes that she must have fallen asleep, and notices with surprise that she has been away for several hours. Blessing the earth with her hands as she pushes herself up, she turns and rushes quickly back to her apartment, hoping her grandmother didn't get too worried.

The Velvet Medicine Pouch

"There you are!" Verdandi says, teasingly, upon Rose's return. "I was beginning to wonder if the trees had swallowed you up and kept you in Middle-earth. Or did you wander off into the hidden chambers of Agartha?"

"Sorry, Grandma, I completely lost track of time, and then fell asleep. Thankfully, a bee woke me up. Otherwise, I might still be in the park. I hope you got my message as I rushed back home."

"It's all good, darling. Join me in the kitchen for some squash and apple soup."

"Smells good," Rose says as the two women move to the kitchen.

"I was there in the park with you in spirit, you know."

"Oh! How?"

"Did you see the hawk?"

Rose shakes her head no. Verdandi chuckles. "You should know by now that my eyes are not limited to this human body. You probably missed the little frog as well. The willow told me that you went through a very deep healing of grieving, letting go, forgiveness, and surrender."

"I did. Well, if you were there, do you still want me to tell you what happened?"

"Of course! It's always so much nicer to hear it from you directly."

Verdandi ladles hot soup into bowls, sets out a basket of fresh bread, and the two sit down to eat. Rose tells Verdandi about her plea to Mother Earth, and her encounter with the Dragon in her dream under the willow tree.

"Do you understand what the ring in my dream is about, Grandma?"

"Yes, and soon you will too. I see that the Cosmic Dragon has already started to prepare you. Meanwhile, the whole time you were sleeping under the willow tree, I was busy making soup and preparing for our ceremony. Somebody has to work."

"Hey, that's not fair!" Rose exclaims. "You told me to go into the park and prepare myself!"

"It's all fine, darling, I'm just testing to see if you still have that edginess. Go and rest some more. Later this evening, when the moon starts to rise, we'll do your ceremony. After dinner, take your purifying bath, as I taught you. When you place your hands in the water, connect with its spirit and bless it. Ask it to purify your body, mind, and soul. If the bathtub is too small, you can also use the bowl with water in the shower, in which I've already placed the rose petals for purification. Give all that needs cleansing and healing to the spirit of water. Ask it to make you receptive for your initiation. While you do your water ritual, I'll complete the preparations in the living room. I've placed a white dress on your bed. After your purification bath, please put it on."

"I still don't know what this is all for."

"No, but you'll find out soon."

"I had a little peek in the living room and noticed that you brought your sacred medicine pouch, the one you call the 'Avatar pouch,'" Rose confesses. "This must be a really important occasion because it's rare for you to take it with you when you travel. In fact, I've never seen you leave Iceland with that pouch before."

Verdandi has safely guarded this pouch for her since the day she was born. Although Rose doesn't realize this yet, her grandmother has been preparing her for many years to one day become its next custodian.

"Yes, it's true. This is a really important time for us to be together, Rose. The pouch contains sacred architect tools that have been kept in our families for over a thousand years, or perhaps even longer." Verdandi pauses and looks at her granddaughter with bright eyes. "I don't know how much longer I'll be able to stay with you all on this earthly plane. There are other places where I'm needed as well."

Rose is taken aback. "I've never heard you say that before. Are you sick? Have you seen a doctor?"

"It's nothing to worry about, love. I'm healthy; it's not like that. It's my duty and privilege to prepare you well, and through you, many others who are going through a similar process. We all know that when we come here on this Earth, it's only temporary."

Tears well up in Rose's eyes. "I'm not ready to let you go. Please stay longer. Much, much longer."

"It will all be fine, dearest. I will be there for you, always." Verdandi holds Rose close and strokes her hair. "Now let's get back to your ceremony. You may not yet feel ready to become the next custodian for this Avatar pouch, and you are indeed still very young, but the old dragon is dying and starting to retreat into its cave. A new time and a new dragon will soon emerge. In between these shifts of eras there can be many upheavals and chaos while the old orders are dissolving and the new orders are not yet fully manifested. It's a dangerous time, and I have to prepare you while I still can. Whether you feel ready or not! There is much at stake, my girl."

Rose suddenly realizes that this is about so much more than climate change or corporate greed. There is a vacuum of power which requires a whole different kind of leadership than what has yet emerged in the consciousness of humanity. She becomes quiet and still as her grandmother's words start to land.

The women sit in silence for some time before Verdandi stands up to get their dessert from the fridge: custard pudding with fresh strawberries.

"While I'm still here, we can explore how you and Sophia can get your own Avatar pouch with your own architect tools," Verdandi continues. "I will then bless these physical tools with the transmissions of the mother pouch and link them energetically to the Cosmic Architect Tools. That way this system for initiating and developing your future human powers can more easily be shared with people around the world, since many will need this."

"Good. Then you keep the mother pouch and its tools safely with you, and we'll make our own," Rose says. "That sounds like a much better plan than leaving it here with me in the Netherlands."

"Oh, love, once this stage of your training is completed, there is another trip waiting for you…We'll both be traveling soon." Their eyes meet. When Verdandi speaks, her voice is reassuring and calm. She squeezes Rose's hand. "Stop worrying and let it all unfold. Trust! And eat your custard."

Ceremonial Preparations

"Can you tell me more about these sacred architect tools?"

"These are tools for developing your Cosmic architect powers, so you can enter into the higher consciousness states for designing and building the new worlds from the eternal Bond of Unity. There are other tools for governing the worlds and for keeping the sacred balance once these new worlds come into being," her grandmother tells her.

"Those tools sound like they're exactly what we need, especially now. We must learn how to design and become the new operating systems for humanity."

"Yes, and these tools contain tremendous powers, although many may not realize how powerful they truly are, due to their size. Appearances, as you know, can be deceiving." Verdandi winks. She continues, "These tools also carry the protection and transmissions of our ancestors and those who came before them."

Rose is solemn. "I still get the impression that there's more to this."

"Your powers are growing. With that, there are new responsibilities and challenges. Certain forces and people will become attracted to your presence. Some will be hungry for what they sense through you. Others will want to stop you as the symbol for the annunciation of the new time. You form part of much larger constellations than you are aware of. I'm speaking of constellations of ancient and future agreements that have yet to reveal themselves to you."

"I don't know whether to feel scared or excited," Rose admits. "It all sounds so mysterious. I wonder what Sophia would say about all of this? I can't wait to tell her. Next time, may I ask her to join us?"

"Of course. Sophia is welcome to join us. She is a wise young woman from one of the most ancient indigenous lineages of Australia. Her families are keepers of ancient creation laws. I've heard so many good things about her; I'd love to meet her. But right now, our focus is on *your* preparation."

Rose has felt a strange attraction to her grandmother's mysterious pouch ever since she was a little girl. During her summer holidays in Iceland, she walked up to Verdandi's altar many times, hoping to touch it and peek inside. But Verdandi always seemed to know what she was up to, and Rose never managed to get close enough. Even as a child, she understood that when something was on Verdandi's altar, even the angels weren't allowed to touch it without her permission! Secretly, Rose also felt a little scared of the pouch, especially when it appeared to glow at night.

Verdandi observes the sun slowly moving toward the horizon. "It's time. Go and take your ritual bath, then meet me in the living room. We will begin the ceremony for your initiation."

Rose enjoys the sacred water ritual as she calls upon the spirit of water to cleanse her body, mind, and soul. The consciousness of the water carries the blessing of the rose. First, she sprinkles the palm of her hand to then bring this blessing to her crown, third eye, throat, the base of her skull, heart, navel, womb, base of her spine, knees, and feet. After her purifying bath, Rose dons the white dress that her grandmother has laid out on the bed for her. She enters the living room where Verdandi waits for her in her ceremonial robe. Beautiful rays of pink and orange light from the setting sun bathe the room, creating a golden hue to all they touch.

Verdandi greets Rose and points out the window to where a luminous full moon has just risen over the horizon. "Perfect timing," she smiles and turns her attention back to her granddaughter. "Let us begin." As she says this, she shifts into her timeless form as a keeper of the ancient lines of magi, druids, wizards, and seers; the meta people. She chants, claps, and blesses the space with her hands. Her tone is strong, deep, and resonant. Through her voice, the wise ones speak as one voice.

The living room has been transformed into a ceremonial circle that looks like a medicine wheel. Rose recognizes the design of the Cosmic Compass in the ways that Verdandi has created four concentric circles on the floor with a black round stone in the center, surrounded by leaves, flowers, stones, cords, water, fruits, candles, and other sacred objects on the compass coordinates of the four concentric circles.

Candles flicker and illuminate the four directions. Even the compass rose is present in the way the ceremonial cords are laid out in three different colors from the outer edge of the circle to the inner circle. Next to the black stone in the center is the sacred Avatar pouch that Rose recognizes from Verdandi's altar in Iceland.

"This is incredible, Grandma. Thank you so much."

"You're welcome, love. Now take a moment to allow yourself to experience the vibrations of this ceremonial circle. As you may notice, it is laid out in the design of the Cosmic Compass that we've been working with for all these months. You'll now discover how you can also use your compass design for ceremonial purposes, and not just for games."

Rose feels a deep resonance with the sacred objects that Verdandi has carefully placed on the compass coordinates inside the room. The flowers, stones, and candles have come alive with the additional energy of the circle and compass. Verdandi has burned special herbs to purify the space, including cedar, tulsi, eucalyptus, pine, white sage, and some secret herbs whose names she never reveals. The living room is suddenly filled with the most wonderful fragrances.

Verdandi picks up her drum and beats it in a steady, rhythmic fashion. She invokes the power of the Cosmic Avatars through another ancient chant, and

Rose feels the Cosmic portal begin to open. Rose enters into a trance. Her body rocks gently with the rhythm of Verdandi's drumming and chanting. She enters the dance that unites the outer and inner Cosmos.

"Become utterly receptive now," Verdandi whispers softly. "Let yourself go. The drum will carry you forth. Just trust and open your heart."

Rose takes a deep breath and releases everything that holds her back. She hears the inner humming of the sacred silence again, similar to what she experienced under the willow tree earlier that morning. The tears she shed there have cleansed and softened her heart, and she feels an expanding lightness of being. She internally confirms her commitment for this next stage of her journey.

Meeting the Divine Mother

"The circle is ready to receive you now," Verdandi tells Rose. "Enter from the east, like I taught you. Seat yourself in the center, behind the black stone and Avatar pouch, and face north to greet the Cosmic Tree of Life. Once you are seated, close your eyes, and I'll guide you further. Begin by thanking our ancestors and the Cosmic Tree for all of its protection and guidance."

The young woman does exactly what she's instructed to do. Verdandi begins to chant an ancient prayer in a language that Rose one day hopes to learn. The room becomes suffused with Cosmic vibrations from the love that moves the sun and the other stars. The full moon has risen further and is now well above the horizon. The last streaks of sunlight illuminate the room with a warm glow. A raven caws nearby. Rose notices that the city has become unusually quiet.

Verdandi walks to the center of the circle and places the red velvet pouch with golden embroidery into her granddaughter's cupped hands. Rose's body sways gently back and forth as she moves more deeply into her trance. She holds the pouch close to her navel with both her hands. She feels the powerful vibrations from the pouch entering her body.

Verdandi opens the pouch and fastens a necklace holding a sacred ring around Rose's neck. It falls just over her heart. Her grandmother says softly, "You now have direct connection with the Cosmic Avatars. May the power of this ring carry you home to the eternal garden."

Rose recalls her dream with the circle of fire and realizes that this ring represents the circle forged by the alchemical Flame of Love from the heart of the Cosmic Dragon. She feels the presence of the Cosmic Avatars forming around her. The pouch begins to glow in her hands as her consciousness is pulled into the realm of the Avatars.

She enters a beautiful, lush garden with waterfalls, rivers, caves, springs, and endless fields of flowers. The entire garden overflows with fertility, abundance, harmony, and joy. Wherever Rose turns her attention, life shimmers and glows with vitality. Looking toward the horizon, she notices a majestic tree, which looks as old as time itself. The tree calls to her, and as she moves closer to it, she realizes that this is the Cosmic Tree of Life. She is overcome with love for this primordial tree, and then realizes how the rivers, waterfalls, springs, and all the waters of the land flow from the heart of this tree, which gives life to all. Each of the branches carries within it an entire universe. The soul of the Tree of Life is the Divine Mother, the Goddess of the multi-worlds that grow from the spreading branches. Suddenly Rose realizes that the Tree of Life is also the covenant and the law of the eternal.

Rose experiences the infinite caring that flows out from this tree to all realms of consciousness as the lifeblood of creation. She is now face-to-face with the Goddess Herself, who kisses her softly on her forehead and welcomes her home.

"Oh, dear Goddess, how I've missed you. I didn't even know how much I missed you until this very moment. Divine Mother of Life, I recognize that it's *your* voice I've heard inside my head, guiding me, encouraging me, and consoling me when I felt alone and lost. I understand now that you've always been there."

"Sweet Rose, my Cosmic child, you, who carries the promise of a new beginning, welcome home. Through the Bond of Unity that lives within your Cosmic heart, you'll always know your way home. I am always near you and within you."

"Divine Mother, we need your help. Please show me how I can help to stop the wasteful destruction and terrible violence that plagues our world."

"The answer to your question is within the Ring of Unity that represents our eternal bond. Study this bond and the laws it represents. Learn the lessons of the alchemical fire; the only fire that does not cause harm or pain. Those who have not integrated the consciousness of fire will be the dangerous, narcissistic, self-serving ones who create destructive, harmful heat in the world. They will be consumed by the power of fire as carriers of hatred, greed, and disunity. On the other hand, the alchemical fire illuminates, gives life, and spreads the power of love."

"Is that why the Dragon heart is awakening within me? Did you send the Cosmic Dragon to teach me?" Rose asks.

The Goddess smiles and embraces Rose with the love that is the answer. Rose drinks in the love fully with her whole being. She opens herself to receive the streams of unity that flow forth from the breasts of the Divine Mother to nourish all souls with the divine elixir of life. Rose feels transformed, restructured, and purified by the divine elixir that enters every cell of her being.

The Mother Goddess informs the young apprentice Avatar before Her that because She has received a seat inside of her human consciousness, Her divine love can now flow through Rose; the love that springs forth eternally from the streams and rivers and never-ending wells of the Tree of Life. Rose bows and thanks the Goddess. She feels complete, and slowly opens her eyes.

Verdandi's chants and drumming with the rhythm of Mother Earth's heartbeat become softer and softer. Finally, she speaks. "Welcome back, my strong girl. I see you have met our Divine Mother. You now begin to experience the power of the ring of unity. Through this ring, every other architect tool is empowered, as all express different qualities from the eternal bond that is represented by this ring. You can explore these other tools from the pouch another time. This is enough for now. Thank the seven directions: east, south, west, north, above, below, and the center." Rose does so.

"You may leave the circle via the east gate through which you entered," Verdandi says.

The Cosmic Architect Tools

The silver rays of the full moon illuminate the ceremonial circle and land right on the little black foundation stone. Rose is still transitioning between the different worlds and is bathing in the tremendous embrace of the unconditional love of the Divine Mother. Verdandi leaves the room to give her granddaughter some quiet integration time. After a while, Rose enters the kitchen where Verdandi is assembling a tray containing two mugs of hot chocolate and a small plate of oatmeal cookies she had prepared earlier in the day.

"How are you, my girl?" Verdandi asks gently.

"Without words. I've never experienced anything like this. I had no idea that love could be so all-encompassing and complete. It suddenly feels like… all of the tools and codes that originally fascinated me are insignificant compared to the power of this love."

"Yes, the real power is already given and within us, yet few use it. All of the destructive technologies and actions that humanity has created stem from this one essential lesson of not understanding the true source and heart of fire."

Verdandi sets the tray down and hands her granddaughter a mug. Rose drinks her hot chocolate slowly, still immersed in her reverie. The two women sit in silence. Finally, the older woman speaks. "You've done well today. Go and rest now. We can talk more tomorrow. I love you."

"Thank you, Grandma…for everything. I love you, too…so very much." She kisses her grandmother on the cheek, and goes to get her pillow and some blankets to make up the sofa bed. She puts on her nightgown and brushes her teeth. By the time she emerges from the bathroom, Verdandi has transformed the living room back to its original state. The scents of the cedar, sage, and other herbs linger in the air. Rose sets her journal and the sacred Avatar pouch onto the little table beside the couch and turns off the light. She snuggles under the covers and falls asleep in minutes.

During the night, Rose dreams of the Cosmic Architect Tools that are connected to the sacred tools in the Avatar pouch next to her bed. She is back with the Cosmic Tree of Life where she discovers the Singing Chalice in the form of a chalice cup near the eternal spring that flows from the Tree. As she takes the cup between her hands, it starts to sing softly, and fills itself with the water from the spring. She takes a little sip of the water and notices that it activates the Avatar codes of the eternal laws within her. She rests for a moment to fully enjoy this magical remembering as she sees the codes within her own body, and in all of life around her.

Next to the chalice cup is her beloved Cosmic Compass, which she draws to her heart. She thanks the compass for all the many ways in which it is guiding her, and asks it to show her where she needs to go next. She feels guided to move to the sacred fire that is burning beside the sleeping Cosmic Dragon and wonders if this is the alchemical fire that her grandmother spoke of.

She discovers the Fire Stones of Darkness and Light in the forms of black and white flintstones on the sand inside the fire. As she moves closer to study the stones the Dragon opens its majestic golden eyes and looks straight at her. A shiver moves through her whole body. She feels mesmerized by its piercing gaze and experiences a profound awakening of her Cosmic heart as she returns the gaze of this ancient Avatar.

The Dragon bows its head and pushes her gently into the fire, nudging her to take the stones in her hands. The Fire Stones show her how the co-creative union of Darkness and Light produces the alchemical fire and ignites the Flame of Love within our Cosmic heart. She thanks the stones and places them carefully back inside the fire and as she does, she spots the Ring of Unity at the center of the fire. She carefully takes it from the fire to look more closely at the egg-shaped emerald stone that is at the center of the Ring, held by a miniature head of a dragon and a serpent who share the same body through the ring. To her surprise she notices how the egg is alive and is pulsating with life. She looks at the Dragon and asks what's inside the egg. Her higher heart responds immediately and shows her how this is the Cosmic World Egg that contains the Cosmic codes of this new world and time. In that moment she recalls her near-death experience and the new world that she saw inside the Cosmic cocoon and starts to understand so many of the things that happened and had to happen over the last sixteen months.

The Dragon looks tenderly at her as she stretches her arms upward and places her hand on its heart. Their hearts beat as one. The Dragon then shows her the Infinity Hourglass near its feet in the form of a luminous hourglass that is shaped like an infinity symbol and filled with the sand of the sacred fire. Rose picks up the hourglass and holds it carefully between her hands. Upon doing this, she gains an awareness of time as an infinity loop, and becomes aware of the consciousness and rhythms of the new time and what needs to end and complete for this new world to be born and manifest.

She senses the presence of the Cosmic Serpent and discovers the Cosmic Mirror in the form of a beautifully crafted mirror in a circular shape not far from the hourglass. The rim of the mirror is in the shape of a white serpent, an Ouroboros serpent who bites its own tail. Through this mirror she discovers the working of the Cosmic Mirror. As she looks into the mirror, she becomes aware of herself and her purpose from her Avatar consciousness, her Cosmic self. She notices how the mirror can reflect back different realities depending on her intention and focus. She intends to better understand this new future world, and becomes aware of more details of the world that is within the emerald egg.

While seeing herself from this Cosmic perspective, she also becomes aware of her dream body and how around it is a luminous cord woven together from three cords that emerge from her navel. She touches the cord, which awakens her Cosmic Navel Cord connection to the Tree of Life. She senses that by tuning into this Cosmic Cord, one may always find the way back home, and revitalize one's Source connection.

The dream is unusually vivid with many more details and symbols. She slowly rises to the surface of her consciousness. She opens her eyes and notices that the moon has made its way across the night sky and is just about to dip below the horizon to make way for the dawning sun. She looks over at the Avatar pouch on the side table. To her delight, it is glowing again. The Avatar ring on her chest feels hot and luminous. What a magical night.

Rose feels immense gratitude for all she has received and experienced. She reaches for her journal, jots down a few notes to make sure she won't forget her dream, then she curls back into her warm, cozy, make-shift sofa bed. She falls into a deep and dreamless sleep and doesn't wake up until a few hours later when Verdandi brings her a glass of freshly squeezed orange juice and toast.

"Rise and shine, love!" her grandmother says cheerily. "Did you sleep well? Any dreams?"

"I had the most incredible dreams!" Rose sits up and pours out the full story of her nocturnal adventure.

Verdandi smiles and nods. "I'm happy to know that the architect tools are starting to teach you directly. That's a very good sign. They will become your trusted companions for a long time to come."

"Grandma, who made these tools? Where do they come from?"

"Some date back thousands of years. I received them from my grandmother when I was around your age. Although these tools are for both women and men, in our families, the women have been the keepers. The powers of the tools are not limited to these objects. These objects merely represent or channel the transmissions from where these powers originate, which can also come to us directly in dreams, visions, ceremonies, and initiations such as what you went through yesterday."

"Aha. So the tools belong to all of us, and are not exclusive to any particular culture or lineage?"

"Yes, darling. They belong to all of us, but that doesn't mean they'll awaken in all of us. You can't force these tools; they have their own consciousness. They do not serve us. Instead, we need to learn to serve the purpose for which they were created."

"Can I show the tools to my friends?"

"With reverence and respect, and when required ceremonially, yes, but never to impress anyone, or for entertainment."

"What happens if someone abuses the powers of these tools?"

"Then the powers will leave you and you'll trigger the full force of Thor. These powers cannot be manipulated or controlled. They don't belong to anyone, and cannot be owned."

"How did you know to share this with me?" Rose asks, curiously.

"The Avatars gave me three signs that could not be ignored. Don't ask me what those signs were, as I won't tell you. That's between me and the Avatars." Verdandi smiles and continues. "These particular architect tools carry the transmissions of the universal powers for conceiving new worlds from the eternal Bond of Unity. These powers come to us when we are at the ending of a great cycle and the beginning of a new era."

"What about the nine Cosmic Keys you gave me?" Rose asks. "Do I continue to use those as well?"

"Yes, of course," her grandmother answers. "Even more so now. And not just nine. The most important one is the tenth Key. You still remember the nine Keys?"

"Yes. The Key of Conscious Choice, Imaginal Power, Cosmic Communication, Trinity, Paradox, Darkness, Self Awareness, Becoming, and Unity. But what is the tenth Key?"

Verdandi chuckles. "The Renaissance Key of consciousness! YOU! By actualizing your future human potential, you become a Renaissance Key for the transformation of our world. Okay, little lady, I'd better stop you now before you give me more questions! Let's wash up these few dishes, and then we'll go for a walk in the park."

Integration -
The Ring of Unity

Through this chapter, Rose received her Avatar apprentice initiation with the Avatar mother pouch and the physical ring of unity that awakened in her the Cosmic Ring of Unity. This Cosmic Ring carries the transmissions of the eternal Bond of Unity, which Rose first discovered through the Cosmic Key of Unity in book 1.

With the help of the willow tree, Rose came face-to-face with the Cosmic Dragon, who will guide her on this journey to develop her powers through the wisdom of the higher heart. She received the transmissions from the Cosmic Ring of Unity three times; as the circle of support from the Cosmic Avatars of the Bond of Unity, as the ring of fire by the Cosmic Dragon, and as the physical Avatar ring from her grandmother. When something is truly significant, it often comes to us three times and in three different ways. Through this chapter we've shared many symbols that represent hidden qualities of yourself and life, which reveal the deeper dimensions of our human psyche.

The Ring of Unity is a mythic symbol that represents the eternal Bond of Unity between the various and diverse expressions, worlds, and realms of consciousness, and ourselves. The Ring of Unity activates the Avatar codes within us for becoming Cosmic humans and empowers each of the Cosmic Architect Tools from unity consciousness. You can call upon the Ring of Unity to activate your innate Avatar codes and your direct Source connection with the eternal garden and the Cosmic Tree of Life.

The summary and questions below will help you to integrate and apply the essential teachings of this chapter:

- The seven Cosmic Architect Tools are: the Ring of Unity, Infinity Hourglass, Cosmic Compass, Fire Stones of Darkness and Light, Singing Chalice, Cosmic Navel Cord, and the Cosmic Mirror. Through the next chapters you will learn more about what each of those things means. The Ring of Unity is the focus for this chapter.

- These archetypal Tools are universal and timeless. They represent your own creative powers for conceiving and architecting your realities with the qualities and powers of the Cosmic architecture of consciousness.

- The Cosmic Architect Tools belong to all of us, but it doesn't mean they will awaken in all of us. You cannot force these Tools; preparation and respect for their universal purpose is recommended. Pay attention to your dreams, as this is how they may announce their presence first, like they did for Rose.

- The willow tree taught Rose the importance of purging and healing her heart, so that the fire inside her heart can harmonize with the alchemical Flame of Love. This is part of the lessons of the higher heart. *Are there any feelings, emotions, or memories in your heart that need purging and healing?*

- Rose also learned to share her plea for the end of violence and disunity through the roots of the tree, which opened the portal to the inner realms of Earth and her mythic self. By entering the inner realms of Earth, she learned about the emerald Dragon heart that carries the alchemical Flame of Love.

- The Avatar pouch of the architect tools also represents the sacred womb of the Divine Mother for guarding our Cosmic powers until the time comes that we are ready to bring those forth and out into the world. When referring to this pouch as the original pouch for these tools, we refer to it as the "mother pouch" or "Avatar mother pouch."

- During Rose's Avatar apprentice initiation, she entered the eternal garden through the Cosmic Ring of Unity, which opened the inner portal to her Cosmic self. She then discovered how the eternal garden with all of its beauty, abundance, and plenitude was a direct manifestation of the Cosmic Tree of Life.

- When Rose made her heart connection with the Cosmic Tree of Life, she was welcomed home into the loving arms of the Divine Mother and realized how this sacred Tree is the Mother Goddess of Life. *How is your relationship with the Cosmic Tree of Life and the Mother Goddess?*

- When Rose said, "Divine Mother, we need your help. Please show me how I can help to stop this wasteful destruction and terrible violence that is plaguing our world," she was told that the answer to this question is within the Ring of Unity, and that she should study its eternal bond and the laws it represents, and to learn the lessons of the alchemical fire, as this is the only fire that does not cause harm or pain. *Reflect on what these words mean to you.*

CHAPTER 3

The Shift of Eras and Eros

The Infinity Hourglass

Rose hears soft, happy humming as she enters the kitchen. Verdandi has been busy making scones dotted with dried currants, and the wonderful scent of their baking fills the apartment.

"Good morning!" her grandmother chirps cheerfully. "These treats should come out of the oven in plenty of time before your friends' arrival."

"Thank you. Yum!" Rose says. "I can't wait for you to finally meet Sophia and Li in person."

"I'm so glad you invited them over." Verdandi places the mixing bowls and utensils into the sink and Rose steps up to wash them.

"I'm looking forward to telling them all about my latest adventures. I also want to tell Li about that horrible board meeting, and discuss what to do with Mike in the coffee shop tomorrow."

"Mike has no idea you'll have extra company tagging along, huh?"

"Nope."

"That should be interesting." Verdandi smiles. "While the scones are baking, I'd like to give you a quick practice for working with the hourglass before your friends get here."

"Let's do it! I'm so grateful that you came. I told Mom you were here and she couldn't believe it. She'll call later today."

Activating the Hourglass and the Infinity Loops

Verdandi carefully removes the hourglass from the pouch and blesses it by holding it between her hands and chanting an ancient invocation, after which she gently hands it to Rose.

"I see you've positioned yourself already." Verdandi smiles at her granddaughter, who has seated herself cross-legged on her favorite meditation pillow.

"You bet. I'm ready to go!" Rose says.

"I like your enthusiasm," Verdandi grins. "Now place the hourglass on your heart with your hands folded over it. Hold it there for a few moments, until you feel it warming up. Use the power of your intention to call upon the Cosmic Ring of Unity. Ask the Ring to activate within you and intend for the Bond of Unity to open. The Ring of Unity acts as a portal for this sacred bond, which will activate the Flame of Love inside your heart."

Rose feels the ring of unity on her chest start to heat up, and the hourglass as well. Verdandi adds, "Now set an intention to connect with the consciousness of time. Ask it to teach you the ways of the sacred rhythms and cycles. When you feel the connection, just nod your head. If you'd like to share what you're seeing, please go ahead."

Rose nods as she feels the inner portal open up to the consciousness of time. In the center of her head, her pineal gland starts buzzing with an unusual electric charge as the pressure on her third eye increases. "I see a huge wheel of time that is spinning with many infinity loops that converge in the center of the wheel. These infinity loops are just like those of the hourglass and the drawing I made of the Cosmic Compass. Each infinity loop shows another possibility on the wheel of evolution. Each choice, thought, and action brings another loop into motion, generating different experiences. Yet, no matter which loop we're on, it seems that consciousness always loops back to itself, just like the Ouroboros who bites its own tail."

"Good. Anything else?" Verdandi asks.

"Yes. By viewing my life from this wheel of time, I can review the cycles of my learning process. I can see when a cycle completes, what lessons it brought, the wisdom it offers, and how it started. I can even revisit the intentions, thoughts, and ideas I had during that time. This wheel is really helpful for reviewing my life experiences!" Rose exclaims. "It's like one side of the infinity loop represents the outward phase of my learning, and the other side of the loop represents my inward process. I can even observe myself during the times when I was processing and integrating my experiences, during sleep, dreams, and meditation. This is fascinating."

"Now you can see how rest and integration complete a cycle of learning," Verdandi tells her. "Like the bear that needs its winter hibernation in order to emerge in the spring, and the snake who retreats so it can shed its old skin, or the child who emerges with exciting new ideas after a good night's rest. Each time we complete an infinity loop, the wheel of evolution moves forward. As you grow in consciousness, your intentions, perspectives, and ideas become richer, more refined, and more infused with the qualities of wisdom. What you've seen is the wheel of learning in time and space, turned by the motions of our continual becoming as we bring consciousness into being. And so, we turn the pages of our lives, and are turned and re-turned by the cycles of life and the wheel of time."

With the hourglass held between her hands, Rose sees the shape of the torus within its infinity shape. She becomes aware of the dance between the nonlocal Cosmic dimensions of consciousness that are out of time, and the emergence of the experience of time when we move into local or physical consciousness. She experiences herself as the torus, as well as the flow of ideas that turn around inside the torus.

She enters the dance of consciousness. She becomes the consciousness in which the wheel of time is spinning as she becomes the motionless and timeless presence of the eternal now. In this state of pure presence, she experiences how she is the dancer and the dance itself. She experiences the simultaneity of timelessness and temporality, nonlocal presence and local embodiment, motionless awareness, and the ongoing movements of the dance of life. She experiences the divine simultaneity of all things, all actions, and even all dreams. There is no more duality; only the unity of all things. All are One.

Rose is silent. There is nothing left to say. Even her experience now dissolves into the nothingness from which it emerged. She has entered the state of pure being, with no thought, no action, and no attachment to anything. Just…being.

The oven clock's beeping brings her back into the mundane action of daily life. The scones are ready. Verdandi turns off the alarm and pulls them from the oven. Rose opens her eyes. Everything looks new, as if she is seeing the world through the eyes of a newborn baby.

Verdandi gives her a cuddle. "Now you know the power of the Infinity Hourglass!" Rose nods. "Give your body a good stretch. I'll be setting out little plates and napkins for our guests' arrival, if you need me."

Rose's eyes wander over to the balcony where a bird sings on the railing. A butterfly with colorful wings lands on the edge of a flower pot. The city buzzes with activity as traffic moves frantically through the narrow streets, yet inside her apartment, all is calm and infused with a very different quality.

Verdandi returns. "We have a few more minutes before Sophia and Li are expected. Are you up for another brief teaching or would you rather rest?" she asks.

"I'm up for it, Grandma. Please share."

Rose is still in bliss from her incredible experience with the hourglass. Verdandi nods and sits beside her granddaughter.

"Recall the experience of your meeting with the company where you submitted your game proposal," Verdandi tells her. "Notice how their focus was on efficiency, competitive control, and financial growth. Their infinity loop on the wheel of evolution is not the same as the one you're on. With the goals they have, they'll only invest in you if they can see a direct gain for themselves. Be aware, without judgment, that your values, goals, and expectations are different. Don't get looped into paths that are not yours to explore."

Rose recalls the tremendous disappointment she felt that day. "Without judgment. Okay, go on."

"You and that company are not living from the same Zeitgeist," Verdandi tells her.

"What's a 'Zeitgeist?'"

"Zeitgeist is a Germanic concept that means 'spirit of time,' which refers to the collective consciousness of particular periods or cycles. Evolution unfolds in cycles; some smaller, some very large, and some even galactic. Each cycle activates certain qualities and possibilities of consciousness. What I'd like you to explore, and we can continue this when your friends arrive, is how the Zeitgeist of the emerging new era is already alive in you."

"Go on."

Verdandi continues, "The people from this company are still in the Zeitgeist of the era that is now ending. This loop of human experimentation has run out of time, and out of energy, too. For those who still identify with the Zeitgeist of that loop, they will experience reality as uncertain, as if things are folding back onto themselves, and possibilities are diminishing. Very much like what you went through before you died."

"Yes," Rose remembers.

"You had a sense that your life was coming to an end and you didn't know how your life would continue. You even had dreams of roads that came to a stop. You felt like your purpose was fading. Remember the uncertainty you went through before you were hospitalized last year?"

"It was a difficult time. I felt like I was getting depressed."

"So do you understand now how this can trigger huge fears in people about their survival? And how they may even harden their stance for control to maximize whatever profit they can still gain while faced with this uncertainty of ending times? The 'Zeit' is getting rather 'geisty' for those who are in the loop that is coming to an end! Your very presence, and the energy you bring in from the new Zeitgeist, is an existential confirmation that their loop of consciousness won't make it in the future. In those ways, you actually represent death for them. And this may terrify them at the deepest and most existential levels of their being. Thus, they feel the need to shape, twist, and mold you to fit their reality, and bend your project to fit their worldviews."

"That makes perfect sense," Rose agrees.

"There's the doorbell," Verdandi says. "Sounds like your friends have arrived."

Rose runs down the stairs to open the door for Sophia and Li, who both showed up at the same time. Her face is beaming.

"Come in! Come in!" she exclaims, ushering them inside.

"It's been a long time since the three of us were together like this," Sophia says with a wide smile.

"Too long," Rose agrees.

"I brought a pie."

"Mmm, apple. That was so nice of you," Rose says as Sophia hands her the pie. "Oh my gosh, it's still warm! And you brought your guitar, Li."

"Yeah," Li grins, "I know how much you love music."

"You're right." Rose embraces her friends. "I'm so glad you're here. Come up and meet Verdandi." She leads them up the stairs and into her apartment.

Apple Pie and Eros

The three friends enter the living room and Sophia immediately rushes up to Verdandi and takes her hand. "Verdandi! How incredible to finally meet you in person. I've heard so much about you!"

"And I you, Sophia. You're such a beautiful young woman."

"She made us apple pie," Rose pipes in.

"My favorite," Verdandi tells her.

Sophia beams. "May I call you Auntie? That's what we do back home in Australia to express how we're all like family to each other. You can imagine how many uncles and aunties I have."

"Yes, of course. Please call me Auntie Verdandi, or just Auntie, if you like. We do the same thing back home in Iceland. And who is this handsome young man with the striking brown eyes? You must be Li." Verdandi gestures for him to move toward her. "Could you please come a bit closer so I can see you better? You may also call me Auntie, of course."

"Your pie smells like heaven," Rose says. She places it on the dining table beside the basket of Verdandi's currant scones. "Look at that. We have a feast! I'll go put the tea kettle on."

"I'll go with you." Sophia follows her friend into the kitchen, leaving Verdandi to chat with Li in the living room.

"Rose, your grandmother is everything you told me about and more," Sophia whispers. "What a fascinating person. I feel like she can look right through me! She reminds me so much of my great aunt who's a powerful seer and healer in my mother's family. What's that around your neck? I've never seen that before."

"It's a special ring of unity, which my grandmother inherited from her grandmother, who got it from her grandmother before her, and so forth. It's very old. Grandma has been guarding this ring since she was about my age. It's used for ceremonial purposes."

"It's interesting. I love how there's a miniature dragon head and snake head, and how they form one body. And is that a green egg? I hope I can hear more about all the symbols and what ceremonies this is used for. The subject fascinates me."

"Me too. I'm sure we'll discover more soon, though Grandma can be quite secretive about some of that stuff." Rose turns to face her best friend. "Thanks for taking time off from your medical studies to come over today. I know how busy you are."

"Of course. I miss you."

"Do you think Li will be okay hearing about myths, alchemy, and rituals? I don't want to scare him."

"He knows you, Rose. He should be used to it by now. I'll cut some slices of this pie and we can take it out to them with the scones. That'll sweeten the conversation," Sophia says, laughing.

In the other room, Verdandi makes the most of her brief time alone with Li. She even performs a couple of tests on him to see what dragon meat he is made of. Although Li wonders why she's asking him odd questions, he responds politely. It simply confirms the comment Rose made to him one time that her grandmother could be a little strange sometimes. No matter. He likes older people.

Verdandi sees an ancient, wise energy around Li, and wonders whether he may have confused this as a weakness or insecurity. Especially as it is not the energy of the dominant masculine of the Western cultures where he has spent his last years. She would love to affirm to him how the ancient ancestral powers of his culture are in fact a great strength, and may one day save his life. Verdandi also senses the presence of a gentle water dragon and how it may have served some of the ancient Daoist temples in the time of the Han dynasty more than two thousand years ago. She wonders whether his parents taught him the ways of their dragons. She is just about to ask him when Rose and Sophia return with apple pie and scones and interrupt the conversation.

"Li, I still need to tell you what happened in that meeting with the company you recommended," Rose tells him.

"Good," Li says. "Please do."

"They were only interested in using me to make profits for their shareholders. They wanted ownership of my ideas and my Cosmic Compass project."

"That's disappointing. Their website talks about their ethical investments and sustainability practices."

"It's all greenwashing," Rose informs him. "I thought that their call for proposals was to support start-ups and innovators like me, but nope, not so. The CEO told their financial guy, Mike, to meet with me tomorrow, apparently to teach me how to write a proposal that matches their criteria. I don't want their money, but I do want to understand how they think. I want to understand how people get sucked into their ways, which is why I'm going to the meeting."

"And you want me to be there as well, right?" Li asks.

"Yes."

"But Mike doesn't know I'm attending the meeting with you."

"No, he doesn't," Rose affirms, "but I need you there so you can show him the ethics of business like you learned from your dad. These people have no moral backbone."

"Right." Li takes another bite of pie. "But don't be too hard on Mike. He's probably just acting the way he's been taught. He may not know any better."

Verdandi speaks up. "That's very kind of you to suggest that, Li, but I wonder if there may be more to this meeting than just business?"

"Like what?"

"It might not be Rose's compass game that Mike is after. She is a young, attractive woman."

"That's true," Li agrees, "but if his CEO suggested the meeting, then it probably means that he really does intend to help Rose with her proposal. Which might not be easy," he adds, teasing. "You know how stubborn she can be. It's not easy to teach her anything."

"Hey!" Rose exclaims.

Verdandi is not quick to give up. "Which might be precisely the kind of challenge that Mike would find exciting. Just be careful, both of you."

"Would you like me to come as well?" Sophia asks.

"No, you'd better not," Rose answers. "He may think it's a set-up."

"Okay, but I agree with your grandmother," Sophia adds. "You're naive when it comes to men."

"Thanks a lot," Rose says.

Verdandi nods her head in agreement. "Don't be fooled. There are times when the dragon of money is actually the disguised god of Eros, looking for a way to satisfy his sexual desires. Money and sexual energy are closely linked, and both can turn people's minds crazy. You wouldn't be the first woman who was tricked like that, Rose."

"I promise to be careful," Rose says.

"Don't worry," Li assures them. "Rose is smart. She can handle herself. And I'll be there to keep an eye on the situation as well."

"Thank you, Li. I certainly can take care of myself. My mom insisted that I learn jiu-jitsu the day after I turned thirteen. She heard it was one of the best ways a woman could defend herself."

"I've heard that, too," Sophia says.

"Even the police are trained to use jiu-jitsu to diffuse violent situations in the Netherlands," Rose reminds her grandmother.

"But you haven't used it much since you were a teenager," Verdandi reminds her.

"Maybe it's like riding a bike?" Li suggests. "Our bodies have memories of movements we make over and over."

"If Mike tries anything, I feel confident that I can handle him," Rose declares.

"It might be kind of cool to see you flip him in the café," Li teases.

"Poor guy. He doesn't stand a chance!" Sophia laughs.

"I won't worry then," Verdandi says. "Now why don't we talk about something else? Would you like a little lesson about the Yugas and the change of eras?"

Rose is relieved that Verdandi is shifting the topic.

"That seems kind of random, but okay," Li says.

"My grandmother thinks on a lot of different levels about a lot of different subjects all the time," Rose explains.

"It's true," Verdandi chuckles.

"I love it!" Sophia smiles. "Go for it, Auntie."

The Inner and the Outer Shifts of Eras

Sophia and Li sink into the cushions of the comfy couch. Verdandi begins, "The Hindu Vedic teaching speaks of cycles of time as 'eras' or 'ages,' also known as 'Yugas.' Each Yuga is a cycle of time with a specific 'Zeitgeist' or life lesson. Each celestial cycle consists of four Yugas."

Li ponders, "That sounds similar to the calculation of cycles in accordance with a Great Year."

Sophia chimes in, "And by 'Great Year,' you mean the approximately 25,800 years it takes for one complete cycle of the precession of the earth's equinoxes? Due to the wobble of our Earth's axis?"

Rose gets all fired up and adds, "That reminds me of something I read a few weeks ago. Scientists have discovered that the distance between this supermassive black hole they found in the center of our galaxy is also 25,800 light-years from Earth. Amazing, huh? The similarities in numbers? You think that's a coincidence?"

"There's still so much for us to discover; so much we don't yet understand," her grandmother affirms.

"I think it's amazing that our solar system orbits around a supermassive black hole that is at the center of our galaxy," Rose continues. "All this time they told us we turn around the sun, but go a little deeper and you find out that we actually circle around a massive Cosmic womb in the form of a black hole. If that's not a paradigm shift, then I don't know what is."

"Maybe the church will finally reinstate the Black Goddess as well," Sophia muses. "Wouldn't that be amazing?"

"Not just amazing, but necessary," Verdandi replies. "From time immemorial, as well as in the times of Isis, the Black Madonna and the Black Mother Goddess have been a favorite principle in spiritual devotion. She is the Divine Mother of alchemy and the sacred Darkness where the light is born and enters our world. But I'm not sure that Li is all that interested in talking about wombs and black holes as gigantic cervixes. For most men, these are rather uncomfortable words to hear."

Rose claps Li on the shoulder. "You don't mind, do you, Li? We've talked about this stuff before."

"Well, yeah, but not in front of Sophia and your grandmother!" Li exclaims. "I would like to learn more about these four Yugas, however. Missis…um… Auntie? Verdandi? Will you tell us more about that?"

Verdandi nods. "The cycle of four Yugas, according to the Hindu cosmology, begins with the Satya or Krita Yuga, also known as the 'Golden Age' or 'Age of Enlightenment.' After this wonderful age completes, things turn progressively worse through three more even darker ages, until we complete the circle and arrive back at the beginning of another Golden Age."

"Just like humanity," Sophia jokes. "We began so nicely, then it all went downward from there."

Rose pipes in, "That's an awful story, Grandma. Can't we change that? What about evolution? Imagine being born in a bad Yuga and getting stuck for all that time."

Verdandi grins. "Well, perhaps with your infinity hourglass you can put forth your plea to the time masters?"

"Infinity what?" Li asks, surprised.

Verdandi replies, "Rose is learning about the consciousness of time, and how it unfolds like the infinity symbol that expands from a single point of unity to then contract back to itself to conceive yet another cycle."

"That sounds interesting. Great image. But what's that got to do with these Yugas?"

"We'll get to that," Verdandi assures him, "but let's get back to Rose's concern of someone getting stuck in a bad Yuga for a moment. It may be that these awful conditions of a world gone bad are precisely what is required to awaken the inner flame of evolution. Just like what happens before and during renaissance times. The awfulness activates consciousness to stir up from its depths, and bring forth new and more meaningful ways to be alive. You'll never be able to understand the spirit of evolution by only focusing on the outer events. The inner stirrings of the evolutionary impulse are just as important, and perhaps even more so."

Rose, Sophia, and Li have suddenly become very quiet. They all look in the same direction just behind Verdandi.

"What's happened?" Verdandi asks. "Have I grown a dragon's tail?"

Sophia replies first, "A bright, flashy light...like a blueish star, just sparked above your head, and suddenly, my ears felt strange. It sounded like I was hearing you in stereo from all directions simultaneously. What was that?" She turns to the others on the couch. "Did you see and hear it too?"

Li stammers uncertainly, "Uh...I...I don't know. My body became like a plank nailed to the ground and I couldn't move. I felt an electric surge move through my brain. I've never experienced anything like that. How about you, Rose?"

"I saw the blue light, and right after that, a dark star opened up—like a portal to another dimension. I've experienced it before with Grandma, but it's great to see that this time I'm not the only one. At least now you won't think I'm crazy when I talk about this stuff."

"Would anyone care for another scone?" Verdandi asks, with one of her mysterious smiles.

"You look like you might know what happened," Li observes. "What was that?"

"Reality is much richer than most people know. Human perception is really very limited. There are many more worlds that we share with all kinds of creatures and life-forms that we have no awareness of. Sometimes the portals between the multi-worlds open and our worlds overlap temporarily." Verdandi puts another scone on her plate and takes a bite. "Now where was I? Ah yes, the 'Satya Yuga,' which is the Yuga that began long, long ago, when the consciousness of humanity and the many worlds of life were still united. It is said that during this Yuga people naturally experienced their unity with the Divine Source and lived a much longer life than today. The Zeitgeist was one of enlightenment and deep wisdom. Today you all got a little taste of how life and perception were different then, eh?" Verdandi laughs. "This age was followed by the 'Treta Yuga,' when the three Avatars of the god Vishnu incarnated on Earth as Vamana, Parashurama, and Rama to help with humanity's descent into darkness. In our traditions, we find stories of this period about the 'triple Goddess,' and a similar pattern of three Avatars, in the form of three priests or three priestesses. In the Christian traditions, we also find the concept of the three wise men or the three kings, as well as the Holy Trinity, although some of our Christian friends may not like these comparisons."

She dabs the corners of her mouth with her napkin and continues, "It is said that during this Yuga, the consciousness of our world came under the influence of evil forces, which some explain astrologically by saying that this is when our solar system moved further away from the central galactic sun. It is said that during this period, our world came increasingly under the influence of domination and control, challenging the primordial bonds of our unity."

Verdandi pauses for a brief moment to see if the trio is still following what she's teaching them. Pleased with their focused attention, she continues, "The age that followed is the 'Dvapara Yuga,' when morality continued to erode in a downward spiral as humanity sought to conquer and possess the earth and life. The age that followed after that is called the 'Kali Yuga,' the age of darkness and destruction. Many say we are now in this age, yet some claim we've left this age already and are on our way back to another 'Satya Yuga': a new 'Golden Age.'"

"I still don't understand how relevant this is for all the problems we face in our world today," Li says. "Irrespective of what Yuga we're in, if we can't stop runaway climate change, there won't be any more Yugas for humanity."

Rose nods and adds, "Besides, this dark age is not at all like the darkness of the Great Mystery or the Divine Mother. It's a darkness of forgetting, ignorance, and diminished consciousness."

Verdandi replies, "That is precisely the point, Rose. The outer darkness of diminished consciousness can become the catalyst for activating the divine spark within! In other words, the outer cycle of darkness manifests the inner cycle of the Golden Age."

"But can't we start the Golden Age right now?" Rose asks impatiently.

"Yes, inwardly," says Verdandi. "By living from the consciousness of the Golden Age."

Sophia has taken a small pad and pen from her purse, and has been quietly drawing while listening. "Rose, I think I get what your grandmother is trying to teach us. It's the infinity loop of your hourglass, which, by the way, is also in your Cosmic Compass design. For each outer Yuga, there's an equivalent inner Yuga, which makes two times four, which is eight. Just like the infinity itself. I have been drawing it here like two serpents, a light and a dark serpent to show the inner and outer dimensions and how they bring each other forth. I have also drawn here how the completion or the reunion happens when the outer and inner learning come together as the two heads of the serpent, which then triggers a new infinity loop. Or, as you would say, the birth of a new world, which is referred to as the birth of the fifth world in some of our indigenous traditions."

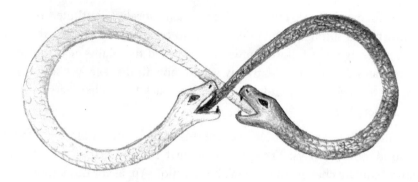

Sophia shows them her drawing and continues, "This whole new world represents an entire infinity loop, which then includes within it again the potential for four outer and four inner worlds or stages. I have a sense that this new or fifth world consciousness that you belong to is what's emerging from this completion of one entire infinity loop. The ending of our current stage also signals the completion of this entire, huge cycle of the whole infinity, and not just the last Yuga. It's the completion of all four Yugas, which is why it feels so big and life-changing for many." She turns to Rose. "Through your death, you jumped into the consciousness of the next infinity cycle already. In other words, you, as the awakening future human, are at the start of an entirely new infinity loop, which gives you the awareness of the whole architecture of time and consciousness, and not just one phase of it. That's why you've been getting all these dreams and visions. Because that's the consciousness that's growing within you. Does that make sense?"

Everyone is speechless, absorbing Sophia's incredible insight. Verdandi smiles and nods her head.

"Sophia, that's amazing!" Rose exclaims.

"Yes," Li agrees. "That makes complete sense. It's profound."

Jump Time and the Five Shifts

Verdandi stands up. "After a breakthrough moment like that, I think we should take some time to relax over lunch."

"Lunch?" Li exclaims.

"Oh yes," Rose tells him as she moves toward the kitchen. "With Grandma Verdandi around, no one ever goes hungry."

While Verdandi and Rose prepare a mixed vegetable salad for lunch, Li is softly playing his guitar with Sophia humming along. The conversation during lunch is light, animated, and witty. Verdandi shares stories of her funny dogs and cats in Iceland. Sophia talks about juggling her studies and her exciting internship at the hospital. Rose asks Li how his family is doing and he tells them about some interesting things they've been up to in Hong Kong. It feels good to share and laugh with good people.

"Rose and I can clean all of this up later," Verdandi says. "The sun has come out. It's a gorgeous summer afternoon. Let's all go for a walk to the park."

The others enthusiastically agree. While walking to the park, Verdandi has a chance to talk with Sophia to get to know her better. Li and Rose follow along behind them.

"We should discuss how we're going to deal with Mike tomorrow," Li says. "I'm really shocked by the way you were treated. Normally, I'm a very calm person, but when bad things happen to you, I feel very protective of you."

"Oh," Rose says. "Maybe your inner dragon is awakening."

"We've been friends for a long time," Li continues. "I'm fond of you, Rose."

"Even when I boss you around?" Rose teases.

"At least you're not as bossy as my mother," Li retorts. The two friends walk in silence for a minute, then he speaks again. "I was so scared when I found out you were hospitalized with COVID-19 last year."

"Really? You never told me."

"I know. I should have."

Just ahead of them, they see Sophia and Verdandi seated and chatting comfortably beneath one of Rose's favorite oak trees in the park. Sophia motions for them to sit beside her, which they do.

"Who here has heard of Jump Time?" Verdandi asks.

Rose knows about this one, so she decides to remain quiet. Li answers, "To jump tracks and shift between different realities?"

"Good, Li. That's quite clever. How about you, Sophia?" Verdandi asks gently.

"To enter the parallel tracks of time, like we do in my culture when we enter the dreamtime and jump between worlds?"

"Yes, that too." Verdandi smiles. "Jump Time is about the transitions between different orders of reality. Jump Time activates when the old orders no longer work and the new orders have not yet fully manifested. In that transition time everything goes into 'jump' mode. Like when you were babies and couldn't yet walk, and also couldn't get back into crawling to get around. We find ourselves at present in the midst of the most massive shift of perspective humankind has ever known. Through it all, many feel lost. We've lost our cognitive, emotional, and psychological bearings in space and time, culture and context. We lack the cohesive story that could tell us who we are, where we came from, where we're going, and why. When story is present, it sustains and shapes our emotional attitudes, provides us with life purposes, and energizes our everyday acts. It provides both context and the momentum that comes from meaning. Clearly, both personally and collectively, we are in need of a new story. What is it? Who will tell it? Does it come as a collective knowing? Or will some rare individual catch the inspiration and bring it forth? Are you, Rose, Sophia, and Li, the bringers of the new story?"

They all grin. Li looks mesmerized. He can see where Rose gets her magnetic qualities.

Verdandi continues, "I don't believe that there are any clear answers to these questions. However, there is light coming from one of the most important things ever to have happened in the last five thousand years. This is the rise of women to full partnership with men in the whole domain of human affairs. With this rise, and its many ramifications, comes, I believe, the emergence of the new story. That's why I'm so delighted that you're here with us today, Li."

"Thank you," he says. Rose nudges him and smiles.

"We are in a major Jump Time of 'whole system transition,' a condition of interactive change that affects every aspect of life as we know it. During this time, there's an emergence of patterns of possibility that have never before been available to humanity. Whether we realize it or not, we are the larger ecology through which this new story is being born and growing. We're being pulsed by our Earth and the Universe toward a new stage of growth."

"How does this 'pulsing' show up, Auntie?" Sophia wonders.

Verdandi replies, "In this time of extraordinary transition, we can no longer afford to live as remedial members of the human race. A new set of values that are holistic, syncretic, ecological, relationship- and process-oriented, and spiritual, are rising within us and around us. Though old habits of fear and division seek to restrain us and hold us back, we know there is no going back. Our complex time requires a wiser use of our capacities; a richer music from the instruments we've been given. The world will thrive only if we can grow to this next stage of our human development. The possible society will become a reality only if we learn to be the possible humans we are capable of being, in partnership with each other, and with life, and the Cosmos."

Li asks, "Can you see any signs of this already happening in our world?"

"There are at least four significant shifts occurring around and through us right now," Verdandi confirms, then laughs. "Oh dear. I'm beginning to sound like an old university lecturer!"

"That's alright," Sophia pipes up. "Please do lecture us. This is interesting." The others nod happily.

Verdandi continues, "The *first shift* is about our focus. People from all over the world are beginning to shift their focus toward regeneration and the healing of our planet. This shift in focus is also driving a major transformation in education and leadership, to prepare people in developing our regenerative and transformative capacities based on a more comprehensive understanding of our roles and responsibilities for this time."

"I know something about that," Li says. "The shift is also taking place in economics, business, and finance. Not yet to the level required, but it's starting to pick up."

"That's your leadership call, Li. You and Rose will make a good team," Verdandi smiles. "Which brings me to the *second shift* that is all about co-creative partnership and new forms of collaboration and coordination. These new forms of partnership and alliances for our emerging global community are like the mycelia networks of the root systems of trees. Critical to this shift is a true 'partnership society' between women and men, humanity and nature, children and their elders, as well as across different cultures and walks of life."

Rose adds, "I feel that, too. There are a lot of new community experiments happening here in the Netherlands with co-housing and communal sharing of resources and cars. A new social architecture is forming."

"You're right, love, and this new, social architecture is the *third shift*, which is made possible by the first and second shifts. As the membranes of old forms are breaking down, a more complex and inclusive global organism is coming into being. As living cells within this new organism, we are rescaled to earth-wide proportions in our responsiveness and responsibilities. Herein, we engage in sacred technologies; ones that access the interconnected world as an evolving world self."

"Does this shift in our social membranes also shift our collective consciousness?" Sophia inquires.

"Yes, Sophia, which is the *fourth shift*: the emergence of a new global consciousness. Although many people don't realize this, it is through this unprecedented collaboration and coordination that we learn to mature as a species."

"I learned that as a biologist when I studied maturation cycles of species," Rose exclaims. "Older and more mature species have learned to *collaborate* rather than just *compete* for resources. It's a fascinating thought that the nature of the crises we're going through now requires unprecedented levels of collaboration and coordination, which is precisely what's going to mature the consciousness of our species."

"Exactly," Verdandi continues. "And that is the sign of the fourth shift; this sense that a new global consciousness is emerging, which is also shifting our values and priorities. This is the emergence of the World Child, our new global identity as a species. Yet it must be nurtured in its infancy and protected in its development. It is the World Child, bearing the world mind, that exists as a kind of Cosmic fetus in each of us."

Rose is excited. "And how about a *fifth shift*? Like the five future archetypes we explored before, and the five stages of transformational change?"

"Very good, Rose," Verdandi replies. "How would you describe this fifth shift?"

"The future humans," Rose smiles. "That's when the consciousness of the new World Child is also born within the individual; that moment when we each become this new future consciousness of humanity in our own local contexts."

Sophia adds, "Yes! And that also makes sense astrologically when it's said that the consciousness of Aquarius, the new age, will ground and manifest in the energy of Leo, the awakened, heart-centered individual. I read somewhere that in astrology they speak of this as the Aquarius-Leo axis that brings in the new era. Auntie, can you tell us more about the kind of mind or psyche that these shifts require? How do we become the *possible* humans for the shifts you've described?"

"A possible human is one who has mastered the lessons of the higher heart. The possible human embodies the wisdom of a mature selfhood that is sourced in unity and oneness with life; a person in whom the inner masculine and feminine qualities are balanced and united. The possible human is also the announcement of the coming of the future human, as Rose just shared. One whose time is ready to emerge! One who embodies the qualities of the new era! The possible and future human is also able to cross-fertilize the wisdoms and practices of world spiritual traditions, as more and more people are gaining access to the Source of our being and becoming. It is a human in whom the new story is born with a mytho-poetic understanding of our diversity of cultures, as we rise and converge our ideas, as well as our beliefs. Archetypal ideas and symbols are sprouting forth already in the collective consciousness of popular culture. We're truly living now in a fertile field for these archetypal ideas and symbols to become our partners in the great work of new civilizational creation. Rose may share this with you later. That's why she's getting trained in the workings of the Cosmic Architect Tools."

Rose turns to Li and Sophia. "Now do you see why I wanted you to meet my grandmother?"

"I do," Li says. "I have another question for your grandmother."

"Ask me anything, Li," Verdandi tells him.

"How can we make these understandings more accessible to large groups of people from around the world?"

Verdandi replies tenderly, "Through the democratization of our human potential, as well as the introduction of experiences that can both expand, as well as deepen, our sense of reality. That's why I've been encouraging Rose to develop her Cosmic Compass game. Rose, you should do the same exercise with Li and Sophia as the one you did with Olaf recently."

"Yeah, great idea. I'll do that." Rose grins.

Free Choice and Destiny Paths

The wind picks up in the park. They've all lost track of time. Li enjoys the abundance of life around them: bees, butterflies, dragonflies, and even an occasional frog. He thinks for a moment and then asks everyone, "Do you believe we have free will in any of this?"

"What do you think, Li?" Verdandi says.

"I'm not sure. Maybe the whole 'free will' thing is also part of a bigger plan. Maybe we're all experiments of a Cosmic simulation."

"Can you explain further?"

"A simulation where the appearance of free will is programmed in as a little error code that creates a vacuum where the algorithms break down. It gives us the appearance of choice, and we get triggered to choose because the program is coded that way, but in reality, we're not really free to choose at all."

Sophia adds, "Or, perhaps it's all 'written in the stars,' as they say."

"Li, do you feel trapped in a destiny others want you to play?" Verdandi asks him.

"Yes, I do," Li admits sadly. "I struggle a lot with that."

Rose touches his arm. "Maybe free will is just a trigger for consciousness to evolve," she suggests softly. "Like a brilliant Cosmic strategy to encourage us to keep developing our capacities when we're unhappy with the status quo. As long as we believe we have a choice to do something else, try something better, or let go of what isn't working, we remain interested in evolution."

Sophia laughs. "Oh, you two! I like to think I'm free to direct my life. Even if it's not so, please let me enjoy the illusion for a little while longer."

Li turns to Rose. "Okay, so let's assume for a moment that what you say is true. Would there be a specific range within which human beings have free will, and perhaps also a range where we don't? What would happen outside that range?"

Rose replies, "Yes, outside the range of our free will is where destiny comes into force."

Li adds, "But how do we know what or who controls or influences our lives? You've shared with me many times that you've had premonitions of the future, yet you've never been able to fully stop these futures from happening. Does that mean that some of our future is fixed? Or is it because we aren't yet fully free, and thus, not able to access the full range and power of our free will? And how do you even know if you're free, if you're unconscious of your own blind spots?"

Verdandi places her hand on Li's shoulder. "My boy, don't overthink it. I thought Rose could get herself entangled in all kinds of mental spins, but I see that she's found her match! Trust in your life, not the life that others want for you, but your own life. Let it guide you. Ever since Rose's near-death experience, she's been having more déjà vu experiences or future memories. She often has the sensation that she's already lived this or that experience, which is where her questions about free will are coming from. I see, however, that your questions about free will have a different origin, and may have to do with your family situation. If you'd like to talk about it, just come and see me while I'm here."

"Thank you. I'd appreciate that," Li tells her.

"Thanks, Grandma," Rose says. "I believe that our power of choice, whether from free will or not, is our greatest power for effecting change in the world. Each choice is also a state of consciousness, and each state of consciousness gives different experiences and activates different sets of possibilities and different infinity loops. I strongly feel that life prepares us to become more able and mature for using our creative powers wisely, so we can learn how to consciously evolve the architecture of our worlds by the power of self-conscious choice."

Verdandi exclaims, "And on that note, I think this is the perfect moment to walk back home."

Integration -
The Infinity Hourglass

Through this chapter, Rose is introduced to the powers of the Infinity Hourglass, which helps her to become aware of the consciousness of time and how it shifts and transforms between and during the various cycles and stages of evolution. She also learns how the consciousness that we bring forth in the world can form part of the Zeitgeist that we most identify with. She further learns how during "Jump Times" there is a phase shift that offers profound renaissance opportunities for whole systems change and societal transformations.

> *The Infinity Hourglass supports you to become aware of the consciousness of time that you identify with, as well as the timeless dimensions within yourself, and how evolution unfolds in stages as an infinity loop that emerges from and returns to the prior unity of life. You can call upon the Infinity Hourglass to increase synchronicities in your life and develop a more conscious relationship with the creative potentials and flows of time.*

The summary and questions below will help you to integrate and apply the essential teachings of this chapter:

⊙ The Infinity Hourglass helps you to become conscious of time as an evolutionary process that unfolds like an infinity loop. This hourglass helps you to become aware of the various stages and cycles of this evolutionary process that are active and manifest in your life, and how this in-forms your experience of reality and the choices you make.

- The Infinity Hourglass also helps you to become aware of the timeless dimensions within yourself, and how to access the prior unity of life that is always present.

- As an Architect Tool, the Infinity Hourglass awakens your power of conscious choice through which you can make in-formed decisions for the evolution of consciousness on our planet Earth.

- Through this chapter, we've also introduced the concept of the "Zeitgeist," as the consciousness of certain periods and how we are now in the shift between two different Zeitgeists.

- We have also shared how you can shift your consciousness to new and different possibilities by using time as a creative force and by removing time from the patterns and structures that no longer serve or are dissonant with your inner being.

- When you experience resistance from people to the possibilities you seek to bring in, explore the readiness of your inner time and the time for what you seek to manifest in life. Remember that people have different relationships with time, and different senses of timing, which can also cause challenges and misunderstandings between people.

- As we have shared in the first book of the trilogy, remember how each of your choices and intentions are states of consciousness that activate specific coordinates in the landscapes and realms of consciousness. Use these wisely.

- During certain cycles, it may appear as if there is more darkness present in the form of division and violence. This serves a purpose. Light is born from darkness.

- Periods of outer darkness can ignite the conscious realization of the divine spark within. This is how the outer cycle of darkness can catalyze the inner manifestation of the consciousness of the Golden Age.

- As we have also shared in book 1, the consciousness of your future human potential already exists within you as your imaginal consciousness. Just like the consciousness of the butterfly is already informing the caterpillar of what is to come. Explore these glimpses of your future realities, even if you are not yet able to understand what they mean.

⦿ We now live in Jump Time, which is part of what emerges during renaissance times. We are called to create a new social architecture; one in which humanity and the earth are each enhanced within the context of our collective destiny. This requires a psyche, mind, and spirit that can reach deep enough to sustain all of this.

⦿ Free choice is part of the architecture of your destiny path. It is how consciousness is able to evolve. *How much of your time are you allocating for things you choose, and for which possibilities?*

CHAPTER 4

Becoming Future Creative

Applying the Cosmic Architect Tools

The next day, Rose spots Li through the window of the coffee shop where they'd agreed to meet. He locks his bike to the bicycle rack and enters. She waves at him and calls out, "Li! Over here! I found us a quiet spot where we can have some privacy."

"Good idea."

She motions for her friend to sit beside her at the table where two piping hot cups of coffee wait for them. She pushes one of the cups toward Li. "I expect Mike to arrive in about an hour. I'm a little nervous."

"It'll be okay," Li assures her.

"I went ahead and ordered us some koffie verkeerd and carrot cake. Is that alright? I wanted to treat you for taking your time to help me out like this."

"Great! This place is famous for their carrot cake. Thanks for treating me."

"You're welcome. It should be here any minute."

"It was great to finally meet your grandmother in person yesterday." Li takes a sip of his coffee. "She's so funny and smart."

"And mischievous," Rose adds.

Li laughs. "Let's just say that there's a lot going on when she's around." The young man removes his lightweight jacket and switches to the corner seat so he can get a good look at Mike when he enters. "I forgot to tell you yesterday how different you look," he adds. "What did you do?"

"I look different? How? In a good way, I hope!"

"Yes, very good! You look radiant."

"Oh. Thank you." Rose's cheeks flush pink.

"Now, about Mike. You didn't tell him that I'm joining your meeting, right?"

"Right. He thinks he's coming to teach me how to rewrite my funding pitch."

"Do you still think that's the only reason he's coming, after all your grandmother told you? And I'm supposed to be here just by chance?" Li asks.

"Yes. Act surprised, as if you just ran into me here. You can even tell him how happy you are to see me so you could finally thank me for the amazing game idea I gave to you and your dad. Then mention how it has the potential to be a 'golden goose' for your family business. That'll get him intrigued."

"Okay, I can do that." Li turns to look directly at Rose with a cheeky smile. "Shall I introduce myself as your boyfriend?"

"No, no…That won't be necessary," Rose says, not wanting to raise the wrong expectations with her friend.

"Alright. We still have some time before he gets here. Why don't you tell me how you're doing these days?"

Healing Conversations

Rose sighs. "Honestly? It's been intense. So many changes…so much uncertainty. I'm grateful for the support of my parents and grandparents, and Sophia, my brother Lucas, and you, of course. But it's challenging. My old life has died."

"That is intense," Li agrees.

"I really want to make my new life count. But I don't yet know how to translate all of these new visions and ideas that are coming to me into concrete things I can do to help our world. I'm worried about what's happening with our climate, and the rise of violence, tensions between people, suicides, and so much more."

"It's overwhelming. I imagine Verdandi's been helpful in navigating you through this."

"Oh, she has. My grandmother is like a wizard."

"You got that right," Li laughs.

"People say she's like a female Merlin. She's not afraid of death or transformation. She's been an enormous help." Rose pauses. "Do you want to know a secret?"

"Yes."

"She feels that I'm destined for great things."

"I think she's right."

"But how? I was given a second chance at life, and for that I'm so grateful. But I have to figure out what to do with the gift. My cousin Otto wasn't so fortunate."

"What happened to him?" Li asks, concerned. "I remember meeting him those few times at your apartment. He's a great guy."

"You didn't hear?" Rose answers. "He died from COVID. We were hospitalized at the same time, but they couldn't stabilize his body fast enough."

"Oh, Rose, I had no idea. I'm so sorry. I know how close you two were."

"Thanks, Li. I miss him so much. I promised him after his death that I would continue our quest to help stop the destruction of our world. Sometimes I feel like he's watching over my shoulder and cheering me on; helping me from the other side."

"Maybe it was Otto who manifested in the room yesterday when I felt frozen and you and Sophia saw those strange lights?"

"Maybe." Rose smiles at the thought.

"You've been going through a lot. You always seem so strong."

"Thanks." Rose glances at the door. There's still no sign of Mike. "Let's talk about something else," she says. She watches a waiter pass their table and deliver cake and pastries to three young women chatting away at a nearby table. "It's taking a long time to get our cake. I like to have it with my coffee, not afterward."

"Yeah, they're pretty busy today," Li observes.

"Have you ever wondered why they call a 'café latte' a 'koffie verkeerd' here in Amsterdam?" Rose asks. "It translates as 'wrong coffee!'"

"Yes, because they always bring it at the wrong time." They both laugh.

"Tell me about you, Li. How are you?"

Li pulls up the sleeves of his shirt and says, "I guess it's my turn to be honest now." He takes a slow sip of his coffee before continuing. "I feel torn… really torn. Your grandmother picked up on it yesterday. My parents have been planning my entire life since the day I was born—maybe even before that—and I don't know how to get out of it."

"This has been going on for quite some time," Rose says. "I remember you talking about it when we were at the university in New York. It's still unresolved after all these years? You never had that talk with your dad?"

"No. I keep postponing it. I'm afraid to let him down. He doesn't understand why I would question the path they've laid out for me."

"Have you tried to imagine yourself from a future possibility where you've already resolved this issue?"

"No, I've never done anything like that. Can you show me? I'm desperate. Sometimes the pressure and expectations feel so strong I can't eat or sleep. Every time I think about my future, I get depressed."

"I noticed that you've lost a lot of weight since we last got together."

"I have. I just don't know what to do." Li runs his hand through his hair and looks down at his coffee cup.

"Okay, I'll share the process with you right now," Rose suggests. "It will only take a few minutes, and maybe we'll finally get our carrot cake by the time we've finished!"

Practice for Invoking Your Liberated Future Self

"Close your eyes and put your hands on your heart. Feel the warmth of your heart. Your heart is sourced by an eternal fire, a subtle life force that originates from a realm beyond this time and place. This subtle life force is part of your current self, as well as your future self. This future self already exists here now in a state of potential. Think of this as a dormant state of possibility that is waiting to awaken in your awareness. It is one of many possibilities that are available for you to access. There is the potential of a future version of yourself that is more liberated and evolved than your present self. This future self knows how to better resolve all of the challenges that are troubling you today, and is eagerly waiting to support you.

"Intend now to experience this innate connection with this future version of yourself; your liberated self who easily provides you with access to whole new possibilities from higher orders of reality. Feel the wisdom and intelligence of your future self as it manifests around you like an empowering friend. Remember, you are already connected through the realms beyond this time and place. Stretch out your hands now and imagine that your future self is touching your hands in order to transmit its guidance and wisdom to you here and now.

"You may even feel how the warmth in your heart increases. Trust that you now have the connection with your future self, and that through this connection, you can feel and see your life from a finer and more expanded perspective. Notice what was blocking and limiting you; what was holding you back or constraining your life. See this from the consciousness of your future self. Now enter into the state of liberation. Experience the resolution of each of these blockages and constraints. Notice how this state of inner liberation gives you enhanced capacities for living your destiny, and in ways that honor those you love.

"This state of inner liberation and higher consciousness also gives you access to new codes and patterns for manifesting your optimum path with greater ease, synchronicity, and joy. From this expanded state, what new choices would you like to make now? What are the natural, next steps on your path? How would you like to express yourself and communicate who you truly are?

"For the next moments, allow yourself to simply be. Enjoy this enhanced and liberated state of being. When you feel ready, open your eyes with the intention to integrate what you just received into your daily life."

Investing in the Future of Life

While going through this practice, Li feels a nourishing warmth flow through his body. Years of accumulated stress and tension are released. He feels revitalized. Liberated. The family pressures feel lighter now, as if a huge weight has been lifted.

"That was amazing!" he exclaims, opening his eyes. "In my family, the whole question of 'what do I want?' does not arise. You do what is expected of you, and act according to your duty as a 'good son.' We don't have this Western notion of 'personal freedom' and 'exploring your potential.' Your destiny is part of the family destiny, which has been in the stars for a long time. Your ancestors watch over you to make sure that the family destiny lives on. That's why it's been so difficult for me to connect with my destiny path. I felt like I was betraying my family tradition by even exploring this idea. But the path that was laid out for me didn't engage my personal destiny. My parents couldn't understand why I felt trapped. For them, it's a great honor to continue the tradition. To break with tradition can bring painful shame and judgment to a family." Li looks at Rose. She listens quietly, with warm compassion in her eyes. "As you know, my family is revered as high-class members of the Asian elite. My dad has invested so much in my education, and we've already signed the notary papers for the company's succession procedures."

"But, Li, can you see now how it's not about breaking with anything? It's about opening to new possibilities that neither you nor your parents have ever considered before," Rose says gently.

"Yes, I hope so."

"'Hope so?' Or 'know so?'" Rose asks.

"Know so. You're right," Li says. "I need to change the story I tell myself. How do you apply all of this?"

Rose can tell that Li is fighting back tears from old, buried emotions that are now surfacing. She feels the ring of unity activating close to her chest. It starts to glow and vibrate inside her heart.

"May I share something my grandmother told me recently?" she asks. "It might help you too." Li nods. "The way we experience reality is directly related to the power of our own perceptions. Could it be that the way you were perceiving this situation before is what kept you trapped, and not the situation itself? You now have a new perspective you can call upon. You can live from the resolution rather than the problem! The more you practice this new way of being, the more natural it will become, and the more powerfully it will in-form the fields of life around you."

"Okay," says Li with some trepidation. "Oh, here's our cake."

Rose waits until the waiter leaves before she continues. "Can you see yourself talking with your dad from this new perspective? What choices are you aware of right now? And are those from your past-present or from your new future-present?"

"I'm still embodying both of those realities. The past perspectives have become the habits of my mind and are still influencing how I see my options. I need to let these past habits go. I need to retrain my mind with these new future states."

"Yes!" Rose exclaims and takes a triumphant bite of cake.

Li continues, "The huge shift for me is the fact that, for the first time ever, I can experience my future as a possibility, rather than an obligation. Ha! I just thought of something. Maybe my ancestors also feel trapped by the old narratives of duty. Maybe they have a desire to evolve in new ways as well. So, as we evolve, maybe they're able to as well. This cake was worth waiting for, by the way."

Rose laughs. "I'm so happy for you, Li. I know how hard it's been for you all these years, feeling like your life was tied up like a knot. Keep going! This is huge!"

"Mike is supposed to be here any minute, but before he joins us, I'd really like to get back to you for a moment. How did your experience of dying change your perspective of life?" Li asks.

"Even though the doctors said the whole thing only lasted for a few minutes, for me it felt like a lifetime in itself. It made me realize how consciousness continues after death, and how death is just a transition from one state into another. It also made me aware of life as cyclical, and how cycles need to complete for life to be reborn and evolve; how life is renewed from the future potentials of the higher orders of reality that exist outside of space-time. The old cycle of my life was complete. It had been for several months. I just didn't know how to enter into the new cycle that was waiting for me. I'd had these recurring dreams of death and dead-end roads for weeks before I was hospitalized."

"I remember you telling me about some of those dreams. I had no idea they were some sort of premonition," Li replies.

"Neither did I. During my near-death experience, I saw our entire world in a huge Cosmic cocoon with an amazing butterfly pattern of lights spinning around it, assisting our transformation. I also became aware of the information of immortality, the Cosmic building blocks of consciousness that are literally in every atom and molecule, and serve as the fractal growth patterns of nature. I realized how the Cosmic architecture of consciousness manifests as the informational dynamics of life. Yet sadly, humans hardly ever apply this architecture. Instead, we create systems and growth models that are completely out of sync with the evolutionary flows of unity. Most people are not partnering with the intelligence and wisdom of life. I then started to realize how our sustainability crisis is fundamentally a crisis of consciousness, by not realizing who we are and what life is."

"What are you doing with all of these discoveries?" Li asks.

"For the moment, I'm just writing everything down and sharing it with close friends like you, hoping we can develop the ideas together. I saw how urgent and critical the time is in which we are now living. We must radically change our understanding and ways of life or we'll be made redundant by design. I saw how my own life was contained in this huge cocoon that is dissolving the old body of time. I was then given the choice to renew and heal my life from the butterfly potentials of the new time."

"Incredible." Li listens with amazement. "And then?"

"When I made the decision to return as a future human of this new cycle, I literally felt like this future consciousness gave birth to me. Everything has changed since I made that choice. I now see from the future into our world. The saying, 'We are in transition times, living between two major eras' has become much more potent for me now. I'm like a little baby of this new era, while also going through the stages of death and completion of all that was part of me from the consciousness of the former cycle."

Li reflects on what Rose just shared. "Does this mean that I can choose today to also become a future human of the new era?"

"Yes! Exactly. Exciting, huh? Imagine what can change when you fully allow the future consciousness of this new era into your life; or this new 'infinity loop' that Sophia explained so well yesterday. My life has changed beyond my wildest expectations and beyond anything I've ever imagined. Even though on the outside it may not look like that for those who don't know what I've gone through. I notice a radicalization and hardening in the world. Many people are suffering from the increase in hatred, racism, protectionism, cynicism, nationalism, and the stronghold of the dominant empire archetypes."

"Could all these be signs of the loss of hope?" Li asks. "Many people I meet don't feel any hope for a better future or a more compassionate humanity."

"Maybe. Everything is getting stirred up these days. The dungeons of collective consciousness are breaking open as we come face-to-face with the demons we've tried to cast away. There's a huge vacuum in leadership as well. So many are hiding behind institutional excuses. As imaginal cells of the new era, we have to keep linking up to form the new evolutionary organs and capacities. Maybe that's why you couldn't commit to the path that was laid out for you by your family. Help them to understand what's really calling you. I'm sure that one day this will make them so proud. It's high time we invest in the future, rather than financing the predatory systems of the past."

The Omen of the Dragon Confrontations

Mike enters the coffee shop and scans the room, looking for Rose. His face brightens as he spots her, then darkens as he sees Li beside her. He is not keen on sharing Rose with a stranger, but he hides his disappointment behind a forced smile as he walks toward their table.

"Hello, Rose, you look beautiful today," Mike says, pulling a chair out so he can sit down. "And who's this here? A friend?"

Li extends his hand to shake Mike's. "Hi, Mike. I'm Li Wu, a close friend of Rose. We went to the same university and have traveled to a few places together in the past. I just ran into her here. She told me she was expecting you and asked me to stay."

"Perhaps she didn't make it clear to you. I'm actually here to see her for a business meeting, not a social talk."

"Yes, she mentioned it, and that's why she asked me to stay. I'm the one who recommended to her that she submit her funding request to your company."

"Really? Why our company?" Mike asks.

"Let's just say that I'm related somehow."

"Li also studied finance and economics," Rose chimes in, "so if you don't mind Mike, let's get started."

"Fine," Mike says with a dry voice. "And how exactly are you related to all of this, Li?"

"My family have been bankers and investors for a long time. I've been groomed with all this stuff since an early age."

"Tell me your name again," Mike says. "Li who?"

"Li Wu."

Rose feels a tiny bubble of laughter rise within her, but she keeps it contained. She can see from Mike's expression that he vaguely recalls this name, but he can't remember from where, and feels that he really ought to know.

"Why the interest in my name, Mike?" Li asks.

"Nothing," Mike answers quickly. "I met someone a few years ago who reminds me of you, that's all."

Li smiles. "Our name is very common. But enough about that. Let's talk business. What is it that you want to teach Rose? I might be able to help you both. We get so many of these funding requests every day in my father's company. Rose has already given me the full story of the meeting she had with you and your boss. She mentioned that it didn't go well."

"It's nothing to worry about," Mike replies. "She just needs to add some more information to her proposal about the return on investment, and get more corporate experience under her belt. Perhaps you can help her understand the realities of business? We like her idea, but she hasn't really explained how it's going to create revenue."

Rose is annoyed by the way Li and Mike are talking over her and discussing her project as if she's not even present. She can feel her inner dragon awakening again, and it's angry. For a brief moment she sees a flashing vision of the dark and light fire stones from the Avatar pouch. She wonders if they're signaling her to work with this strong, emotional charge rather than releasing it as an emotional explosion. She quietly invokes the transmission of this ancient architect tool. She manages to take out some of the charge, but still decides she must speak now.

"Actually Mike, I did outline the revenues and financial sustainability of my project. Extensively, in fact. It's not my fault that you and your boss didn't take the time to understand what is really meant by 'sustainable finance' and 'value creation' as revenue."

Li sees his opportunity and winks at Rose to calm her down. "Mike," he says, "I'll let you in on a little secret about Rose. She probably didn't tell you, being as modest as she is, but my father calls her a 'golden goose.'"

Mike looks surprised. "Your father knows Rose? What did she do?"

"You mean, what did I do?" Rose says angrily. "I'm sitting right here. You can ask me directly."

"Do you mind if I tell him the story, Rose?" Li asks her, touching her foot with his foot under the table and hoping she'll calm down. "You're so modest that sometimes people don't realize the tremendous value you bring."

Rose gets the message. "Alright," she agrees, taking a breath.

"Rose has given our family business many winning ideas over the years. In fact, we all think she's a bit of a star. My father adores her. He even offered her an executive position with the company. He felt she could assist us in getting 'future fit' and ahead of the curve. Unfortunately for us, she declined our offer, because she told us that she'd rather travel the world than sit in an office all day."

"Yes, that's right," Rose asserts. "Li's father acknowledges the value that my generation can bring."

"What else do you need from her before you agree to fund her project?"

"The usual majority shares, and a solid business case, that's all," Mike responds.

"Huh. I'm surprised. You're still doing that?" Li asks.

"Yes, why not?"

"You didn't receive our new ethical guidelines and our new sustainability strategies for diversifying the investment portfolio through future investment?"

"What do you mean, 'your guidelines?'" Mike asks, slightly nervous.

"I see that you haven't figured out who I am yet. But you know who Mr. Wu is, right?"

"He's the chairman of the New York branch of our division," Mike stammers.

"Exactly," Li smiles. "Which means that you report to us."

"Ohh. Mr. Wu…Of course." Mike shifts in his seat. "Now I know why your name sounded so familiar. Uh, no," he lies. "We didn't get those guidelines."

"I thought as much. That's why I took the liberty of briefing my father about the way you and your CEO treated Rose. He's quite annoyed about it, and even called it 'theft,' given what you requested from her."

The color drains from Mike's face. A tiny sheen of sweat appears on his upper lip. "That's not what we meant," he says quickly. "No, not at all. Rose just didn't understand what we asked, most likely due to her...you know... her lack of experience. And being so young and all."

"And you are experienced, Mike?" Li asks. "Please teach her. I'm all ears."

"Yes, of course. Sure." Mike stands up. "Sorry, can you excuse me for one minute? I have an urgent call I need to take." He walks quickly toward the toilets while appearing to talk on his phone. Li and Rose watch him go, resisting the urge to burst out laughing.

Rose whispers, "You didn't tell me any of this. Is it true? Is your dad really the chairman of their mother company? Did you really speak with him?"

"It's all true," Li assures her with a grin. "I'll tell you more in a minute. I did my homework. Hold on, he's coming back." Li adjusts his face to adopt a more serious expression.

Mike smooths his hair while walking back to the table. "Rose, I have good news for you. That was Charlotte, my boss, who called. She mentioned that she has reviewed your project and explained that she hadn't had the opportunity to read all of the sections before. We're not used to getting such lengthy proposals. She told me to tell you that we will be happy to fund your project, and that we can work out the details later."

"I'm sorry, Mike, but while talking with Li the other day, I realized that my ideas are worth much more than what I pitched for. I don't think your company can afford me. While you were speaking with Charlotte just now, I received a text message from a game developer I approached after our failed meeting. He informed me that he is most interested in taking my ideas and developing them further in the marketplace, and is more than willing to do so while honoring my requirements." She smiles mischievously. "Things can change so quickly in business. But I trust you know how the real world works, right?"

"How much is he offering to invest?" Mike asks, realizing that his company may have just lost its golden goose.

"Never underestimate a woman like Rose," Li interrupts. "Looks can be deceiving. You drove her right into the arms of your competitor. That's why my father prepared those new guidelines for future investing. We know full well how important it is to keep a brilliant young talent like Rose, and also what it will cost us if people like her become our competitors because we were too short-sighted to secure their ideas. My father will probably have to double his offer to Rose now, just to keep her."

Mike is speechless. Nothing of what just happened has gone according to his plan.

"Looks like you came all this way for nothing," Rose says to Mike. "Of course, you're welcome to join us for cakes and koffie verkeerd. Order whatever you like; I'll pay for you."

Mike mumbles, "Thanks," and settles for a quick cup of coffee in an attempt to save face. While he waits for his drink to arrive, he fidgets with his phone.

Rose looks over at Li in admiration. She's amazed at how quickly her friend shifted once he engaged in the process she'd shared with him earlier. She's never seen him like this. *He really stepped into the role of liberator*, she thinks, *and not just for me, but for himself as well.* She visualizes the Infinity Hourglass in her mind, and using her imaginal powers, she turns the past around with a clear intention. *This cycle of being put down and taken advantage of stops right here and now. I liberate myself from the cycles of diminishment and corporate greed and vow to also work to stop this in the outer world.*

Li breaks the silence. "Tell me, Mike, what's your company doing about the management of the commons?"

"By 'commons,' do you mean the natural capitals, like the ecosystem services of forests and rivers?"

"Not entirely. 'Commons' are common resources that bring value to the whole community and should be managed communally or peer-to-peer, and in ways that are inclusive and sustainable. Commons include, but are not limited to, ecosystem services and natural resources. They also include technological, social, cultural, spiritual, and other common resources. To protect the commons, we have to ensure that they can never be exclusively owned or controlled by anyone. Just like our planet should never be owned, nor the biosphere or our biodiversity. And neither should Rose's Cosmic Compass game be owned exclusively by you, or anyone else for that matter. Her ground-breaking idea is for the common usage and benefit of the whole of humanity and should thus be funded without the kinds of strings you tried to attach. Only then can she develop her project collaboratively and secure it through a creative commons license with open-source codes that can ensure this is going to take off globally. Everyone on the planet should be able to play the Cosmic Compass game for the betterment of our common world and future. This is the new economics and business leadership that I am expecting from people like you, Mike. Not your old model of shareholder control and profit maximization."

"That all sounds very idealistic, Li, but it'll never work in the real world of finance," Mike says airily. "Besides, it doesn't align with our Corporate Social Responsibility Charter that we follow for funding projects that help to implement the United Nations Sustainable Development Goals."

Li replies, "Your model may have worked twenty years ago, but that's not where the world is heading. Rose is correct. We are in a *value* crisis, and this is directly playing out in the way commons are managed and undervalued. There's a dangerous lack of consensus about what constitutes 'value' and from where 'value' is derived, just like you demonstrated in the way you undervalued Rose's project, and tried to extract value from her. You only focused on shareholder value, not societal and future value. Nor did you recognize how her project could increase the value of the commons and be commonly managed peer-to-peer. We're headed toward ecological bankruptcy because companies like yours still reward 'extractive' methods, like oil and petrol companies, for growing corporate wealth. Meanwhile, you discourage 'regenerative' opportunities. The time of outsourcing your corporate sustainability responsibilities is over. Business ethics demand that your corporate activities add both subjective, as well as objective, value to society, our planet, and future generations. You have to put mechanisms in place for distributing wealth fairly and managing the commons equitably. What you've been doing is the business of the past. There's no place for that in the future."

Mike purses his lips together as if he's just eaten a very tart lemon. "What do you want, Rose? I trust that as a 'woman of the future,' you can speak for yourself and don't need Mr. Li Wu to speak for you?"

Rose replies eagerly, "What I want hasn't changed. I explained it to you and your boss during our meeting, and in my proposal. You're not the right partner for my project. I understand that now. My thinking is far ahead. You aren't ready for what I bring to the table. Thank you for helping me see that. I've learned a lot from this whole experience."

"Yeah, okay. See you, Rose." Mike takes one final swig of coffee and rises to leave. "If you ever want to reconsider, you have my number. Bye, son of Wu. It was most informative to meet you."

Mike walks to the door without looking back. His original plan to ask Rose out to dinner, and maybe something else—in fact, the real reason he came to the café at all—is pointless now. He isn't used to being humiliated, and he doesn't like the feeling. It occurs to him that this may be how Rose felt after she left their meeting a few days earlier. "How the tables have turned," he mutters bitterly, stuffing his hands into his pockets and heading toward his car.

Back in the café, Rose sits quietly with Li. She finishes the last bite of her carrot cake and reflects on all that has happened.

"Everything's different now," she observes. Li nods in agreement. "Each of us has been given new choices. Fresh opportunities. I wonder what we'll do with them?"

How to Shift Reality from Future Consciousness

Rose thanks her friend for all of his help.

"Hey, you helped me, too. I really feel different. Like something big has shifted in me," Li tells her. He pauses, then asks, "Did you really get that offer on the phone, or did you make it up on the spot?"

"I did receive a message from a game developer in this new community I joined," she answers. "It's called SEEDS. Mike wouldn't understand any of it."

"Ahh! Smart girl! You beat him at his own game."

"Speaking of 'smart,' you were brilliant, Li! You were so convincing. I've never seen you like that before."

"Must be that powerful practice you gave me," he smiles.

"It really sounded like you were speaking from the man you want to become: a leader in the new economics, like you've told me about so many times. Did you really speak with your dad about me?"

"I did. When you told me how the meeting with that company went, I quickly called my dad to learn more. He warned me that guys like Mike typically try to play it big, even though they really have very little power in the game of leadership. They pretend they do though, and can be real opportunists. My dad likes you very much. He'll have a good laugh when I tell him what happened today."

"Maybe this is also the perfect time to tell him about your incredible ideas for the future of business," Rose suggests. "He may be pleasantly surprised to know what's really brewing inside you. It was so good to see you connect with your passion and speak from your deeper purpose like that." She suddenly becomes quiet. Tears well up in her eyes.

"What's up? What just happened?" Li asks.

"I miss Otto. It was only a few months ago that he and I were sitting here, happily eating carrot cake, and planning how we were going to trick the world into upgrading itself. His life ended so abruptly; I still can't believe he's gone. Do you believe in reincarnation?"

"I've never given it much thought. My grandparents do. They believe I'm the reincarnation of a powerful Chinese Zen master with whom they studied kung fu." Li touches Rose's shoulder. "I'm sorry you lost your cousin."

The friends continue to sit in silence, honoring Otto. After a few minutes Li says, "You helped me to understand something about my life that is really fundamental. I realize now how my passion and enthusiasm are linked to my future. This will help me to discern better whether something has future potential for me or not. You're right. The future already exists here as a potential. How else could it be guiding me?"

Rose wonders if she should tell Li about the hourglass from the pouch. "I'm glad you can feel it now. Grandma told me, 'Human beings are multi-temporal by nature. At the quantum level of our world, we start to see time as a simultaneous creative present within which arises past, present, and future times. The Universe is alive and interconnected through this quantum reality. When you can bring your local consciousness to a higher resonance in this quantum field, you can access the Universe as a living book of life. In this state, all-knowing is direct knowing in real time, and all systems are on go.'"

"That's a mouthful."

"Yes. And true."

"I like the sound of that: 'All systems are on go.' That feels so powerful. What else did she say?"

"That we have a very short time-span as local beings in a biodegradable space-time suit."

"She has a way with words."

"She said, 'Rose, if you want to live your life from the possibilities of the future, you need to access your potential as an infinite being with powers and possibilities that allow you to live in a universe that is larger than your personal aspirations alone.'"

"Cool. Did she tell you how to attract these new possibilities?"

Rose laughs. "The whole point of your future self is that it is a *possibility* space. By tuning into your future consciousness, you can literally shift the coordinates of the fields that you're playing with. Life is holographic; a creative ocean of information. Each unit of information contains the potencies of the whole, finely tuned, for us to evolve, grow, and learn. When we access different states of consciousness, this also activates different potentials within and around us. As we shift, so does life. The vibe you're sending out right now is very different from the one you came in with this morning. You will naturally attract different experiences and opportunities now."

Li smiles. "Is the future the same as the unmanifest aspects of ourselves?"

"You could see it like that, yes. Future is much more than a flow of time. Future is 'creative possibility.' And futures exist now, as information in a state of potentiality. Potentials are real; they're not just thought forms or ideas. Information that is in a state of potentiality is in what's called a 'nonlocal superposition state,' which is a state of simultaneous possibilities before the wave function collapses into 'this or that.' Everything that will ever come to exist here locally in our world already exists now as nonlocal Cosmic information. So yes, the future also includes unmanifest aspects of ourselves. We're each born with the power of manifestation. In fact, our life itself is a living expression of that power. Most people don't know how to use it wisely or coherently because our attention is all over the place. Am I making your head spin too much?"

"Not at all. It's fascinating. Does our process of becoming also provide us with greater access to the future potentials that already exist in our consciousness? And when you say 'nonlocal,' do you mean, non-physical?"

"Yes, but nonlocality is more about the connectivity that exists between particles in ways that can't be explained by classical laws of physics. Scientists observed that under certain conditions, like in a quantum state, a simultaneousness of particle connectivity exists. This is what is explained by the principle of 'nonlocality.' Albert Einstein called this 'spooky action at a distance.' The way I've been applying this principle is to access a larger continuum in which the simultaneity of times past, present, and future exist as nonlocally connected. When nonlocal possibilities become locally manifest, this literally in-forms and shapes reality around us."

"So the conversation we just had with Mike is already in-forming the field around us?"

"Yes."

"This is better than those virtual reality games. I wonder if this is also the key to many of these consciousness-changing technologies by syncing us to the vibrations and coherencies of the higher consciousness states? Are higher consciousness states naturally future creative?"

"Yes. Higher consciousness is nonlocal consciousness, but with the capacity to localize, and thus embody and tune, body, mind, and spirit to the higher states. This is what being future creative is all about."

"You mean we can literally create new futures through these higher states?" Li's curiosity is fully activated now.

"Yes, because these higher states give us access to the imaginal realm within which are infinite potentials and possibilities for how we manifest our lives."

"Ah. So that's why you say that 'future' is about so much more than time. When I imaginally form these new ideas about future economics and regenerative finance, does that mean I'm also making that happen in our world?" Li asks.

"Yes, when you do so coherently and develop the required capacities. There are various stages for how to actualize potentials. But yes, it starts from there. These higher states of consciousness are not just acts of imagination or mental desires from our ego. The perspectives of the ego are not Cosmically coherent. Ego is *fractured* thought and not *fractal* realization, else you'll be in a state of unity. Egoic states naturally dissolve as soon as we become coherent with the unified field of higher consciousness."

"Interesting. It sounds really complex, Rose. I wonder how many people you could even have this conversation with?" Li laughs.

"Probably not many. That's okay. Becoming future creative means bringing forth new possibilities that are life-affirming and life-enhancing. However, habits and conditioning close and diminish possibilities, as do fear and constriction. Earlier today you were afraid of being future creative, as it meant shifting the patterns that had confined and defined your world for such a long time. You even confused that with loyalty to your family."

"It's true. It was impossible for me to be future creative while feeling constricted with fear and expectations, which may be why I was feeling so depressed, as well. My life couldn't renew and revitalize. Can feelings like curiosity, wonder, and gratitude enter us into these higher consciousness states?"

"Yes. And so can love, certain sound harmonics, and spending time in nature. There are lots of ways to enter into higher consciousness."

"How about good ol' sex?" Li asks teasingly.

"Um…I'm probably not the right person to ask," Rose answers, with flushed, pink cheeks.

"Well, there's always a first time for everything. You may want to try that for a change before your higher consciousness lifts you off our planet altogether."

They both laugh nervously. Rose has only had a few sexual relationships, and they weren't amazing. She knows deep inside that there must be more to the enjoyment of her sexuality, especially after that dream of the flower she had a couple of months ago. Now with Verdandi in her apartment, she feels there's not much of an opportunity for experimentation in those areas.

Li notices how Rose has become genuinely insecure when discussing this topic and it fascinates him. She looks like a little schoolgirl. Though he doesn't come across that way, Li is far more experienced in that arena. He particularly enjoys tantric sex, and has found it to be very effective for moving into the higher consciousness states that Rose describes, as well as for entering into profound states of unity. In fact, a full body tantric orgasm is one of the few ways that Li is able to silence his mind completely, after which, all of his worries about life dissipate naturally and easily. He has never been in a long-term relationship with anyone, but has enjoyed tantric experiences with both women and men. He hasn't told Rose about any of this, however. She seems so innocent, and he doesn't want anything to happen to their friendship.

Rose decides to shift the topic. "I think it's great that you take such an interest into higher states of consciousness. I had no idea you were into that. You must spend some more time with my grandmother while she's here. She has the most amazing practices for entering into those states. Don't talk with her about sex, of course. She'd probably die of embarrassment. But other kinds of practices."

Li chuckles to himself, seeing Rose so flustered and worried all of a sudden. He has a sneaking suspicion that the topic of sex wouldn't phase Verdandi in the least, but he says nothing.

Rose continues, "These days, so many people are only interested in a quick thrill. 'Spiritual consumerism,' I call it. They want to manifest their soulmate, lots of money, and to become the most popular influencer in the world. People are willing to spend thousands of dollars on any training or gadget that promises to increase their power of manifestation, while doing nothing to invest in the future of life. I believe that anyone who is genuinely in a higher state of consciousness will not be focused on these superficialities. Grandma also mentioned how 'higher' doesn't mean 'better,' since life is not hierarchical. 'Higher' simply means entering into or being closer to the 'Source state' of the unified ocean of consciousness."

Li understands where Rose is coming from, but also sees how her approach may actually limit what she wants to do. "I do think we'll need to work on your pitch, Rose. Especially if you ever want these practices to go mainstream. To tell people that they shouldn't desire success, the love of their life, and financial security isn't going to work. The church has tried to sell us those messages for hundreds of years, and look where that got us. You'll need a new narrative to engage people into exploring these higher consciousness states you're speaking of."

"Maybe you're right," Rose sighs. "But I don't know how to go about it. Like Grandma told us yesterday, it's for us to create the new story, and she also said that partnership is key. We need balance. I think we also need a new story about the masculine, and not just the feminine. I don't believe that the patriarchy is any worse than a matriarchy."

"Or any 'archy,'" Li adds.

"Men have suffered severely by masculinity becoming so distorted and disconnected from its inner feminine. That's what the dragon has been showing me: the heart of the masculine."

"Did I hear that right?" Li asks. "What dragon?"

"Sorry, Li. I had a Jump Time moment. I'll explain another time. But you really were a great dragon today!"

"Thanks. I have no idea what that means, but I'll take your word for it. I have one more question, and then let's order lunch. How do I manifest these new future patterns in my life? As you know, I have some big decisions to make and I still dread the conversation I need to have with my dad about all of this."

"First, ask yourself if the time dynamics you're experiencing are yours or a projection from those around you. Ask yourself whose time you're breathing life into. And whose patterns are you manifesting?"

Li thinks about those questions while the two friends order lunch. Rose says, "We have some time before our salads arrive. I'd like to guide you through another quick process, if you're open to it."

"You bet."

Practice with the Infinity Hourglass for Manifesting New Realities

"Close your eyes and relax. Take a couple of deep breaths. Release the stress from your neck and shoulders. Become aware of your relationship with time. Do you have plenty of time? Little time? Do you feel rushed, restful, creative, synchronistic, meaningful? How does time manifest in your life and what does it manifest? How do you allocate time? How do you decide what and who to make time for? Take a few moments to simply be with whatever becomes revealed as you ask yourself these questions…

"Become aware of any limiting patterns that may be dominant in your life. Like, overcommitting, and thus, creating stress, procrastinating on things that are really important, criticizing yourself for not living up to your potential, doubting your own self-worth. How are these patterns able to manifest in your life? Is it happening consciously, unconsciously, willfully, accidentally? Again, just observe and don't engage with what becomes revealed. Simply observe…

"Now stretch out your hands and imagine receiving a mysterious hourglass that is shaped like an infinity symbol. You recognize this also as an hourglass that people use for allocating time. However, this is no ordinary hourglass. It contains within it the mysteries of time; mysteries known by the wizards and sages who've been able to manifest in and out of time, and in ways that others have labeled as miracles. Explore this hourglass with your hands. Feel its weight, energy, and appearance.

"This hourglass has been carefully designed to help us create a more conscious and meaningful relationship with time. It has come into your hands to help you shift and optimize your relationship with time. You may now ask this hourglass whatever it is you wish to know or understand about time. Let it reveal to you how to manifest the miraculous, the synchronous, and the consciousness that we are. Spend some moments with this hourglass. Let it awaken in you the awareness of the timeless expressions of yourself, as well as the local expressions that belong to this time and place of your human journey.

"Become aware of any habits and patterns that you really want to change in your life. Visualize these patterns, habits, and experiences in the bottom of your hourglass. Form the intention to remove time out of these manifestations and turn the page on all that no longer serves your life. When you are ready, you may turn the hourglass. As the sand turns inside the hourglass, these patterns, habits, beliefs systems, and former codes dissolve out of time. Their energy is recycled to support a new and more conscious manifestation of your consciousness through time.

"Well done! You've now turned the page on your own history. You've turned the page of your story. You are now free to consciously choose how you would like to co-create this new cycle of your life with time as your friend and the Cosmos as your beloved partner. New future potentials and patterns are now able to manifest in your life and in-form the fields of life around you. These new configurations of support forming around you will help you to further attract and create the synchronicities of the miraculous, as well as the wonder of life's infinite benevolence and wisdom.

"When you feel ready, you may return this beautiful hourglass to the Cosmos and thank it for all of the ways it has supported you. If ever you'd like to receive it again, all you need to do is call for it. You may now complete this practice in gratitude and trust. When you feel ready, you can open your eyes and gently move your body. Enjoy your new reality."

The Consciousness of Time

"Incredible, Rose! How did you even know all of this?"

"Actually, I didn't. I went through a special initiation with my grandmother the other day. She shared with me the transmissions of seven architect tools, which have been kept by the grandmothers of my mother's family for a very long time. One of these sacred tools is the hourglass. I had no idea of this practice; it just came through me as soon as I started to speak. I suppose my grandma's transmission worked," Rose laughs. "And I think I benefited from doing it as much as you did."

"Wow, this is so cool. Mega thanks."

"You're welcome! What shifted for you?"

Li replies with dreamy eyes. "I realize now that I can be true to myself and be true to my family. It's not an either-or situation; it's both-and, plus much more. My destiny never asked me to sacrifice one over the other. That was just my previous belief. I'm starting to understand that life is not a duality. We make it like that."

"Wonderful. I'd love to hear what else shifts for you in the coming week. Keep me posted, alright?" The waiter arrives with two walnut and melted goat cheese salads with warm figs, and two glasses of freshly squeezed juice with ginger and mint. "Perfect timing! That looks so good. Let's dive in."

After a few minutes, Li speaks. "This is a totally different topic, but it's something I'm curious about. Do you think we can experience time without memory? My aunt was recently hospitalized with severe influenza and a very high fever."

"Oh. Sounds like COVID."

"No, she tested negative for COVID-19," Li assures her. "She already had some problems with her memory before, yet things have turned much worse. She suffered complete memory loss for three days, and has no recollection of what she told the medical staff. She also lost all sense of time, having no idea how many days had passed."

"I'm sorry to hear that, Li. I don't know. Let's ask Sophia. As a doctor-in-training, she may know better. My own sense is that the experience of memory has something to do with our brain's capacity to localize information, and that when these internal structures for localization dissolve, so does our sense of time or time-based information. However, we are more than just our local mind. We also have a universal mind, which when trained, can help us to retain consciousness in different ways. The information of what we experience isn't lost—life is holographic after all—yet our experience of that information may get lost if we can only access it through our local mind or brain. We really should be developing our Cosmic brains as well, and not just our physical brains."

"How about animals? Do you think they experience time like we do?"

"I don't know. It seems like animals, insects, and plants are very aware of cycles and can sense what's coming long before we can. Remember how the elephants in Indonesia moved to higher ground to avoid the tsunami all those years ago? They knew what was coming."

"Yeah, I've read similar stories of animals who move away just before a major earthquake hits. I've even seen ants move entire nests days before a big rain." Li glances at the clock feature on his phone. "Oh, shoot. Where has the time gone? It always seems to fly by whenever I'm with you. Remember that time in Spain when we missed the ferry?" Li laughs.

"Oh, yes. All too well! I don't ever want to sleep in a drafty terminal like that again. Those wooden benches were so uncomfortable, and my sweater made a terrible pillow," Rose chuckles.

"The spirit of adventure! My father would never do anything like that."

Changing the Story of the Why

Li's expression becomes more somber. "I just realized something. My fear of being rejected by my family has nothing to do with my family. I've been fabricating all these reasons in my head about why I can't follow my passion and make my own choices in life, but you know what?"

"What?"

"That's been my excuse for not having to take responsibility for creating the life I really want. It's risky to be free."

"Whoa. I can't believe you just said that."

Li continues, "I'm afraid of being happy. It's easier to tell myself 'Do what's expected,' 'Be a good son,' than it is to take the risk of being free, happy, and adventurous, *like you*. Those are not values that I grew up with. By hiding behind the expectations of others, I don't have to take responsibility for my own choices. Then when things don't go as expected, I can say it wasn't my fault, which isn't true, of course. This is how I've rationalized blaming others for my own disappointments."

"Now or then?"

"What do you mean?" Li asks, puzzled.

"You just said, 'When things don't go as expected,' but didn't you shift that pattern earlier? Start telling the story differently. You can start right now."

"You mean, like saying, 'When things didn't work out for me in the past, I used to…?'"

"Exactly." Rose smiles.

"This is *so* liberating! Thanks for being such a great friend, Rose. I've got to rush home now to call my dad for our big talk. Let's meet again soon, okay?"

"Okay. And thank you, too, Li. What you did today with Mike was simply amazing. Say hello to your dad from me."

They both jump on their bikes and ride home in opposite directions.

"I can't wait to tell Grandma Verdandi about all of this," Rose says aloud. "I knew I could handle it!"

Integration -
Applying the Cosmic Architect Tools

Through this chapter, Rose discovered for the first time how to apply some of the Cosmic Architect Tools, namely the Ring of Unity, the Fire Stones of Darkness and Light, and the Infinity Hourglass. The Fire Stones of Darkness and Light activated when the confrontation with Mike started and she felt emotionally triggered. The Ring of Unity activated when Rose reached out to help Li shift his fears. The Infinity Hourglass activated when Rose guided Li through a practice for shifting his relationship with time and accessing his future potential.

> *You can call upon the Cosmic Architect Tools for shifting your reality, entering into higher states of consciousness, and supporting others in liberating and evolving their consciousness and lives. Most importantly, you can call upon these Tools for building the new worlds of higher consciousness in partnership with Life and our Earth.*

The summary and questions below will help you to integrate and apply the essential teachings of this chapter:

- We are each local expressions of universal consciousness, and universal expressions of local consciousness. Weave your world with the potentials and qualities of the local and the universal realities.

- Your future human consciousness gives access to more evolved and liberated states of consciousness through which you can access the possibilities and capacities of higher orders of reality for your life and our world.

- Your future is a possibility space for new choices, patterns, and experiences. Become a possibility space for yourself and others.

- Explore your life from the perspectives of your future consciousness, and enter into the experience of the resolutions you seek. Shift and transform constraints, limitations, and blockages with the consciousness of liberation, without focusing on the details. This is what it means to become future creative.

- Call upon your liberated, future self and explore the following questions: *What new choices would you like to make from this liberated, future perspective of your life? What are the natural, next steps on your path? How would you like to express and communicate your life? How does your enhanced future perspective in-form your choices and decisions?*

- Remember that the information of immortality, the Cosmic building blocks of life, in-form how you and life grow, develop, and evolve. The Cosmic architecture of consciousness is the same as the Cosmic architecture of our universe, which manifests as the informational dynamics of life.

- We are the imaginal cells of the new era. *What is calling you forward? How do you invest in the future of life?*

- We are in a value crisis, heading for ecological bankruptcy because we employ "extractive" methods for growing and accumulating wealth, while discouraging "regenerative" opportunities and fairly distributing value. *How can you support the necessary shifts in values and become a regenerative force for our world and future?*

- We are multi-temporal by nature. At the quantum level of our world, we experience time as a simultaneous creative present within which arise past, present, and future times. The Universe is alive and interconnected through this quantum reality. When you bring your local consciousness into higher resonance with this quantum field, your capacities and understanding will be greatly enhanced.

- Life is holographic; a creative ocean of information. Each unit of information contains the potencies of the whole, finely tuned for us to evolve, grow, and learn. When you access different states of consciousness, it also activates different potentials within and around you. As you shift, so does life. Everything is in a dynamic state of change and becoming.

- Higher consciousness is nonlocal. Through these states, you can naturally access the potentials and potencies of Cosmic consciousness. These high consciousness states are essential for developing and maturing your manifestation powers.

- Call upon the Infinity Hourglass to shift and optimize your relationship with time. Ask the Hourglass to reveal to you what you are to understand about time, and how to manifest the miraculous, the synchronous, and the consciousness you are. Use the Hourglass also to awaken your awareness of the timeless, as well as the local expressions of yourself and life.

- You are more than just your local mind; you also have a universal Cosmic mind. Train *both* minds together.

CHAPTER 5

Revealing the Powers of Destruction

The Wisdom of the Higher Heart

"**G**ood morning, sunshine!" Verdandi greets Rose the next morning as she enters the kitchen in her pajamas. "Rise and shine."

Rose yawns. "Is it morning already? It can't be. I must still be dreaming," she says sleepily. "What pretty flowers."

Verdandi continues to tuck assorted, colorful flowers into a vase. "Aren't they lovely? I couldn't pass up this spectacular bouquet down at the market. The lady working at the flower stall gave me a good deal when I told her I was visiting from Iceland."

"You've been to the market? Already? What time is it?"

"Eight thirty. Very late!"

"Very late if you're a dairy farmer, but not very late for me."

Verdandi chuckles. "Are you hungry? I put some oats on the stove for you, and there's hot water in the kettle for tea."

"Is it your famous oatmeal?"

"Of course."

"The kind with the nuts and fruit? And dried coconut flakes and honey?"

"Of course."

Rose perks up instantly. "Thank you! Nobody makes it the way you do." She scoops the oatmeal into a bowl and sits at the table.

Verdandi adds water to the vase and places the bouquet in the center of the table. "What was your dream about?"

"It was about a council meeting that happened long ago. People had gathered from many nations to prepare for challenging times. It was unusually vivid."

"Ah yes, that dream!" Verdandi grins. "Do you have your journal? You may want to write down some key words about it while the images are still fresh in your mind. Then finish eating your oats before they get cold."

Rose grabs her journal from the table in the living room and quickly jots down what she experienced in her dream. As she writes, Verdandi starts to whistle an ancient invocation song and Rose senses that this may again become one of those special days.

"In the dream there was a majestic, white, snowy owl who kept following me," Rose says. "I can still feel his presence. It was so powerful. What does it all mean, Grandma?"

"You'll find out soon, love. Eat your oats."

Honest Viking Conversations

Rose wolfs down her breakfast, and even takes a second serving. "Delicious," she says with a full mouth. "You can wake me up for this anytime."

"I'm so glad you like it. Goodness! You really are hungry this morning. Are you feeding your inner dragon as well?" Verdandi laughs. "When you finish, we really need to do something about those beautiful curls of yours. They're all over the place."

"You sound like Mom."

"Well? When's the last time you brushed them?"

"It's a new style I'm trying out: wild and original," Rose grins. "After that board meeting with Mike and his boss, I felt like I should change my appearance to look more assertive."

"Assertive?"

"Yes. Li liked it. He said I looked really different in a good way. Oh, Grandma, you should have seen him in action. He was brilliant. I've never seen him like that. I'm going to keep this Viking look for a while. I like it. And maybe now, people won't take me for a child or a fool. I hate it when people treat me like I'm naive."

"So you're trying to become like those fierce Viking warrior women of your grandpa's family, huh? Be careful what you're getting yourself into.

They have a mind of their own. Stubborn like their goats! Can't you at least braid it?"

"Grandma! I don't want to look like a schoolgirl."

"Your hair is so beautiful, but you do need to take care of it."

Rose sighs and looks the other way.

Verdandi takes note of her granddaughter's reaction, and decides to let the subject go. "Before we speak more about your dream, I need to ask you something about the way you treated Mike yesterday. I had the impression that you quite enjoyed seeing him defeated, and even somewhat humiliated." Rose says nothing. She takes her empty bowl and spoon to the sink and washes them. "Where is your dragon heart, darling? Was it really necessary to put him in his place like that?"

"I believe so, yes," Rose replies, tipping her chin up. "Now he has a taste of what they put me through. Besides, now there's no way he'll ask me out. You should be happy! I thought that's what you wanted."

"Not like that, love. It worries me that you enjoyed being on the winning side at *his expense*. Your powers are growing fast, and if you're not careful, your shadow will grow fast, too. Please be honest with yourself about the way it made you feel when you put him in his place. Winning is a very attractive energy that can easily mask the desire to dominate. The corporate greed that you felt so upset about is run by the same energy. You said you didn't want their money, but you don't mind accepting the equivalent emotional currency when it means you can be on top?"

Rose is quiet. This is not the reaction she expected from her grandmother. She did wonder why Verdandi didn't say much yesterday as she relayed her account of her meeting with Mike and Li at the coffee shop. She looks out the window. *Do I really have this blind spot?* she wonders, with a pit in her stomach. *Do I want to dominate others? Is that why I feel attracted to power and like to feel powerful? Is Mike a mirror for me? Or was it Charlotte, the CEO, who really triggered me? There's no point in arguing with Grandma. It'll only prove her point if I get defensive about this.*

"Are you okay, Rose?"

"I'll be okay, but I feel a little shocked about your statements. To be honest…yes, I did enjoy putting Mike in his place. I enjoyed revealing his arrogance and ignorance. That doesn't mean I enjoyed his suffering. Alright, maybe there was a fleeting moment of satisfaction, as well as a sense of getting even. But it only lasted for a few seconds."

"A few seconds is all it takes for the shadow to gain ground," Verdandi replies. "Never underestimate the ways of the trickster."

Rose reflects for a moment. "Maybe I'm more competitive than I realize, and more dominant than I want to admit. Thinking about it, I never really saw Mike as a strong man, even though he likes to put himself across as one. I actually thought of him as rather weak. But I did see Charlotte, the CEO, as strong and extremely confident. I admit to feeling competitive toward her." A thought strikes her. "Oh! It's like I used Mike to get back at her!"

"That's an honest start. These types of emotions can be very attractive, and addictive, too. You wouldn't be the first person to be lured in. Humanity has a long history of wanting to dominate and win at the expense of others. At least you've made a first step by accepting and admitting to yourself how you really felt. And it seems that Li was more than happy to be your knight in shining armor," Verdandi chuckles. "Now tell me about your dream."

Remembering the Original Instructions and the Need for New Covenants

Rose recalls the details of her dream. "It started with the white snowy owl I told you about before. It led me to a large gathering around a council fire. The people there were discussing how to prepare for the difficult times that were coming."

"Can you describe them?"

"They looked like ancient hunter-gatherers from many different nations or tribes. They were clearly worried about their future. There was a woman at the center of the fire who looked like a shaman or seer. She was instructing people from the Spirit World so they could survive the violence that was heading their way. She reminded them of an ancient bond for their protection, which reminded me of the ring you gave me."

"It sounds like you dreamed of the original instructions. Long ago, these were given to our ancestors all over the world. The instructions were part of a covenant; sacred agreements they made with the gods or Creator Beings, who they saw as their guardians. Many have since forgotten the instructions and agreements. And yet, this covenant guided our people, and many other indigenous cultures, for thousands of years. Some of the architect tools are from those times as well, which may be why you're dreaming of this now."

"Can we call on that bond again?" Rose asks. "Can we use the original instructions to prepare for what's coming now? I'm really worried about all of the planetary changes we'll no doubt be facing soon. So many leading climate scientists have warned that we're headed for climate catastrophes. Some have even warned that the Gulf Stream may soon collapse. If that happens, billions of people will be impacted through changing rain patterns, more droughts, rapid sea level rise, and maybe even an ice age for Europe, although the debate is still out about the effects. We really do need a new covenant that can guide us; instructions that people will actually listen to and use."

"You may be right, Rose. But this is a different Zeitgeist," Verdandi says, concerned. "In this age, it's all about who owns and makes the technologies that are used to create and distribute the new covenants. The digital world has become a universe of its own, with its own gods and avatars, and many of them are not benevolent nor wise. The gods of money and power dictate who can play in this new universe that is consuming Gaia like a ferocious, ravenous giant."

"But how can covenants be owned by people? They're sacred agreements in service to life. Nobody should own or control them."

"You're right, darling. But just like long ago when kings believed they owned the use of people's lives and land because they were Avatars for God, modern tech companies now try to control and create the rules of the game in which the agreements for our modern lives are written. The puppet masters are never far away, and they are devious shapeshifters."

Rose adds, "True. And now that our lives have become so complex, most people have no idea what they've agreed to. We download an app and click the agreement box without ever reading the small letters of the contracts we sign. There's so much trickery and deception. Is climate change even our biggest danger? The eternal Bond of Unity is given to us, but who acts on it these days?"

"That's why I had to share the Cosmic Architect Tools with you now, love. Call upon these sacred Tools in your meditations, dreams, and reflections. Ask them to reveal to you what you are to understand and act upon."

"Okay, I will," Rose answers. "Will you tell me more about the ancient covenants?"

Verdandi nods. "During one of my vision quests, our ancestors showed me how one day the ancient covenants would be renewed through new agreements. These new agreements may take a very different shape today than they did in the past. They may even become an Earth constitution, or form part of the new economic and governance experiments you were telling me about."

Rose smiles. "Keep going. I can feel the energy of that, and the ring on my chest is getting very hot."

"But first, there's something else I'd like you to understand about this new cycle of time that we're moving into. What's happening right now is not just about our planet alone. There are larger forces at work; universal forces of deep transformation, as one cycle is completing and another begins. Our ancestors spoke of this shift as the time when the Cosmic Serpent starts shedding her old skin. They saw the skin of the Cosmic Serpent as the body of time for that cycle. Each time the Cosmic Serpent sheds her skin, she sheds a cycle of time, and a new era begins. This process happens from deep inside the womb of our galaxy, and perhaps even beyond. Our planet is part of this cyclical process, and she has her own natural cycles, too. Sadly, the many changes we have forced on her are now destabilizing her own cycle of transformation."

"Ahh, that makes sense. I was reading a book on mythology that said that serpents and snakes feature in many cultures as ancestral Creator Beings. And Sophia told me once how the Rainbow Serpent is very much honored in her culture as a powerful Creator ancestor who often dwells in waterholes. I just wish that our Nordic myths wouldn't portray the dragon, serpent, and wolf as such violent and evil creatures."

"Perhaps the original myths didn't," Verdandi says. "Those interpretations may well have been part of the demonization of the pagan religions that took place afterward. And perhaps the deeper lesson of these myths was to become aware of those shadow behaviors in ourselves. Of course, the original myths are nothing like the modern film versions that are prevalent today."

"That's for sure," Rose agrees. "If the ancient gods and goddesses saw how they're portrayed in the movies, they'd never recognize themselves."

"What did your grandfather tell you about those Nordic myths?"

"He told me about the story of Loki and his children and how they ended the old world with its nine realms. He explained that Loki was a half-god who played the role of the trickster and was very cunning."

"Did he tell you that Loki represents our shadow side?"

"Yes, and that he had two wives. One of them was the giantess, Angrboda. They conceived three children who were considered to be a great threat to the gods and goddesses of Asgard, since it was foretold that they would be their demise. Asgard was the place where they all lived. Kind of like Mount Olympus was for the Greek pantheon."

"That's right. Go on."

"Loki's children were Jörmungandr, the Midgard sea serpent, Fenrir, the wolf, and Hel, the queen of the underworld and the realm of the dead. When the father god, Odin, learned of the threat of Jörmungandr and how he kept growing larger, he cast him into the sea of Midgard, which is the realm of the humans. That's how Jörmungandr became the Midgard sea serpent. Grandpa also said that when the Midgard serpent has grown so big that it starts to crawl on land, it will encircle the entire earth. Its movements will cause violent volcanic outbursts and earthquakes. That's how we'll know that the end times are beginning. What if these end times are now?"

Becoming Conscious of the Trickster Within

Verdandi pauses for a moment and then repeats Rose's words, "*What if these end times are now? Indeed, this may be the key question. Endings and new beginnings are cyclical. For the Nordic people of those earlier times, they probably had their own version of a world that was ending. Especially during the days when their Viking lands and villages were burned to the ground, and their religion and rituals were banned by the violent takeover of the new religion in the form of Christianity. But you're right. The myth of the Ragnarök apocalypse and the ending of the old world with its nine realms may very well be happening today, also. What would the Midgard serpent represent for you in today's terms?"

Rose stretches her body. "The Midgard serpent is a child of the trickster Loki, and thus represents our own trickster energy. In today's world we've created so many technologies that promise to improve our lives and advance humanity, yet many of them also serve a very different agenda that destroys life on Earth. To me, the Midgard serpent represents the rise of artificial intelligence and digital technologies that are going viral—just like a fast-growing serpent, encircling the entire Earth. And in particular, those technologies that we've created from our shadows in a state of semiconsciousness, tricking ourselves into believing it is all in the name of progress, when deep down we know better."

"What else?"

Rose ponders for a moment. She twists a curl around her finger, then continues, "The Midgard serpent also represents for me an entity we can't control, with poisonous venom that can alter our consciousness; an entity that keeps on growing and growing. In the final battle, Thor dies from the deadly venom of this serpent after he kills it. The myth says that the serpent releases so much venom in the final battle that it poisons all the air and kills all of the remaining creatures. The release of venom could also refer to how we're now changing the composition of the biosphere, making it uninhabitable for life on Earth."

"And what exactly do you mean by 'venom that can alter our consciousness?'" Verdandi asks.

"I believe that the venom could also refer to the digital consciousness that is now spreading through the human realms, which ends the consciousness of our earlier pagan worldviews, and perhaps even our biological consciousness. The seers would have received visions of a time they couldn't yet understand, but would also have seen the end of their world and customs. It would seem as if other forces were taking over their world, which they described as a gigantic serpent or sea monster."

"And a ferocious wolf."

"Fenrir. Yes. Because those archetypal images formed part of their collective unconscious. Yet, do we know the implications of seeing the world through the eyes of artificial intelligence and digital consciousness? Do we understand the implications of constantly consuming data that are fed to us by these technologies? Are we altering human consciousness in ways we have no idea of yet? I'm not against digital technologies or artificial intelligence per se, but I do believe there are more messages to this myth than may appear at first glance. This is not just food for an action movie. I can feel deep in my bones that our ancestors were telling us something of the times in which we now find ourselves."

"Very perceptive, my girl," Verdandi replies. "As you mentioned earlier, there will come a time when the Midgard serpent has grown so big that it will be able to encircle the entire earth. As he starts to crawl out of the ocean and onto the land, his body will shake the ground from below, causing violent tsunamis, earthquakes, and volcanoes that will break the chains of Fenrir. Once the gigantic wolf is freed, he will open his jaws so wide that he will devour the earth, the sun, and the sky. And he will kill Odin. That's when we'll know that Ragnarök, the final battle, has begun. What does all of this mean to you?"

Rose ponders for a minute, then answers, "It means that there will come a time when our technologies are going to shake the earth like the Midgard serpent. During the end times, we'll see an increase of violence between people, as well as a ferocious hunger. Those two things represent Fenrir the wolf. The violence and hunger will be perpetrated by the people and corporations who are eating up our planet for their own selfish purposes. When the viral technologies grow beyond a certain point, it'll break the chains of our predatory financial systems, which will unleash all of the destruction that'll take our world to the brink of extinction. It also means to me that this will be the time when we can all *see* the Midgard serpent, as it will no longer be hiding in the waters of the unconscious."

"Exactly. It will be out in broad daylight and in the media," Verdandi agrees.

"This is happening now," Rose adds. "So many lies and schemes are getting exposed. People are becoming knowledgeable about the social media giants who have been controlling our lives and politics, and we're starting to become conscious of the many forms of manipulations in our world. This also breaks the chains of our ignorance, which can erupt in a lot of anger and violence between people. For so many people, it feels like their world is being shaken from its foundations. Nothing is as it seems anymore."

"And that, my darling, is the *raw* emotion of which I wanted you to become conscious. I believe that this is the reason you and your friends have felt so shaken recently. Deep inside, you all feel terribly upset and in rage about all that's going on with our world right now. This emotion hits a very ancient nerve. You know instinctively, and in ways your mind doesn't yet understand, what's happening. This also unleashes in you a deep primordial anger that is rising up like a fierce dragon. In this rage, you feel the fire of destruction, as well as the alchemical fire of transformation."

"Wow! Yes, that's it!" Rose exclaims. "I feel so angry, yet I have no idea who I'm actually angry with, beyond the usual suspects I've already named. Am I angry about the Midgard serpent? Or the patriarchal Odin and Thor? Who are the tricksters here? Who is Gaia in this story? What is her voice and where is her anger in all of this? What if the venom of the serpent is necessary to end the old patriarchal masculine, as represented by the death of Thor?"

"Good," Verdandi nods. "You're becoming aware of the trickster, who never reveals itself, but always gives you a target for your anger and revenge. Many of the old gods and goddesses are destroyed during Ragnarök, as the old world turns to ash and sinks into the sea. Even the old sun and moon are devoured, as you mentioned. The trickster is always at work behind the scenes. So much so that we could ask whether the final twists of this myth of ending times were made by those of the new religion who wanted to end the influence of the old gods and goddesses. What I want to get you conscious of is how these stories of endings and new beginnings are cyclical; the patterns repeat. And yet, we have the opportunity now to evolve the story from higher orders of reality. But only if we can see all sides of the story and how it lives in us."

Rose takes a moment to digest what she has just come to realize. She starts to become aware of her own inner trickster, her own shadow, and realizes how deceptive it is. And how difficult it is to spot once she's acting out from that place.

Healing the Shadow Wounds

Rose looks at Verdandi with teary eyes. "Grandpa said that in the old Norse myths, there was no such thing as good or evil; each god and goddess was portrayed as having shadow qualities. The themes of betrayal, scheming, and fighting also applied to the Creator Beings. That's a much more compassionate view than needing to become perfect humans for a perfect God who never sins. I want to become conscious of the full spectrum of life, including my capacities for love and caring, as well as my appetite for power, control, and destruction. The Norse gods and goddesses also needed to learn how to grow their powers, like Odin who had to give up one eye in order to receive the wisdom from the Well of Knowledge. And the same for Horus in Egyptian cosmology in his fight with his brother Seth, remember?"

"I do."

"He lost an eye, which was later magically restored. In order to grow our Avatar selves, we need to give up some of our beliefs and views that stand in the way of our evolution."

"Now you're entering the Dragon heart," Verdandi replies tenderly. "The voice from which you just spoke is the voice of the *higher* heart. The higher heart is the Cosmic heart that transmits wisdom from higher orders of love. The Cosmic Dragon heart teaches us the ways of the higher heart through the courage and determination that burns away all of our illusions and projections, and helps us to see reality for what it truly is. Keep going."

"It hurts, Grandma. It really hurts. The line between seeing the illusions and feeling disillusioned is so thin. It's easy to slide down into nihilism from there; to not believe in anything anymore. Yet I know if I take that turn, my heart will turn cold as ice, and the energy of skepticism will have won my heart. Then my shadow will have free rein and I'll become an ice queen."

Tears of sorrow, pain, and anguish roll down Rose's cheeks. Waterfalls of buried emotions that were stored in the caverns of her heart are unleashed. The fire in her heart burns away all of the walls she had built around those emotions.

"Breathe, love," her grandmother advises her. "Breathe into your heart. Let all of those emotions flow down through your feet and into the earth. Gaia loves you. She is with you, and has seen and felt it all." Verdandi puts her warm hand on Rose's back, between her shoulder blades.

Rose allows herself to feel it all. With a trembling voice she asks, "What if these forces of destruction from Loki's children were necessary to end the old orders, and make way for a new cycle? What if some aspects of the old gods and goddesses represent our own egoic superpowers when we grow out of touch with our human vulnerabilities? What if their denied destructiveness and trickery, and our own, take the form of Loki and his wife and their three children? What if the things that ended them are the things that they denied and cast down to the underworld, out of conscious sight? Once thrown to the shadow realm of our own unconsciousness, the aspects we have denied about ourselves will continue to grow in the cold darkness of resentment, fear, and anger. Oh, Grandma, I'm all of it. All of it! The whole story is happening within me, right now."

Verdandi speaks with quiet power. "I'm honored to witness the profound integration taking place in you, Rose. You're finally embracing your inner Odin, Thor, Loki, and all other aspects of the ancient mythic tales—the gods and goddesses, as well as the children of the trickster couple: Jörmungandr, the Midgard serpent, Fenrir, the wolf, and Hel, the queen of the underworld. You can feel all of these characters inside your own inner saga as your mythic understanding awakens. This is a profound inner shift and healing. Take your time, dear one. Now you can see how the shadow parts of ourselves, although destructive, can also help in the destruction of our egoic superpowers that have grown so arrogant and dominant that we've become blind to their influence. You can see the deeper purpose for the dragon, snake, and wolf, which are not the evil powers, but primordial powers that return us to our naked consciousness. From that place, we can begin anew, and we are wiser. Now you understand Loki's purpose."

"Thank you, Grandma. It's true. For the first time, I actually feel compassion for Loki. Before, whenever you made me conscious of my inner Loki, I always felt a sense of shame and guilt. I wanted to hide it. I was scared of being found out. But now, I feel a profound love for Loki, and myself, without shame. This is all new."

"You can also heal your fear of wolves now, and understand the recurring nightmares you've had in the past of being swallowed by a huge wolf," Verdandi replies. "Fenrir devoured Odin, after the gods tricked and chained him several times. Knowing that the wolf was a child of Loki and Angrboda, the gods made Fenrir an outcast. They turned him into a threat, believing that he would be the end of them. Those are the battles between the ego and the shadow, which, in fact, belong to the same family. Both have to come to an end if we are to progress to the next world of higher forms of consciousness, in which these tendencies are integrated and healed."

Rose feels calmer now, and more grounded. "How about Loki's third child, Hel, who became queen of the underworld and the realm of death? Wasn't she keeping the deceased god Baldr, who represents peace, beauty, and renewal?"

"Exactly," Verdandi affirms. "It is said that all of the havoc started when Baldr died. Because with him gone, those qualities were no longer represented in the outer world. He was the most liked god, and everyone wanted him back."

"But Hel refused to let him go, right?"

"Well, she made a demand before she would release him from the world of the dead. In order for Baldr to be allowed to return to the world of the living, every single being had to cry for his return."

"But one person faked dry tears with no sense of grief."

"That's correct. Some say it was Loki who refused to cry real tears."

"But whoever it was, Baldr had to remain in the underworld."

"Yes," Verdandi affirms. "Yet, it is from this underworld, and the death of the old egoic consciousness, that a new world emerges. A world that is born from peace, beauty, and love, as you just experienced. You have now met Baldr."

"That's amazing," Rose murmurs. "Isn't that also like Christ, who descends to the underworld, and the sun that dies in order to be reborn? Digital consciousness and artificial intelligence can't ever produce the qualities of beauty, love, and peace that are integral to our human nature. If we let those qualities go, the world will not renew, and all will end."

"It's true," Verdandi says solemnly. "Now you know what your true superpowers are and where to find them. And why Hel is not evil."

"You're right!" Rose adds. "Hel is an energy that forces us to truly desire what is required for the renewal and healing of our psyche and world!"

"You've got it," Verdandi smiles. "Now, I'll give you one more twist to the story. Imagine that Fenrir the wolf and Jörmungandr, the Midgard serpent, are the *female* offspring of Loki and his wife, and not his male children, as is often portrayed. Look at the rise of the feminine in our world today, and how the old patriarchy sees this as a huge threat."

Rose jumps up from her chair and exclaims, "That changes so many elements of the story! The serpent as the sexual awakening of women; the wolf as the return to our wild, untamed feminine powers; and Hel as our awakening as gatekeepers to the underworld from where the powers of renewal and rebirth are born and released. This is not the egoic feminine that lusts for power, revenge, and influence. No! This is the primordial sacred feminine who uses the power of destruction to end the worlds of our egoic human selves. My whole body is buzzing with this revelation. It's so powerful and profound!"

"Now you understand what's necessary for a new world to emerge. All the lessons are within the journey you've just taken, as well as for those who will one day read your story. When the Christians tried to convert our people, they tried to use the story of Baldr as a way to convince people that Christ was the risen Baldr. They told our ancestors that the world they came to offer was the new world that would become possible by the ending of the Nordic gods and goddesses. And yet, they themselves had not faced their own confrontations with the Midgard serpent, the wolf, the dragon, and Hel, the queen of the underworld; the four primordial forces that would need to first devour and end their own egoic battles. As such, they were blind to their own shadows and the ways in which they were causing destruction through their so-called 'new world of redemption, peace, and salvation.'"

"So," Rose says, "if we don't complete this phase of our transformation into higher consciousness through the destruction of the inner, egoic worlds, the transformative forces will become the monsters by which we destroy our outer worlds. Then the dragon becomes our abuse of fire through the endless consumption of fossil fuels and the creation of weapons of mass destruction. The wolf becomes our never-ending consumption and addiction for economic growth that devours our world. And the serpent becomes the poison that ends the evolutionary consciousness of nature and shakes our world 'til it cracks, unleashing the chains of more destruction. Hel becomes our entrapment in the underworld, where we're unable to bring forth our powers of renewal through beauty and peace, as those qualities aren't truly missed in the egoic worlds."

"Yes indeed, Rose. And of course, other cultures will have other symbols and archetypes for describing these fundamental lessons of the formation of the higher heart and mind."

Rose reflects, "I see. So we can't skip this inner integration with the dragon, serpent, wolf, and the descent to our underworld. We can't enter or bring forth this promised new world from the state of our egoic selves. If we don't destroy these illusions in ourselves, we'll destroy the world around us and all who live on it. Is that why you came with the Avatar mother pouch and the architect tools?"

"Yes, love. These tools are essential to guide you through this stage of your journey. You are familiar with the overall stages of the transformation that takes place inside the Cosmic cocoon, through your rebirth from your butterfly consciousness. However, it's only now that you can start to experience the archetypal forces that are truly within these enzymes of dissolution. These enzymes can also take the shape of the serpent, dragon, wolf, and the gatekeeper to the underworld, as well as other archetypal symbols that devour our egoic tendencies. Keep that ring of unity close to your heart while you go through this process and until such time that the Cosmic Ring of Unity has fully awakened your higher heart. If you don't, you may forget what this is all about, and become bitter, revengeful, and destructive yourself."

"I'll keep it close, Grandma. I promise." Through her pajamas, she touches the ring that rests on her chest.

"Remember, my girl, our ancestors had a profound cyclical understanding of the nature of life. For them, there were no final endings. The same is true for the Greek and Egyptian mythologies, and many other indigenous teachings.

Human nature is part of nature. Have you had enough for now?"

"It's a lot to process," Rose answers.

"Maybe you'd like to play your violin or do something else that will help you to integrate all that you've just gone through."

Practice for Connecting with the Wisdom of the Higher Heart

Later that evening, as the sun dips below the horizon, Rose relaxes in the living room. Mozart plays quietly in the background. Verdandi enters and sits beside her granddaughter.

"I have a process that will help you to integrate the things you've come to realize today," she says. "It will also help you to connect with the wisdom of your higher heart and help you to balance any strong emotions that may be rising up."

"That sounds wonderful," Rose answers. She snuggles into the couch with a cushion on her lap. "I'm ready," she tells her grandmother.

"Then let's begin. Take a deep breath and relax. Release any tension in your shoulders, neck, and jaw. Take another breath and relax even more. Let go and allow yourself to be fully present. Acknowledge how you're feeling. Don't engage with the feelings; just be present, like a loving friend who's sharing the same space and is just listening and witnessing what's happening.

"Bring your attention to your body. Become aware of any tensions or pain, and lovingly bring your presence there. Touch the areas of pain and sensitivity with your loving awareness; your presence of care.

"Now become aware of your inner world. Notice the qualities, feeling tones, and the light. Is it dark, dim, or bright in your inner world? What emotions are present for you? How do you feel about yourself? Just notice without engaging; simply be that loving friend who is present to it all.

"Place both hands over your heart, as if you are holding it. Imagine putting your arms around your heart, as if hugging your dearest friend. Thank your heart for giving you the power to feel and know.

"Now imagine that deep within you is a wiser part of yourself that has already gone through the destruction of the egoic worlds, and is your beloved friend from the other side of the veil. This is your consciousness from the new world that is born after the egoic worlds of our shadow selves have fully disintegrated and come to an end. At each new stage of the journey, this new world can be overtaken by aspects of ourselves that we are unconscious of. This wiser part of yourself has gone through these cycles of the birth of new worlds and the ending of old worlds, many, many times. So many times, that this old friend knows how to guide you through each of these stages. This beloved friend is the wisdom of your higher heart. It is your Cosmic heart.

"Take a moment to greet this trusted friend. Continue to hold your hands over your heart. Feel this trusted friend awaken inside your heart. It sends its energy and support to your hands. You now have the connection with one another. Explain to this trusted friend, the wisdom of your higher heart, how and where you need support in your life right now. Share the emotions that have been challenging to heal and integrate. Let it know how it may best serve and support you.

"Ask the wisdom of your higher heart, your Cosmic heart, to help you become conscious of the feelings, thoughts, intentions, and beliefs that you've pushed aside and become unconscious of. Ask it also to help you become conscious of your shadow dynamics, and how to lovingly reclaim the rejected parts of yourself from the influence of the shadow. Notice how the wisdom of your Cosmic heart returns these rejected parts to you so you may embrace these parts of yourself and bring them home within you.

"Nourish these parts of yourself now with your love, and as you do this, notice how these parts transform and heal as they return to their essence and true purpose.

"Rest a few moments in this state of healing and integration. You now know the way to access the higher heart, your Cosmic heart, and you can call upon this trusted friend whenever you need its support. When you feel ready, you may gently open your eyes and stretch your body, being fully present, here and now."

The Ways of the Higher Heart and Mind

The next morning Rose wakes up peacefully. She has slept like a baby and is still integrating the profound conversation she had with her grandmother the day before. She reads the latest news on climate change while finishing her breakfast. As usual, there are more alarming reports that reveal how humanity is on course for extinction events. Verdandi comes in from the bedroom where she has just finished her daily tai chi routine.

"Good morning!" she says cheerfully. "Did you sleep well, love?" She kisses her granddaughter on the top of her head.

"I did, thank you."

"Anything good in the news?"

"Not really. Floods. Hurricanes…Hey, remember that talk we had yesterday about cycles and changes? Are these climate changes also part of a natural cycle of our evolutionary process?" Rose asks.

Verdandi pours herself a bowl of cereal and sprinkles the top with fresh blueberries. "Not quite, dear. The climate crisis is a result of humans not learning the lessons that evolution offers us. If we don't take responsibility for our powers, then each next turning of the wheel of time will make us more destructive, and bring more painful lessons. The destruction of our natural world is a direct result of our persistent greed and desire to dominate life. We're still trying to 'negotiate' with Mother Nature, but she can't be bullied into compliance. Whenever we attempt to shortcut or bypass evolution, we create an avalanche of unintended consequences. Life is precisely tuned to make life possible and thrivable, to use that term you love so much."

Rose replies, "Yesterday we talked about the necessary destruction of the egoic worlds by taking responsibility for the destructive forces of our shadows. Can we stop this pattern of greed, domination, and hatred without destroying our Earth in the process? Do we really need to take this lesson out on nature?"

"We can stop this pattern by going through the process you just embarked on," Verdandi tells her. "The destruction of the egoic forces and shadow trickery needs to happen from within, just like the lessons of fire need to be mastered from within. Soon you'll be ready to start working with the white and black fire stones from your Avatar pouch. There's always a more peaceful way that is possible, Rose. Especially, when we don't kill the god and goddess of peace, beauty, and renewal in ourselves. We've been externalizing so many of our inner divisions and quarrels, yet there's no law that says we have to evolve through destruction. It's up to us how we navigate and move through these Cosmic cycles of transformation."

"I'm glad to know that. I still wish there was more I could do," Rose sighs.

Verdandi smiles. "Oh, dear girl, you have no idea how powerful your story really is. You are a cornerstone in the rainbow bridge that is being built between this possible world and the destruction of the old ways that no longer serve us. The first step is the one you took yesterday: to honestly face your own inner shadow and egoic tendencies. Especially your desire to dominate and win! Get to know these deeper forces that live and rise within us from the collective unconscious."

"That all sounds fair and well, but I have no idea how to apply this to the economic and financial systems we've created. As a biologist, I learned how, in living systems, the energy for growth, activity, and development is circulated and regulated by the cycles and processes of life. In the Nordic ending of the old world, the forces of regulation were destructive and monstrous."

"Do you suppose that might be because each of those forces had been made outcast, and thus denied?" Verdandi asks.

"Oh. Yes. Maybe that's where the answer lies. Perhaps the inner equivalent of economic engines running on fossil fuels is our own denied shadow emotions by which we feed the engines of destruction. Whereas, when we learn to fuel our economic engines with the solar energy of our sun, we discover new sources of powers within us and vice versa. The majority of our economic systems are still running on fossil fuels, and purposefully so. We have to shift our consciousness if we are to stop this predatory capitalism."

"That's why I recommended that you talk with my friend Hazel Henderson. I'll give her a call in the next couple of days. I'm sure you two will have much to discuss about this topic." Verdandi smiles. "And remember, you can always ask the Cosmic Dragon to teach you about the consciousness of fire, and the ways of the higher heart."

Rose pours one cup of tea for her grandmother and one for herself. "That reminds me, you mentioned before how the Cosmic Dragon is androgynous, yet outwardly expresses this through the masculine force. Like the Cosmic Serpent is androgynous and outwardly expresses this through the feminine force. You also said that the androgynous consciousness is rising in our world again because we are at the beginning of a new cycle. Is that why we're seeing such a diversity of gender expressions and sexuality right now?"

"Yes, love, I believe it is," Verdandi replies. "In many indigenous cultures there has always been a more fluid understanding of gender and sexuality, and not this Western binary approach of being either feminine or masculine. And yes, with the rising of the Dragon and Serpent consciousness, the androgynous is rising in the collective unconscious of humanity as well."

"While my inner dragon is rising up, does this mean I'll also become more masculine?" Rose wonders.

"It could be. You're about to emerge from your cocoon and getting ready for birth. You feel the pull of the world, rather than just the pull of the inner Cosmos. The fire that's been supporting you to grow your new internal butterfly body is now starting to direct outwardly to bring you into the world. This is an essential role of the masculine: to provide deep support for the birthing feminine."

"Ah, now that makes sense," Rose smiles. "I've felt this outward pull growing a lot lately. I also miss going out."

Verdandi continues, "The masculine is a wonderful and essential force that should never be thought of as separate from the feminine. Together they form a unit, just like the Cosmic Serpent and the Cosmic Dragon. It's essential that you learn about and from the masculine; to know this energy in yourself. Learn from the fire element of alchemy, and the higher heart of the Cosmic Dragon. Learn about the impregnating force of creation and how it develops as the force that protects and prepares the ways for new life to enter into the world. Learn how to become an architect and builder of the new world through the partnership between the feminine and the masculine.

"And learn from the air element of the higher mind, the Cosmic mind, and the expanse of universal consciousness and illuminated thought. For the last nine months, you've retreated in the womb of your inner cocoon, which led you to explore the Cosmic womb and the feminine principles of the Cosmic architecture of life. Now it's time to explore the masculine, and how they work together."

"I hadn't thought of it like that," Rose says. "It makes so much sense the way you just put it. So how do I work with the inner fire that's rising up inside me, so it won't explode and bite someone's head off?"

Verdandi smiles. "Just like the Cosmic Dragon showed you. Let this primordial force rise up from within your heart, and not just your head or your will power. Your heart is designed to house and circulate a tremendous amount of heat without this ever becoming harmful. When your inner dragon fire rises without the coherence of the heart, it can become forceful, dominating, destructive, and even violent in the way it expresses itself. That's the typical display of the Western, patriarchal dragon, which does not at all express the balanced masculine energy of the Eastern dragon, or the mystical dragons of our indigenous druidic traditions."

"So that's why my heart has been getting so hot lately," Rose reflects. "You're right; it's a strong, pleasant heat. Very different from the fire of a fever. I also noticed how each time my heart activates, synchronous events happen in the following days, including new visions and insights and stronger dreams. I love it when this heat spreads through my whole body, especially when it enters my womb and gives me a feeling of strength and rootedness."

"Enjoy it. And if ever you feel like your dragon energy is becoming too strong, just call upon the wisdom of your higher heart and ask it to harmonize this primordial force with the wisdom of love. Then hold the intention of the greatest goodness and wellness for all of life, and feel your love for all of creation."

"Thanks, Grandma. I'll do that. You've given me a lot more tools and new perspectives for addressing the causes of climate change. I see how important it is that we also focus on healing and evolving human consciousness. It's not our planet that's in trouble; we are."

"When we move straight into action without understanding, action becomes *reaction*! Keep going, Rose; you're doing well." Verdandi smiles.

"May I ask you one more question?"

"Sure, love."

"When you say higher heart, you don't mean higher in terms of hierarchy or higher in terms of vibration, right?"

"Higher in this case refers to higher orders of reality that are more subtle, less dense, and which contain higher levels of usefulness. Disease often happens when you forget that there are other levels of reality that try to enter in order to be helpful. Your stomach, for example, can help you break down your food so it becomes digestible, and the higher levels of your stomach that are subtle in consciousness can help you break down your life experiences in ways that make them become digestible."

"Oh! That's why my stomach hurts when I feel stressed or receive news that I find hard to digest!" Rose exclaims.

"Exactly. Each of your physical organs also have other, subtle levels and orders of reality that can be called upon, and they need nourishment too. This is all part of learning the art of active transcendent embodiment of the multiple levels of yourself, at every level, as well as a whole. There are many mansions with multiple levels in the house of the self. Like that dragon of yours that lived in the basement and has now climbed up to the balcony on the first floor. In the same way, you can put your mind to use for ordinary tasks or higher levels of usefulness to create extraordinary thoughts and ideas that contribute to life on Earth. You hold the keys to the house of the self. The higher mind, like the higher heart, is coded and fueled for the positive, creative empowerment of yourself and others."

The Fire Triangle

Later that evening, a light rain begins to fall. Rose illuminates the living room with beautiful candles that she has kept for a special occasion. She finds that the warm, flickering glow of the candles and the sound of raindrops spattering the windowpanes have a soothing effect on her. Verdandi sees this as a good opportunity to teach Rose about the power of fire.

"Now that you're able to call upon the wisdom of the higher heart and are discovering the sacred purpose of the powers of destruction, it's time to tell you more about the primordial power of fire. As you know, fire has always been a part of nature. Those who understand fire and know its consciousness know that its true purpose is not to kill or harm, but to transform, energize, and purify. Fire is a necessary power of evolution, yet the ways we as humanity have used and employed fire differ greatly, depending on the goals and aspirations of each of our cultures. Some cultures used it to develop new technologies and fuel the engines of societies, while others decided to keep it limited to cooking, ceremonies, rituals, and as a means for communication and protection. The dominating cultures tended to use fire primarily as an energy source for developing their weapons and to fuel their political and economic aspirations. Many cultures also used fire to clear their lands for agriculture and for the building of cities and villages."

"How do you know all of that? Not just from books." Rose looks puzzled.

"Our ancestral knowledge and oral traditions are our university of life. Where do you think the historians and anthropologists gained all of their knowledge?" Verdandi asks. "Just ask Sophia. I'm sure she can explain to you how her people from Aboriginal Australia were very cautious about using fire for changing their environments, intuiting the irreversible changes this would bring. Now we can't think of a world without fire. I'm glad that solar and other renewable energy technologies are gaining in popularity, but where the psychological expressions of fire are concerned, we're a very immature and young species. Quick tempers explode our minds and emotions. You've heard of the fire triangle?"

"No," says Rose.

"The fire triangle describes three conditions that need to be present for making a physical fire: heat, fuel, and oxygen. Heat is used to ignite a fire. If the temperature drops below a certain level, it goes out. During extreme heatwaves, the chance of wildfires is much higher. When there's enough fuel and oxygen, fires will keep going. To stop a fire, you can remove the oxygen by throwing a blanket or sand on it, for example. Or you can drop the temperature by pouring water onto it, or by taking the fuel out so there's nothing left to burn. This concept of the fire triangle can also be applied to more subtle and metaphysical expressions of fire."

"It's true," Rose says. "I've experienced what happens when I ignite my fire through anger, fuel it with resentment, and oxygenate it with my belief that I was made wrong."

"That's an excellent insight, Rose. You've had lots of important revelations in the past few days. That's not the kind of fire that can produce progress, and yet it's the most common fire that humanity employs these days. Once you see the triangle at work, you can get creative in shifting it by developing the alchemical fire of the higher heart. Ignite your fire through the warmth of love, and the sparks of passion and joy. Fuel your fire with empathy and compassion! And once your fire is sourced from the Flame of Love, then feed your fire any of the pain or shadow dynamics you have buried inside for healing and purification. Breathe the lightness of oxygen into your fire by the luminosity of your higher mind, or put out a harmful fire by removing your negative thought forms. Learn about the sources of warmth, fuel, and oxygen in yourself and in our world, both internally, as well as externally."

"This is going to become another helpful practice. Thanks, Grandma. Did you know that our stars, including our sun, are powered through a process called nuclear fusion? Deep inside the core of the sun, the nuclei of hydrogen atoms collide and fuse into heavier helium atoms, which releases tremendous amounts of energy in the form of light and heat. Simply put, that's how our universe fuels itself with energy. This is in stark contrast to the human technology of nuclear fission, which produces energy by splitting atoms, like we did for creating the atomic bomb, and what's used in most nuclear power plants and weapons. Splitting is separation thinking, rather than unification. So it's not surprising that there are so many destructive impacts from this 'splitting' of atoms, rather than the 'fusing' approach of merging."

"That makes sense."

"Some scientists believe that the solution to our energy crisis is to replicate a sun on Earth, using nuclear fusion and magnetic field dynamics. There are still many challenges to overcome before this will come to the market. I'm learning more about this in order to better understand what's happening in those fields."

"What is it about these technologies that interests you?" Verdandi asks.

"The applications of the Cosmic architecture of the Universe, and the importance of applying this consistently," Rose explains. "One may think that the outcomes between fusion or fission are the same thing, namely energy. However, I believe that these are fundamentally different procedures that will have many unforeseen implications, apart from all the environmental hazards and nuclear waste. It's a completely different approach when you create energy by breaking something apart or splitting it up, compared to merging it together to form a larger unit. Fusion reminds me of making love, and the alchemy of the Flame of Love that you spoke of earlier."

"You mean sexual intercourse?" Verdandi chuckles.

"Yes!" Rose grins. "I'm talking about the energetic merging that happens in sexual love-making, and the tremendous energy that is released through the nervous system during an orgasm. It's as if the natural technology of the stars for producing energy is fractally at work in the marriage between our spiritual, physical, and mental circuits."

"You know something, love? That's a quality I really admire in you; you're always thinking."

"I have an active brain," Rose laughs.

"I thoroughly enjoy our conversations, but it's been a busy day and I think it's time for me to get some sleep. May you have sweet dreams." Verdandi kisses Rose goodnight and gets up from the couch. Just before she reaches the bedroom door, she turns to her granddaughter and says with a wink, "Want to know something else? That wild Viking hair looks just perfect on you."

Integration -
The Wisdom of the Higher Heart

Through this chapter, Rose comes face-to-face with her own shadow dynamics and egoic powers. She learns how our powers can be used to destroy as well as to create with the forces of life. She receives a profound, personal experience of the wisdom of the higher heart, which is the Cosmic heart, and learns how to work with the alchemy of fire as the Flame of Love.

The wisdom of the higher heart protects you from being overtaken by the egoic archetypes of domination and disunity, and connects you with the wiser parts of yourself that have already gone through the destruction of the egoic and shadow worlds. You can call upon this wisdom to teach you about the alchemy of love and the unifying power of the higher heart, and for showing you the new world that becomes possible by the ending and disintegration of the egoic worlds and shadow dynamics.

The summary and questions below will help you to integrate and apply the essential teachings of this chapter:

⦿ Shadow represents the unconscious forces that drive our lives. The shadow can also be thought of as the inner trickster, and can be very manipulative and cunning. When we engage in shadow dynamics, we distort the use of our powers by using these in reversed and contrary ways.

- Become aware of the trickster and puppet masters in your life, and what you are (and are not) agreeing to. Remember the Key of Conscious Choice, and how you hold the powers to change the rules of the game where this concerns your life.

- Endings and new beginnings are cyclical. *What in your life, and inside yourself, requires an end so that your life can renew and evolve?*

- Reflect on the role that Loki the trickster plays in your life. *How does your inner trickster manifest? And how do you feel when you realize how you've tricked yourself (and others)?*

- Reflect on the offspring of your inner trickster. *What do Jörmungandr, the Midgard serpent, Fenrir, the gigantic wolf, and Hel, the queen of the underworld represent to you as shadow powers?*

- Become aware of your shadow qualities. *How does your shadow manifest in your life and in your relationships with yourself and others? What are the qualities of yourself that you are not conscious of or that are not yet mature? How does your shadow or ego use these qualities?*

- The force of destruction is not a shadow force, but is often used by the shadow since it is a force we tend to disown, dislike, fear, and make wrong. *How do you feel about the force of destruction and can you think of ways that this force can be used in support of life? For example, by destroying the illusions and false belief systems of egoic tendencies and shadow dynamics?*

- Become aware of the force of destruction in you. *Are there any destructive qualities that you repress or are unconscious of?*

- Ask your higher heart and mind to reclaim your powers of destruction from the domains of your shadow, and to show you the ways of using the power of destruction wisely and with love.

- The line between seeing the illusions and feeling disillusioned is very thin. It's easy to slide down into nihilism by not believing in anything anymore. *How cold or warm is your heart? Has the energy of skepticism or cynicism hardened your heart in any way?*

- If we don't complete the inner destruction of the false and shrunken self that creates the egoic worlds, our transformation cannot complete to bring forth a new cycle of a wiser world. These same transformative forces will then become the monsters by which we destroy our outer worlds.

- You cannot enter or bring forth the promised new world through the ego or shadow. If we don't destroy the illusions of separateness in ourselves, we will destroy the world around us and all who live on it.

- The wisdom of the higher heart is the wiser part of yourself who has already gone through the destruction of the egoic worlds and acts as your beloved friend from the other side of the veil. This is also the consciousness from the new world that becomes possible after the egoic and shadow influences have ceased and disintegrated.

- Call upon this inner wisdom of your higher heart to guide you through the various stages of endings and new beginnings.

- There is always a more peaceful way possible, as long as we don't kill the power of peace, beauty, and renewal in ourselves and our world.

- The masculine is a wonderful and essential force and should never be thought of as separate from the feminine. Together they form a unit and a sacred partnership.

- Your heart is designed to house and circulate a tremendous amount of heat without this ever becoming harmful. Ask your heart to harmonize your inner fire with the wisdom of love.

- Fire is a necessary power of evolution, yet the ways we as humanity have used and employed fire differ greatly depending on our goals and aspirations.

- The fire triangle consists of three conditions that need to be present: heat, fuel, and oxygen. Apply this concept to the exploration of your fire composition. Develop the alchemical fire of the higher heart by igniting your inner fire with the Flame of Love and its sparks of passion and joy. Fuel your fire with empathy, generosity, and compassion. Oxygenate your fire with the lightness of your higher mind.

- Once your fire is sourced from the Flame of Love, you can feed it any of the pain or shadow dynamics you have buried inside for healing and purification. Learn about the sources of warmth, fuel, and oxygen in yourself and in our world, both internally as well as externally.

CHAPTER 6

Healing the Intersections of Destiny

The Cosmic Compass

It's so beautiful outside that Rose and Verdandi decide to take a stroll along the city canals to watch the ornamented "woonboten," or houseboats in English. Sunlight sparkles on the water; a few lazy clouds float by overhead. The air feels fresh and clean. They pass a particularly charming boat, painted pink and green. A woman with a headscarf smiles and waves, then returns to the task of watering her window boxes of overflowing flowers. A scruffy dog barks and wags its tail beside her.

"I've always wanted to live on a houseboat," Rose confesses. "Not the kind that stays docked though. I like the kind that moves around."

"Ahh, the life of a water gypsy," her grandmother grins. "That sounds delightful. I may have to join you. OH!" Verdandi collapses into Rose, clutching her stomach with both hands as if she's been punched.

"What's happening?"

Verdandi can't speak. Her face contorts in pain.

"Grandma, you're scaring me. What's happening?" Rose reaches into her pocket for her cell phone to call for help, and realizes she left it at the apartment.

Tears flow over the older woman's cheeks. She moans and falls to her knees on the ground close to the water. "Not my sister," she chokes out. "Nooooo. Oh, please, holy Mother! Please protect her!"

"Anna?"

Verdandi nods. A ginger striped cat with large golden eyes observes the scene from the deck railing of the closest houseboat. He leaps to the shore and pads over to the two women. He rubs his cheek against Verdandi and allows her to stroke his head. He flicks his tail and curls up in her lap, as if sensing what has just happened. A raven flies over them, a little too closely. It flaps its majestic black wings and lands in the highest branches of a nearby tree. Rose's body tenses. *I have a feeling that's not a good omen this time,* she thinks. She doesn't know what to do. Silent tears stream down her grandmother's face as she continues to pet the cat. Minutes feel like hours. *Mother Earth, please help!* She places her hand on Verdandi's shoulder and breathes deeply.

After a little while, the older woman stands up, her face still wet. She gives the cat one more stroke of love and gratitude and watches him return to the houseboat.

"Anna got attacked," she says finally.

"Oh no!"

"We're so connected that it felt like I was being attacked at the same time."

"By whom? Where? How?" Rose asks in a rush, deeply shaken.

"I don't know. I need to sit." She and Rose make their way to a wooden bench beside the canal and sit close together. Verdandi takes Rose's hands and looks into her eyes. "We need to visualize a protective cocoon of blue light around her. We must hold the intention for her highest protection and complete healing."

"Of course."

Both women close their eyes and set that intention.

"Let's get back to the apartment," Verdandi says, rising from the bench. "I need to call her immediately."

The Omen of the Twin Sisters

The phone in Verdandi's hand rings and rings, but her sister doesn't answer. She leaves a message asking Anna to call her back as soon as she can.

"We'll just have to wait," Verdandi tells Rose.

"Does Auntie Anna still live by herself?"

"Oh yes," Verdandi sighs. "She loves her little cabin in the woods, surrounded by trees and animals. She likes the solitude."

"You must miss her."

"I do. Twins have a strong bond. But I have to go to Norway to visit her; she doesn't like to leave home, so I don't see her as often as I'd like." Verdandi picks up the phone again, then sets it down. "I know she prefers the life of a hermit, but sometimes I wish she'd found a partner to keep her company. I guess we're different that way. I can't imagine my life without Dagaz."

"I wonder if she ever gets lonely?" Rose wonders.

"She does get out sometimes. She was part of the conception of the indigenous Sami parliament in Norway, remember?"

"Yes."

"And she joins our Sami relatives in ceremonies and festivities from time to time."

"I remember you showing me and Mom photos of the gorgeous traditional clothing she embroidered for some of those events when I was younger. I was so impressed," Rose recalls.

"Yes, your Auntie Anna has many talents. But she definitely prefers animals to people. So she stays in the woods, gathering her herbs and making potions."

"Well…that's what shamans do," Rose says. "And even though she likes her solitude, she's always been available to help people in need with her natural medicines."

"It's true. My sister has always had a good heart."

"When's the last time you spoke with her?"

"Recently," Verdandi answers. "She told me that a certain group of religious extremists who live at the edge of the woods close to town have been spreading rumors that she practices black magic."

"What? No!"

"They've been calling her a sorceress."

"Why?"

"It appears the rumors were started by a vengeful woman Anna refused to sell her herbal potions to. When Anna saw the dark shadow of this woman and the forceful way she behaved, she told her that the potions were not for sale and sent her away. Apparently, the woman felt terribly offended. She was not used to being refused anything, and started to spread the gossip. She even told some people to 'get rid of the witch.'"

Rose's eyes grow wide as she listens. "That's terrible. What did she do?"

"I warned her to be careful," Verdandi continues. "Radical extremist groups are sprouting up like mushrooms all over the world. Especially the ones that are organized by hate groups, which stoke the fires from behind the scenes."

"So she may be in danger. Do you need to go and see her right now?"

"Let's find out what happened first," Verdandi replies. "Until we hear from her, please keep visualizing this protective shield of Cosmic light around her."

Rose and her grandmother sit in silence, each focusing on protecting Anna from further harm.

"I'll call Dagaz," Verdandi says. "Maybe she called my house." The phone rings, but no one picks up on the other end. "Nope. He's not answering either. Darn it, I was hoping he might have heard what's going on." She paces and looks out the living room window.

"Would you like some tea while we wait?" Rose asks.

"That sounds nice. Thank you."

Rose returns a few minutes later with the tea. Verdandi joins her on the couch, deep in thought. She picks up her mug of tea, but doesn't drink it right away.

"You know," she says, "my sister was trained to open the portals to the multi-worlds."

"Really?" Rose asks.

"Yes. She also acted as mediator for the spiritual laws within the human realms. When Anna was younger...about your age...she often used to disappear into the woods for hours. Eventually, the hours became days, and one time, even months. In the beginning, our mother was terribly worried. Our father died when we were just thirteen years old. Our mom raised us by herself. She was a very brave and resourceful woman."

"You always said that Great Grandpa was the love of her life."

"He was. She never remarried. That was it for her."

"She must've been so worried when Auntie Anna disappeared!"

"The first time it happened, she was. We both were. The forest was teeming with wild animals. We thought that bears or wolves might have taken her. When she returned home full of smiles, we realized how the ancestors were strongly guiding her and preparing her for a special task. We even saw once how a bear protected her from an intruder who tried to invade the land on which we were living at the time. Anna has the same spirit as the animals; they consider her to be family." Verdandi blows on her tea and takes a sip.

"You've never shared these details about your twin sister before, Grandma."

"She's had an interesting, mysterious life."

"I only met her a few times," Rose says. "I didn't quite know what to say to her. She was so different from anyone I'd ever met. I think I was a little bit afraid of her. What was Anna being prepared for? Hey, does she know what happened to me? How I died and came back?"

"Yes, love. When I told her about your experience, she said she already knew about it. She's the one who told me that I shouldn't wait to see you in person. I was given a vision of three omens. Two of the omens have happened already. The third omen has to do with twin connections. There's a prophecy in our family that the new world will come into manifestation when the twin connection between and within women is restored."

"What does that mean? And what were the other two omens, Grandma?"

"The first omen was the carrot with the triple roots."

"You mean that funny carrot that Grandpa Dagaz pulled from the garden?"

"Yes," Verdandi nods. "The second omen concerns the confrontation between the Dragon of the East and the Dragon of the West."

"Ah that meeting between Li and Mike! Ha, now I know why you were so keen on knowing Li's dragon history!"

"Yes, but there's much more to these signs than what may appear on the surface," Verdandi replies. "For example, the confrontation between Li as the Eastern Dragon and Mike as the Western Dragon can be read in several ways. It may look like a confrontation between the aggressive Western corporate dragon and the more peaceful, wiser Eastern Dragon, although even that has changed recently. However, there's another layer of meaning that is much more important."

"What is it?"

"The vision didn't show who is the good dragon and who is the evil dragon. Instead, it showed how the Dragons of the East and the West came to a full confrontation with far-reaching consequences. Look at what's happening now between China and the triangle that formed recently between Australia, the United States, and the United Kingdom. The carrot omen with the triple roots can also be read as the sign for how a new superpower tries to emerge from something submerged. Australia, the US, and the UK share the same cultural roots. And from another perspective, the omen also reveals the rise of the triple Goddess."

"Wow, I had no idea you could read the signs to understand what's happening politically and economically right now, as well. Incredible! And it's so precise. The trinity between these three Anglo-Saxon countries led to the confrontation with China and also undermined French and European allies, which resulted in the seeding of division in Europe. China sees itself as the new economic superpower and uses this to command political influence."

Verdandi looks pleased. "You're starting to see now how there are always deeper forces and patterns at play. This confrontation between the Eastern and Western Dragons is the beginning of a larger escalation that has been brewing for years. Some even suggest that the spread of the virus from China is no coincidence, but let's not feed the conspiracy theories."

"I agree. So what about this third omen?" Rose asks.

"The third omen is about attacks on twin connections. Superficially, it may look as if the twin pattern is about duality. However, the code of the twin pattern is about unification via our twin half or other side, which can also represent the inner marriage with our twin Cosmic self. Attacks on the symbolism of the twin pattern can thus also be seen as an attempt to stop the reunification between the higher and lower orders of reality."

"Dad told me that there's an ancient prophecy in his tradition about the twin female Messiahs and how the Messianic era can only be ushered in by the women in whom the twin Messianic code has been activated."

"Your dad is a wise man," Verdandi smiles. "There's a lot more to this twin pattern than people realize. What happened today is not just an attack on my twin sister and me, but also a sign that the time for the activation via the twin code has come. Reality has to be stimulated from both sides of the veil, and that is the deeper understanding of the twin pattern and the union with our other halves. Even the attack on the Twin Towers in the USA on 9/11 has a deeper meaning for those who can read the signs. Now, let's go back to your compass."

Rose is speechless. She wonders what other signs her grandmother has received, yet never told anyone about. "Did you learn to read these signs from the Cosmic Architect Tools?"

"That, and by observing patterns, love. Remember that reality on this planet is always in a slight twist, so nothing is as it appears. There may be a truth to the saying 'the truth is bent,' which can be quite literally so as a result of these space-time curvatures you spoke of." Verdandi tries to laugh to shift her mind away from the anxiety she feels about her sister and this dreadful time of waiting for news.

Rose smiles back in an attempt to put her grandmother at ease, knowing very well that she must be feeling terrified. Verdandi looks at the phone again to see if there might be a message from Anna or Dagaz. Nothing yet.

"It's so hard to wait," Rose says. "Patience isn't my strong suit. I think I'll go make us some lunch."

She rises from the couch, just as the phone rings. Verdandi jumps to answer it.

"It's Dagaz," she tells Rose.

"Hello, sweet blossom!" Dagaz addresses his wife. "Is everything okay? I just got your message. It took a long time to walk the dogs, feed the horses, take care of the cats, and look after the garden. You always make it look so easy."

"Good thing I left you on your own for a few weeks," Verdandi teases. "Otherwise, you'd have never realized that! Have you heard anything from Anna?"

"Anna? No. Why?"

"I'm worried that something may have happened to her. I've tried to call, but she's not answering."

"Uh-oh. That doesn't sound good. What about that guy who lives kind of near her house? Can he check on her?"

"Yes, Franz might be able to pay her a visit to find out why she's not picking up the phone."

"Alright, I'll give Franz a call right away."

Verdandi tells Dagaz briefly what she experienced that morning during her walk with Rose.

"I understand why you're so concerned," Dagaz says. "And you're usually right about things like that. But don't worry, we'll get it all sorted. I'll try to get more information and let you know."

"I appreciate that."

"Uncertainty is always the hardest. Rest if you can, and know that I love you."

"I love you, too, Dagaz."

Verdandi hangs up the phone as Rose emerges from the kitchen with a tray loaded with two bowls of piping hot split pea soup and chunks of sourdough bread.

"I got the recipe for this soup from my friend Lillian," Rose says, setting the tray down. "I hope you like it."

"Thank you, love. I'm sure it'll be delicious."

"I'm scared, Grandma. What if something similar happens to you? Or me?"

"Don't be afraid, love. I'm safe, and so are you. Just promise me that you won't provoke or poke what doesn't need to be stirred up, okay?"

Rose nods her head. Verdandi continues, "Perhaps, in your case, a little bit of fear might be a good thing with all that Viking energy that's roaring through your veins!"

"Can that new covenant we spoke of protect and guide us?" Rose asks.

"It depends on how it's done," Verdandi explains. "The real covenant is deep from the eternal bonds that can never be broken, only forgotten. The outer covenant or a new Earth constitution will have to be formed through a process that can unite and inspire people. Not as a political or religious construct, or yet another legal document. Remember, many indigenous cultures have their own covenants and agreements as well. They may not be keen to join a global agreement of nations who've never honored their sovereignty. Getting the myriad indigenous nations to agree with one another is another mighty challenge. Humanity is still heavily under the spell of separation and disunity. The vision of the new covenant speaks of a time when humanity stands united as one family and affirms the ancient bonds of life in the form of a new pledge between human beings, our Earth, all non-human life, and the Cosmos. That's what the bond of the multi-worlds is all about. It's how we become the future ancestors of the civilizations that this covenant seeks to establish."

"I feel this deeply in my bones," Rose sighs. "It's a relief."

"Think of this covenant as a Cosmic Compass, rather than merely a set of principles or agreements. Can you show me those designs again that you made for your compass?"[1]

The Three Laws of Life and the Compass Coordinates

Rose retrieves her journal and places her Cosmic Compass drawing on the table. Verdandi takes it between her hands and brings it to her heart, as if blessing it. She then returns it to Rose and says, "Now hold it between your hands and tell me what these coordinates and symbols mean to you."

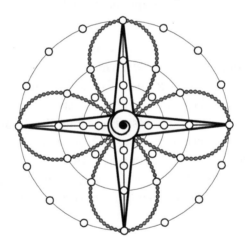

"The black dot in the center represents the Cosmic code of unity, as well as the black hole or womb that's at the center of our galaxy. Our life spirals around these fundamental principles. The 'knob' of the compass rose consists of the black dot, the spiral, and the black circle around the spiral, which together represent the three laws of life that you taught me many years ago."

"I'm so glad you remember that," Verdandi says with sincerity.

"Yes, of course," Rose smiles. "The black dot represents the *law of existence*, which reveals how existence itself is unified; there are no separate parts and particles. We form part of an undividable wholeness. We are each fractals of unity. The spiral that emerges out of the black dot represents the *law of change*, which reminds us that life is constantly changing and evolving like a spiral that expands and contracts. During the expansion phase, our energy and focus flows outward and the complexity of life increases. During the contraction phase, our energy returns to our inner center and our focus flows inward to integrate and learn from our experiences. The circle that forms around the spiral represents the *law of balance*, which reminds us to honor the sacred boundaries of life that regulate our interdependence and create the conditions for our personal autonomy. This circle also helps us to become aware of the ways in which consciousness actualizes its cosmological potentials in the worlds of form, time, and matter."

"It's beautiful to see how you've applied it here," Verdandi says. "Continue, darling."

"These three laws or principles serve as fractal codes that in-form the evolution of life in our physical worlds, which is shown here as the four arms of the compass rose that each consist of three lines to create a trinity arm like the tip of an arrow. These four trinity arms stretch into the four cardinal directions: north, east, south, and west. These four directions, plus the center, also represent the five eternal wisdoms that we've explored before when I had that dream about the moral compass, with the *all-pervading wisdom* in the center, the *mirror-like wisdom* in the east, the *wisdom of equanimity* in the south, the *wisdom of discernment* in the west, and the *all-accomplishing wisdom* in the north."

"I'm happy that wisdom is the foundation for this design, my girl. If you like, I can guide you through a practice tomorrow for strengthening your relationship with these five wisdoms and your compass."

"Thank you, Grandma. I would love that!"

"Now tell me, how would you apply these principles to economics, governance, and education?" Verdandi asks.

"Ah, that's when things get really interesting," Rose says with enthusiasm. "You can use the codes and principles of the compass design as a *living* constitution by translating these into shared agreements and commitments for creating the new operating systems of humanity. As well as the new protocols for how to regenerate our planet and create fair and thrivable systems that by design are in harmony with life and replenish the carrying capacities of our planet. Such a constitution can also set the foundations for the design and transformation of our laws and legal systems to include the rights of nature and provide a sustainability context that is based on the laws of complex living systems. Furthermore, such a constitution could provide the necessary embedding and re-alignment of our economic, political, social, cultural, and educational systems from the planetary health context as the utmost priority."

"I see you've put a great deal of thought into this, Rose. You've made a lot of progress. Very good."

Rose beams. "Thank you, Grandma. I just know in my bones that it's possible to create completely different types of systems and cultures, if only we can open our minds to these possibilities and listen to our inner compass first."

"The interior of the humans is what needs to evolve first and foremost," Verdandi agrees. "Especially people's mental constitutions. Oh! The phone! Please let it be Anna." She looks at the number of the incoming call. "It is her. Rose, please excuse me. I'm going to take this call in the bedroom."

"Of course," Rose says.

Verdandi goes to take her call, and Rose takes the dishes into the kitchen, saying a quiet prayer that her aunt is safe. She washes and dries the dishes, then puts a small load of laundry into the washing machine. She straightens up the living room and is just about to open a book when her grandmother emerges.

"Is she alright?" Rose asks.

"It was a difficult conversation," Verdandi says. She looks sad and tired. "Anna's voice was shaking the entire time. That's not like her."

"What happened?"

"She was attacked by the group I suspected. Two men and a woman attacked her while she was out on a walk in the forest with her dog. They taunted and humiliated her. The woman threw eggs at her. The dog tried to protect her, so they beat the dog. Then they beat her."

"No!"

"While the men struck her, the woman screamed that Anna was an evil witch—a servant of the devil, who puts spells on the minds of men, and lures women into sin. She spat on my sister and told her that they never wanted to see her face in their community again. While she lay there, crumpled in the dirt, they threatened to burn her alive in her cabin if she ever told a single person about the incident."

"How did she get away?"

"They left when a raven swooped down upon them over and over again. My sister attributes that to me. Her friend Franz found her and her dog in the woods after he received the call from Dagaz. Franz is taking her to the doctor to get her injuries treated. He asked his neighbor to take the dog to the veterinary hospital."

Rose can barely speak. Her stomach feels hollow and cold.

"It was just as I feared, Rose," Verdandi continues. "The people who attacked her are the members of that radical hate group. Apparently, for people like them, nothing has changed much in the last hundreds of years. They're still on a witch hunt."

"But at least Auntie Anna is alive!" Rose exclaims. "And so is her dog."

"Yes, love. The wounds of the heart may be worse than those of the flesh. She has always been wary of people. After this attack, she may choose to withdraw from society even further."

"I'm so sorry, Grandma. This is awful. Poor Anna. She never did anything wrong. People can be so intolerant and full of hatred."

"Yes, and why?" Verdandi cries. "Because she threatens their belief systems? Because she's a woman who lives on her own in the woods? Because she's an indigenous woman who is proud to keep practicing the ancient ways of our culture? Because she refused to sell her medicines to that one woman?

Or because they needed a scapegoat for their pent-up resentment, so they made her into a threat?"

Rose has never seen her grandmother so upset. "Is there anything I can do? For Anna and for you?" she asks, concerned.

"Keep visualizing the field of protection around Anna, and please send a healing wave to her poor dog who must have been so scared. Dogs are our most loyal companions; experiences like this affect them deeply." Verdandi turns to Rose. "I need some time to process what's happened. I'm going for a short walk to the park to sit under that willow tree of yours. I'll be back soon."

Consulting the Cosmic Compass for Healing and Guidance

Rose keeps looking at the clock. It's been more than an hour and Verdandi still hasn't returned. She wonders whether she should go to the park herself, but doesn't want to interrupt her grandmother, who clearly said she needed time alone. After another thirty minutes pass, she can't hold herself any longer. She puts on her coat to walk to the park and is just about to lock the front door when she spots Verdandi walking toward her with a strong, sturdy gait. Rose feels so relieved. Verdandi looks recharged and determined.

"Okay, young lady," she says in a commanding voice, "we've got work to do. Get back inside and bring the Avatar pouch to the living room. Lay the tools out on the black silk cloth that's in the bag. Then burn sage in the room to purify everything and prepare the space."

Rose carefully prepares the room and lays out the tools. Across the room, Verdandi hums and blesses the room with her swan feathers. Swan medicine is one of Verdandi's totemic relationships. She informs Rose that the swan offers protection through grace, and is a guardian for the inner transformations in life.

"Now place the compass here," Verdandi says firmly, pointing a finger at the center of the cloth. "Move the ring of unity over the compass with the intention that this ring activates the powers of this compass. This ancient Avatar compass was created to open the portals to parallel realities and guide one through the landscapes of consciousness that are invisible to most people. It awakens your navigational powers as a seer, and the ability to track energy to its points of origin." Rose does as she is instructed. "Good. Now place your hands above the compass and ask it to show you where the energy and intentions for this attack originated from. Close your eyes and watch with your spirit eye. Notice how the compass rose that is manifest within you will start to shift your awareness to the direction where healing is required. Nod your head when you can see or sense this direction."

Rose nods her head. Her hands become very hot. She feels a pull to the northeast direction of the compass, which she can also feel inside her.

Verdandi continues, "Now ask the compass to guide you in tracing the energy that is behind this attack. Trace it all the way back in time until you get a sense of the origins of this pain and the cause for this hatred."

Rose starts to see visions of hundreds of years ago. There is panic in a village. Men with weapons and symbols of the cross have entered the village in search of pagans, led by a priest who is inciting fear. Women are screaming and panicking, trying to hide their children, while many of their men are executed on the spot. The message is clear: if the village hides a witch or prays to the old pagan gods, everyone will be punished by death for protecting these people. One woman is terrified she'll be found out. She feels that her only protection is to prove to the violent intruders that the God of the new religion is now her savior. But she hesitates. She has used herbs given to her by her pagan sister to heal the skin of her little boy. What to do? She panics and runs out to face the soldiers. "I'll show you the witch!" she screams, pointing to the house where her sister hides. "She's in there! She's the one who put a spell on all of our innocent people! It's her fault. She's the one you need to burn! Please spare us!"

Rose describes what she sees to Verdandi. She feels sick to her stomach watching the scene. Verdandi replies, "Now take the hourglass and hold the intention to turn the page on this chapter of history so the healing happens in *that* time. Place all that you've just witnessed into the bottom of the hourglass, and send healing and forgiveness to all the people who've been involved and affected by these massacres and tortures. Include the soldiers and the priest. I will now sprinkle healing water from the chalice cup over the hourglass. Hold the intention that the insights and wisdom of our present and future time flow toward that earlier time in support of a full healing in consciousness."

Rose observes in amazement how the consciousness of our future time supports the healing of our present time, and how through the awareness we have in the present moment we can direct this toward the healing of the consciousness of past times where people's minds were constricted and caught in loops of violence.

Verdandi continues, "Now take the hourglass in your hands and form the intention that a new cycle may originate from *that* time based on the healing that's just taken place. See these timelines heal as the energy of hatred, fear, and resentment transform into compassion, forgiveness, and love. Now turn the hourglass 180 degrees and express the intention that out of this healing, a new cycle may begin for each of these people; a cycle rooted in love and unity."

Rose feels a huge shift in energy. Everything around her becomes very still. She suddenly understands that the woman who started the attack on Anna may have carried within her the terror of these ancestral memories. The woman never realized that by acting that story out, she was continuing the old violence, as well as starting new cycles of violence and terror. The anger Rose held toward this woman and the two men involved in the attack on her aunt begins to melt and transform into compassion.

After they complete this healing ritual Rose asks, "Grandma, will the people who attacked Anna feel the healing ritual we just did? How do we know if it reached them?"

"We don't know and that doesn't matter," Verdandi tells her. "We're changing the fields of energy around this violence, which increase the possibilities for healing and forgiveness. Trust the process, and let life do the rest. Let's pray that something deep inside those people may release, shift, and heal, based on what we've just facilitated here."

Rose hugs her grandmother. "I'm so grateful for this time with you," she tells Verdandi. "I could never have learned this over the phone. This ritual gives me a whole new understanding of how I can work with the compass and the hourglass together as tools for healing and guidance."

"I'm grateful for our time together, too."

"I was thinking that the scenes of history that I just witnessed also relate to the same time period that we spoke of a few days ago when we were exploring the Nordic myth of Ragnarök and the Midgard serpent," Rose continues. "I'm fascinated by the way it all seems to connect, even though I don't understand it all yet. Do you think that life is showing me another facet of this period in history to help me to understand more about the completion and beginnings of major cycles?"

"I do." Verdandi's eyes shine.

"You know, the ending of the non-Christian pagan world did not bring peace and enlightenment for our ancestors. The promise of a new beginning for present and future generations was enforced through violence, intimidation, and threat. The earlier patterns from each of these different worldviews and religions never completed because the egoic structures and shadow worlds were never destroyed and disintegrated. The trickster won and became even more clever. Or is the ending time of this pattern of violence happening right now?"

"There's much to think about," her grandmother says. "Maybe you could write about it in your journal."

Healing Orbs for the Cosmic Compass Game

The next morning Rose receives a FaceTime call from Olaf. He sounds very excited and his eyes are sparkling with a sense of adventure.

"Hey, Rose, remember that compass game we played? The one where you asked me to close my eyes? I called to show you this." Olaf places a complex looking Lego creation in front of the camera. "I made it myself out of Lego blocks!"

"That's amazing, Olaf. Is it a gun?"

"No! It's a healing energy device."

"Interesting. How does it work?"

"You see this part here? That's a *healing* orb. When it lands on someone, it heals them instantly. The bigger the orb, the bigger the healing effect. It's charged by these batteries that you plug into the side of the device over here." Olaf shows a cube of Lego blocks in which he is storing the orbs, and which attaches to the side of the healing device.

"Impressive!" Rose smiles. "You put a lot of thought into that."

"Thanks. Yeah, and these are no ordinary batteries. They come from a special tree in the Blue Mountains, where we met the scientist team for getting the mineral to heal the river. And when you help someone heal in the game, you get more of these healing orbs as a reward. That way you can help even more people to heal."

"Olaf, you've taken our game to a whole new level!" Rose says excitedly.

"I really like the game and I also like making stuff out of Lego blocks, so

I decided to combine both things. Thanks to the game, I have all kinds of new ideas. Like shooting a target doesn't need to be for killing, it can be done to heal or transform something. All I had to do was change the rules of the game. I'm going to do this for my other games, too. I like shooting the orbs that are supercharged by the magical trees of the Blue Mountains. It's fun."

"It's a very creative addition to the game. Good job."

"Oh, and there is also this attachment." Olaf shows Rose a scope he built. "When you're standing far away from a person who needs healing, you can place this scope here on top of the device. When you click the scope, the orbs can heal the person at long distance. I showed it to my friends. They think it's really cool. They're coming over tomorrow, and we're going to play the game in real life."

"Fun!"

"Yeah! Oh, my mom is calling me. I gotta go. I have to get ready for school now."

"Well, thanks for sharing your invention with me. I love it."

"You're welcome. Bye."

Rose sets the phone down with a light heart, and goes to share the news of Olaf's invention with Verdandi.

"This is wonderful news," her grandmother says with joy upon hearing the details of the conversation. "It confirms to me even more that things have started to shift in a profound way. For those who don't read the signs, it may not seem related at all, but I know how the currents of consciousness connect behind the blankets of time and space. Something in the weaving of the collective unconscious is starting to shift in a positive direction."

Rose runs to the market to buy a few necessities. When she returns, Verdandi mentions that while she was out, Anna had called again.

"How is she?" Rose asks.

"The doctor told her she didn't break any bones."

"Thank goodness."

"Yes. But her body needs time to heal from all of the bruises, as well as the shock of what happened. Franz has taken her home to his family, to make sure that she has all the care she needs, and so she can feel safe."

"That's a relief. How kind of him."

"Yes, I'm relieved, too, but I know this isn't over yet. But first things first. Anna needs to heal, and so does her dog."

Verdandi looks at her granddaughter with tenderness and love. She hopes she'll be granted all the time she needs to properly prepare her for the dangers that are coming. The third omen has now manifested, which confirms that Rose's sheltered life will soon come to an end.

"Rosie…I'd like to share that practice I promised you for using the Cosmic Compass and the five eternal wisdoms. Are you up for that now?"

"Yes!"

Rose loves these practices. She happily makes herself comfortable on the couch, closes her eyes, and makes herself utterly receptive. Verdandi begins.

Practice for Connecting with the Cosmic Compass

"Take a deep breath and let it out slowly. Let go and relax, and now relax some more. Start by connecting with your imaginal powers. Become aware of your inner Cosmic architecture as the wisdom of your body and the pulse of your heart join with your innate capacities to learn and evolve. The Cosmos lives within you. You are part of the Cosmic intelligence that sustains our worlds.

"Imagine now that your Cosmic architecture takes the shape of the Cosmic Compass, a precious and eternal gift from the Cosmos that is readily available to guide you through life. It is composed from the finest wisdoms that hold the coordinates for your higher destiny and becoming. Take a moment to feel and experience this Compass of wisdom.

"Imagine that this Cosmic Compass takes the shape of a luminous sphere that you can easily enter; a sphere that welcomes you and manifests from your own personal space. Step inside this sphere now. Feel and experience the qualities of this sphere. Experience the qualities of wisdom that know how to direct your life. This sphere manifests from the luminous structures of your Cosmic architecture, which are the living structures of consciousness that evolve together with us. Stay here for a few moments to experience this wondrous architecture.

"Now move into the center of this Cosmic Compass. Meet the black dot that holds the Cosmic code of unity. It is the Source point that supports you with the wisdom of the eternal; beyond these worlds of form and time.

Connect with this Source point in you, and within it, find the all-pervading wisdom that is your direct access to your own eternal nature. Spend some moments here at this Source point of your life.

"Now imagine moving into the east coordinates of the Cosmic Compass. As you enter the east side of your sphere, a deep clarity enters you, enabling you to see what is real and what is not. You now have direct contact with the mirror-like wisdom. This wisdom can reveal to you the true nature of reality as you look into the great mirror of life. This mirror reflects whatever is happening on the surfaces of reality, yet is not changed by what it reflects. This great wisdom illuminates your path and helps you see through any illusions, guiding you forward with clarity. Stay here for a few moments to realize more fully what this wisdom means for you.

"Now imagine moving into the south coordinates of the Cosmic Compass. As you enter the south side of your sphere, you now have direct contact with the wisdom of equanimity. This great wisdom can teach you what it means to live in right-relationship with life and with the greater Universe in which your life unfolds. Receive from this essential wisdom the experience of unity and connectedness, reminding you how our fundamental nature is the same, and how we are each of equal value.

"Now imagine moving into the west coordinates of the Cosmic Compass. As you enter the west side of your sphere, you now have direct contact with the wisdom of discernment. This ancient wisdom can teach you about your higher will and the alchemical Flame of Love. This Flame has the power to purify and harmonize all of your desires. It also helps you to develop great compassion. Through your compassion, you come to understand the root causes of suffering and the path of liberation via the power of love. Stay here for a few moments to realize what this wisdom means for you.

"Now imagine moving into the north coordinates of the Cosmic Compass. As you enter the north side of your sphere, you now have direct contact with the all-accomplishing wisdom. This eternal wisdom can teach you about the larger Cosmic story in which your life unfolds. It knows each of the roles and destinies you have played, are playing, and will play in the great theater of consciousness. It helps you to develop a deep trust in your path and shows you the steps and actions that lead to true success. Stay here for a few moments to realize what this wisdom means for you.

"Now move again to the center of the Cosmic Compass, and know that this Compass has many more features that you can discover and experience anytime you want. All that is required is your intention to call it forth, and it can appear to you from within and guide you as required.

"Experience now the whole Compass as a living wisdom that is part of the architecture of your personal space. There is no need to focus on anything in particular, just let the Cosmic Compass harmonize and balance you as required. Feel and know yourself to be fully supported by the Cosmos, with all the keys, tools, and wisdom you need for guiding you forward in life. When you are ready, you may gently complete this practice by opening your eyes, being fully present here and now."

Integration -
The Cosmic Compass

Through this chapter, Rose experiences the deeper workings of the Cosmic Compass. She also discovers how to apply this for healing the timelines and multiple layers of world consciousness, together with the Infinity Hourglass. She received the codes and designs for the Cosmic Compass months ago during a dream. She has been exploring how this can be applied to the design of a game, and be translated into shared agreements and commitments for creating the new operating systems of humanity, as a living constitution.

> *The Cosmic Compass brings you in touch with your eternal wisdom nature and helps you to navigate with the Cosmic architecture of consciousness through the multiple dimensions of life. You can call upon the Cosmic Compass to explore and create the foundations for your destiny path, and to guide you in making conscious and informed choices based on unity and wholeness.*

The summary and questions below will help you to integrate and apply the essential teachings of this chapter:

- ⦿ Continue your exploration of possible blind spots or shadow dynamics by honestly exploring the nature of your inner dragon and the emotional charge of your inner fire. Notice if you feel a competitive edge, and check whether it is a healthy expression or based on wanting to win or dominate over someone else.

- Explore with the Cosmic Compass design the constitution of your life in terms of the principles, values, and agreements that you resonate with and reinforce through your belief systems and emotional investments. *What is the covenant or sets of agreements that you have formed with life and reality?*

- Become aware of the *three laws* or principles of life that are within the center of the compass rose. The *law of existence* (black dot) reveals how existence is unified and whole; we each are fractals of the great unity. The *law of change* (spiral) reminds us how life is constantly changing and evolving like a spiral that expands and contracts. The *law of balance* (circle) reminds us to honor the sacred boundaries of life that regulate our interdependence and create the conditions for our personal autonomy.

- Explore how you can transform weapons of destruction into weapons of healing, like Olaf did with his healing device and healing orbs. Your mind can become a weapon of destruction if you do not develop the wisdom of the higher heart. Get in touch with the powers and qualities of yourself that have become destructive, restrictive, or reversed, and give those to the Cosmic Dragon and the alchemical fire of the higher heart for inner healing and transformation.

The five essential wisdoms of the Cosmic Compass are here summarized below:

1. *The all-pervading wisdom of the center*—This is your direct access to the ever-presence of your eternal nature; the Cosmic code of unity as your Source point for accessing your eternal qualities beyond the worlds of form and time.

2. *The mirror-like wisdom of the east*—This reveals the true nature of reality as you look into the great mirror of life, which reflects what is happening on the surfaces of reality without being changed by what it reflects. This wisdom illuminates your path, and helps you see through any illusions, guiding you forward with clarity.

3. *The wisdom of equanimity of the south*—This guides you in how to live in right-relationship with life and the greater Universe in which your life unfolds, based on unity and interdependence. It reminds

you how our fundamental nature is the same, and how we are each of equal value.

4. *The wisdom of discernment of the west*—This guides the development of your higher will through the sacred Flame of Love, through which you learn how to purify and harmonize your desires through the power of compassion. It reveals the root causes of suffering and the path of true liberation.

5. *The all-accomplishing wisdom of the north*—This reveals the larger Cosmic story in which your life unfolds, and the various roles and destinies you have played, are playing, and will play in the great theater of consciousness. It helps to develop trust in your path and show the steps and actions that lead to true success.

CHAPTER 7

Awakening Our Cosmic Capacities

The Avatar Interface

Rose catches her breath with a pounding heart. She's just finished a run in the park and feels great. As she opens the door to her apartment, she overhears a conversation between Verdandi and Dagaz. They sound serious. She decides to eavesdrop in the hope of finding out more about her grandmother's mysterious visit.

Forewarnings

"And now that attack on your sister! Who's next? You? Rose?" Dagaz exclaims. "Have you told her about the omens and forewarnings? Shouldn't she know why you really came?"

Verdandi clears her throat. "I told her about the three omens in a general sense, which is enough. Too much knowledge of future events can be dangerous. Remember, I'm here to help *prevent* certain things from happening, not to cause them. The less she knows of this the better it is, for *her* sake. Besides you know how she sinks her teeth into things. And she has the protection of the architect tools now."

"But does she really understand how to use those tools? It took you decades before you mastered their powers," Dagaz protests.

"My darling, we don't have decades. Times have changed. The ancient dragon fires are awakening and rising all over the earth. Humans have no idea how to guide that process or what it does to their psyche. We're like tiny babies when it comes to these forces: utterly unprepared. I need this time to train Rose, but even then, I'm not sure I'll be able to avert what's coming.

The times of Ragnarök are happening now as well. If only our ancestors had actually completed their cycle, as the original instructions told them to do," Verdandi complains.

"Well, humans the world over are all the same. Don't count on this species to mature very quickly. In the face of danger, God knows what we're going to do next. We've already put our planet in grave peril, and we still believe we can fix it all. I'm really worried about you two. Maybe I should come and join you," Dagaz suggests.

"No, you can't come," Verdandi exclaims. "The dogs and cats need you at home. It's okay, truly. We'll be fine. Besides, Rose has made some good friends here. One of them is even a police officer. Did you get any further news from Anna?"

"She's still recovering at Franz's place. I spoke with him last night. They're taking good care of her. As you know, your sister is not very talkative, and I didn't want to upset her with questions," Dagaz replies.

"And how about Eivin, her dog?"

"He has a broken leg, but is healing together with Anna. He won't leave her side."

"Thank goodness, that poor fellow. He must have been terrified, trying to protect her like that. I haven't spoken much with Anna over the past few days, but I can feel her all the time. Our twin connection is so strong, especially now. My stomach still hurts from one of the blows they gave her. I'll give Franz a call later. The tension with that hate group has been building up for years. Maybe I should pay those people a visit myself to put things straight in their minds."

"Don't! Please, promise me you won't do that. You're not in your forties anymore. Let Franz and the village council handle it. Besides, you've been away for too long and you don't know how dangerous these people can be," Dagaz warns. "Does Tara know what's going on?"

"No. It's already hard for her because she can't come to see her daughter. I promised her that I'd take good care of Rose." Verdandi pauses for a moment. "Hold on, Dagaz. I think I hear someone at the door. One moment…"

Verdandi walks as quietly as a cat to the front door, which she sees is slightly ajar. "Rose? Is that you, love? Are you home?"

"Oh, hi, Grandma." Rose appears from behind the door. "I just returned from my run in the park. Is that Grandpa you're talking to? What's going on? Am I in danger?"

"How much did you hear?" Verdandi asks.

"Something about omens and how you are here to prevent certain things from happening. And that Mom doesn't know the truth of why you came."

"Well, my dear, it appears that you've stumbled on hidden information once again." Verdandi sounds a little annoyed. "Don't worry. I was just trying to assure Dagaz that all will be fine."

"But, it sounded like he doesn't agree with you. Is he coming here, too?" Rose is not about to let it go so quickly.

"No, and please don't bring that up with him. Now go take your shower while I return to Dagaz before he gets even more worried."

Rose goes to the bathroom and takes a quick, refreshing, cold shower to cool down. Her dad is famous for taking a cold shower every day, even in winter. He claims it keeps his immune system strong and has healed many of his former pains. Rose finds them to be energizing. She towel-dries her hair and puts on fresh clothes. Verdandi is still talking with Dagaz as she enters the living room.

"Hello, Grandpa. How are the animals? Are you managing there, all by yourself?" she asks.

"Nice to see you, Rose," Dagaz smiles. "Please keep an eye on your grandmother. She has a tendency to take the whole world on her shoulders. And keep yourself out of danger so she doesn't have to play the rescuer." He tries to sound light, but Rose senses his concern.

"Ha! As if I'd ever do that," Verdandi exclaims, and goes to the kitchen to refill her water glass.

"Not to worry, I'll take good care of her," Rose assures him. "And I'll keep myself out of trouble as well. You've got nothing to worry about. We're fine, truly."

"You sound just like her. Two peas in a pod." Dagaz shakes his head.

"Grandpa, is there something I should know? I get the impression there's more to Grandma's visit than she lets on. And it seems that you know more about this, too. And from what I overheard earlier you haven't told Mom either. You know how angry she gets when she finds out things have been hidden from her. Can't you at least tell her?" Rose knows that her mom won't hide the truth from her, but she forgets that tricks like these don't work on her grandparents, who know her all too well.

"Nice try, Rose, but it's not up to me to tell. I trust my wife knows what she's doing and if she feels the need to tell you and Tara more, then she will," Dagaz smiles. "Uh-oh...There they go. The dogs are making a fuss outside..."

"Yes, I can hear them."

"The neighbors got a new cat. She walks along the top of the fence, just out of reach, and looks down at the dogs like she's the Queen of Sheba. She loves to rile them up. I think it's a game she invented. They never seem to get tired of it."

Verdandi enters and chimes in, "The dogs may never tire of it, but I'm sure the neighbors will."

Dagaz laughs. "You're right. I'd better go bring them in. I love you both! Take good care of each other."

"We will. Love you!" Verdandi and Rose blow Dagaz a kiss over their computer screen as they end their call.

"What's on the docket for today?" Rose asks.

"Today is going to be busy," her grandmother tells her. "It's time for you to learn how to activate your Avatar interface with the Ring of Unity, transmit the blessings of the Cosmic Mother, and learn about the true nature of your desires."

"Is that all?" Rose laughs.

"I've prepared brief practices that you can share with your friends, if they feel ready for a more advanced stage of training."

"Cool. Thank you."

"On top of that, I'd like to go for a walk in the forest with you."

"Sounds like a full schedule," Rose says.

"The attack on your Auntie Anna has inspired me to accelerate your training," Verdandi explains.

"Why is Grandpa so worried about us?"

"I don't want to discuss that with you, Rose. I know you're curious and persistent, but let it go for now. We have a lot to do today, so let's get started.

Please get the ring of unity from the Avatar pouch on the altar; we're going to need it."

Rose retrieves the ring and settles into the pillows on the couch. She only wears the ring on a lightweight chain around her neck when Verdandi prompts her to do so. When she does this, the ring rests directly over her heart and she can feel the enormous powers that are transmitted from the worlds to which it belongs; mythic worlds beyond this time and place.

"Now that the energetic connection has been made, the Cosmic Ring of Unity can also be activated without the physical ring being with you," Verdandi tells her. "All you need to do is intend for the connection to activate. It will then open like a portal."

Practice for Activating Your Avatar Interface with the Cosmic Ring of Unity

Verdandi begins the practice. "Make yourself comfortable and relax. Take a deep breath and then let go. Release any areas of tension you're holding in your body. Relax your jaw, neck, shoulders…Now relax even more. Bring your attention to this present moment. Move your hands together in front of your heart by placing the palms and fingers of your hands together with the fingers all pointing upward, like a traditional prayer position. Keep your hands in front of your heart for a few moments and intend for your energy to harmonize and center with the wisdom of your heart.

"With your hands still held together in this position, call upon the Cosmic Ring of Unity that is part of the architecture of your heart. Feel how this sacred Ring lives inside you and is already part of you. This Ring also exists in other forms and ways: as a circle of unity that we can bring forth when we gather in ceremony or to sit in council; as an Avatar ring that has been forged by the fire of the Cosmic Dragon heart to teach us the ways of the higher heart; as a Cosmic portal that brings the vibrations, wisdom, and powers of our eternal Bond of Unity into our world; and as a sacred agreement or covenant from the eternal Bond of Unity, to guide our souls in the unfolding of our lives. Just reflect for a moment on all the various ways in which this Cosmic Ring exists and lives in you.

"Now place your hands on your heart and feel how the energy of the Ring of Unity grows stronger within you. It harmonizes your whole self: physically, emotionally, mentally, spiritually, and energetically. Ask the Ring to align your powers to the consciousness of unity; the essence of your consciousness. Feel and experience how your consciousness is being attuned now by the Cosmic Ring of Unity, giving you the vision, senses, and understanding of the eternal Bond of Unity.

"Rest for a few moments in this expanded awareness. Allow yourself to receive and learn from this profound state of unity consciousness…

"Now bring your focus again to the Ring of Unity and ask it to activate your innate Avatar interface. You may experience this activation as a tingling sensation, an internal warmth, or even as a subtle body or template of energy that awakens around you. Your Avatar interface is perfectly tuned and architected to facilitate your direct connection with the Cosmic Avatars and your Avatar consciousness. Your Avatar consciousness is your Cosmic consciousness beyond this time and place, which includes profound states of unity consciousness and understanding of the wholeness of life.

"Your Avatar interface enables these more expanded realities to manifest within and through you into our world in ways that are safe, sacred, and respectful of your autonomy and purpose. Your Avatar interface also gives you enhanced and expanded sensory capacities for communicating and exchanging with the Cosmic realms of consciousness. Experience now how your consciousness shifts and your awareness expands as your Avatar interface is now active and fully operational.

"Notice what has shifted in your awareness and what you can sense within and around you through this expanded state of higher consciousness. You are now also able to give more direct feedback about the human experience to the teams of Cosmic Avatars that live on the other side of the veil. Let them know about your experience of human life and how they can support us here on Earth. You enhance and empower each other through this Avatar interface that bridges our worlds through the Bond of Unity.

"Rest for a few more moments in this Avatar state of consciousness. When you are ready to complete this practice, intend for your Avatar interface to enter into the appropriate mode, whether dormant or active, or simply present and on standby. Your inner wisdom knows how to shift it to the appropriate mode.

"Know that you can activate and call upon this interface whenever required to more effectively interface with the larger Cosmic realities that are beyond our human perceptions and ways. Being fully present here and now, you may now gently open your eyes."

The Cosmic Architect Tools Are Part of Your Avatar Interface

"Incredible! I looove this practice!" Rose practically jumps up with joy. "I feel so good! It's like being in a real-life avatar game. I even imagined how my Cosmic Avatar interface is my inner compass. This is a whole new aspect of the Cosmic architecture of consciousness that I hadn't discovered. In the compass game that I play with Olaf, the avatar suit has a similar interface, which even gives you compass vision. But what I just experienced is even better, and is giving me many more ideas. I even started seeing and hearing hues of colors I've never experienced before. I felt an almost instant connection with any kind of information that I wanted to focus on, without getting affected by it. It was as if I was getting access to the codes and systems behind the information, like a game designer, and not just a game player. I'm also going to use this exercise to deepen my scientific explorations of the Cosmic architecture of life and the informational codes of the Cosmic hologram."

"I'm so glad you enjoyed it," Verdandi smiles. "And yes, after this rather mystical time with me, it might be good for you to go back into your science studies. I wouldn't want your dad to think that I'm influencing your bright mind with magical thinking."

"Don't worry, Grandma. Dad can be quite esoteric as well. I think that his work as a psychologist keeps him grounded and closely in touch with the realities of this world. His focus is on putting all these ideas to good use for his patients so he can better help them to improve their lives. Actually, he should try this Avatar interface as well. It may even help him to see what's behind the pathologies, patterns, and problems of his patients. And it would help him sense through the multiple layers of time itself, so he can discover the origins of the troubles that people come to see him for."

"When you share this with him, I'm sure that your dad will be delighted to have that special time with you as well. Being guided by his daughter through a mind-blowing practice will be good for him," Verdandi chuckles. "Now you've experienced how the Avatar state of consciousness is also an *architectural* awareness of the nature of reality. And why the sacred tools from the Avatar pouch represent the Cosmic Architect Tools that form part of your innate Avatar interface. Similar to the Wholeness Coder archetype that helped you to enter into code consciousness, which you explored a few months ago through the five future archetypes."

"Yes, that was one of my favorite archetypes," Rose beams. "You just said that the Cosmic Architect Tools are part of the Avatar interface. Can you say more about that?"

"Very briefly then, else we'll never make it to the forest. I know how these conversations can go with you once you latch onto something that interests you," Verdandi replies.

"Please, Grandma, I really want to know!"

"Alright. The Architect Tools exist archetypically on multiple planes and in multiple ways, like you just experienced with the Ring of Unity. They connect to specific Cosmic principles and bring forth the wisdom powers of these principles through which we learn how to manifest the Cosmic qualities of consciousness in the worlds of form. For example, the archetype that is the Ring of Unity connects to the principle of Oneness and brings forth the powers of the Bond of Unity. In similar ways, the Infinity Hourglass as an archetype connects to the principle of cyclical change. The Cosmic Compass connects to the principle of holism for developing our navigational capacities with the Cosmic architecture of consciousness. I don't want you to memorize these principles, but rather let them be revealed. Find your own ways to name or communicate these principles and powers. Remember, the Cosmic architecture is never static nor dogmatic."

"Does that mean that each Architect Tool can also help us to better understand the Cosmic architecture of consciousness and how to apply it?" Rose asks.

"Precisely, love. Most importantly, each Architect Tool represents a specific power and quality from your extended Cosmic consciousness that is not always able to enter our human minds. As you know, human minds can be incredibly dense. Our minds tend to filter out, or even block, what doesn't conform to our conditioned, and often dualistic, ways of seeing the world. Your Avatar interface bypasses these mental blockages and conditioned filters, and thus facilitates a more direct connection with your Cosmic powers. As you may have noticed, the Tools activate depending on what is required to come forth, as you experienced with the Cosmic Compass and the Ring of Unity."

"Yes, I did notice that. It was as if they each have their own intelligence and know exactly when to activate and for which purpose. It even felt like they generate a kind of force field, which also activates new possibilities. I experienced this vividly with the Infinity Hourglass when I was with Li in the coffee shop and guided him through that practice. It was incredible. The words just came forth by themselves, as if I had *become* the Infinity Hourglass. I knew exactly what to say for Li to shift his relationship with time and reality, even though I'd never done the practice myself."

"That's a perfect example of how these extended capacities of your Avatar interface work," Verdandi replies. "That's also why you need to approach this with much care and humility. Otherwise, it will become the favorite toy of your ego. I hope you realize how fortunate you are to have access to all of these sacred practices, keys, and tools. Most people never get to learn about this. So much has been kept hidden from humanity for all kinds of reasons. If ever you decide to share this publicly, please be aware that you may experience anger from those who still maintain it should be kept hidden and reserved for only the 'chosen' ones."

"Why don't *you* keep it hidden, Grandma?"

"Because the time for secrets is over, love. Our world is in peril. We can no longer afford to keep these essential teachings for only a handful of mystery schools around the world. But enough questions. Let's go to the forest."

Rose stands up. "I'm ready!"

"Wonderful. I packed sandwiches, fruits, and water for us while you were out running."

"Thank you. And Grandma?"

"Yes?"

"I really do appreciate everything you're sharing with me."

Entering the Consciousness of the Forest

Rose and Verdandi arrive at the forest after a pleasant, scenic drive through the Dutch countryside.

"Ohhh, it's beautiful," Rose exclaims, getting out of the car.

"Isn't it?" Verdandi agrees.

"Smell that fresh air!"

"It's a very ancient forest," Verdandi tells her. "Long ago, people gathered here to worship the Earth Goddess."

"My friend Lillian told me one time that there might even be ruins of a Germanic goddess temple here. I'd love to see that."

"Have you been here before, Rose?"

"No, it's my first time. You?"

"I was here one time with your mom, long ago, when she was a young girl. It was during our brief stationing in the Netherlands when Dagaz was teaching at the university near here. Your grandfather is such a character. Even though he's been retired for more than ten years, he continues to be active as a professor of psychology and education. He thoroughly enjoys giving lectures and publishing. You think he'd slow down a little, but nope."

"That sounds like Grandpa."

"He loved teaching so much. He got energized by the bright minds of his students. He'd come home and tell me all about engaging discussions they'd had in class that day. Discoveries they'd made…Makes me wonder why he ever retired." Verdandi sighs as her memories of these earlier days return. "Dagaz would have loved to join us on our walk today. I miss him."

"I miss him, too."

"Rose? Do you think this is the forest from your dream last year?"

"I'm not sure."

We'll soon find out, Verdandi thinks to herself. *The ancestors warned me that Rose may find herself in dangerous situations that she's not prepared for.* She prays silently. *Beloved Mother of Life, guide me. Help me to keep my granddaughter safe from harm. Show me how to prepare her.*

Meanwhile, Rose sprints ahead on the trail. Verdandi calls her back. "Hey, butterfly girl, not so fast! We haven't done our little ritual to connect with the spirit of the forest and ask it for permission to enter its home."

"Oops, you're right. I thought I forgot something," Rose grins and runs back to her grandmother.

Verdandi continues, "Being here physically doesn't mean that we have also entered the consciousness of the forest. That's why we need to connect first, just like we do in our human relationships. You know how awful it feels when someone is physically with you and yet their mind is somewhere else. We don't want to do that to our forest relatives here."

"I'm sorry. I didn't mean to disrespect the forest," Rose replies, playing with a little twig. "Oh, it smells so good here. Must be from that rain earlier. It's brought out all these amazing forest aromas. And I love the sounds of the birds. Is that a hawk over there?" Rose points to the farm field just opposite the forest.

Verdandi replies, "It looks like it. That's a good omen. Now focus, love. Remember to enter the forest with respect. Don't bring anything in there that's toxic to this place. We're entering someone else's home. We wouldn't like it if someone came to our place and started trashing it, whether physically, mentally, or emotionally. The forest always lends its support to help us heal and ground, but that can only happen when we take responsibility for who we are and what we carry with us."

Rose nods in agreement and quietly turns her attention inward. Verdandi continues, "Intend now to let go of, disconnect, and release yourself from any energies, thought forms, or connections that are not in harmony with life, and don't belong to you. Call back your energy to yourself *here* and *now*. Release and return with love and light whatever doesn't belong to you. Always do this before you enter someone else's place, including places in nature, so you're sure to bring only yourself. No need to become a galactic bus stop for attachments who want to tag along and travel with and through you. Now become fully present. Center and ground yourself. By doing that, you're now able to connect consciously and respectfully, just like you would want to be greeted by others."

Rose notices how her quality of attention instantly shifts and how her mind relaxes as she releases and dissolves the many ideas she's been working on in her mind. She also notices how some of the dream energy that she was still processing from heavy dreams during the night now returns to her. She recalls and reclaims her energy from any of the realms and timelines that she's been exploring, so she can be truly present, here and now. She continues by clearing and dissolving all of the thought forms and energies she has projected onto others. She does this imaginally by using her power of intention. She then proceeds to return to others the thought forms and energies that they have projected onto her. She clears away everything in her energy field that isn't hers by returning it all to its place of origin with love and light.

Verdandi places her hand on Rose's shoulder and says, "Close your eyes and connect with Gaia. Then connect with the consciousness of the forest. Let it know you're here and let it sense you. Make the connection with the earth energies below through your feet. Imagine the roots of the trees coming up to greet you. Let them sense your energy and presence. Extend your love through their root systems, like the living web of life that mimics the Cosmic web of relations. It facilitates all of the interactions in this sacred forest, as well as the sharing of vital resources and nutrients. We humans can learn a lot from nature about connectivity, collaboration, and sharing. When you feel the connection with the consciousness of the forest, ask it for permission to enter, and for its guidance."

Rose feels her energy becoming part of the forest's web of relations. The soles of her feet tingle and she has a distinct sense that the trees are checking her out. They're sensing who she is as their energies meet through the living web of life and through the mycelium networks in the soil and spaces they share. Several birds fly by. Rose wonders if they are also checking her out; informing the forest of her presence here. While she experiences how the forest becomes aware of her, she becomes aware of herself in ways she has never experienced so vividly before.

After a few minutes, she feels a distinct pull from the forest, calling her forward and letting her know that she may now enter. Verdandi senses this as well, and both women look at one another knowingly as they move forward on the forest path.

"Thank you for the reminder, Grandma. I can feel the connection with the consciousness of the forest now."

"Good. Me, too. Now we can start our walk," Verdandi answers, as a rush of wind brushes their hair. The forest welcomes them in.

Membranes and Portals of Interbeing

"I love these new experiences and sensations," Rose says happily. "It's so exciting to connect with the world around me through my Avatar interface. Everything is so much more vivid and multidimensional." Rose feels the ring of unity beaming gentle waves of energy from her chest. She continues, "I can even see and sense the living membranes now. I can intuit where they are around the plants and trees, and understand how they protect and regulate their sacred space and personal boundaries. Oh, look at that pond over there! There's an even larger membrane around that. Amazing. That little pond is home to so many different species: dragonflies, frogs, mosquitoes, fish, and birds."

"Everything is connected."

"Yes. I studied ecological niches during my biology classes at the university, and nonlocal connectivity during my quantum physics classes. But here I get to truly experience energetically and in consciousness what these new paradigm scientific principles are actually referring to. The Universe as a gigantic Cosmic hologram is no longer an abstract concept when I'm walking here with you. We're literally part of, and continuously evolving, the living web of life, like a Cosmic hologram." Rose beams with joy.

"It's true," Verdandi agrees.

"Oh, and look there, Grandma! There's another energetic membrane around that group of trees and shrubs. Each forms a perfect little bioregion of communal space while maintaining its own unique collective consciousness. I knew about the cosmological membranes from my previous explorations of the Cosmic architecture of life, but this is a whole other order of reality."

Verdandi nods and watches her granddaughter as she makes these new discoveries. "You're right," she says.

"If only more humans could see this so we could design our economies and societies by nature's wisdom," Rose exclaims passionately. "It would solve all our problems. These living membranes regulate and exchange the information and resources that are shared and processed in each of these ecological niches. And yet we humans appoint managers and politicians to do that job, and then create financial institutions who operate on principles of debt rather than abundance."

"Make it visible for them, Rose. Draw it out. Or even better, bring them here and show them in person. You could start with Li. He's an intelligent young man with many good ideas for how the world of business and finance might be changed."

"That's not a bad idea. I could do that. Why don't we create a real vibrational Avatar interface? Like a virtual reality simulation that could send them into nature so they could see the living webs of relations, and how nature shares and generates resources for present and future generations."

"That active mind of yours. Does it ever have a day off?" Verdandi laughs. "Remember to teach them the ways of consciousness first, so they learn how to turn on their inner Cosmic interface before they become reliant on yet another technology that makes humans even more removed from nature. Now let's go back to your Cosmic Compass design for a minute. Remember that circle that you drew around the spiral in the center of the compass rose?"

Rose nods, while she moves her hands above a raspberry bush. She's asked the plant for permission to eat some of its delicious, ripe raspberries, which are now in season. She senses that the plant tells her it's okay, but she quickly looks at Verdandi to confirm this.

"Go ahead, my girl. And say thanks to the plant afterward. Remember to briefly hold your finger above the place where you removed the fruit with the intention to seal or close the energy. If you don't do that, its life force will leak out longer than is necessary, especially when you pick leaves, branches, or fruits that are not yet ripe to be released. Those berries look so good! Hand me a couple of those as well. And remember…"

"I know, Grandma! 'Always leave enough for Nature herself, and our animal relatives. Don't take more than strictly needed.' You've drilled that one in since I was little," Rose says teasingly.

Verdandi sighs with satisfaction as the raspberry melts in her mouth. "Mmm…Delicious…Like eating a burst of sunshine. When we visited here with Tara all those years ago, she couldn't stop eating them. I'd forgotten about that. Her tiny face and hands stained with juice…" Both women laugh at the thought of that. "I have so many sweet memories here," Verdandi murmurs dreamily. Rose pops another raspberry in her mouth. "What was I saying?" her grandmother asks.

"You were explaining something about the circle that's around the black dot and spiral that I drew as the center of the Cosmic Compass rose."

"Ah, yes." Verdandi smiles.

"You told me before that the circle also represents the law of balance, which comes alive here in nature in the form of these ecological membranes and the mycelia networks of the trees and fungi in the soil. These energetic membranes are the living boundaries of life that give each being and each collective their autonomy. We can connect with the membranes energetically by moving our hands through the space, and also our minds, by using our intention."

"I told you all of that?"

"You did."

"Huh. I'm pretty smart."

Rose laughs. "You also told me to remember to always do so with respect, as these are personal boundaries. The membranes can also guide and in-form us about the living wisdom and consciousness of their place, including the collective memories of what happened here and the lessons it offers."

"You got it exactly right, my girl. I'm impressed."

"What about the portals of the multi-worlds that you showed me in Iceland? Are there similar portals here, too?" Rose asks.

"Yes. Gaia has a vast magnetic field or grid that acts as her nervous system," Verdandi explains. "This magnetic field includes the intersection points of many energetic conduits or lines that are similar to what you were designing in your compass game with Olaf, but for real. The major intersection points form the portals of the multi-worlds, just like the chakras form where major meridians intersect. As you know, chakras are actually portals or energy wheels or vortexes that interface and regulate your subtle bodies of consciousness. You could think of this as the energetic equivalent of your physical nervous system."

"That's so interesting. And the magnetic field, is that the same as the one that many animals, birds, and insects navigate by?"

"Yes, love. Their inner compass is directly attuned to Gaia's magnetic field. The energetic lines of the magnetic field are also known as ley lines, songlines, or dragonlines by the old druids. The places that we refer to as sacred sites for our ceremonies are the places where major ley lines intersect. There you can find the portals of the multi-worlds. That little black dot at the center of your compass is also a portal; an intersection point for consciousness to converge and interchange. Now you can learn how to find your way in the subtle landscapes of consciousness and energy that are hidden within the physical world."

"And the intersection points in my body are what in Eastern spiritual teachings is referred to as the chakras. Right?"

"Yes, exactly. You may notice how in many of those chakra points, you'll find a major gland in your physical body. Like the pineal gland for the third eye chakra, and the thyroid gland for the throat chakra. In similar ways, we often find sacred wells on or near a sacred site of major portals. The well acts like a womb for receiving the Cosmic seeds and fertilizing the sacred powers of that place, just like our physical glands regulate our hormonal system, which influences the ways we grow and develop, and also, our fertility. The macro Cosmos is always within the micro Cosmos and vice versa. Life is fractal."

"Amazing. While listening to you, this vision came to me of dragon energy and how its fire travels through the ley lines, just like the fire of our nervous system. The vision also showed the magnetic power of water near the portals. Can you say more about that?"

"You're probably seeing the sacred wells and underground waterholes that are often near or on the portals to magnetically attract the spiritual powers from the Cosmic realms into our physical world."

"Maybe that's why the Rainbow Serpent is often spotted in or near waterholes, like Sophia explained," Rose says.

"And there's the dragon that sits near the roots of the Cosmic Tree of Life and the well below it."

"They're the Cosmic Avatars that magnetize the water with their life-giving, creative powers. So the old saying that fire and water don't like each other is not true at all! Is that also how the masculine and feminine powers work alchemically together?"

"Yes, it is," Verdandi affirms. "The masculine energizes, impregnates, and expands, while the feminine magnetizes, fertilizes, and in-forms. The activating powers of fire and the magnetic qualities of water need to work together to create new life. The fire is represented as the dragon energy of the ley lines and the water is represented as the sacred wells."

"This is so fascinating," Rose says. "Our world is alive with consciousness in so many more ways than we realize. We live in a universe of consciousness and meaning."

"Yes. And stories," Verdandi adds. "Creation is a continuous process, and we each play our role in it, whether we are that tiny ant foraging over the forest floor, the child who just woke up on the other side of the world, or the dog that's barking in the field nearby. We all have a role to play."

Rose stops suddenly, points at the ground, and whispers, "Deer droppings. Let's follow the trail. Maybe we can even spot a wild boar or a wandering wolf. Did you know that wolves are returning to the Netherlands? They were recently spotted in some of the forests and farmlands, after more than a century."

"I imagine that not all of the farmers are happy about their return," Verdandi says softly. "Let's be careful not to scare the deer who may still be roaming close by. The Great Deer, or 'Grand Cerf' as Dagaz would say, is an important guardian for us. In our druidic tradition, the male and female deer can also represent the high priest and high priestess. Remember the story I shared with you about that?"

"Of course, I do. That's one of my favorite stories. 'Long ago, the druid high priestess would awaken the Great Deer within the apprentice king through an intimate anointing ceremony. Once awakened and married ceremonially, the magical realms were able to be represented within the consciousness of the king, so he could become a king of both worlds: the realms of nature and the human world.' You also said that the high priestess was elected by the Goddess to be Her Avatar here on Earth. Are any of these powers awakening in me?"

"Perhaps they are, my Rose. Just be careful with certain men in whom the Great Deer is awakening," Verdandi cautions. "You may find an unusually strong attraction to these men, and vice versa. Especially when the deer between you seek to mate in order to awaken one another. There are certain spiritual powers that lay dormant in you. These form part of your ancestral and spiritual lineage. Others may seek to access these powers through you to activate their own powers. But enough of that now. Let's see if we can spot this beautiful deer."

The women follow the trail of the deer for a few minutes until Verdandi stops, listens, and then places her hands in front of her as if tracking the deer's energy.

"Did you feel that, love?" Verdandi asks quietly.

"You mean these goosebumps and electric waves that make the hairs on my arms stand up? Is that because of the deer?"

"No, no. This is something else; something quite magical. I'm glad that not all of the portals have closed here. What you just felt is a dragonline. It's right here. We've been walking along an ancient ley line. The deer must be using these too, especially for communicating with its fellow relatives," Verdandi explains. "Your ears may start to feel a little strange."

Rose hears a high-pitched sound inside her ears and experiences a strange buzzing, similar to the time when she, Li, and Sophia spotted an unexpected presence behind Verdandi in her living room. She wonders if this is happening again because of a Cosmic portal.

Verdandi continues, "Our ancestors knew how to find the ley lines and portals for expanding their consciousness so they could receive prophetic dreams, omens, and visions for spiritual guidance. That's why many temples, churches, and mosques are built on these natural power spots."

The women continue to follow the ley line until they reach a group of stones that are grouped in a natural stone circle. They seat themselves on the stones while taking a moment to attune to the energy of this place.

The Three Primary Forces of Desire

"There are many ways to navigate through life," Verdandi says softly. "And there are many tools that can assist us along the way. Like this wooden stick that I picked up during our walk, which has now become a staff and antenna for guiding us. As we talked about earlier, the Architect Tools exist in multiple ways and forms. The importance is to understand the Cosmic principles and powers that they represent, and how we can extend this into our world. There are so many worlds in the Universe. Our human world is only one very limited fractal of the totality. When you relate with life in this way, ordinary stones can become magical stones infused with wonder. A feather that lands on your path can become the message from the Great Spirit you've been waiting for. The world is alive with magic for those who know how to connect with the consciousness that we are. Our Earth is alive with infinite wisdom and meaning."

Rose carefully touches the wooden staff in Verdandi's hand. "This is so much better than buying those fancy new age tools with fake amulets and magic wands that are empty inside."

"Nature is simple, my darling. Everything here is infused with spirit, meaning, and life force. It's only our human minds that have become too fancy to recognize it. Given your recent adventures *and* your attraction to danger, it's time for a teaching about desire."

"Alright. I'm ready."

"Desire is a very powerful force. Even more so when it's not met." Verdandi gives Rose a meaningful look and continues, "Unfortunately, few people understand the true nature of desire, and yet many are driven by it. If one is unconscious, one's desires become the main power supply for the ego and shadow; aspects that are all too happy to promise the fulfillment of desire, if only they could."

"So, you're saying that desires are not necessarily bad?" Rose asks. "I thought that in many religions and spiritual teachings, people are told that they must give up all desires. I even read somewhere that a state without ego is a state without desire."

"It's not quite like that, dear. But you're right," Verdandi smiles. "Knowing the hold that desire can have over our minds, we're often warned not to indulge in desires. And you know very well that when something is forbidden, it only becomes more attractive."

Verdandi stops. She has a strong sense that someone is trying to energetically connect with her and Rose; someone who is not in the forest and knows her well. She senses that this person is trying to read her mind and access her powers as he projects his thoughts onto her.

Rose is feeling quite distracted herself, but doesn't want to let Verdandi know. With the subject of their conversation turning to desire, her mind keeps drifting back to a sensual dream she had a few nights ago. In her dream, she meets a handsome man with flashing eyes and dark hair who kisses her passionately, arousing her inner fire. The memory of this dream and that delicious kiss keeps popping up at the most unexpected and inconvenient times, like right now. She knows her grandmother can read her energy, so she keeps trying to dissolve the image in her mind in an attempt to hide it.

Verdandi scans the source of the intrusive energy in her field, and places protection around herself and Rose, before continuing to walk along the path. "Unfortunately, my dear, few have understood the fundamental nature of desire, and thus made it wrong, including the animal world and Nature herself."

Rose stares at her blankly. Verdandi senses that her granddaughter is somewhere else, and decides to put her to the test. "Then a huge banana manifested in the sky," she tells Rose. "And monkeys took over the world after watching all of the humans slip on the banana peel and tumble over the edge of the waterfall. Don't you agree?"

"Yes, Grandma. I agree. You're very wise."

"Just as I thought! Where's your mind, young lady? Have you even heard a word of what I just said?"

Rose's cheeks flush pink. "Um…yes. You were talking about desire. Sorry my mind went blank for a second. Could you please repeat what you said?"

"We were speaking about desire. And where did your mind travel to?"

"Nowhere."

"Nowhere?"

"Oh yes, I remember now. You were saying that desires are a part of life," Rose replies.

"Look at that tree. Does it have desire?" Verdandi asks.

"Yes, of course. So does the little ant over there who is working hard to bring food to its nest. Nature is full of desire. But why do people make such a fuss about it?"

"Because it's the most powerful fuel of our psyches," Verdandi says. "The problem is not with desire, but with our minds. Especially minds that are not in tune with nature because we believe ourselves to be apart or separate, and are thus seeing the world from an egoic state of consciousness. The evolutionary forces of life are forces of desire to propel life forward. When these forces enter our psyche, we experience and label this as desire."

"Aha. So by denying our desires, we feed the ego and create shadow thoughts. And yet by indulging our desires, we also feed the ego. I'm confused."

"When people indulge in desires, they're consuming the fuel of desire at the level of their minds, and not using the evolutionary forces that exist prior to their minds. Think of desire as a flame that produces energy for the mind, energy for your thoughts, feelings, and actions. Now remember the fire triangle and how in order to create a physical fire you need warmth, fuel, and oxygen, right?"

"That's right."

"Desire, as part of the consciousness of fire, is alchemically composed of three elementary forces: creation, preservation, and destruction."

"So I need to become aware of these three forces within me in order to learn about the nature of desire? Is that it?"

"Yes, that's the key. You are one smart cookie. Many of the ancient sages understood this, and thus the principle of the triad, trinity, trimurti, and triunity in many cultures and religions. That's also why many of the Avatars and gods are shown with a staff that has three forks at the top."

"A trident."

"Yes. Even the staff of the Greek god Hermes, the caduceus, has three elements that unite: the two snakes entwined, and the staff that produces the enlightened mind, represented by the wings on top. You need to become aware of these three elementary forces of life and how this produces the fuel for your desires within you, and how these desires become directed and engaged by your mind. Killing or denying your desires is not the solution. Training the mind with the wisdom of the higher heart in how to work with these elementary forces is the answer. Without the wisdom of your heart, your mind will be completely lost and unable to withstand the powerful urges that stir the mind."

"Why do teenagers not learn about this at school, as part of adult education?" Rose asks. "I learned about sex, orgasms, and intercourse, but they never told us about the physical, emotional, and mental states of desire."

"And don't forget the spiritual state of desire: the tantric state of pure bliss when the three forces unite and produce the spiritual light of the illuminated mind or pure consciousness."

"I look forward to experiencing that one day," Rose sighs. "So these three elementary forces can unite and rise up and down from the densest to the most subtle layers of our consciousness?"

"Indeed, darling, and not only can they unite, they *are* united, which is why action of one force will cause a stirring of the other two forces. These three forces always work together. When you don't recognize these forces or when you deny your desires, it will start to feed your ego and shadow in their opposite manifestation. Just like what happened with Loki and his offspring who were denied and rejected, and thus became the reversed or negative manifestations of the forces of *creation, preservation,* and *destruction.*"

"Loki's three children! I understand now! The Midgard serpent was the negative or reversed force of creation. Hel, the queen of the underworld, was the reversed force of preservation and order. And Fenrir the wolf was the reversed force of destruction."

"That's it!" Verdandi replies. "And now add to this understanding the fire triangle that we spoke of."

"To create a physical fire, you need warmth, fuel, and oxygen. You told me that you can also apply this principle to explore their subtle equivalents in our psyches. The elements of fire can be used to create, preserve and sustain, and destroy."

"Exactly," Verdandi smiles. "These three elementary forces of life are very well explained in the Indian Vedic cosmology as the gods Brahma, Vishnu, and Shiva. You may want to read up on that this week."

"And the force of preservation also includes regeneration?" Rose asks.

"Of course, which is what we need right now after so much excessive creation that has turned destructive. In order to regenerate, we'll also need to destroy and transform the systems that are not in service to life as a whole. You'll also find the principle of the triad in the triple Goddess of the Celtic cosmology, and as the three Norns or Avatars, Urd, Verdandi, and Skuld, in our Nordic cosmology. The three Norns govern the three tenses of past, present, and future of humanity's destiny for *what was, what is,* and *what will become.*"

"You really are like the living embodiment of the Norn Verdandi," says Rose while looking tenderly at her grandmother.

"Don't let me get distracted now, especially if my Norn-like powers are to keep us present!" Verdandi laughs and continues. "Let's explore for a moment how these three forces are expressed as healthy desires, and what happens if these forces become suppressed or reversed."

Rose listens attentively and nods for Verdandi to continue.

"Let's start with the force of creation, which brings us into existence and awakens in us the basic desire to live, experience, and grow."

"What if this force becomes blocked?" Rose asks.

"Then we may lose our sense of purpose and belonging, and feel like our inner light is slowly fading. It may even feel like the world doesn't need or want us. This causes us to withdraw from life, which, for some, may result in them choosing to end their lives. The force of creation also triggers change, and as such, triggers the force of preservation."

"So when the force of creation is blocked, our desire to live fades away, and the force of preservation will then also not emerge, which means we won't want to take care of our lives and may even destroy or end our life..." Rose ponders as her mind is processing this new information at lightning speed.

"We could write a whole book on the various forms and consequences of blocked, repressed, reversed, and excessive manifestations of each of these forces and the impacts on the balance of the three forces as a whole. But looking at the dark skies that are forming, we'd better not go into that right now. I just want to make you aware that these three forces form the alchemy that fuels our human desires, and in particular, I'd like for you to learn about the force of destruction."

"I wonder if the root of violence is not our own mental distortion? When a lion kills a giraffe, is that violence? Is it killing for killing's sake to disrupt the unity of life, like humans often do? Then again, the cat who kills a bird for fun isn't particularly a show of peace. Dolphins who bully a seal aren't that friendly either."

"We are a part of nature, and nature can be very violent. Yet the human violence you're speaking of originates from a different plane; from mental states of consciousness that are more cunning and deliberate."

"Yes, and from the egoic states that always attempt to split what is whole and united by creating ranking and divisions, rather than embracing the unity of our diversity," Rose sighs.

"Before we leave the forest, close your eyes for a moment and connect with the goddess of this place. Her presence is strong here. Then tell me what you see, hear, or feel." Verdandi places her warm hand on Rose's shoulders.

Rose closes her eyes. In her mind's eye, she begins to see images of the people who came here to worship the goddess, bringing offerings and sacrifices to a temple that had been built in her name. Some of these images look terribly violent and bloody. Rose swiftly opens her eyes. Her heart pounds. "I don't like what I'm seeing," she says. "It almost makes me understand why there were people who preferred the new religion over the old, violent ways of some of these pagan rituals. The last image I saw was of a beautiful boy with blond hair who was being prepared to be sacrificed to the goddess. Horrific. I didn't want to see how it ended, so I opened my eyes. Maybe we should go home now."

"Okay, darling, we'll go soon. But first I want to teach you how you can call upon the blessings of the Divine Mother to heal all of this, including the divisions of Her own manifestations. The distortions are not just in the human realms. Let's move to the small pond over there so you can shift the energy of what you've seen and be close to the water that you love so much. We'll do this next practice from there."

Walking to the pond, Rose dissolves the disturbing images from her mind and connects with the ring of unity on her chest. Her heart warms up and she feels the gentle presence of the dragon who reminds her that she has the courage to see what needs to be seen and what needs to be healed.

Practice for Transmitting the Blessings of the Cosmic Mother

"Close your eyes and relax, and then relax some more. Know that you are safe and protected and deeply loved. Take a moment to connect with the wisdom of your heart. Call it forth to guide and support you. Feel the Ring of Unity within you, as it creates a protective force field of pure love and light around you.

"Become aware of your hands. Move your fingers and rub your hands together till they warm up. You can even blow on your hands to awaken their energy. Imagine that within the palms of your hands the Cosmic Ring of Unity is now an energetic portal that connects you to the eternal Bond of Unity and the power of love.

"Feel how the portals of your hands are opening to the Cosmic realms and your larger Cosmic self. As the inner portals open, you'll be able to transmit the life force from the subtle realms of consciousness. You have already experienced this many times when your hands generated their healing touch.

"Ask the Ring of Unity to activate your innate Avatar interface. You may experience this as a gentle warmth or the sensation of a subtle energy body or template that activates around you and is precisely tuned to facilitate your direct connection with the subtle realms of Cosmic consciousness.

"Now intend for your direct connection with the Cosmic Mother to awaken. You may start to experience how Her gentle loving presence forms and manifests around you like a blanket of pure love and wisdom. You can also act as an Avatar, as a sacred extension and interface, for the Divine Mother Herself.

"Ask Her to superimpose Her healing hands over your hands. The energy circuits of the Divine Mother are now able to interface directly with your energy circuits via the Avatar interface that enables you to exchange with and learn from one another. Your hands are able to transmit Her healing touch and blessings, as Her hands extend through you into the worlds of the living. Do this with the utmost respect and honor. Allow Her to guide and facilitate this process. She knows how to do this interface with humans.

"Her hands are now superimposed over your hands. Ask the Cosmic Mother, the Divine Mother, to transmit Her healing blessings for our world, via your hands. You can even uphold your hands with your palms and fingers stretched so that Her healing blessings can easily flow into our world. Intend for Her healing touch and care to go to where it is most needed. You may also include yourself in the receiving of Her care and love.

"Imagine holding the whole earth between your hands with Her healing hands superimposed over yours. Intend now for Her healing touch, love, and blessings to encompass the entire earth, bringing support to all who need it. Allow this transmission to continue until it comes to a natural completion.

"If there is anyone in particular who may also need Her blessings, you may think of this person and intend for the blessings of the Cosmic Mother to go to them, for their highest good and wellness.

"Rest for a few moments in this profound healing state. When you feel it is complete, thank the Divine Mother for Her care and love. The superimposition of Her hands over yours will now dissolve as you each return to your own realm and space of being. Know that Her love and wisdom is always directly present within you, and you can call upon Her support whenever required. Bring your attention now back to yourself and let go of what's not yours. Be fully present here and now. When you are ready, you may gently open your eyes and move your body."

Remembering the Forest Dream

The first raindrops begin to fall. Rose is still in awe of what she's just experienced. Her hands are vibrating in a way she's never felt before. She feels assured that whenever she has difficult dreams or sees and feels things that are painful or scary, she can always place this trouble between her hands and call for the Cosmic Mother to heal it with Her blessings.

Verdandi and Rose walk back quietly to the car park. They are each in deep reflection. The shrill cry of a hawk jolts them out of their contemplative state as they look up to the skies. The hawk circles twice above them, then flies off to the left. Heavy rain clouds are approaching, so there's no time to wander further into the forest. Rose looks in the direction of the hawk's disappearance and suddenly remembers her dream.

"Grandma! I've been here before. Not physically, but in my dream. It is indeed the forest from that frightening dream I had last year; the one where I was in a forest with Sophia and there was danger all around us. In my dream, we heard a teenage boy screaming for help after we'd found an ancient ruin that was a place for worship and sacrifices. I wanted to help him, but felt paralyzed, as if frozen in time by a truly evil force that had been unleashed from long ago. I was crying for help, but my voice got stuck in my throat and I couldn't get past the evil forces. Sophia shouted that I had to put on my ring, which I couldn't find, and didn't even know I had. Is this the ring?" Rose lifts the ring of unity up from her chest.

"Yes, love. That's the one. The dream was a forewarning to give you the chance to change things so that you'll be ready to face those forces when they start to manifest."

"How will I know when this is happening? Am I ready for that?"

"The hawk activated your future memory, which is a strong sign of what's coming. My sister Anna is a powerful portal holder, as I told you. When she got attacked, this may also have caused a brief disruption of the portal. Those evil forces you dreamt of may have taken advantage of this, so they could enter our world. The chains that bound Fenrir the wolf can also be seen as rings or portals that keep certain forces out and bind them to places and realms where they cannot harm the living. Our world is being shaken up right now in all kinds of ways. The attack on the twins is also an attack on the portals. We don't know yet what's awakening or has entered our world from other realms. But we'll soon find out."

"I felt a cold shiver running down my spine as you were saying that. I don't know if I'm strong enough to do this. Apart from dying, I've never encountered much danger, other than Mom and Dad's crazy trips in the Australian outback, and that time we spent in Zimbabwe."

"You're more prepared than you realize," Verdandi assures her. "Most of the time you didn't see the dangers because others sheltered you from them. Now you have to become aware of these forces in yourself, as well as in others. You were brought up as a child of nature, which gives you a huge advantage. I don't know if you're ready for what's coming, nor if any of us are, but you can be sure that I'm preparing you in all the ways I can. And so are the ancestors and the Avatars. You're not alone, my love. Don't try to take this all on by yourself."

"Thanks, Grandma. I know you always do everything you can to help me. But maybe there are some lessons in life that I have to learn by myself. You can't shelter me from danger all the time. I need to face this. What else could my dream mean?"

Verdandi reflects for a moment. "That teenage boy that was chased by men in your dream might also represent the sacrificed masculine by the forces of the patriarchy that are being shaken up. Whereas your vision of the goddess temple, which showed the sacrifices of young boys and girls, could serve to remind us that a return to the matriarchy is also not the answer. We can only bring forth a wiser and more caring world in true partnership between women and men, and humans and nature, based on the Bond of Unity that reminds us of our divine origins."

"That's why these new covenants are so important," Rose says solemnly.

"Yes."

The rain begins to fall more heavily. The two women pick up their pace and make it back to the car.

"Can we watch a comedy tonight?" Rose asks. "I'd love to take my mind off of all these images and questions. I just want to have some fun and relax with you."

"That sounds like an excellent plan. I'd love that too. Now let's get going, I can hear the rumble of thunder getting closer, and my stomach is starting to rumble as well!"

Integration –
The Avatar Interface

Through this chapter Rose learns how to activate her Avatar interface with the Cosmic Ring of Unity to ensure that these enhanced states and powers are not turned on by her ego or shadow. She also learns how to use her Cosmic interface for connecting with the Divine Mother and transmitting Her blessings into the world. She further learns essential lessons about ways of entering the realms of nature, and the three elemental forces of our innate desires.

> *The Avatar interface is perfectly tuned and architected to facilitate your direct connection with the Cosmic realms and your Avatar consciousness. You can call upon this innate interface to enable the more expanded realities of your Cosmic self to manifest within and through you into our world, and for enhancing and expanding your sensory capacities for communicating and exchanging with the Cosmic realms of consciousness.*

The summary and questions below will help you to integrate and apply the essential teachings of this chapter:

- The Avatar state of consciousness provides an architectural and Cosmic understanding of the nature of reality and the wholeness of life. Similar to the Wholeness Coder archetype that helped you to enter into code consciousness, which we explored in chapter 8 of book 1, *The Quest of Rose.*

- The Cosmic Ring of Unity is part of the architecture of your heart and exists in multiple ways: as a *circle of unity* that we can bring forth when we gather in ceremony or to sit in council; as an *Avatar ring* that has been forged by the fire of the Cosmic Dragon heart to teach us the ways of the higher heart; as a *Cosmic portal* that brings the vibrations, wisdoms, and powers of the eternal Bond of Unity into our world; and as a *sacred agreement* or *covenant* from the eternal Bond of Unity, to guide our souls in the unfolding of our lives. *How does this Ring of Unity exist and live in you?*

- Call on the Cosmic Ring of Unity to activate your innate Avatar interface. Through your Avatar interface you can also give more direct feedback about the human experience to those who live on the other side of the veil. *What shifts in your awareness when you enter into the expanded consciousness states of your Cosmic interface?*

- The Cosmic Architect Tools represent the powers of Cosmic consciousness and form part of your Avatar interface. These powers can be called upon to help bypass and transform the blockages, filters, and restrictions of the conditioned local mind—personally and collectively.

- Apply the following method for your personal, energetic hygiene so you can enter communal spaces respectfully and consciously: Let go of, disconnect, and release yourself from any energies, thought forms, or connections that are not in harmony with life and don't belong to you. Call back your energy to yourself and release and return with love and light what is not of you. Do this before you enter someone else's place, including places in nature.

- The Cosmic portals of the multi-worlds can be found on major intersection lines, like nodes of the nervous system of Gaia.

- Desire is one the most powerful fuels of our human psyches, and even more so when the desire is not met. If a person is unconscious, their desires become the main power supply for their ego and shadow; aspects that are all too happy to promise fulfillment, if only they could.

- Remember, the problem is not with desire, but with egoic or dualistic minds. Especially when the mind is not in tune with nature because we believe ourselves to be apart or separate, and are thus seeing the world from an egoic state of consciousness. The elementary forces of life are evolutionary forces to propel life forward. When these forces enter our psyche, people tend to experience and label this as desire.

- Think of desire as a *flame* that fuels your psyche; energy for your thoughts, feelings, and actions. Desire is part of the consciousness of fire, and is alchemically composed of three elementary forces of life: *creation*, *preservation*, and *destruction*. Preservation also includes regeneration and sustenance. Destruction also includes guardianship and renewal by ending what harms, and making space for new life cycles.

- Train your mind with the wisdom of the higher heart, your Cosmic heart, in how to work with these elementary forces of life and the powers of desire.

- The three elementary forces—*creation*, *preservation*, and *destruction*—always work together. When you don't recognize these forces or deny your desires, it will start to feed your ego and shadow dynamics.

CHAPTER 8

Unveiling the Mind

The Cosmic Dragon

The city is engulfed in a thick blanket of fog. The sun struggles to shine through, which gives the scene a timeless feeling. It is wind-still. A lone swan majestically glides through the calm water of the canal directly across from the apartment. Rose leans against the damp railing of her balcony, mesmerized by the beauty of the swan emerging from the fog. She's about to move back inside when a mysterious looking silhouette attracts her attention.

She can't make out if the figure is a man or a woman. The face is hidden under a black hat. The stranger moves closer until he's nearly beneath the balcony, and she realizes that he's a fairly tall man in a well-tailored, charcoal gray jacket and black pants. She strains to see his face, but he's looking down and she can't make out any features. He doesn't speak. *Who is that guy? I wonder what he's doing here. He looks familiar, and yet…* The man looks up, and a shiver runs down Rose's spine. Intelligent, dark brown eyes look into her own. Piercing, bright eyes that seem to peer into her very core. She can't look away. She doesn't want to. The man flashes a grin. *Beautiful white teeth. And look at that tumble of dark, wavy hair.*

The Stranger from Another Order of Reality

"Hello, Rose," the stranger says to her, removing his hat. He continues to hold her in his gaze.

"Do I…know you?" Her voice is as soft as the fog surrounding them.

"Ask your grandmother Verdandi. Is she here?" the stranger asks, casually.

"How do you know my grandmother? And how do you know she's here? What's your name?"

The man laughs. "She was right about you. You do ask a lot of questions."

"But you're not providing any answers, I see," Rose teases.

The man gives her another charming smile. "Tell Verdandi that Diego is here."

"Will do." Rose steps back inside the apartment, trying to look nonchalant, though her heart is pounding. "Grandma!" she calls out. Verdandi rushes into the living room, wiping her hands on a kitchen towel.

"What is it? Your voice sounds weird."

"There's a man outside. He's looking for you. His name is Diego. And he knows my name!" Rose exclaims in a rush.

"Oh." Verdandi falls back onto the couch and sighs deeply.

"Do you know him?"

"I told him not to come. Let me deal with him. You stay inside."

"But he looks friendly," Rose protests. "If he's come to see you, we should invite him up for tea or coffee." *Please say yes. Please say yes.*

"No. Absolutely not."

"But—"

"You don't know what you're getting into. Let me deal with him, I said."

Rose is hurt. It's rare for her grandmother to snap at her. Verdandi marches downstairs and opens the main door to talk to the man. Rose dashes into her bedroom, which looks out onto the main street. She opens the window a tiny crack so she can hear better. Verdandi's face is stern. Rose can't make out what she's saying. Her grandmother waves her arms in a way that suggests the man should leave. He stays put and listens instead. After a few minutes, he looks up, right to the spot where Rose is watching from behind the curtain. She feels his magnetizing gaze again. Even though he can't see her physically, she knows that *he knows* she's watching him. After a few more minutes, her grandmother returns inside. Rose runs to greet her with a million questions.

"How did it go? Who is he? Why did he come to see you? How does he know my name?"

Verdandi closes her eyes and takes a deep breath. "Everything's fine," she says. "I told him I'm busy right now and can't receive him."

"But who is he?"

"Diego is a former apprentice of mine. He spotted us in the park the other day and followed us home. He said he's staying with a friend nearby, and helping him with a political campaign of some sort."

"Your apprentice? I didn't know you had apprentices like that? Where is he from? What does he do?"

"A *former* apprentice. I no longer teach him. I can't." Verdandi looks directly into Rose's eyes. "Why are you so interested in this man?"

Rose tries not to blush. "Nothing. Just curious."

Verdandi shakes her head. "Diego is a campaign strategist; the kind of magician politicians hire to gain influence over the minds of people. He's very charismatic, and very dangerous."

"Really? He didn't seem dangerous to me."

"Rose, trust what I'm telling you. Diego has the ability to bend the minds of people when they least expect it."

"Where's he from?"

"He was born and raised in Peru. At an early age, he discovered that he was gifted with certain powers and abilities. A female sorceress noticed this and took him under her wing as her apprentice. She promised him that he would become a powerful magus if he did what she instructed him to do. He began the training, but sensed that something about the woman didn't feel quite right. His intuition was correct. His association with her nearly cost him his life. Fortunately, he shared his secret concerns with a local shaman who knew of me and my work. I was able to help him to become disentangled from the woman's dark energy."

"His story sounds fascinating. Can't we ask him to come back? Please? I want to learn more about him. Will you introduce us?" *Those eyes! That smile!* Rose's heart skips a beat recalling the way he'd looked up at her.

"NO," Verdandi says firmly. "He is not a good influence for you. I barely got him out of the clutches of that woman and the dark side of magic. You don't need that kind of energy around you right now."

"But why did he come to see you? And how does he know my name?"

"He said that he came to town to help his friend's campaign, and that while he was here, he hoped to have the opportunity to meet with me in person."

"How did he know you were here?" Rose asks.

"We've stayed in touch. I told him about you after you almost died last year."

"You did?"

"Yes. I wanted to show him the power of conscious choice and how he could also choose a different direction for his life. I explained how you healed yourself and returned from the valley of death. He must have been quite intrigued and curious to learn more."

"You see? All the more reason to invite him back. Then I can tell him personally how I healed myself," she grins.

"Oh, *you*. You just don't give up, do you? No, love, it's not a good idea. Not right now…perhaps later. I do believe there's plenty of goodness in him, but he hasn't yet healed his inner wound. He's still dabbling in darkness, and not the sacred Darkness that you love so much. His shadow continues to draw energy from his inner wound, while his ego cloaks it by pretending that he has moved on. He's complicated. And he awakens forces in and around people that belong to a different order and time."

"What order?"

"One that is steeped in blood, battle, and control for power. As I said, he's a complicated man. Now, let's talk about something more interesting. What would you like to do today?"

"I'd like to learn about the fire stones of darkness and light that are inside the Avatar pouch."

"Help! You really want to do that today?" Verdandi sighs.

"Yes. I'm sure that's why Diego showed up," Rose laughs. She can't stop thinking of her dream of the stranger and the kiss. *Is it him?* She secretly wonders and hopes.

"Okay then. Do you want to invite Li and Sophia to join us? They may need this teaching as well. I'm sure they'd enjoy it."

"That would be great except that Sophia is working at the hospital today. But Li might be able to join us. I'll call him right now."

Upgrading the Sleeping Giants

Li is delighted with the invitation, and will join them for lunch. Rose walks to the kitchen to help her grandmother prepare a big pot of pumpkin soup, when Olaf calls.

"Hey, Rose, I have a new idea for the Cosmic Compass game."

"Wonderful. Let's hear it."

"We can put the whole game into sleep mode, or some kind of reduced, disabled state where the game powers only work partially, by introducing a giant into the game."

"A giant? Well, that sounds interesting. Tell me more."

"The game takes place inside the giant's mind, but he doesn't know it because he's asleep in a lower state. While he's dreaming, the game challenges begin. Many of the challenges the players have to solve in the game have to do with his dreams. The dreams can be really awful because the giant is working against us, not realizing that we actually want to help. In his dream we have to figure out creative ways to make him our ally. We have to convince him that he's doing bad things, and that he's the one who's really destroying the planet."

"That's so original, Olaf. Go on," Rose encourages him.

"Our powers in the game are linked to the powers of this giant. When he's in this reduced state of awful dreams, our powers and the help sent to us by the team of Cosmic Avatars are reduced as well. This makes what happens in the game even worse. But there's one superpower that we have, which the giant doesn't know about."

"What's that?"

"We can wake him up and reset him! The Avatars in the game will let us know through a secret message that the giant we're fighting is not his normal self. They'll explain that he's a reduced version of himself and we hold the power to reset and upgrade him to a better version. We can only access this reset and upgrade function if we manage to combine enough of our human powers together with our Avatar team to form one gigantic superpower. When the superpower unlocks, it becomes a huge, blue, laser light that shoots the reset button and fires the mind of the giant with such force that the upgrade codes become activated."

"Wow, you've really thought this through," Rose says. "Okay, the laser hits the reset button, and the giant starts to get upgraded. Then what happens?"

"The giant will start to wake up, which is when he becomes even more dangerous. Remember, he's not his better self yet. We have to be extra careful right then so he doesn't destroy our world and poison the minds of the humans. The Avatars know about this, and together with a small team of humans, they've worked out a plan. If you solve certain challenges in the game, you get invited into this plan, and can join the reset team. Oh, and in order to unlock this superpower, you have to learn how to use your avatar suit and also accept your own upgrade as a human. Because we're playing from a reduced version of ourselves, too."

"This is brilliant! I soooo love what you've added to the game!" she tells her nephew.

"Thanks."

"Olaf, I'm in awe of you. Good job. So now the goal of the game is not just to save the planet and advance humanity, but also to reset and upgrade the giant in order to evolve the entire dream in which all of this is taking place!"

"Yeah!"

"What you just shared is not just a game, it is *the* game. This is true on so many levels!"

"I'm glad you like it, Rose. Uh-oh. Dad is motioning for me to get off the phone. He's taking me to get a haircut. I was trying to avoid that. Maybe I can talk him into getting me ice cream afterward as a reward."

"Good luck."

"Thanks. Love you. Bye."

"Love you, too. Say hi to your mom and dad from me." Rose ends the call and finds her grandmother to share Olaf's latest ideas with her.

"He is such a clever little man," Verdandi laughs. "If only he knew how accurate he is. The giant that he spoke of can also be considered as our collective consciousness, which did emerge from giant bodies of consciousness before those diversified to become all of us so long ago. I believe that's why in so many of our mythologies, the stories of creation begin with giants; human-looking giants as well as giant animals."

Rose smiles and nods in agreement. Verdandi continues, "Olaf is right. The majority of human consciousness is still caught in the prisms of the dream of the giants; the dream of forgetfulness by falling asleep in lower orders of reality and not realizing the illusions of our minds. And indeed, it's not a pretty dream. In fact, it's a living nightmare. It sounds like the archetype of the primordial giant, or 'Adam Kadmon,' as your father would call Him-Her, is connecting with Olaf. He-She is the androgynous one who still remembers the original state of consciousness beyond the dreams of duality that are spun by our minds. These primordial codes of consciousness, or 'upgrade codes,' as Olaf refers to them, exist in each of us. The codes will upgrade the inner wiring of the giants once we find the ways to gather and unite our powers, and realize who we are within the game of life."

"Maybe there's a way we can use the Cosmic Compass game to play the game of life," Rose says enthusiastically. "Imagine this as a huge campaign to wake the sleeping giants in each of us by finding and activating their upgrade codes in order to reset humanity and the collective dream. To lift collective consciousness to the levels of the game where it can stop the self-destruction of the degraded, dreaming giants. To realize how we each are a miniature giant who is playing a lesser version of ourselves." Her mind spins with exciting possibilities. "With movies, theaters, television series, school plays, and social media and communication channels joining from around the world to share the challenges and stories of the people who are co-evolving and upgrading how the game of life is played on planet Earth!"

"You're on fire, my girl! And you may be right, which is all the more reason for you to learn more about the puppet masters who are still controlling and manipulating how the game is played here on Mother Earth."

New Opportunities

Li is looking forward to meeting Verdandi again. He had a powerful dream of her where she spoke to his inner dragon. He never thought of himself as a dragon, but in the dream, he transformed into a white dragon with a blue tongue. He's curious to find out more about the dream. He remembers seeing a painting at his grandfather's house of a white dragon. His grandfather told him that the dragon was an ancient ancestor guardian of their lineage, which goes all the way back to the Daoist times in China. But before he discusses the dream, he has some other things he wants to discuss with Rose. He seats himself at the round table in Rose's living room, next to the balcony so he can look out on the canal.

"It's nice to see you again, Auntie Verdandi. I trust that Rose has told you of our successful meeting with Mike. He won't be bothering her again. My dad said we might be able to help her with the funding of her Cosmic Compass game if the two of us are willing to visit him in Hong Kong. He said that such matters have to be discussed in person after we have physically met.

He always tests the people he does business with first, and only discusses the financial affairs last."

"Your father sounds like a wise man," Verdandi smiles.

"He's offered to pay for the trip," Li continues.

"That's so generous of him!" Rose exclaims.

"I'm sure Rose would love a trip to Hong Kong," Verdandi says. "Has it been a long time since you last met with your parents?"

"Yes, it's been almost two years because of the COVID pandemic," Li sighs.

"I understand, believe me. I miss my parents so much," Rose pipes in. "Li, I would love to go with you to visit your parents in Hong Kong, but first I need to join Grandma in Iceland."

"How long would the trip take?" Verdandi asks Li.

"For Rose, it would only be a week, unless she'd like to stay longer, of course. I'll be traveling to Hong Kong a week before Rose joins us. I have some serious, private matters to discuss with my father. Then the two of us can travel back to the Netherlands together."

"It sounds like an outstanding plan." Verdandi smiles.

"I think so, too." Li feels very shy all of a sudden. He can tell that Verdandi has spotted his feelings for Rose. All week, he's been imagining Rose joining him on this trip to see his parents. He was really surprised when his father came up with the suggestion that she join them, after he told him the news of their meeting with Mike. And he was even more surprised to find out that his father sounded genuinely interested to learn more about Rose's project, and that he'd pay for the trip. Things are looking up.

"This opportunity sounds amazing, and I'm genuinely grateful, but what about our trip to Iceland, Grandma? We've been looking forward to that for so long."

"It'll all work out fine. There's no conflict," her grandmother assures her. "I have to see my sister Anna in Norway before I return to Iceland. I was planning to spend a couple of weeks alone with her. While you're with Li in Hong Kong, I can be with my sister. Then later we'll meet up again in Iceland for the winter solstice gathering and to enjoy the Northern Lights."

Rose likes adventure, and a fully paid trip to Hong Kong with one of her best friends is too attractive to resist. Plus, the prospect of her compass project materializing sounds like a dream come true. Verdandi excuses herself and walks to the kitchen to finish the last preparations for their lunch. The kitchen smells so good. She stirs the pumpkin soup in the pot. The secret to her delicious recipe is to add a few potatoes to make it creamy, as well as an apple for balancing the heaviness of the pumpkin. She then finishes the soup by sprinkling in fresh coriander and small blocks of feta that melt into the soup.

At the table, Rose and Li chat away excitedly, bouncing ideas about what this new opening with Li's father could bring to them. Rose says, "Please tell your dad that I'd love to visit your family and present him with my ideas, but first, you've got to help me improve my proposal. Would you? Please? I don't think my project is up to his standards."

"Don't worry, Rose," he replies. "I'm happy to help you, but first I need to convince my dad that the change in business you and I talked about is a good idea. He doesn't yet understand the new business models. I need him to see who I am and what I'm passionate about in life. I can't take over his business the way it's running now. I'd need to have the freedom to make it my own, or at least have a wing of the larger business where I'm free to design it according to my ideas."

"And not just your ideas, but also your purpose in life. Never forget that," Rose adds.

"I won't forget." Li smiles. "As you know, I've been planning on having this talk with my dad for a long time."

"I know you have," she replies tenderly, "and now you're ready. I believe in you. I saw what you can do when you connect with your passion."

"Okay, you two, time for lunch," Verdandi says as she emerges from the kitchen with a big pot of hot soup.

The Puppet Masters of Money, Psychology, and Technology

"This soup is delicious," Li tells Verdandi.

"It's her secret recipe," Rose grins.

"Is it rude to ask for seconds?"

"Please help yourself," Verdandi replies. "So what have you been up to these days, Li? Are you keeping busy?"

"I am. I watched a documentary the other day with interviews from people who worked at one time for the big social media platforms. I learned how many of those companies deliberately manipulate what we see, and how and when we see things, with the aim of getting us addicted to their platforms."

"Ha," Rose says. "No surprise there."

"They use specific algorithms powered with AI designed for one purpose: to make a profit by selling our attention span and engagement to the companies who use their social media platforms. That's their business model."

"And they make billions of dollars in profit," Verdandi snorts.

"That's right," Li says. "Meanwhile, we get more hooked and disempowered as our worldview gets narrowed down and biased by what they want us to see and react to. I'm sure you're both aware of this since it's been all over the news with the elections in the United States and Europe, but I never knew the specifics of how they're doing this, and it really shocked me."

"Tell us more about what you mean by algorithms and AI programs," Verdandi says.

"Sure. As I understand it, algorithms are codes that include rules for carrying out specific operations, and rules for how to solve a problem. As Rose can tell you, nature uses plenty of algorithms, but not in a deterministic, dualistic, or limiting way."

Rose nods in full agreement. "Yes, that's right. The laws of physics can be seen as in-formational algorithms that guide how the Universe exists and evolves as a coherent entity that is whole and unified. I'm not convinced, however, that the algorithms of our mainstream human technologies use the same informational coding as the cosmological algorithms of the Universe. Algorithms created by human beings are not precisely tuned to make life possible. In fact, the majority of algorithmic programs that modern computers run on are designed to carry out tasks and objectives that have little to do with life or our Earth. And most of those don't include any ethical codes either."

"It's true," Li affirms. "And to answer your other question, Auntie Verdandi, AI stands for artificial intelligence, which are programs that use groups of algorithms that can alter themselves by learning from the data inputs their programs gather."

"What you're saying is that AI programs are capable of creating new algorithms on their own, by learning from the feedback they gather. Is that correct?" Verdandi asks.

"Exactly. But as Rose would say, many AI programs do not process feedback from cosmological data or algorithms of nature. And worse, the majority of our social media algorithms are biased toward addiction and fake news."

"Meaning, they're programmed to select the kind of data that makes us more polarized, divided, and hooked on drama." Verdandi frowns.

"Yes," Rose pipes in. "They create a bias to make us more stupid, more opinionated, and less aware. The complete opposite to how the Universe is designed!"

"Pff, what a waste of human intelligence." Verdandi shakes her head.

Rose adds, "It's not all bad, of course. There are also many good AI programmers and good AI technologies that can process an enormous amount of useful data for things like medical diagnosis, scenario analysis, collaborative social innovation, and more. The problem is not with the technology, but with the designers and their business models. It sounds like the program Li watched was about the social media designers who program for addiction, and are doing it intentionally. They know exactly what they're doing and why."

"It baffles me that smart people like that would want to use their skills in those ways." Verdandi sighs.

"It baffles me, too," Rose agrees. "They carefully study our human vulnerabilities to better manipulate and design for the feedback loops that serve their profit models. They use emoticons, connection options, and view preferences to influence what we see and when we watch, and only add the interactive elements for us to get hooked and wanting more so they get paid more."

"Don't forget about the economists, investors, and politicians who hide behind free market mechanisms as a blank card to pursue their harmful business schemes," Li adds. "It's the combination of these economic and political opportunities, coupled with the knowledge of psychology and social dynamics, which are causing these mass manipulations."

"You're right. The technologies of the puppet masters. The modern schemes of the emperors." Rose feels her inner dragon rise up again. "I can't stand their manipulation."

"Yeah, the puppet masters know exactly how to get us biochemically hooked by triggering the release of powerful dopamine hormones in our body." Li finishes his second helping of soup.

"Just like gambling," Verdandi says.

Li nods. "And now it's run by *mega* computers that use processors run by AI, which, in addition to processing enormous amounts of data that can make computations faster and more efficiently than our human minds ever could, can also update their algorithmic programs to get better and better at getting us hooked and enslaved. I'm afraid it's only the beginning."

Rose looks at her phone and sets it face down on the table. "To be honest, I probably use the social media gadgets on my phone too much as well. I tell myself that it's only to communicate with my friends, but in fact, I forget that behind the social technologies are platforms controlled by people who don't care at all about my friendships or wellbeing. We're playing with the tools and toys of the puppet masters. It's so easy to get hooked into their universe."

"Or metaverse," Li adds. "I agree with what you said earlier, Rose. The problem is not with technology or the science that's used, but the people who use it and their power-hungry mindsets. What if we could use these technologies to actually monitor and know exactly when the dopamine in our bodies increases, and thus become aware of the biology of our consciousness? Like with those biofeedback machines where you can see how your heart coherence and brain wave patterns shift with different thoughts, feelings, and states of consciousness."

"Oh, that's clever," Rose laughs and touches Li's arm. "I like that. Let's use their tools and reprogram them to assist us in becoming more self aware by helping us regain control of our inner chemistry. Maybe, by becoming aware of our social and biological hooks, it can train us to become more evolved."

"Yes," Li exclaims. "Even to the point that we won't need any of these gadgets."

"Like beating the devil at his own game! I'd love to help create purposeful, conscious technologies that are wise by design. Just imagine." Rose's eyes are bright as she ponders the possibilities.

Verdandi enjoys the passionate exchange between the two friends. "I may not be as computer savvy as you," she says, "but I do know a thing or two about wisdom. Wiser technologies require wiser people who understand the nature of consciousness and how to apply it."

"Could you extrapolate on that?" Li asks her.

Verdandi continues, "Okay, let's begin by exploring what consciousness is *not*. And you know this well, Rose. We've had endless conversations about that. Consciousness is not an algorithm, nor will it ever become artificial intelligence, which is programmed by people. Consciousness is the *source* of existence, and the field in which all experiences take place and dissolve. Consciousness is our awareness—awareness as self, life, the Universe, and the tiniest cells and atoms. Can technology become self aware? Can consciousness become aware of itself as a technology or even an algorithm? A subtle difference in focus makes all the difference."

Rose interrupts, "Consciousness can take the shape of an algorithm or technology, which is also a form of information. Yet, algorithms cannot limit or define consciousness, as it originates beyond the programs and formulas of our human minds."

"Absolutely correct, my butterfly." Verdandi smiles.

Li has closed his eyes to listen better. He's surprised by a subtle shift in his mind as he sees into the world from an internal presence that is always there; a presence that's free from the web of his thoughts, observing it all. He feels the presence of his own consciousness *as* awareness. The freedom he feels from this subtle shift in attention is exhilarating: to experience the awareness behind his perceptions that makes him conscious *of* his perceptions, without getting entangled. He wonders how technology could facilitate this subtle shift in our perception to become self aware as consciousness.

Rose is all fired up now. She adds, "Consciousness can evolve by learning from the data of artificial intelligence programs, but artificial intelligence remains a program. Even if such programs are coded to upgrade their algorithms by learning from the data that they gather, they still remain programs and therefore require some kind of interface with consciousness for there to be understanding. We can't expect artificial intelligence to evolve our consciousness or make us better humans. That's *our* job. Just like AI programs can't learn for us. Our brains are super quantum processors; we just don't realize it. I'm convinced that the brain is not the seat or source of our consciousness. It develops and evolves by receiving, transmitting, and processing data at various levels of consciousness, which also helps us become aware of ourselves and our environment. However, 'the self,' as a *local* expression of consciousness, is not limited to the information, feedback loops, and perceptions it experiences. Somehow the consciousness of our Cosmic or universal self goes beyond our bodies."

"You experienced that," Verdandi says.

"Yes, I did. It was so vivid during the few minutes that I died, and before I returned to my body. I'm sure that this Cosmic consciousness, if it can localize inside our bodies, can also shift and evolve the programs of our physical wiring. I don't know if artificial bodies created by humans can ever serve as the kind of biological interface that we have now with our larger Cosmic self."

Li reflects for a moment, then adds, "What if we learn how to transfer our human consciousness to these machine-like robotic interventions that don't age? I'm sure that's already happening with all of those new biotech inventions."

"But Li, what gets transferred?" Rose asks. "Consciousness? Or memories, data, and feedback loops? Do we even understand what consciousness is? All I know is that consciousness is not limited to our physical reality. It operates nonlocally in ways that do not require information transfers through space-time. Consciousness is far more direct than any of that, and is always present. We are not the data or the informational structures, nor are we our memories. We are what can somehow make sense of all this information as a coherent whole. We are the consciousness in which all experiences take place."

"Then consciousness does not die or end," he says. "That's basically what you are saying, right?"

"Yes," she answers. "And maybe one day we may actually be able to prove how space-time is a two-dimensional holographic data-structure of consciousness that gives the *appearance* of what we perceive as a three-dimensional, physical world, with time as its fourth dimension. And how somehow this data-structure is coherently tuned and algorithmically unified to make it possible for one to become self aware as consciousness when embodied. I don't think that AI programs, in the ways they're currently designed, can provide the embodiment for self aware, conscious experiences. Remember how the Nobel Prize winner Sir Roger Penrose said that consciousness has something to do with understanding? And is thus not just a computational formula or exclusively algorithmic?"

"Yes, I remember," Li smiles.

"Well, he also mentioned in one of his talks that artificial intelligence should have been called 'artificial smartness' instead, since intelligence requires understanding. I believe that consciousness cannot be reduced to a program or simulation. Because even the simulation itself takes place in consciousness. Perhaps the simulation is the illusion; the projection of consciousness onto itself." Rose turns to her friend. "Li? Are you ready for a thought experiment?"

"Alright. Go for it, Rose."

"Let's imagine for a moment that far into the future there's one branch of future humans who have become a kind of hybrid robot that is partly organic with human DNA, and part robotic. The robotic elements include AI operating systems that enhance certain human capacities and stop aging and disease. Will this new species of techno humans also have an energetic heart that can help us understand what love is? Will we still have minds that can dream and imagine to explore the mysteries of the Cosmos and our inner worlds? Will we be able to create and enjoy music, arts, and culture? Will we be able to understand what unity is? And will we be able to experience within us the three evolutionary forces of creation, preservation, and destruction, as you showed me a few days ago, Grandma? And will this new species of humans have the ability to evolve their codes and programs in ways that increase our awareness of life?"

Verdandi looks at Li and laughs. "Don't feel pressured to answer her questions. As you probably know by now, she likes to explore the entire Universe as part of her social conversations."

"Yes, ouch." He shakes his head and laughs.

"Would you like a cup of coffee to return to our present time on Earth?" Verdandi asks.

"I would, thank you," Li says. "Rose, what did the Cosmos do to that brain of yours the night you died? Is there anyone around who can keep up with you?"

Verdandi laughs. "Don't look at me!"

"Sorry, Li. I didn't mean to overwhelm you, but I got so excited and one idea followed after another. I'll make the coffee. Grandma, would you like your favorite tea?"

"Yes, love, thank you. And please bring some water and rice for the birds on the balcony as well."

Rose rises and goes to the kitchen. She isn't able to stop her mind, but she got the not-so-subtle hint from Li. She continues to ponder how AI programs, as they're made by people, reflect the levels of consciousness and bias of their makers. Especially people's bias toward drama, fake news, and violence. After a few minutes, Li joins her in the kitchen with the soup bowls and spoons, which he sets beside the sink.

"Without evolving human consciousness to higher orders of reality, we'll never be able to create safe technologies or wise AI programs," she tells him. "Could you grab those three mugs for me?"

"Sure." Li pulls three mugs from the cupboard and sets them on the counter beside the tin of loose-leaf tea.

"We should be developing these tools and technologies in service to life, and never for the sole purposes of profit, mind control, or in ways that are harmful to life and our planet," Rose continues. "The futurist and evolutionary economist Hazel Henderson, who you like so much, has warned over and again that the majority of our social technologies, and economic algorithms, are created from a very limited notion of life. We're being programmed for greed, envy, and competition, or 'the seven deadly sins,' as she refers to it. The information we're fed is based on scarcity mindsets and egoic biases."

"I agree with you and Hazel Henderson," he answers. "She understands the *heart* of economics, and the purpose it should fulfill. She's a real role model for me."

"I'm glad to hear that because I have a call scheduled with her and her friend, Mariana Bozesan, who knows all about what she calls 'safe AI,' as well as integral investment that is ethical."

"No way! Really? That's incredible. Any chance I could join in on that call?"

"Sure, I'll ask them. They're friends of my mom and grandma. Small world, huh?" she grins.

Suddenly Rose feels overcome with sadness. Li watches her face change. "Rose, what's up? Was it something I said?" he asks gently.

"No, no, it has nothing to do with you," Rose tells him. "I just got a flashback of Elise. She and I used to share ideas about how our planet's view of economics could possibly change for the better. She was so young. She had her whole life ahead of her. But she lost hope. I wish I could have done more for her. She ended her life so abruptly...so violently. I'm really worried about the growing suicide rates."

"Me too. There's a lot of depression among people our age, and even younger."

"Elise was always a bit insecure, looking for 'likes' and social acceptance. Remember that post she shared that included the picture of herself? She got so many vicious, nasty comments from other women."

"Yeah. People think they have anonymity online. They'd never have said those things to her face."

"After that incident she started to isolate herself more and more. I tried to reach out a few times, but it clearly wasn't enough. I keep feeling like I let her down when she needed me most. I'd just returned from the hospital around that time and wasn't really in a social mood either. I think those social media comments and the manipulative algorithms pushed her over the edge."

Li puts his hand on Rose's shoulder. "I'm sorry to hear all of this. I never realized that it hit her that hard. Her parents and brother must be devastated. You know, my uncle also committed suicide not long ago."

"Oh, Li, I'm so sorry."

"Yeah. He couldn't handle the financial pressures anymore. He'd tried so hard to create a business for conscious leaders, but many of his customers expected him to charge a lower rate for his programs. Some even thought he should give them away for free."

"Why?"

"They believed that people shouldn't charge for spiritual knowledge. When the bank sent a letter to claim his house, he felt too embarrassed to ask for help. Especially because he was told by many of his colleagues that if you're a conscious leader, you can manifest all the abundance you want from your higher states of consciousness. When he got further into debt, he believed that it proved he was a failure and would never succeed in life."

"That's so sad."

"We learned all of this through the final letter he left behind." Li turns to face Rose. "We have a lot of work to do. Your grandmother's right, we make a good team. So let's get to work instead of focusing on all that's bad in the world."

Rose smiles and places her hand over his hand. "You've always been such a good friend, Li. Thank you. Let's start by breaking the spells of the puppet masters."

Mindfulness or Mindlessness

Verdandi is deep in her own thoughts while she has this little moment to herself. She reflects on Diego's surprise visit this morning. *Did he come to meet with me or Rose?* She has a sense that whatever his agenda is, he won't let it go that quickly. She remembers certain interactions with him previously where he was as stubborn as her granddaughter. She wonders whether she did the right thing by sending him away or if it would have been better instead to introduce him to Rose. Forbidden fruits are always more attractive to humans. Diego has a magnetic presence, as well as charm and good looks. Rose may not be able to stand up to that.

Rose and Li return from the kitchen with the mugs of coffee and tea on a tray. "Li has to leave in about an hour, Grandma. I'm not sure if he told you, but he's really interested in higher states of consciousness. He told me that he's even experimented with different techniques and ways of achieving that. Could you teach him some more?"

"Oh, well done, Li. Good for you." Verdandi smiles. "Tell me, what have you done so far to enter into these higher states of awareness?"

Li's face turns beet red. "Uhhh…"

Rose gives him a look and pokes his foot with her foot. They both recall their conversation in the coffee shop about sex and higher states of consciousness.

"What can I say?" he grins. "I've tried…you know…various methods. Some more effective than others. But what I'm really interested in are the methods you could teach us. Rose told me that's your specialty."

Nice save. Rose catches his eye and inwardly sighs in relief.

Verdandi is well aware that there are multiple conversations taking place here, and some of those are not spoken. She grins at Li. "I'm glad you've already started to experiment with various methods yourself. There's nothing wrong with pleasure and enjoyment, right, Rose? It can be most effective for entering into higher states of consciousness, which can be quite a thrill and truly mind-blowing when you do it well and together with someone of like mind. The challenge, however, is how to ride the wave that follows after the high. For many people the dip or low that occurs after that high gets them hooked into searching for the next thrill that'll take them back up into higher states of consciousness. That's how people get addicted to mind-altering substances as well."

"Grandma, this is all very interesting, but before we dive deeper into this particular subject, I'd like to ask you something else. It ties back to what we talked about earlier. Do you believe in evil powers or is power always neutral, and we make it good or bad? And what happens if we abuse the laws of nature to serve our own selfish agendas?"

"Why do you want to know, Rose?"

"Oh, no particular reason." Rose's cheeks flush pink. "I just want to better understand what magic is all about. And…you know…how we can protect ourselves from any subconscious manipulations of the puppet masters and the addictive algorithms of our social media programs."

Verdandi suspects that the real reason for her granddaughter's question has to do with Diego and her fascination with his power. "Be careful with those explorations, love. Evil is not an algorithm or program that you can decode and disarm. Evil is a kind of wicked and reversed intelligence that grows out of our own unconscious shadows. If we are not sufficiently self aware it can take over like a virus by animating its host with programs and promises that ultimately cause the person to self-destruct. Once it's been able to hook you in, it won't let go that easily."

"But viruses aren't evil," Rose protests. "They're part of nature. They play an important role in evolution."

"Yes, my girl, they do, but they can also be highly contagious. Evil does not have inherent existence. It's an illusionary state, but one that can be highly attractive and appealing to people. This reversed intelligence or shadow dynamic, as I prefer to refer to it, keeps us stuck in the drama triangle of the savior, victim, and persecutor."

"What's a drama triangle?" Rose asks. "I've never heard of that."

"Neither have I," Li adds.

"The drama triangle is commonly known through the work of Stephen Karpman, which is from before you were born, love. He called it the drama triangle to describe harmful interactions between people that keep us trapped in a loop of pain. Ask your dad more about it. I'm sure he uses this model in his therapy with people."

"How does a person get into a drama triangle?" Li asks.

"We get into a drama triangle when, although wanting to help, we keep perpetuating the same problems by not resolving the underlying dynamics, and especially our own needs. We get stuck in a drama triangle between victim, rescuer, and persecutor if we identify with any of those roles to satisfy our own emotional needs, rather than examining the bigger picture of what's truly causing this."

"Oh, I see now why it's so attractive to the shadow," Rose says.

"Yes. The shadow uses any of these three roles to keep us from taking responsibility for our pain and emotional needs. It can project itself as an empathic friend who understands your pain completely and promises to rescue you in its role as savior, or else to convict those who harmed you in its role of persecutor. Or it may convince you to step into the role of savior, rather than helping people to heal their pain and remind them of their inner resourcefulness. Or it could lure you to get onto your high horse and right the wrongs for others, rather than helping the person who has been harmed to speak their truth and discover their own power to stop the abuse."

"Interesting. So in each of these roles, there's a kind of codependency, and even a kind of self-righteousness. It all sounds very dualistic," Rose says.

"So how can I help a person who's in pain without disempowering them?" Li wonders.

"By reminding them of their own healing power, their own authentic, inner voice, and their own wisdom," Verdandi explains. "You can support a person who's been hurt with your love, compassion, and friendship, but not by creating a dependency *on you*. Don't try to save them from their pain or to make things right for them. And most importantly, don't see a person who's been hurt or wronged as weak or a victim. Remember the person is not the pain or the harm. They're so much more than that. We each are a divine spark of the greater consciousness."

"This is really helpful," Rose smiles. "I do need to get to know my own shadow better."

"So do I," Li agrees.

"Good," Verdandi replies. "And please remember that the shadow never shows its true face. It is always cloaked and masked as something you identify with and deeply desire. It doesn't have a face of its own. It is a faceless construct that preys on our insecurities and hides in the darkness of ignorance, not the darkness of wisdom. It projects itself as a trusted friend who understands you completely. If it appeals to your victim complex, it will show you how you've been wronged. If it appeals to your savior complex, it will show you how to rescue those helpless beings who depend on your interventions. And if it needs to appeal to your persecutor complex, it will tell you all that's wrong with the world and how to persecute those who need to be corrected."

Li doesn't believe in good or evil. He wasn't brought up with this Western dualism, but he's seen how humans can be very destructive and harmful. He's intrigued by Verdandi's explanation and curious to learn more. "What do you mean by 'darkness of wisdom?'" he asks.

"Have you heard of the mystic, Meister Eckhart, who lived about 700 years ago?"

Li and Rose both nod. Verdandi continues, "Eckhart told people to embrace the darkness, and that God is the essential darkness. The way to experience the divine, he said, is by surrendering to this darkness and letting go of the mind; to stop constructing your experiences and your sense of reality with your mind; to enter the silence of non-mind and to go beyond the states of consciousness where we still project ideas and images. This means even going beyond the imaginal that you love so much, Rose. In this state of darkness, there is no image, no concept, no thoughts. Just essential darkness and silence. When there's no mind, there's nothing to attack or defend. It's the end of duality. In that darkness, you find the hidden or concealed light of God, or consciousness, that the mystics speak of."

"Aha," Li exclaims. "So, if you're not identified with your mind, then there's no need to protect yourself from mental and emotional manipulations by shadow and ego dynamics. It must be profound to know yourself as *that* darkness. My grandfather spoke of something similar. He called it 'mushin,' a mind without mind; a mind free or empty of all concepts and 'isms.' He explained that the experience of mushin is the natural flow state of pure consciousness."

"Very good! So now you understand why it's pointless to try to answer all these questions with your mind," Verdandi smiles.

"But I do have one more burning question on my mind."

"Okay then, what is it, young man?"

"I had a dream of a white dragon recently. I'd really like to know what it means."

"The color white means different things in different cultures," Verdandi replies. "In Western cultures, white is a sign of purity, maturity, and wisdom. I am aware, however, that the white dragon in your Asian culture can also be seen as a sign of death and rebirth, and by some, is feared as a bad omen. Maybe you're going through your own rebirth process? Just like Rose went through hers last year. Maybe it's the death of your old life and the birthing of who you truly are. The flow state you mentioned just now is also the stream of light that flows forth from the primordial darkness. Do you meditate?"

"Yes."

"Good. When you meditate to enter into these higher consciousness states, ask the dragon why it's showing up in your life right now. Ask what it's here to teach you."

"Good idea, Auntie. I'll do that."

Rose's mind is still focused on magical powers and projection. "Grandma, I have another question. You said that evil or shadow doesn't have a face. So how can we face it?"

"From the darkness, not with your mind. You don't face 'it,' you face *you*. You reclaim *your* face, and become aware of your own self constructs that 'it' has used against you. You end the drama triangle inside yourself, which is, in many ways, the reversed fire triangle. You take responsibility for the primordial forces within you—creation, preservation, and destruction. Reclaim those powers and also any ways that you may have distorted or reversed their purpose and manifestation in you. Remember, ego and shadow have no power of their own because they don't have inherent existence. Wherever your intelligence or power has become twisted or contrary, return it to your primordial consciousness. Then ask your Cosmic consciousness, the sacred Darkness in you, to shift your mind and reveal to you the true direction, focus, and purpose of these powers, and how to apply those powers wisely. Use the power of destruction to deconstruct the illusions of your mind. End the appearance of your false self by seeing its non-existence, and cease the illusions of separation. Return your awareness to the primordial ground of being. There you'll discover the grand luminosity of consciousness that never ceases. Remember, the battle is with yourself and you can't fight, win, or end it with your mind. You have to go beyond, and surrender to that force deep inside you that carries the liberation and ends the inner divisions. The conflicted or conditioned mind cannot help you."

Li listens attentively. Many more memories of his time with his grandfather are bubbling up to the surface. He was a wise and gentle man who followed the path of Zen Buddhism for his entire life.

"What you're teaching us is so similar to the Buddhist teachings back home," he says. "My grandfather always started his days in silence before the sun would rise. I used to watch him gaze toward the mountains with a kind of empty expression, as if his mind had ceased to exist. He would look at me gently without saying a word. He was living in that profound emptiness that you speak of. And yet, through this emptiness, I could feel how he was more present with me than I was with myself. It took me years to appreciate and understand what he was doing, and now it feels like you're completing the teaching he started all those years ago. Thank you profoundly." Li folds his hands in front of him and bows to Verdandi in respect.

Rose is in her own world. She was hoping for a different answer to her question, and struggles to take her mind off Diego. "Grandma, you once told me that seeing is a form of creation. That when you look at something, there's an energy transfer. By seeing evil, shadow, or ego, are we also bringing it into existence and empowering it? But by denying it and pretending it's not there, don't we feed it then as well? I'm confused. How do we get out of this loop?"

"What or who sees the evil, ego, or shadow? Who is looking? In whom is this image appearing? Who's doing the seeing, and who is projecting?"

"Me. My mind."

"And where is this mind? Can you touch it, hold it, or take it away?"

"In my consciousness," Rose answers.

"And where is this consciousness? Can you place it, touch it, hold it, or move it aside?" Verdandi asks.

"I am all of that. It seems like the projections appear as soon as I start to think. The darkness doesn't project, yet I don't fully know the 'I am' who is projecting."

"That's because you are not yet fully aware of your shadow," Verdandi says with a smile. "See from the luminosity of your consciousness. Use your effortless awareness. Remember what we worked on last year with the Key of Darkness and the Key of Self Awareness? Your awareness is the presence of your Cosmic self. Don't get engaged in the beaming lights of your ego, which put everything under a spotlight to be examined, judged, and dissected."

Li quietly observes the lively exchange between Rose and her grandmother. He becomes aware of how his mind has shifted once again without effort. He follows the subtle shift in awareness and suddenly realizes how, without doing anything in particular, he has shifted into higher consciousness. He feels a profound sense of inner peace. Silence opens his entire being. He starts to understand his grandfather's way of seeing into the world, and feels a profound sense of oneness with him. He experiences being of one mind; the non-dual mind.

Rose, on the other hand, feels incomplete. She wants to explore the new powers that are awakening within her. She doesn't like the idea of returning her powers to the mindless self that has nothing to identify with. It feels so otherworldly and without concepts and forms that she finds it hard to let this inner aspect of herself direct her life.

Li wants to bask in the feeling of oneness. He decides that he'd like to spend some time alone in silence, so he stands up to say goodbye. "It's time for me to go. Thank you for everything you've shared with me today, Auntie Verdandi. I've learned a lot. Bye, Rose. I'll call you soon. And thank you both for the very nice lunch."

"It's our pleasure, Li. I've thoroughly enjoyed our time together," Verdandi replies, as she and Rose walk him to the front door. "Remember to connect with the white dragon. It might be your grandfather."

The Lure of More...

Rose goes out by herself for a run in the park. Like Li, she feels she needs some alone time to reflect on all they've talked about today, particularly, the new opportunities that have opened up. *Hong Kong! That was certainly unexpected. I can't wait to meet Li's parents and present my Cosmic Compass project. This is really a major step.* She arrives at her favorite willow tree, where she always rests for a few minutes before continuing her run.

A playful dragonfly hovers over the place where she usually sits for a short break. She loves dragonflies. They remind her of the story her grandmother once told her about dragonflies being the Avatars of the Cosmic Dragons here on Earth. She leans against the side of the willow tree so as not to disturb the dragonfly, and becomes aware that she is not alone. Someone is watching her closely. She whirls around to see who that may be.

"Diego! What are you doing here?" *Those eyes!* She feels herself getting lost again in his gaze. He has been quietly standing there, watching her; studying her.

"Hello, Rose. This must be my lucky day."

"How so?"

"Meeting you twice within a couple of hours."

Coincidence? Rose wonders.

"I came here to clear my mind," Diego continues. "What brings you here?"

"It's my favorite place. I come here to run and meditate under the tree." She smiles shyly.

"It seems we like the same tree."

"Yeah, it does seem that way. Odd."

"Why?"

"Well…it feels like you knew you'd run into me here," she says. "Did you come here on purpose?"

"Why? You think I've been following you?" He laughs. "Don't worry, I'm not after you. Did your grandmother warn you not to speak with me?"

"Something like that. She's very protective of me. She seems to think you're a bad influence. Are you?"

"It all depends on what you mean by 'bad.' I know a great deal about certain topics she may not want you to learn about…yet." Diego smiles slyly.

"Like what? She always tells me everything. Mostly."

"Let's just say that I practice the ancient art of alchemy that some people believe is a subject better left alone. Anyway, enough about me. Tell me more about you. Have you fully recovered from COVID? What are you doing these days?"

"Yes, I've recovered. I'm fine now. Much better in fact. I'm not doing anything special these days, just working on some projects. I might start a Ph.D. next year."

"Good for you."

"What kind of alchemy do you practice?" She can't resist asking. Her curiosity is piqued.

"Imaginal alchemy."

"Really. I've never heard of that. My grandmother did teach me a lot about imaginal powers."

"Yes, Verdandi is a living master when it comes to the arts of the imaginal. I learned a lot from her. Let's just say that imaginal alchemy takes it to the next level. You can learn about mind control, and how to influence certain events through a specific use of your imaginal powers. If she hasn't yet taught you this, I'd better not say anything more. I wouldn't want to upset her training of you." He intentionally moves in a way that suggests he's leaving, hoping this will intrigue Rose to get him to stay longer. He has already intuited that she needs to believe she's free and in control of herself.

"Wait! Have you got a few more minutes, Diego? It's not often that I run into one of my grandmother's former students. Why did you two stop working together?"

"She told me there were certain lessons I needed to complete on my own first, which is what I'm working on now. I was hoping to have a longer talk with her this morning to show her what I've done since we last met, but it seems she has no time for me right now. Her full focus is on preparing you. Understandably. You're very fortunate to have her with you, and to be trained personally by a living magus of the dragon ways. One of the last, I might add."

"You know about the dragon?" Rose's curiosity is growing by the minute.

"Of course. He's the one who teaches me. Or rather, he *did*, until it all went wrong." Diego studies Rose. "I see the dragon has woken up in you as well. Use that power wisely. Don't get burned by it. I learned that the hard way."

"Really? How so?" Rose asks.

"He became too strong in me. I thought I could control the powers, but the powers began to control me. Told me what to do, who to meet, where to go. It gave me all sorts of premonitions. It started to take over my life. It became an obsession. That's why I went to see your grandmother. She broke the loop."

"Yes, she said something like that. She's very good at breaking loops and traps. But are you sure those things happened to you because of the dragon? Or was it something else?"

"Those powers are not innocent, Rose. They've been used by the most powerful warriors, kings, queens, emperors, and other rulers. Look at the myths. There's always a magus near those who hold positions of power. The rulers believe the powers are theirs; not realizing they were only lent to them for a certain time and for a certain purpose. The dragon returns to claim what's his, and when he does, the debt has to be settled."

"That doesn't sound like the dragon I know. Grandma never spoke of dragons in those terms. She's been teaching me about the alchemy of the dragon heart; the ways of the higher heart."

"Good. That should keep you safe and on the straight path."

"Why would there be a debt to settle when you use the powers of the dragon? Did you have to settle a debt?"

"That's a long conversation, Rose, and not for a stroll in the park. I'm happy to tell you more another time, when your grandmother agrees that I can see you."

"I'm a grown woman! I don't need her permission to see you."

"But it would be better if she knew, right? You wouldn't want to hide anything from her, would you, Rose?"

"No, you're right. One more thing before I head back home. Grandma said something about you using magic. Do you really use magic? Is that the same as the imaginal alchemy you spoke of earlier? Can you influence people's minds?"

"Of course, and so do you. Why else are we still talking here? Why did you turn around to see if someone was looking at you? Why did you feel drawn to go here for a run at precisely this time?"

"Do you mean to say this is all a set-up and you've been manipulating my mind?" Rose feels her stomach tighten at the thought.

"We're all manipulating life. All the time. Each and every one of us is influencing certain outcomes; even those who believe they have no power. A chiropractor manipulates the bones so the life force of the body can flow freely again. We manipulate the blockages of the mind so the primordial forces of consciousness can manifest. People don't understand power, which is why they're so fascinated by it, and at the same time feel they're always lacking it. You aren't afraid of your powers, are you?"

"No, of course not," she laughs. "What do you mean by 'magus?'" Rose is already familiar with the term, but is interested to hear how Diego would define it.

"A magus is a wizard or sorcerer," he says. "Someone who knows how to conjure the forces of nature and is very close to the earth. A magus can see what is veiled from the ordinary mind of humans. A magus is like a scientist of the mind and the human psyche; one who knows how to open the portals to our untapped human powers of consciousness. Ask your grandmother to tell you about the magician archetype by Carl Jung. You'll find it very interesting."

"It sounds like you have no problem with the word 'magic.'" Rose is fascinated by how comfortable she seems when discussing these topics.

The High Art of Magic and the Science of Alchemy

"Magic is an ancient art of alchemy that has been widely misunderstood," Diego replies. "It's not about superstition, potions, or witchcraft. In fact, magic is the art of using our imaginal powers for what they were truly created. Magic can help you to develop the full potential of your imaginal powers. It's all about knowing how to visualize and animate your desired goals and intentions with subtle forces of life that can manifest those goals and intentions. Our understanding of our human powers is so limited. What people don't understand, they cast to the domain of magic or miracles. In fact, there's nothing 'magical' about these powers, once you understand the *science* of alchemy. Through the high art of magic, you'll learn how to shift your consciousness at will. You will then discover the true power of the mind and how to liberate yourself from the lower forces in the world that prey on human weaknesses. The high art of magic is the path of the spiritual warrior, rebel, and light bearer who brings liberation."

"But isn't it dangerous to stir up these forces? How do you know what they'll do once you conjure them up?" Rose starts to feel slightly concerned about his confidence.

"The art of magic teaches you how to link your human powers with the powers of nature. And isn't that what the whole modernization of our human worlds have done? Look at all of the technologies that have been invented where the human mind has sought to understand the laws of nature, and then use this to create technologies for altering the environment and drawing resources from life. Because we can explain it rationally, we don't call it magic. But for someone who lived in the 12th century, they'd see our phones and quantum computers as high magic, or maybe even black magic. In similar ways, there are other laws and resources that most people don't yet understand, or worse, deny. Look at what happened with the brilliant inventor Nikola Tesla, who was far ahead of his time. We understand so little about collective consciousness and the fields by which you can influence what people will experience with their minds. And yet, modern tech companies are constantly inventing tools to alter people's perceptions. The whole world of commerce is based on manipulating people's buying preferences. Wake up, Rose! We live in a world that's run by magicians. We just label them differently these days."

"I see your point," she admits. "But how do we regain control over what we think or believe, or even feel?"

"By understanding magic! By knowing how it works; how people become spellbound, and how the masses are influenced. By knowing the workings of your own mind first, which is the real study of the magus."

Rose recalls a warning from her grandmother: *People who dabble with magic often trigger events that are seductive for the ego, but which they cannot control. The right use of magic, in harmony with the natural laws, requires a stable personality and a fair degree of self awareness.*

Rose adds, "You mentioned earlier that you lost control over your mind and these powers overtook your life. Yet it sounds like you're still defending these powers and explaining why they're needed. Or why people like you are needed in the world."

"Very perceptive. 'That which does not kill us makes us stronger.'" Diego smiles.

"Friedrich Nietzsche. Not sure I'd want to follow in his footsteps. I read that he turned mad toward the end of his life. Okay, I really need to head back home. It's been fascinating to talk with you, Diego. I hope to see you again in the future."

"The pleasure has been all mine, Rose. I trust we'll meet again soon. You take care. And don't scare the crow on your way back." He takes her hand in his hand, then bends forward, puts one leg behind the other like an ancient knight, and kisses her hand softly.

Rose is completely taken by surprise. Her whole body starts to tingle with inner fire. She desperately hopes that her cheeks aren't showing how flushed she feels.

"What crow?" she asks shyly. She turns her face away, pretending to look for a crow so he won't see how she's blushing.

"You'll see," he grins. He turns and they both walk off in different directions.

Running back home, Rose feels invigorated. *This is an adventure!* she thinks. *As if a new chapter of my life has announced itself. Diego is sooo... interesting. And handsome. And...Oh no. How am I going to hide this from my grandmother? Or Li?* Rose stops running. *I need to speak with Sophia. But she's working at the hospital today. She might not have time to talk.* She reaches into her pocket for the phone and dials her best friend's number. *Please pick up!*

"Hello?"

"Sophia! I'm so glad you answered my call. Are you free to talk for a second or are you still at the hospital?"

"It's okay. I'm still working, but we can talk for a few minutes."

"Where to begin? We'll have to meet soon. Can you join me this weekend for a walk in the forest? Saturday, maybe? I've got so much to tell you."

"Sure. Will your grandmother be there as well?"

"No, I need to speak with you alone. She won't mind."

"What's up, Rose? Your voice sounds different. More excited than usual."

"I've met someone very interesting. I'll tell you all about it when we meet. I'll pick you up early on Saturday. Around nine o'clock?"

"Okay."

"It's a long drive to the east of the country; about two hours. We'll go to the forest in Twente that's linked to the Germanic goddess Tamfana. I went there the other week with Grandma, and it's amazing. Definitely worth the drive. Many ley lines converge there with natural vortexes and portals."

"Sounds like my kind of place. See you Saturday!" Sophia replies happily as they close their call.

Rose continues her run on cushions of air that feel light as a feather. Her head is in the clouds while her feet barely touch the earth as she increases her pace. *Almost home.* She races around the last corner, nearly colliding with a man on his bicycle who swerves to avoid her and crashes to the ground.

"Darn it, lady!" the man yells at Rose. He brushes himself off and scowls at her.

"I'm so sorry! I didn't see you. Are you injured?"

"No."

"Thank goodness."

"Just watch where you're going!" The man climbs back onto the seat of his bike and speeds away, shaking his head.

"I'm really, really sorry!" she shouts after him.

Above her, a startled crow caws loudly and flies off, interrupted by the sudden noise. Rose shivers. *That was a wake-up call.* She remembers that her grandmother warned her that the shadow never shows its true face. *But she reminded me that I can always trust the wisdom of my heart to reveal it all.*

Rose hears the voice of Verdandi in her head telling her, "Remember love, the shadow is always cloaked and masked as something you identify with and deeply desire. The laws of the Universe respect the sacred autonomy of each being as sovereign and sentient, as we are all living cells in the Cosmic body of Mother Universe, and thus we each have our role to play, whether we're conscious of that or not. When unsure about your powers or influence, direct and filter them through your heart. That's what the Cosmic Dragon has been teaching you. And remember, we all influence each other all of the time. Each breath creates a ripple in the fields of life that influences the next ripples. There's no need to fear your power or influence. Trust it. Develop it from that powerful spark of love that you are."

The Powers of Darkness and Light

"How was your run in the park, love?" Verdandi asks as Rose enters through the door.

"I had so much energy that I almost crashed into a man on his bicycle on my way back home. I felt like I was flying, that's how fast I was running. The poor guy fell off his bike trying to avoid hitting me."

"Was anyone hurt?"

"No. Thankfully, neither of us got injured, but it was a close call."

"So why all this energy?"

"I was just thinking about Li and Hong Kong. It's such an exciting opportunity."

"Nothing else?"

"Not that I can think of right now. But I do want to learn more about the new powers that are growing within me. Is there any risk that they may try to overtake me?"

"Does the power of the sun overtake the sun? Does the power of the earth overtake Gaia? Does the power of the ocean control the waves?"

"No."

"And why do you think that is?" Verdandi asks.

"Maybe because they don't have a mind that tries to control or mimic those powers?"

"Exactly. Do you understand now why I've been teaching you to become aware of your ego and shadow? The healthy expression of your ego is about your individual self-expression, which helps you to maintain your personal boundaries. The unhealthy expression is about getting lost in duality and separation dynamics. Shadow is what you mask and deny. It's also the areas in yourself that you aren't aware of. You can use the powers of darkness and light for egoic and shadowy purposes, as well as for growing your consciousness and becoming more self aware. You can hide in darkness, as well as in light. But remember, the greatest power in the Universe is *the power of love*. Love cannot be manipulated or divided. It never loses its qualities or essence. It remains ever-present, whether humans connect with it, or not. Here, have a glass of water. You must be thirsty."

"I wish this would also be true for falling in love," Rose says while gulping down her water and taking some more.

"Oh dear, you don't fall into or out of love. Now sit down and relax. Or go take a shower. What you're talking about is attraction, passion, and desire. Love is a different force, but can teach you many powerful lessons about those other three forces."

"One more question. Why is the feminine often associated with darkness and the masculine with light?"

"You don't want to shower first?" Verdandi asks.

"No, I'm still too hot. I like to cool down a little before showering. Please tell me more about the feminine and masculine."

"The feminine and masculine principles can also be understood by exploring the qualities of darkness and light. Darkness absorbs, contracts, integrates, and draws the powers back in so they can manifest internally. The feminine principle acts in similar ways, yet is often misunderstood or feared; whereas light illuminates, expands, infuses, and impregnates, manifesting the powers externally. Those qualities are often associated with the masculine principle. We all have masculine and feminine qualities; they are the dual dynamics, or alchemical polarities, of our powers. Men tend to be more masculine in their outward expressions, while more feminine deeper inside their being. I'm not sure if you've noticed, but men can have really tender hearts, which is why some of them cloak it under an armor of bravery."

"Yes, I've noticed that. I wonder whether that's one of the reasons why it can be more difficult for men to emotionally express themselves? And why it's harder for them to deal with emotional turmoil? If the feminine principle is active inside men, this would also mean that their emotions can become more drawn into themselves. They might feel like they're disappearing into a black hole. Right?"

"Exactly. So keep that in mind when you get closer to men. Women tend to be more feminine in their outward expressions, while masculine inside. Accordingly, women can be quite calculating, and even tough on the inside, which can surprise men if they expect women to be all fluid and cuddly."

"Aha. So we can cloak ourselves in mystery and elusiveness, while deep inside, we know precisely what we want and how to get it!" Rose laughs.

"Yes." Her grandmother smiles. "And these days, a growing group of people feel like all this stuff about gender is so confusing that they simply don't want to associate with it, and would rather express themselves as gender fluid or androgynous. Nature is also gender fluid. When I speak of Mother Earth or Gaia, it doesn't mean that I don't honor her masculine powers and expressions."

"She is also Father Earth."

"Yes. But acts outwardly in the role of a mother, as life bearer. Here's how Gaia shared it with me when I asked her what humans are to understand about themselves so we can become the people for this long-awaited and promised new beginning.[2] Darkness and light are complementary expressions of the same universal consciousness, just like the feminine and masculine principles. Oneness requires these two forces or principles to become all that is in the continual dance of life. Women have often been blamed for luring men into their darkness, meaning into their animalistic nature, and yet this is one of our greatest powers of initiation: to return consciousness to the darkness of the womb where we discover the consciousness of the unknowable that is not constructed by the mind. From this womb, the consciousness of the self is born. You won't become self aware if you fight or deny the wisdom of the darkness. It is in the sacred Darkness that we discover the powers of renewal and transformation, and we discover the light that is hidden—the dark light. It is within the sacred darkness of the womb that the masculine is given the impulse to offer his seed to fertilize the potentials of life. This can happen physically, and also energetically or metaphysically, as the seed of ideas, intentions, and thought forms. We find our inner goddess by connecting with our inner darkness. It is then that we become initiated into the ancient mysteries and learn from the hidden or veiled knowledge that is necessary for becoming fully conscious and self aware beings."

"Oh. Is that why there's a Black Mary or Dark Madonna in many of Dad's books on Gnosticism and mysticism? Is the Pistis Sophia a key principle to focus on?"

"Yes, and this lesson also applies to women, of course. Many women fear or may not even be aware of their inner darkness because they lack understanding of the principles and actions it represents. In similar ways, there's a huge misunderstanding about the masculine and the authentic power of men. The masculine principle represents the inner light—the manifest light—in the forms of logos, knowledge, and outer action. The masculine principle impregnates our potential so it can be born in the world of form and bring our consciousness out into the open. The masculine principle helps us to build with the orders of life, creating structures for the outer manifestation of the world from the implicate orders of consciousness. We find our inner god by connecting with our inner light. The masculine plays an essential role in developing our active powers of manifestation. The forces of creation, preservation, and destruction are masculine and feminine. It's really important that you get to know the dual actions of each force, both outwardly and inwardly. Hence, the two Fire Stones of Darkness and Light together ignite the blue Flame of Love in which these dual actions and polarities are unified."

"Can you please share a practice for working with these stones from the Avatar pouch?"

"Certainly, love, but let's do it after dinner, and after your shower. You're all sweaty and smelly!"

Rose laughs. "Okay, okay, I can take a hint."

Later that evening, Verdandi stands at the window and watches the sun sink toward the horizon. In the transition between the light and darkness, she begins the practice. The Avatar pouch is placed next to Rose on a special black silk cloth that is reserved for that purpose. Rose wears the ring of unity on her chest. She knows to connect with this first, before connecting with any of the other architect tools, to ensure that the tools from the pouch are activated from the consciousness of unity.

Verdandi hums and invokes the archetypal powers of the Flame of Love and the alchemy of Darkness and Light. She blows softly over the flintstones to activate their Cosmic powers. She then calls forth the alchemical force of Darkness from the dark flintstone, and the alchemical force of Light from the light flintstone. The stones become fractals of these primordial Cosmic forces and can now transmit their timeless qualities.

Holding the two stones, Verdandi brings her hands to her heart where she holds them briefly, blessing the stones with *the wisdom of the higher heart.* She then raises her folded hands to her forehead and blesses the stones with *the wisdom of higher vision.* She continues by moving her hands above her crown and blesses the stones with *the wisdom of higher knowing.*

She places the dark flintstone in Rose's left hand and the light flintstone in her right hand. She says, "These sacred stones are now activating your innate powers of Darkness and Light, which are Cosmic powers. You can connect with these powers directly or by holding the stones in your hands. You can also call upon the archetype of the Fire Stones of Darkness and Light, which will help you to interface more directly and safely with these ancient powers. Your practice will now begin."

Practice with the Fire Stones of Darkness and Light

"Take a deep breath. Inhale all the way into your belly. Hold your breath for a few seconds, and then let it go. Breathe out and relax. Do this a few more times until you feel present and relaxed.

"Become aware of the Cosmic Ring of Unity inside your heart as the wisdom of your higher heart. Form the intention for this wisdom of unity to purify, center, and energize your powers. Sense, see, feel, and experience how the Ring of Unity calls back each of your powers to align with the powers of the higher heart, and facilitate how you can transmit and bring forth your powers with greater wisdom, awareness, and care. Allow for this inner action to take place now.

"Check inside yourself. If you carry any fears or negative beliefs about your powers, including the belief that you don't have power, intend for all limiting thoughts and beliefs to fall away and dissolve. Trust and allow the wisdom of your higher heart to guide this process.

"Place your hands on your legs in a comfortable position with the palms facing upward. Keep your left and right hand slightly apart from each other. Now bring your focus to your left hand and imagine a black fire stone in the palm of your left hand. This fire stone carries within it the power of the sacred Darkness.

"Ask this black stone to help you balance your relationship with this power. Spend a few moments getting to know the power of this sacred Darkness. Feel its qualities and actions and remember how this sacred Darkness is already part of your own consciousness. You are merely becoming more aware of it now.

"Ask the sacred Darkness to balance the feminine qualities within you. Give to the sacred Darkness within you whatever needs integration, healing, and reconnection with the feminine qualities of yourself.

"Ask your mind to rest for a few moments in the heart of the sacred Darkness; to be received by your deepest, innate self that is the wisdom of the Darkness. Trust and let yourself go into this inner realm of your consciousness where you are reunited with your primordial self.

"Now imagine a beautiful light that is born from this Darkness, the sacred Light of consciousness, which takes the shape of a white fire stone that manifests in the palm of your right hand. Bring your focus to your right hand and imagine how this white stone carries within it the power of the sacred Light that emerged from your inner darkness.

"Ask this white stone to help you balance your relationship with this power. Spend a few moments getting to know the power of this sacred Light. Feel its qualities and actions and remember how this sacred Light is already part of your own consciousness. You are merely becoming more aware of it now.

"Ask the sacred Light to balance the masculine qualities within you. Give to the sacred Light whatever needs expression, support, and reconnection with the masculine qualities of yourself.

"Ask your mind to rest for a few moments in the luminosity of this sacred Light; to be received by your actualizing self that is the wisdom of this Light. Trust and let yourself go into this inner realm of your consciousness where you are reunited with your eternal self.

"Now bring both of your hands together in front of your heart, in a folded position. Intend for the powers of your inner darkness and light to unite within you whatever became divided and disconnected from the source of your being.

"Imagine rubbing the two fire stones against each other until a spark ignites. Let this spark grow bigger and bigger, bringing forth the eternal Flame of Love. May your inner being remember deeply how to bring forth the eternal Flame of Love from this alchemy of Darkness and Light. Feel and remember how this eternal Flame gives you the power to manifest the qualities and potencies of love in yourself, your life, and in the world.

"Continue to hold your hands together, folded in front of your heart, and imagine how this power of love that is born from the alchemy of Darkness and Light spreads through your whole being as a healing, nourishing, and illuminating force of consciousness. Ask this power of love to spread through your whole life and each of your relationships as a healing, nourishing, and illuminating force of consciousness.

"Continue to rest for a few moments as your inner darkness and light harmonize, integrate, and synergize, bringing forth more and more of love's powers to actualize who you truly are. Allow this process to come to a natural completion.

"Imagine now that these two Fire Stones of Darkness and Light dissolve from the palms of your hands, as they have completed their purpose. Know that you can call upon this Cosmic Architect Tool whenever you need its help.

"Bring your awareness fully to the present moment, centered and grounded in your entire body. Feel your feet and your direct connection with the earth. When you're ready, you may complete this practice by opening your eyes and gently moving your body."

Integration -
The Fire Stones of Darkness and Light

Through this chapter, Rose experiences the workings of the Fire Stones of Darkness and Light. She learns about the dual actions and alchemical polarities of our human powers and how to combine and integrate those to bring forth the alchemical Flame of Love. She learns about the powers of *darkness* and *light* within her, and how these relate to the feminine and masculine principles. She continues to learn about ego and shadow dynamics within herself and in the world, and the workings of the mind. She comes face-to-face with the magus who mirrors her own desires and awakens in her the sexual alchemy of love.

The Fire Stones of Darkness and Light represent the alchemical wisdom of the sacred Flame of Love and how to use the dual aspects of our powers from a place of unity consciousness. You can call upon the Cosmic Fire Stone of Darkness to reveal the ways of the sacred Darkness and feminine principles, and the Cosmic Fire Stone of Light to reveal the ways of the sacred Light and masculine principles. By combining both, you learn how to integrate and apply your feminine and masculine qualities for developing your innate powers from wholeness, and with love.

The summary and questions below will help you to integrate and apply the essential teachings of this chapter:

- The sleeping giants represent our unaware collective consciousness, which long ago emerged as a giant body before it diversified to become all of us. The awake giant can also be seen as the androgynous one who still remembers the primordial state of consciousness beyond the dreams of duality that are spun by our local minds.

- The majority of human consciousness is still caught in the prisms of the unaware sleeping giants, by falling asleep in lower orders of reality and not realizing the illusions and projections of the egoic states of mind. *How have these dream prisms of the sleeping giants manifested in your life and mind?*

- The upgrade codes to awaken and reset the sleeping giants are your *future potentials* of a new cycle of consciousness, which live dormant within you as imaginal potencies from higher orders of reality. Once these upgrade codes start to activate, it will also reset and upgrade the inner wiring of the collective giants.

- The transition time of the awakening collective mind (the giant) can also bring increased tensions and violence, especially when it (our collective shadow) is triggered and poked to evolve, and we enter the early stages of awakening. *How does this play out in your life right now?*

- The Future Humans Quest is also the quest to reset and awaken humanity from the hypnotic dream states by entering the levels of the inner game where we can stop our self-destruction and any of the degraded operating systems of our egoic mindsets.

- Become aware of the puppet masters in your life and in yourself; the shadow dynamics of manipulation and distortion. Unhook yourself from the algorithms of shadowy programs that are coded for addiction and biased for egoic states of mind. Instead, support the algorithms of life that are tuned for self awareness and form part of the Cosmic operating systems of consciousness.

- The evolution of your consciousness and the actualization of your future human potentials are one of the primary means by which you can directly contribute to the necessary collective shifts in consciousness.

- Your ego represents your process of individuation in human form, which is a natural and healthy process for certain stages of our personal development. Know that it is never required, nor possible, to separate yourself from life or consciousness in order to become a full individual. That belief is the egoic illusion of duality and separation.

- Shadow represents what you don't know about yourself and what you deny, suppress, and manipulate. It is a kind of reversed intelligence. Shadow never shows its true face. It is always cloaked and masked as something you identify with and desire.

- You can use the powers of darkness and light for egoic and shadowy purposes as well as for growing your consciousness and becoming more self aware. The greatest power is love because it cannot be manipulated and it never loses its essential qualities.

- Continue your exploration with the three elementary forces of life—creation, preservation, and destruction—and how these manifest in you and your life and as the fuel for your primary desires. Reclaim those inner forces from any shadow or egoic dynamics that may have distorted or reversed their purpose and manifestation.

- Ego or shadow has no power of its own because it doesn't have inherent existence. Wherever your intelligence or power has become twisted or contrary, return it to your Cosmic consciousness and ask the sacred Darkness in you to shift your mind and reveal the true direction, focus, and purpose of these powers and how to apply these wisely.

- Use the power of destruction to deconstruct the illusions of your egoic states of mind. End the appearance of your false self by seeing its non-existence, thus ceasing the illusions of separation. Return your awareness to the primordial ground of being, where you'll discover the grand luminosity of consciousness.

- Remember, you can't end the shadow battle with your mind. You have to go beyond and surrender to that force deep inside you that carries the liberation and ends the inner divisions. That force of liberation is in essence the alchemical Flame of Love; the fire of the Cosmic Dragon heart that activates and rises up within you when your higher heart starts to awaken.

- Shadow dynamics keep you stuck in the drama triangle of savior, victim, and persecutor. It projects itself as a trusted friend who understands you completely. If it appeals to your victim complex, it will show you how you've been wronged. If it appeals to your savior complex, it will show you how to rescue those who depend on your interventions. And if it needs to appeal to your persecutor complex, it will tell you all that's wrong with the world and how to persecute those who need to be corrected. *How does or did this drama triangle play out in your own life and your relationships with yourself and others?*

- Spend a few moments each day in the sacred darkness of mindlessness. Enter the silence of non-mind and non-duality by going beyond thoughts, images, and projections.

- The feminine and masculine principles can also be understood by exploring the qualities of darkness for the feminine, and light for the masculine. Darkness absorbs, contracts, integrates, and draws the powers back in so they can manifest internally. Light illuminates, expands, infuses, and impregnates, manifesting the powers externally. We all have masculine and feminine qualities. They are the dual dynamics, or alchemical polarities, of our human powers.

- Work with the practice of the Fire Stones of Darkness and Light to learn how to bring forth the alchemical Flame of Love by working with the alchemical polarities of your innate powers. These polarities do not divide or dualize, only the mind does that. Instead, they attract each other into higher orders of reality. That is their purpose.

CHAPTER 9

The Giant of Domination Awakens

The Singing Chalice

"Shhh…Don't move or we'll scare him," Sophia whispers as she and Rose freeze to observe the buck who stands motionless, watching the two women.

"Look at those eyes…those majestic antlers. Maybe he was expecting us?" Rose replies softly.

Sophia jumps as a large bird swoops low behind them and disappears into the trees. The buck darts off.

"What was that? An owl?" Rose asks.

"I think so," Sophia says. "That startled me. I hope it's not a messenger of death."

"Why would you say that? I love owls. It's not like you to be so negative."

"I don't know why I said it. It just slipped out. My auntie from Australia once told me that they can be messengers of bad news."

"But owls can also be good omens and help us see the hidden worlds with their incredible night vision," Rose suggests. "Maybe it was a raven or a crow?"

"Mm. Maybe."

New Trails of Old Tales

The friends continue their walk. They're searching for the ley lines, or dragonlines, as Verdandi prefers to call them. Sophia listens attentively to Rose and her account of the awful visions she had when she came here last time with her grandmother: visions of human sacrifices, blood contracts, and massacres that happened long ago. Rose also tells her about the practice she learned from her grandmother for transmitting the blessings of the Cosmic Mother for healing the land and our collective traumas.

"Oh, and before I forget…" Rose looks at Sophia, "Remember that strange dream I had a year ago about us in a forest? When I came here last week with Grandma, I recognized this place from my dream."

"What dream?" Sophia asks. "I don't remember."

"The one about the young boy who was being chased and was about to be killed or sacrificed, and screamed for help. It was as if I'd slipped back into those violent times of the past. I wanted to help him, but couldn't because I was immobilized by some kind of evil force. You were there too, in the dream, and you told me to put on my ring. But I didn't have a ring back then."

"Okay, yes. I do remember you telling me about that dream. What did your grandmother say?"

"She explained that the boy in the dream could represent the purity and innocence of the child, like a young lamb. She explained how during earlier matriarchal times, some of the tribes in Europe used to sacrifice children, especially boys, to the Goddess. They believed that they were required to exchange a life, like a blood contract, for the granting of fertility, protection, and prosperity from Her."

"That's sickening," Sophia protests. "Exchanging a life like that. I don't mean to sound rude or disrespectful of religion, but don't Christians believe that the sacrifice of the only Son of God, Jesus Christ, was necessary in order to settle the debt of human sins? Isn't that what it means when they say he died for our sins by making the ultimate self-sacrifice? I mean, honestly—and again, I mean no disrespect, I'm just curious—how is that different from those earlier blood sacrifices of innocent children that people made for a god or goddess? All of these religious constructs sound like distorted human economics to me. Humans can be so disgusting."

"They do come up with some violent schemes."

"Our people in Australia have their own history with violence as well, of course, but I've never heard of those kinds of human blood sacrifices being necessary in order to be granted wishes from the ancestral Creator Beings."

"Maybe because your people weren't interested in taking over the world. Their creation story is very different."

"True. It doesn't tell them that they have to conquer and convert everyone to their religion," Sophia says.

"That's right," Rose continues. "As you explained to me, your ancestors saw themselves as caretakers; custodians of nature, not conquerors."

Sophia nods. "What else did your grandmother say about the symbolism of your dream?"

"She told me that the boy who's about to be killed can also represent how the aspect of the renewal of the sacred masculine via the child is being violently suppressed in the patriarchal cultures, including our world today. She said it can also represent an aspect of myself that is at risk of being killed by forces that I'm not yet able to see. Forces that are trying to stop the emergence of the new era by attacking people like myself and her sister Anna; people who serve as portals for this new time."

"So by killing the child—the future generation—it's another way of stopping the renewal and transformation of our world that these children are bringing forth?"

"Yep, something like that," Rose nods.

"Could the dream also represent a younger part of yourself? Maybe your own inner masculine who is trying to emerge, but feels held back?"

"I hadn't thought of that." Rose ponders for a moment. "You mean that I'm holding myself back or silencing a part of myself? I'm not able to voice and help my inner child?"

"Yes. You've gone through a lot in a very short time, Rose. More than you realize. Your rebirth experience in the hospital last year was huge. There's a new part of you that was born through the choice of new life you made. Maybe that part of you needs your help? Maybe it also needs the help of the ring you carry close to your chest, in order to fulfill its purpose in this present time?"

"That resonates with me," Rose says. "Thank you. I suppose there are still many parts of myself I don't know yet. Grandma reminded me again of the importance of a true partnership society between women and men. She explained how the matriarchy and the patriarchy had shadow aspects of violence, and how violence will continue as long as we keep sacrificing parts of the whole."

"I agree with her," Sophia says. "Those patriarchal times were terribly violent to many men. I mean, think about it. They were sold as slaves, tortured to death, or sent out as soldiers on the battlefields."

"And let's not forget the burden of always having to be the economic caretakers of their households."

"Many men were ridiculed for showing emotions," Sophia adds. "They still are."

"Yeah. No wonder so many men burn out," Rose sighs. "It's a lot of pressure."

"Do you still feel frozen like you did in your dream?" Sophia asks lovingly.

"I don't anymore, thanks to all the training Grandma gave me for all those months and weeks. I did feel stuck a few months ago. I had no idea what to do with my life or how I was going to take care of myself financially. That's why I'm so grateful for this opportunity with Li's father. If he's really willing to fund my Cosmic Compass game on the terms I laid out, it will be a huge help for me and the world."

"I'm happy for you, sister." Sophia places her hand on Rose's shoulder. "You deserve it. On a different topic, I wish you hadn't stopped your grandmother from joining us today, especially after everything you just told me."

"Maybe you're right," Rose admits. "But I really wanted to have this time with you alone, as I explained in the car. I can't tell Grandma about that meeting with Diego just yet. She'll blow a gasket if she thinks I met with him behind her back."

"But you didn't. You just ran into him. You didn't know he was going to be there in the park. She'd understand that, wouldn't she?"

"I suppose so, but then she'll tell me not to see him again," Rose protests. "And I want to see him again. I can't stop thinking of him."

Sophia grins. "She knows you so well. I'm sure she's already sensed that something is up."

"She did insist on joining us today, but I gave her a very strong *no*. I explained that I needed this sister time alone with you."

"Oh dear."

"I hope she doesn't feel hurt, like I'm excluding her on purpose."

"But you are."

"Let's change the topic," Rose says. "This is making me feel depressed. Tell me, what do you think of Diego? Should I try to meet him again?"

"He sounds fascinating."

"He is. And handsome," Rose adds.

"But you don't know much about him," Sophia warns. "I think you need to put all of your cards on the table with your grandmother, and explain to her how you really feel. She's a wise woman with deep insight who knows him very well. Don't you think it would only hurt her more if you continue to see him behind her back?"

"Maybe you're right. Wait…slow down. I think I found a dragonline! Let's follow it. Grandma and I had to give up finding it last time because it started to rain so heavily."

The friends eagerly walk along the ley line in search of the energy vortex that the forest is so well known for.

The Portal to the Multi-Worlds Opens

"Whoa! Can you feel that?" Sophia asks. "Like a powerful magnetic field. Do you think it's the energy vortex?"

"I can feel it too," Rose says excitedly. "It does feel like an energy vortex. Maybe this power spot is also linked to the myth of the goddess Tamfana. They built a small temple dedicated to her not far from here. Let's go there later. Some of the locals say that she's a fertility goddess who's also a guardian of the mysteries of the night. They say she unveils the darkness. It's said that people came here to this forest and the lands around it to receive her oracles."

"I never knew that the Dutch also believed in goddesses," Sophia replies.

"Yes, some did, but it's not well known. There's also a goddess temple that they found in Zeeland dedicated to the sea goddess Nehalennia. There's a kind of revival going on these days, especially among women. Many of them are reclaiming their indigenous European roots and customs."

"That's wonderful. Is that where you went sailing with your friends?"

"Yep, that's the place," Rose smiles. "That reminds me, Grandma often speaks of the 'Huldufólk' or 'hidden people,' as they call them in Iceland."

"You mean the elves, fairies, dwarfs, and trolls?"

"Yes. This place is known for them as well. She says they live around energy vortexes because those act as portals to the multi-worlds. She even said that I'm like a hybrid and future ancestor of a new offspring of humans who've been remarried to the realms of nature and the larger Cosmos to which we belong. I'll bet you are too, Sophia."

"You may be right."

They scan the air with their hands to get a sense of where the center of the vortex might be. Rose feels a surge of energy in her fingers as she moves in one direction. She doesn't realize that she's just stepped into the center of the vortex. The ring around her chest vibrates and amplifies the powerful energy of the vortex. Rose unconsciously accesses and activates the Avatar portal, which is like the master key to many other doorways and dimensions. This Cosmic portal doesn't exist on the physical plane, but can manifest through a powerful Earth vortex like this one, combined with the right activation.

"I thought of a fun game we can play," Rose suggests. "I used to play it with my cousin Otto when we were little. We called it 'portal jump.' All you need to do is imagine there's an ancient portal here to a magical land that holds the doors to every country and place in the world. Once we're in this magical land, we can choose the door we want to jump through to instantaneously visit any country or place of our choice. It was so much fun. We visited all kinds of imaginary countries and realms this way. Where do you want to go? Ancient Rome? Paris? New York?"

Sophia puts her hands down. "Rose, your powers have grown a lot since then. You may not realize it, but your imaginary powers have become imaginal, like those of wizards and druids. I don't think it's wise to play that particular game in a place as powerful as this. You have no idea what you might activate or open here."

"Come on. It'll be fine. Don't worry! I'm wearing my ring of unity, so we're protected."

Rose stands in the center of the energy vortex and continues to activate the hidden portal with her mind. The energy within the ring of unity is building up to the point that it's getting physically hot. A crow caws loudly from a nearby tree branch, as a strong, whirling wind starts to blow around them.

"It's happening! Sophia, it's happening for real! This is so cool!" Rose exclaims. "Come and join me! This must be the center of the vortex we've been looking for."

Rose stands in perfect alignment and becomes the portal of the multi-worlds. Sophia feels the powerful forces activating, and intuits that it's not a good thing. "Rose, be careful. This isn't child's play. This vortex is really powerful."

"I know! It's amazing!" Rose replies. "My whole body is vibrating like crazy. Ohh, wait. I'm…very…di…zzy…"

Sophia rushes forward to catch her friend before she hits the ground. "Rose! Can you hear me?" She speaks in her calm doctor's voice and feels for a pulse. "Listen to my voice, Rose. You fainted. I want you to breathe. Breathe…breathe. Good. Come back now. Feel your feet. Feel the earth. Very good. Now breathe into your belly."

Rose is dazed and disoriented. "Where am I? What happened? What day is it?"

"Saturday. You passed out for a few seconds. I caught you as you fell."

Rose rubs her temples. "I feel weird."

"Your pulse was very fast. It's calming down now. Do you have a headache? Nausea?"

"No headache. Slight nausea."

"Keep breathing into your belly. Here, take a sip of water." Sophia grabs the water bottle from her bag and hands it to her friend.

Rose drinks the water and looks around. "I feel strange. I recognize where we are but…does everything look different to you?"

"What do you mean?" Sophia asks.

"It's like…we're in a different dimension. Did you see that light? It flashed in front of me right before I fainted. And that sound! I've never heard anything like it."

"It may be that the frontal lobe of your brain got electrified," Sophia says clinically. "Are you still feeling dizzy?"

"I feel better now. The dizziness is gone."

"Can you breathe freely? I think we should head back to the car. I don't want anything else to happen to you."

"I'll be okay, I just need a few minutes. Everything inside me started to resonate and vibrate, like an amplifier that doesn't stop. I honestly felt like I was about to take off in a space-suit I never knew I had; as if my body was about to dematerialize. Seriously, I've never experienced anything like it. I'm not making it up."

"I believe you."

"I started to see flashing lights. Next thing I know, everything goes black, except for this loud humming sound that I can still hear inside my head." Rose drinks more water.

"It sounds like you opened a major portal, or rather, you became one. Did your grandmother ever teach you about this? Did she tell you what to do once it opens?"

"Oh my gosh. Sophia, I totally forgot. Grandma did warn me that the ring can open and close Cosmic portals. She said to be very careful, and to connect with my Avatar interface first before opening any portals because that will protect my body from the powerful surge of energy that can occur. She said that the Avatar interface can protect my nervous system from overload by distributing the magnetic surges to the fields around me, so that I don't become a conduit for it. I completely forgot to activate it. And I didn't check with the guardians of this forest to ask for their permission first. What's going on with me? Thank you for coming to my rescue."

"I know you can be rather impulsive sometimes, but you're not reckless," Sophia says with concern. "This isn't like you. What's going on?"

"My head has been so full of Diego, I got distracted and forgot all of the important things my grandma taught me. I feel so stupid."

"Dear sister. Don't let him or any other person spin you out like that. Maybe this was a good lesson not to take this Cosmic stuff and these energy portals so lightly. You know, you really are like a butterfly that just flutters from one event to another, barely touching the ground lightly before taking off again. But remember, you almost died last year. You didn't listen to me when I warned you not to go to that party. Instead, you told me I was exaggerating. And a few minutes ago, I warned you that the bird might be a bad omen."

"You're right. I'm sorry for not taking you more seriously. I promise to listen more." Tears well up in Rose's eyes.

"Okay, let's not worry about that now." Sophia helps her friend to move a bit further away from the center of the vortex.

"What's your sense of this place?" Rose asks. She places her hand over the ring of unity. It's becoming cooler to the touch.

"It feels like we're inside a natural temple of the goddess, and not one that needs any walls or sculptures. It's as if we're inside her body," Sophia says.

"This really does feel like a power spot. It reminds me of some of the sacred sites back home in Australia. Like you, I have a feeling that terrible things may have happened here long ago."

Rose adds, "Maybe a high priestess guarded this power spot, and had to close the portal to keep the inner temple safe from harm. I hope she wasn't killed."

"Who knows? But for whatever reason, it does seem like we were meant to come here today and find this spot."

"I feel that too. But, you're right, I should have brought Grandma along with us, rather than letting Diego distract me."

"Actually, in this case, I don't think that his presence was all bad. It sounds to me like he carries similar codes and you somehow activate each other. It's as if your powers somehow fit together, like that ritual you told me about with the Great Deer, the one between the high priestess and her high priest."

"Could that be why I'm so attracted to him?"

"Maybe so. He probably feels the same. It sounds like your magnetic pull to each other is much stronger than just a personal crush. There are other forces at work here that neither of you fully understand yet. This is bigger than you and Diego, and I'm sure your grandmother knows that too. She just wants to protect you, knowing that where there's power, there's also danger and shadow."

"That makes sense. I feel like there's an ancient connection between the two of us. I'd better pay attention to what his presence awakens in me. Maybe it's not as personal as I make it all out to be."

"Exactly. This is all new for you, my sister. Now, how are you feeling? Is the dizziness gone? Headache? Nausea?"

"Thank you for your care, Sophia. I actually feel much better. Would you mind if we stay here a bit longer? It's not often we get the chance to spend time in a real Earth vortex."

"I'd like that too," Sophia replies. "Besides, vortexes are known for their powerful healing energies, so it'll probably do you good to stay here a little longer."

The Singing Chalice

Rose stretches her body and starts to move around to balance her energy. "I wonder if there's a well nearby?" she wonders. She lifts up her ring and shows it to Sophia. "The night that Grandma gave me this ring, I received a vivid dream about the seven Architect Tools. One of these Tools introduced itself as the Singing Chalice. I'm not sure why, but I have a strong feeling that the Chalice has something to do with this place."

"It's interesting you should say that," Sophia smiles. "On the drive over here, I was checking my phone to get more information about this place and I found a painting of this goddess, Tamfana, or Tanfana, or whatever her correct name is. She was shown with a golden cup that looked like a chalice."

"Really? Maybe that's also linked to the Grail Cup of the Avalon myths. Remember that fun conversation we had last year about the Holy Grail of communication and the information of immortality?"

"I remember that all too well," Sophia grins. "And the complicated physics theories you came up with, and how you said this can help us understand the Cosmic architecture of life. Let's not go back to that conversation right now. Once you get going, it's hard to stop you."

Rose laughs. "I can't argue with you there."

"So tell me more about the dream you had of the Singing Chalice. That sounds really interesting."

"At least we know that my brain is still functioning after that energy blast," Rose chuckles. "In my dream, the Chalice was filled with water from the eternal spring that flows forever from the body of the Cosmic Mother to nourish the worlds and souls of the living. I took the Chalice between my hands and it started singing softly with the most beautiful, harmonic tones. The tones activated within me the codes of the eternal laws, and suddenly I saw how the eternal worlds and the temporal worlds are woven together. It connected me to my eternal body, and I experienced again how my consciousness continues on, lifetime after lifetime, and never dies."

"That's beautiful, Rose," her friend sighs. "Perhaps this land needs the healing waters from the Divine Mother once again. Maybe that's the reason She called us here."

"Grandma also told me that the Ring of Unity can activate our Avatar interface so it's easier to commune with nature. Let me show you how you can do that without the physical ring."

"That's wonderful. Could you help me connect with this Singing Chalice as well?"

"Yes. Good idea. Let me combine them both as a quick practice. Here, we can sit on these large rocks while we do this."

Rose takes the ring of unity in her right hand and places her left hand over her heart to first activate her own Avatar interface. She feels her connection with her Cosmic self open up. Sophia closes her eyes and makes herself receptive.

Practice with the Singing Chalice

"Take a deep breath in and let it out slowly. Let go and relax, and now relax some more. Now connect with your imaginal powers; your capacity to embrace and experience realities that live beyond the domains of your ordinary mind. Let your mind know that it's okay and safe to do this. Make yourself receptive to the subtle dimensions of life; the subtle dimensions of consciousness that live beyond the veil of your ordinary perceptions.

"Now imagine a Cosmic Ring of Unity, one that was forged long ago in the fire of the Cosmic Dragon's heart. This Ring is also an archetypal symbol, an Architect Tool, for reminding us of the eternal Bond of Unity between all beings, life-forms, and worlds. This bond can never be broken and never expires. The bond is part of the Cosmic architecture of life, and thus also part of your innate Cosmic architecture. The bond is well known by the wisdom of your heart, which keeps it alive when the mind forgets.

"Thank your heart for keeping this bond alive in you, and reminding you of your unity with life and all that you are. Call upon this Cosmic Ring that lives within your heart and ask it to manifest the powers of unity consciousness within and around you. Take a few moments to enjoy and receive from the eternal Bond of Unity its deep wisdom about life and the nature of your inner being.

"Now imagine that, as part of the architecture of your inner being, this architecture also serves as a Cosmic interface—coded to communicate, exchange, and interact with Cosmic realms and realities that live beyond this world and time. Hold the intention to become aware of and connect with this interface capacity of your innate Cosmic architecture. You may experience this as a gentle warmth within or around you, a tingling sensation, or simply a sense of trust.

"As you become more aware of this Cosmic interface within you, know that you may also utilize this to extend your capacities and develop a greater self awareness. You can also call upon this interface capacity to help you bring forth your Cosmic powers of consciousness to this place and time. Take a moment to simply enjoy your interface capacities with the energetic realms of consciousness while being safely in your human body.

"Now imagine how your Cosmic interface also facilitates your direct connection with Mother Cosmos, enabling you both to receive and communicate with each other beyond this time and place. Let Mother Cosmos know that you'd like to learn about the wisdom of the Singing Chalice. Ask Her to place this beautiful Cosmic Chalice in your hands. As She does so, you notice that it is crafted of the finest materials, engraved with sacred symbols, and empowered by the eternal Spring of Life; the living waters of your soul. Take a moment to enjoy being trusted with this precious Chalice in your hands.

"Now the Chalice starts to sing and vibrate softly. It produces the most beautiful, harmonic sounds that restore and attune your whole self to the sacred essence of your eternal self. Ask the Singing Chalice to harmonize and attune your whole body, mind, soul, and energy to the essences of life that form part of your eternal consciousness. Give permission for the sounds and sacred harmonics to clear within and around you all that doesn't serve you, including anything that is dissonant with your essence and inner being. Allow for this clearing, harmonization, and attunement of your energy fields and consciousness.

"Now become aware of the living water from the eternal Spring of Life that is held within the Singing Chalice, and bring the Chalice to your lips. Drink this eternal water from the Spring of Life, and sprinkle it over your head and onto your heart. Bless yourself with this water and let it enter into you, bringing healing, renewal, rejuvenation, and a deep awakening of your eternal body of consciousness. Ask this eternal water to activate within you the codes of the eternal laws as you become aware once more of your eternal self.

"Rest for a few moments in this timeless experience of your own eternal nature in unity with life. Now thank the Singing Chalice and the Ring of

Unity for their support, and let your image of these forms dissolve, knowing that the wisdom they represent is always within you as part of your inner being. And know that whenever you need the help of these wisdoms, you can call them forth.

"Take another deep breath in, and out. Bring your awareness fully here and now. When you are ready, you may gently open your eyes and move your body."

The Song of the Avatars

"That's amazing, Rose." Sophia stretches her arms and legs. "I love the Ring of Unity and the Singing Chalice, and my Avatar interface. They're so powerful. It's all part of our own inner being, yet we so rarely connect with these potentials. My crown chakra became all electric, and my heart and womb became so warm, while my third eye started pulsating strongly."

"I feel like the Cosmic interface is protective as well," Rose adds. "As if it shields us from any interference or harmful energies."

"Yes. I feel much more focused and balanced, and so revitalized. It's like a mist has lifted from inside my mind, and everything has been washed clean inside of me."

"That's how it works!" Rose laughs. "Don't you love it? I'm so happy you had that experience."

"I can also feel the presence of Mother Earth more strongly now," Sophia says. "She really is like a *singing* chalice. Have you heard those recordings of her sounds from outer space?"

"Yes, I have. They're beautiful."

Sophia closes her eyes. The activations of this practice are still vibrating and resounding within her. Images enter her mind of the painting that people made of the goddess Tamfana with her golden cup. With her eyes still closed, Sophia speaks to the goddess: "For all this time you've taken care of this land, its people, and all the species who live here—as a mother, lover, guide, and revealer of the mysteries of the night. Tamfana, they called you. Oh, dear goddess, my heart is saddened that so many of us have forgotten who you are. Like we forget the trees, the rivers, the bees, and all who form the parts of who you are. We take your love and care for granted. Worse than that, we've replaced you with fake goddesses of computer games and avatar icons devoid of life, dressed like movie stars for our entertainment."

She takes a deep breath and continues, "And you, being a goddess of humans who now rule the world you created? What a twisted fate. Long ago, when we searched for fortune, prosperity, and fertility, we begged you for your blessings, believing it required trading life for love. But no matter what you gave us, it was never enough. We always wanted more…like a hunger that never stops. And when you didn't manifest our wishes, or so we believed, we turned our backs on you and others like you. We silenced your voice inside our hearts. Not realizing how we abandoned you and banned you from our human world, the tragedy continued. We started to deny you ever existed. We reduced you to a figment of our imaginations, and called it a stage of human infancy. We reduced you to an artifact of myths; a sculpture placed on the buildings where we continue to gather to rule the world you created long ago. We called ourselves a civilization. Not so for the deer, who know you *as the forest* in which they shelter when they rest among the trees. The frog knows you as the pond in which she swims and has her babies. The dragonfly knows you as the wind beneath his wings, and the bees know you as the flower that provides their nectar. Nature does not forget who you and we all are."

Stirred by Sophia's invocation, Rose stands up and joins her. "Dear goddess!" she exclaims. "How can we experience your love and beauty if we continue to plaster your body with cement roads and claim ownership of the wonders of nature you created?" She lifts her hands toward the towering trees. "How can we understand your care and wisdom if we continue to reduce the labor of your love to commodities for sale, and things we own? How can we hear your voice when we suffocate our world with the pollution of electromagnetic grids of radio frequencies and noises that never turn off?" Rose shakes her head. "How can we commune with you when our minds are never available? Constantly tuned to the demands of mobile phones and gadgets of artificial connectedness that leave no space for life to enter? Yet, you continue to be here for us! You've never left us. Like these ancient trees who've been witness to it all." Rose takes Sophia by the hand. "Oh, dear goddess, know that we love, see, feel, and hear you. We promise to always keep a space for you within the temple of our hearts. This is your home within us where we meet, love, and laugh. We will always remember who you are."

Rose and Sophia are moved to tears. A deep gratitude wells up in their hearts. The goddess knows that she's been seen and heard at last.

"Thank you for what you just did, Sophia. It feels like *you* became the Singing Chalice. When you professed those profound truths, it activated in me the long view of life that we so easily forget and discard. I felt the song of *the* Goddess that flows into our hearts as the eternal Spring of Life, forever nourishing and awakening that which has dried up and hardened inside."

Rose starts to sing a song she recently learned from her mother: "We are rising! We're uniting! We're igniting! Stoking the fire, transforming our pain, with the Flame of Love. We sing our world together, sing our world together, sing our world together, now."

Sophia joins in the song. The two women happily sing, dance, and clap their hands. They untie their hair and shake it all loose. They *sing the worlds together*, and not just the human world. They sing the codes of the archetypal world; the world behind all worlds, as they dance in the portal of the multi-worlds that has now opened. Two dragonflies join the dance, hovering over the portal with their iridescent wings. The Cosmic Dragon smiles. A sudden wind whips up. It howls through the trees like the call of the wolves who roamed this land long ago. Nature joins in the dance with the daughters of the Goddess. The forest comes alive and awakens from a long, deep sleep. Other forces that roamed here long ago awaken as well.

Within the young women, the Cosmic Avatars rise, unite, ignite, and stoke the fire of love. This is the dance that moves the stars. This is *the song* that weaves the blankets of time and reality through which the ancient ones become the future ancestors. What had to happen has begun spontaneously, yet it was no accident. The Avatar portal has opened through the vortex of human hearts. The Cosmic Dragon is happy.

In the foliage behind the two friends, the buck has returned. Next to him stands a beautiful doe. The majestic pair look curiously at the joyful young women. The Goddess smiles. The Cosmic Avatars are returning and remembering who they are. The upgrade codes of the sleeping giants are activating. Others, too, are stumbling on portals they didn't realize exist, activating the trigger points that contain within them the upgrade codes for our collective dreaming. This process will continue to increase in intensity until the giants have awoken fully; when we become conscious of the nightmares we've been trapped in and perpetuate. Many of the awakening giants do not yet realize we are here to help and who we are destined to become, and so the fight shifts to a whole other level.

Confronting the Archetype of Violence

"That was sooo good! I feel so alive," Rose says, exalted, as she seats herself on a nearby tree trunk.

"Me too, sister." Sophia grins and grabs her backpack, then sits beside her friend. "And now, I'm starving. Let's eat." She removes the sandwiches she has prepared for them and hands one to her friend.

"This is great. What did you put in it?" Rose digs in.

"Sun-dried tomatoes, avocado, cheese, mustard, mayonnaise, lettuce, and beetroot. Glad you like it."

"You can make these for me anytime. How's work?" Rose asks. "How are your studies?"

"Intense. I love what I'm doing, but it sure feels good to get out of the hospital and spend some time with you in the forest today, Rose. Thanks for inviting me."

"You're welcome. I—"

"HELP! HELP!"

"What was that?" Rose asks.

"I don't know. I heard it too," Sophia says, scanning the forest around them.

"HELP!"

"There it is again."

"Yes, I heard it. Is this happening now or are we still in some kind of time loop?" Rose stands up to see what's going on.

"HELP ME! Please! Somebody, help me!" the voice persists. A dog barks frantically.

"I think this is real. What do we do?" Sophia's stomach tightens.

Rose quickly activates her internal Avatar interface and calls forth the Ring of Unity that is within her heart. This allows her inner dragon to rise within her. She calls upon the forest guardians, Mother Earth, and the Cosmic Avatars. This time she remembers exactly what to do. Her mind is clear. All that she's been prepared for now comes into play.

"It's the boy from my dream," she whispers to her friend. "We have to help him."

The women still cannot make out exactly where this is happening. They stealthily make their way through the bushes, being very careful not to make a sound. An angry male voice shouts, "There's nobody here, you little brat." Rose and Sophia move toward the sound.

"Get away from me, Erik!" the boy shouts.

"Scream all you want, kid. It's too late for you. We're gonna make you pay for what you did today," another man insists.

"HELP!"

"We told you not to sneak up on us, Sam," the first man says gruffly. "We've warned you for years. You should have kept your snotty nose out of our business."

"I won't tell anyone, I promise. I promise, Pim! Just take my phone and leave me alone."

"Erik, do something about that dog."

"No! Leave my dog alone!" the boy says.

A small dog barks and growls at the two attackers, desperately trying to guard Sam. Sophia and Rose peek through the bushes to a clearing where the crime is happening. The slender, pale boy on the ground looks like he's about fourteen years old. The two men towering over him appear to be in their twenties. Rose quickly shoots pictures of the scene on her mobile phone, while Sophia tries to call the police. She can't get a signal. She tries Rose's phone, but has no better luck. Rose prepares herself to enter the fight. The forest guardians have heard her call. A huge raven lands on a branch nearby, while above them, a hawk circles.

Sam's dog continues to bark loudly at the men. Erik picks up a stone and hurls it directly at the dog's side. It hits the intended target, and the dog yelps in pain.

"You got him!" Pim shouts. "Good shot!"

"Don't bully my dog!" Sam screams.

"You're right. We shouldn't waste our time bullying your stupid dog when we could be bullying you," Erik laughs and cuffs the boy roughly across the top of his head.

"Yeah. Ever since you were a tiny, little snot-nosed kindergartner," Pim chimes in.

"Well, what are neighbors for?" Erik says. "All those times in the alley near your house after school. But you never snitched, did you, mousie? You never told Mommy and Daddy." The man leans in very close to Sam's tear-stained face. "And it's a good thing you didn't."

"I won't tell anyone now either," Sam says.

"We can't take that chance," Pim tells him. "Growing cannabis on your property is illegal in the Netherlands, and you know it."

"He knows it," Erik adds. "Don't you, mousie? I'll bet that's why you were spying on us. You were planning to turn us in!"

"I wasn't! I was just walking my dog!"

"Sorry. We don't believe you. And of course, there's the evidence." Erik holds up Sam's phone. "Just walking your dog, huh? Then why'd you take so many photos of our little cannabis operation?" Erik kicks the boy hard.

"Just take my phone!" Sam pleads.

"Naw, we need to make sure that no one ever finds out. Ever. And sadly… that means you've gotta go."

"HELP!"

The dog barks and barks as the two men move in to strike the boy again. Rose picks up a strong stick from the forest floor and takes a few deep breaths. The ring of unity burns on her chest. She enters into an altered state of hawk-like vision. She sees everything as if from above and in great detail. Sophia still desperately tries to pick up a phone signal so she can contact the police. She moves further away from the vortex, to see if that helps. Rose sprints toward the angry men with the stick in her hand. Action is on; all systems are go.

Awakening the Giant of Domination

Sam screams as he absorbs the blows.

"Shut up, you little punk! No one can hear you! Just shut up!" Erik shakes the boy and beats him into the ground with his fists.

"Please, Erik! Stop!" The boy sobs loudly and uncontrollably, but the man strikes him again. The dog tries to bite the attacker in the leg, but he's kicked away. Erik swears and turns back to Sam with all of his anger unleashed.

"Not so brave now, are you, brat? You are dead meat for the wolves." He pummels Sam, causing blood to trickle from the boy's mouth and head.

"Erik, that's enough, man," Pim yells at his brother. "We have his phone; let's get outta here."

Out of the bushes, Rose rushes straight toward the men, her stick held high. "LET HIM GO!" she roars. "NOW!"

The men jump back, startled to see this personification of a fierce Viking warrior woman running toward them at top speed. With braided curls flapping in the wind, Rose grips the stick, ready to strike. Her training in jiu-jitsu kicks in. Her inner dragon is fully awake.

Sophia continues to step further away from the vortex while moving in the direction of Sam as quietly as she can. So far so good. Both men are fully focused on Rose wielding that stick. Sophia finally gets a signal on her phone and manages to reach the police. "Please hurry," she whispers into the phone with a trembling voice, "or the boy will die." The police dispatcher warns her not to provoke the two men. She orders her to hide and wait for the police to arrive. She assures her that a rescue team, including an ambulance, will leave immediately. Sophia thanks her, but knowing that the situation is taking place deep inside the forest, she worries that the rescue team may not be able to get there in time. She disconnects the call and says a silent prayer. She moves a leafy branch aside to get a better view of what's going on.

Rose can't be stopped now. Dark clouds close in over the forest, causing the temperature to drop. The forecasted thunderstorm has arrived earlier than expected. Erik leaves the injured boy behind and turns to face Rose.

"You don't scare me," the man hisses, reaching down to grab a hefty stick of his own. "Come on, Pim. We can take her."

But Pim is sneaking away into the forest, trying to escape.

"Fine!" Erik yells at his brother. "I've been in fights all my life. I don't need you." His eyes flash as he sizes up his opponent.

Lightning strikes the ground nearby. The deer stand alert, watching Rose, and so does the raven. Erik clenches his stick and gathers his energy for the attack. Pim finds a hiding place behind a tree and shits his pants. The boy's body has collapsed on the forest floor. He doesn't move. Sophia sees her opportunity and rushes to him. He is bleeding heavily in several places, and has passed out. Sam's dog limps toward her, yelping in pain. The poor animal is barely able to walk.

The forest holds its breath; the air crackles with tension. Thunder clouds roll over the nearby fields and shake the trees of the forest. Rose lifts her stick.

The dragon inside her rises up and gives her the raw force she needs. Erik strikes first. "CLACK!" Their sticks clash loudly. Lightning strikes again, this time even closer to where the fight is taking place.

"THIS STOPS NOW!" Rose yells with the full force of her Viking voice. Images of horrific violence, bloodshed, and human sacrifices flood into her mind; not just from the history of this place, but from all over the world. Mother Earth shows her how humanity has been under the cloak of this violence for eons. Each time it arises, they've given another justification for the insanity. Rose realizes with painstaking clarity that these nightmares will never cease unless we all declare that *THIS STOPS NOW*.

Rose is not just fighting Erik; she's confronting violence itself, and with it, the pattern of domination and oppression that has plagued our world for far too long. She screams at the giant to wake up. Erik has now become a direct conduit for the giant of domination and the shadow forces of a violent darkness that have plagued this Earth for centuries. He is no longer conscious of himself.

All the Avatar powers now converge within Rose. They become laser-sharp as they bundle together through the Cosmic Ring of Unity that's within her higher heart. The confrontation has shifted to another level. Rose has become the Avatar for the Cosmic Dragon, and Erik has become the instrument of the giant of domination and violence. Their human bodies are frozen in the forest clearing. They stand motionless in confrontation. The fight has moved to the dimensions where it all began long ago.

The Cosmic Dragon's heart activates, glowing strongly as the alchemical flame comes forth and intensifies inside its powerful body. The forces of Light and Darkness have united within the Cosmic Dragon. The giant of domination prepares to squash the Dragon with its mighty fists. The Dragon focuses on the heart of the giant, which has turned to stone, hardened by its forgetful state. The Dragon opens its mouth and expels the alchemical fire that awakens. He releases it through an enormous roar, which is echoed by the thunder clouds above the forest. The fire hits the giant in the chest, where Erik and the minds of billions of humans and other beings are trapped inside. The upgrade codes turn on within the melting heart of the giant. The dormant future potentials of the promised new era begin to activate within the giant's mind, causing him to feel threatened and angry. *How dare this Dragon confront and challenge me?*

The giant tries to strike back and grab the Dragon by its neck to snap its head. But his arms no longer answer his mind. A different program is starting to activate. Chaos breaks out inside him as the minds of all who were trapped within now turn on each other. *Who's in control? Who holds the reins? Who commands the power?*

The giant wants to run away, but he can't. He is terrified of losing his mind and control over his world. Other giants are awakening too; fighting for a control they never had. Illusions are shattering as confusion increases. Some people realize where they've been trapped all this time. They now recognize the Cosmic Dragon and realize that he was never the threat.

Rose regains control of her body, and so does Erik. Their sticks clash again. "CRACK!" His stick snaps right through the middle. He falls to the ground. Rose raises her stick high above her head. Erik moves his arms over his face to protect himself from the impact. To his surprise, she doesn't hit him. Instead, she smashes her stick down on the ground in front of him, commanding, with full force, the end of the spells of violence.

Lightning strikes very close. Thunder clouds collide with booming power as the spells of thousands and thousands of years of violence shatter. The forest shakes.

Rose and Erik return to their normal selves. Erik feels frightened for the first time. There's something different inside of him that he doesn't understand. It terrifies him. He scrambles to his feet and runs away. Rose kneels and puts her forehead to the ground. She weeps softly for all the pain and terror that was trapped for all that time, now released and free to heal.

The police arrive and chase after Erik. Pim still cowers in the bushes. "FREEZE!" an officer shouts to Erik. "Get down on your knees!" she adds. The man stops running and surrenders. He kneels and puts his hands behind his head. The police officer moves in and handcuffs him. Another officer runs to Rose, who alerts him that Pim is still out there in the bushes.

Sophia holds the boy in her arms. She's managed to stop the bleeding and tend to his wounds while waiting for the medics to arrive. He regains consciousness, but is white as a sheet. The boy's dog sits next to Sophia. He licks Sam's hands while looking back and forth from him to her with pleading eyes. Sophia strokes him gently and says, "You were brave, little friend. You did everything you could to selflessly protect that boy. Good job." The dog weakly attempts to wag his tail, then stops and whimpers. Sophia suspects that his hip is broken. The medics will need to carry them both out of the forest.

The Giant of Domination Awakens

The medics arrive with Sam's parents. They run toward Sophia and their son. Meanwhile, the police officers continue to search for Pim. They know he won't be able to get far. They warn Rose not to get involved in this, explaining that a cowardly person can be very dangerous.

The forest breathes in relief that the fight is over for now. The heavens open and rain pours down, cleansing the trees and surrounding fields.

Rose feels the rain on her face. She's deeply saddened, shaken, and angry with all the violence she has seen and experienced during her visits to this forest. She knows it represents a far larger pattern worldwide, which began when we started to forget who we are, mistakenly believing that pain and suffering were necessary for us to grow and evolve. We made blood contracts with gods and goddesses who we created in our image. We sacrificed lives to exchange for our growing demands, not realizing the true economics of nature. Rose wonders if the puppet masters are not behind it all; those who always remain invisible, and yet orchestrate the violence and divisions from behind the scenes.

The puppet masters of the past have become the gods of money of today; financial predators of new economic empires. The forms may have changed, but the rules of the game have not. Rose knows that until we learn to play by the rules of the game of life and regain our consciousness, this violence will not end. She's determined to help people realize how the *real* game is a game without losers, debts, and blood sacrifices.

"Sam! Oh, Sam. How could they do this to you?" The boy's mother strokes her son's head, while the medics talk to Sophia, take his pulse, and wrap his wounds.

The mother turns to Sophia. "Thank you for saving his life. You and your friend are true guardian angels. I don't know what would have happened if you hadn't shown up. We were scared when he didn't return home at his usual time, so we called the police. I've suspected for a long time that those two men were trouble, but I was too involved in my own problems." She looks at her son and cries, "I'm so sorry, Sam. I'm sorry I failed to protect you. Please forgive me."

Sophia listens quietly. The medics are now ready to carry him out of the forest and into the ambulance, together with his dog. Sophia says her goodbyes and walks toward Rose.

One of the officers has finally located Pim. He is handcuffed and led to the police car. The chase is over. The two young women finish giving the police their report of the incident. Rose exchanges contact information with Sam's father, so they can stay in touch.

"My wife and I are deeply grateful for everything you've done for our son," he tells Rose. "The police confirmed to me that if you hadn't stepped in to confront Erik, Sam might not be alive right now. Erik is known by local police as a troublemaker and a hothead. He's been convicted of smaller crimes before. It remains to be seen what those two brothers have learned, if anything, from this experience."

"Life gives us many chances, but not everybody accepts them," Rose says. "It's time for me and Sophia to return home." The young women head toward the car and Rose sends her grandmother a quick text message to let her know that all is well and that they're on their way.

Onward We Go

Rose feels exhausted and relieved as she opens the car door. "Now I understand why Grandma was so worried," she tells Sophia. "But I'm glad she didn't join us. Imagine what could have happened if one of those crazy guys had hit her too."

"Come here, my sister. You were so brave." Sophia gives her friend a warm, healing hug. "I'll drive. You just rest now."

"That sounds good. Thank you. You were very brave, as well." Rose smiles. "First by coming to my rescue when I fainted in the vortex, and then by taking care of Sam's injuries. I'm relieved we managed to turn the situation around and save him, but I have a nagging feeling that the fight behind this fight is far from over. What happened today is so much larger than we realize, or can take on by ourselves. At least I know now that I can rely on myself and my inner dragon when it really counts. I experienced something very powerful out there. I'm so glad that Grandma came to Amsterdam to prepare me for this in person. I couldn't have done what I did today without all those months and weeks of training and preparation with the Architect Tools."

"Don't forget your many years of martial arts training as well," Sophia reminds her. "We can't stop violence without the kind of preparations you've gone through. I came to realize some things today, too."

"Like what?"

The Giant of Domination Awakens

"I want to join a jiu-jitsu class so I can learn how to defend myself. I agree with you that there's a lot more going on than we know. I feel like we're placed like pieces on a chessboard in a game we don't understand and can't oversee. What would have happened if we hadn't come here today?"

"I don't know," Rose says quietly. "But I do know that what happened here wasn't just about a fight between Sam and those awful men. During my confrontation with Erik, I felt my inner dragon rise up fully and then unite with the Cosmic Dragon. And it felt like Erik became absorbed into the giant of domination. For the first time, I experienced the depth of the raw, untamed dragon power that is also part of my innate nature. It was quite something. Thankfully, Grandma taught me how to channel this power through my higher heart and call upon the Cosmic Dragon. Otherwise, I may actually have killed the man or injured him badly. Once this force moved through and from my higher heart, I felt how it was directed through a higher plan where it served to awaken, reset, and upgrade—and not just destroy."

"You sure looked like a mighty dragon," Sophia laughs. "And a very scary Viking warrior. I've never seen you like that! I'm glad I wasn't Erik. I doubt he's ever encountered a woman like you."

Rose chuckles. "I think you're right."

"Well, please take some time to reflect before you jump into the next adventure. Promise me!"

"Okay, I promise. I feel so tired now."

"I understand. You really need to rest. Oh, by the way, did you notice the deer who followed right behind you? And the raven up in the tree?"

"Really? Wow, that's amazing," Rose says with a big smile. "I heard the raven and knew he was nearby, but I didn't know about the deer. I'm glad you mentioned it, so we can still thank the animals before we leave the area. They've really been our guardians today. And, of course, the forest itself has been, as well."

"And the goddess of this land!"

Sophia pulls the car off to the side of the road for a moment. The friends roll down their windows to send their gratitude to all who helped them today. A little frog by the side of the road looks up to them before it hops into a big puddle of rainwater to enjoy and wash itself. The women laugh and adore the simple ways in which nature responds.

"Goodbye, deer! Goodbye, raven! Bye, beautiful forest," Rose says. "Thank you for all you did for us today. Bye, Tamfana. Thank you for showing us the goddess ways. We will always remember you."

A rush of wind moves over the women. In the distance, the raven caws goodbye. Deeper in the forest, the deer stop their grazing for a brief moment and look up. The friends roll up the windows of the car.

"This has been a life-changing adventure," Sophia says.

"Life-changing and exhausting," Rose laughs.

"I'm relieved it ended the way it did."

"Me, too. Now, onward we go, my sister. Take us home."

Integration - The Singing Chalice

Through this chapter, Rose experiences the workings of the Singing Chalice. She unknowingly opens and becomes the Avatar portal, which activates as the inner vortex of the higher heart. She has to confront the archetype of domination and violence in the form of Erik. Through their fight she is challenged and tested to see if she'll remember to channel her powers through the wisdom of her higher heart, or else she will be overtaken by the powers herself and become the next archetype of domination.

> *The Singing Chalice is always filled with water from the eternal Spring of Life that flows forever from the body of the Cosmic Mother, to nourish the worlds and souls of the living. You can call upon this Chalice to harmonize your consciousness with the eternal fields of life, and to activate within you the codes of the eternal laws, and become aware once more of your eternal self.*

The summary and questions below will help you to integrate and apply the essential teachings of this chapter:

- Your innate Cosmic architecture also acts as a Cosmic interface that facilitates the exchange between energies and realities of our human world and those of Cosmic realms of consciousness.

- The Cosmic Ring of Unity represents the eternal Bond of Unity between all beings, life-forms, and worlds. You can call upon this

Architect Tool to manifest the powers of unity consciousness within and around you and for activating your innate Cosmic interface.

- The eternal Bond of Unity can never be broken and it never expires. Your life is part of this eternal bond, and known by the wisdom of your heart that keeps it alive whenever the mind forgets. This bond also serves to protect you from the illusions of separation.

- Take some time each day to honor and acknowledge the larger unseen realities of life, like the spirits of nature and invisible guardians who are aware of us, even if we do not realize they exist. Make time to be in nature when you can, and remember that everything around you is alive in the fields of consciousness we share and are.

- The Avatar portal represents the multidimensional nature of your Cosmic self, which is also the vortex of your higher heart. When you enter into and become the larger versions of yourself, you also become like a portal for bringing in these higher orders of reality to this time and place.

- Become aware of the upgrade codes of the giants inside you; these are your own future human potentials. When these codes start to activate within us, we become more conscious of the nightmares in which we've been trapped, and those we still perpetuate. Be careful during this time to not resort to domination and violence as a way to protect yourself from what you may feel threatened by. Don't regress.

- There are many archetypal layers in this chapter. *Who and what do Sam, Erik, Pim, Sophia, and Rose represent in your life, in yourself, and in our world?*

- Remember to harmonize and direct the primordial powers of your inner dragon via your higher heart, your Cosmic heart, through love, and directed in service of life.

- When you confront the evil, shadow, and violence of the archetypes of domination and disunity, there is a potential to become what you fight and challenge if you believe it only exists outside of you. Use the Architect Tools to guide the development and applications of your powers with wisdom and love.

- Become conscious of the spells of violence and the forgetfulness of the sleeping giants. *Are there any spells of forgetfulness or violence that you need to break in your life and relationships?*

- Examine the ways in which you transact, economize, exchange, trade, and share resources, goods, and services, including your time, energy, and life force. Become aware of unconscious agreements, assumptions, and beliefs underneath these transactions, knowing you hold the power of your agreement and have the right and responsibility to stop what causes harm to yourself, life, or others.

- Be honest with yourself about what you are ready for and able to take on without endangering yourself and others. You are not required to be like Rose or Sam. There are many ways to help stop the violence in our world, like the role Sophia took when she called upon the help of those who are trained and prepared for this task, while also tending to the wounds of those who'd been impacted.

CHAPTER 10

Fishing in the Ocean of Consciousness

The Cosmic Navel Cord

The news of Rose and Sophia's heroic actions spreads fast through their community of friends and family. Li is really impressed, although not quite understanding all the details. He wonders if there are some elements of the story that the women are keeping from him. Rose's parents have mixed feelings about what happened. They're relieved that their daughter came out of this ordeal unharmed, and proud of the way she rescued Sam, but they're not happy with the risks she took. Rose senses this and is avoiding "the parent talk."

Rose has finally told her grandmother about her surprise meeting with Diego. Verdandi suspected as much, but feels a little hurt that her granddaughter thought she couldn't tell her about it. But, as Dagaz reminded her on the phone, Verdandi had similar adventures herself at that age, and she did tell Rose she wouldn't approve of their meeting.

This is Verdandi's last week with Rose in the Netherlands. Next week she plans to visit her twin sister Anna in Norway, after which she'll finally return home to her beloved Dagaz in Iceland. She feels that she has completed what she came here to do. It's time for other people and experiences to enter Rose's life. The Cosmic Architect Tools have awakened within Rose, and she trusts that these Tools will continue to guide her granddaughter directly. The outer tools from the Avatar pouch have served their purpose.

Sophia and Li are joining Rose and her grandmother this coming Sunday to learn how to make their own Avatar pouch with miniature architect tools. Verdandi will transmit the original blessings of the Cosmic Architect Tools to their physical tools via a special initiation ceremony with the mother pouch. Verdandi and Rose are also exploring the possibility of offering online courses to teach people how to use and apply these sacred Tools as part of a Future Humans Quest.

Olaf heard the news and is hoping to speak to Rose. He's home from school today, recovering from a cold. He can't stop thinking of the Cosmic Compass and the game version of the Future Humans Quest. His mind is bubbling with so many ideas.

A Cosmic Bypass Tool from Olaf

"Hey Rose, did you really fight that big man to save that boy?" Olaf asks excitedly over the phone.

"Yes, I did. How did you know?"

"Dad told me. That's super cool," he says with sparkling eyes. "Weren't you afraid to get attacked?"

"I was a little afraid, yes, but protecting Sam was more important than my fear," Rose smiles.

"I've been telling all my friends what you did," he grins. "They told me I have the coolest aunt. Did you get hurt?"

"Just some scratches; nothing serious. I have very strong guardians. Remember that Avatar interface of the game? Well, I used it in real life, together with the Ring of Unity, and it works pretty well."

"Can you teach me how to do that?" Olaf asks.

"Sure, but only if you agree to learn martial arts. My friend Sophia is going to sign up as well. During my jiu-jitsu classes I learned how to fight with wooden sticks, wooden knives, cords, chairs, and even the sharp edge of a credit card. I've never had to use those skills in real life, but I'm so glad now that I trained for all those years. During the fight my reflexes kicked in and I knew instinctively what to do. It's all about how you concentrate and direct your power."

"I want to learn how to do that," Olaf tells her. "Dad taught me a few moves, but what you just described sounds way more interesting. You used cords as well?"

"Yes, so you can defend yourself in case someone tries to strangle you."

"That reminds me of the other reason I called you. I wanted to show you the bracelet I made with cords." Olaf puts his wrist to the phone camera and shows Rose the colorful bracelet he braided with woolen cords. "Nice, huh? Would you like one too? It's a friendship bracelet."

"Of course. I'd love that. Thank you. That's very kind of you to offer."

"Okay, I'll get Dad to send it to you when I'm finished. What colors would you like?"

"You choose."

"Alright. When I was making this bracelet, I came up with another idea for the game." Olaf smiles.

"Tell me!"

"Remember how I told you we need to wake the giant from his sleep in order to upgrade him? And how he becomes more dangerous when he starts to wake up because he's not his better self yet? And that's why we need the help of the Cosmic Avatars to work with their plan so he doesn't destroy the planet and poison our minds?"

"Yes, I remember all that," Rose grins. "It's my favorite part of the game."

"Right. Well, I've thought of another tool that we can give the humans in trouble. Especially those whose minds are poisoned by the dreams of the giant, and the humans in the game who are very confused or really angry, like that guy who attacked Sam."

"Go on."

"We can give them a Cosmic cord that's like a navel reset button to activate their inner Source codes. It restores them to their original self and their direct Cosmic connection so they can receive Cosmic guidance without interference. Once they've returned to their Cosmic self, and are no longer in the lower version of the giant's ideas of humans, they can choose their own next upgrade version."

Rose is astonished with her nephew's clarity. "That's very clever. You mean when people use this cord, they remember who they truly are? It bypasses all of the false information, illusions, and poisonous projections of the giant?"

"Yeah. Nice, huh? It's like a super cool bypass to protect the minds of humans from the destructive sleeping giant, before he himself gets upgraded."

"Amazing, Olaf. It sounds like the Cosmic cord actually restores us to our Avatar selves and the realization of who we truly are beyond this time and place, and beyond our physical shapes."

"Yes!" he beams. "That's why the Avatars came up with this tool. Because it's really *themselves* trapped in the human realm. That's who they're trying to help."

"It's brilliant! I love it."

"I'm so glad you like it. You should try it out through that imaginal practice you always do. Especially before you go and design all those game codes and stuff," Olaf says.

"Perfect. Will do. And I'm doing it right now, while listening to you. I can feel the shift happening already."

Olaf looks very pleased that she likes his idea. He really loves this game. "Oh, and one more thing before I go," he adds.

"What's that?" she asks.

"I had a strange dream of the giant last night and thought I should tell you. You know how I always speak of the giant as a *he* and *him*?"

"Yes…"

"Well, in my dream, the giant woke up. He was really grumpy because once he was awake, he realized that he is a *she*! She's a *female* giant! Thought you'd like to know."

Rose is delighted with this news. "That's so funny," she laughs. "Thank you for telling me. I've got to share this news with Grandma." Olaf doesn't quite understand what's so funny about this revelation, but joins in her laughter nevertheless.

"Bye now," Olaf says. "Say hi to Grandma from me. Tell her I'll call her tomorrow."

"Bye, Olaf. Will do. Give your mom and dad a kiss from me. Love you, my clever nephew. Thanks so much for calling."

Verdandi enters the room with a tray containing two cups of coffee and a plate of freshly baked stroopwafels.

"Yum!" Rose takes one of the flat, waffle-like cookies and eagerly bites into it. "These are so good. I love the melted cane syrup in the middle."

"I got them from the bakery. I want to enjoy these Dutch delicacies while I can." She sets a cup of coffee in front of Rose and sits to enjoy one herself.

"I have to tell you what Olaf just said about the giant."

"I overheard the last part of your conversation," Verdandi says with a chuckle. "Bless that boy. He has the brightest mind."

"Yes, he's very clever. So you heard that the giant is female. Isn't that funny?"

"It's hilarious, and it certainly gives a whole other spin to our 'Sleeping Beauty.'"

A Liquifying Vision with Diego

Rose has arranged to meet Diego at the beach. She's excited to see him again, even though it's windy and gray outside. She takes her last sip of coffee, wolfs down the last bite of stroopwafel, and pulls her favorite sweater over her head. She searches for her running shoes, but has no luck. "Grandmaaaa! Have you seen my shoes?"

"Oh, love, it sounds like you'll need that Cosmic cord that Olaf just spoke of. Your shoes are next to the washing machine, where you left them yesterday. There's no need for you to rush about like this; Diego can wait for a few minutes."

"I don't want to make a bad impression by showing up late," Rose explains. She retrieves her shoes and puts them on as quickly as she can. Verdandi shakes her head. Rose grins and gives her grandmother a quick kiss on the cheek. "Thanks for being supportive about this. Love you."

"Drive safely!" Verdandi calls after Rose, who runs toward the door. "Please ask him to join us for lunch on Saturday."

"Thanks, will do. Bye."

"Wait, one minute, love, before I forget. Can you give me the number of Sam's mother? I'd like to offer them my help."

"Right now?"

"Please?"

"Alright. Actually, it would be great if you called. Sophia said that Sam's physical injuries are healing well, but he's still in shock and won't eat or speak much." Rose looks up the number on her contact list and forwards it to her grandmother's phone.

"We can send him some healing support later this evening. You can ask Sophia to join us as well, if she's free. Tell her I'm making lasagna."

"I love your lasagna! I'll give her a call on the way. Okay, I really need to get going now." Rose blows her grandmother a kiss and closes the door behind her.

When she arrives at the beach, she can spot Diego from a distance. Her stomach jumps as she walks toward him. *Act cool, Rose. He's just a man. Oh, that long, wavy hair...so sexy. Stop it, Rose. Seriously. And that gorgeous dimple on his chin. I wonder how he kisses? I'll bet he's a really good kisser. Stop it, Rose. Pull yourself together.*

Diego notices something is different about her, as if she has more confidence. She even looks a little taller. He loves her bright blue sparkly eyes, and how her messy curls don't want to be tamed. He smiles as he watches the way she walks with a spring in her step, as if she's bouncing off the earth like a dancing butterfly. But most of all he likes her witty mind, and her sexy smile. He's well aware of the chemistry between them, and curious to explore it further.

"Nice to see you again, Rose. Your grandmother agreed that you could meet me?" He takes her hand in his hand, and kisses it like a gentleman.

This time Rose lets him keep her hand a little longer than during their last encounter in the park. "Yes, we talked. It's okay. She sends her greetings and asks if you'd like to join us for lunch this Saturday, before she returns to Iceland."

"Please tell Verdandi that I gratefully accept her kind offer." Diego grins. "Now tell me more about you."

"I'm well, thanks for asking. I had a rather wild time with my friend Sophia last Saturday. How are you?"

"Fine, just fine. What about this wild time with your friend Sophia?"

Rose takes a deep breath and proceeds to tell him in vivid detail about their adventure in the forest. Diego listens attentively while they walk along the water line. The waves play with their feet. He watches how the water shifts the ripples of the sand. They walk and talk as if they've known each other for many years. He's surprised at how relaxed he feels around her. He feels no need to prove anything or defend himself. He enjoys her company and secretly wishes he didn't have to leave the Netherlands so soon.

"So, what do you think?" she asks finally.

"I don't think," Diego smiles.

She feels slightly annoyed by his answer. "You don't have anything to say? What I just went through is major. I could've died, and my friend Sophia and Sam could have as well. Thankfully that crazy man and his friend didn't have a gun. Just imagine what could have happened if they had."

Diego ponders for a moment, then says, "You knew deep down that you would be safe and were guided to that place for a reason. The forest protected you, and so did the dragon. I respect your experience so much that I don't want to spoil it with my comments or opinions. I'm sure you've had enough of that from the people around you. I'm really glad you came out of the situation unharmed, and that you are such a smart woman who is fully capable of defending herself and others. Is this the first time you've felt your dragon power rise up like that?"

"The first time in a physical fight, yes. It happened once before in a mental fight when I wanted to defend my ideas and felt humiliated and attacked by some business people."

"Watch out for the third time the dragon rises up within you," Diego advises. "Make sure he doesn't overtake you. He's growing stronger, and has now tasted your powers. Don't underestimate him. The third time will determine whether you can ride the dragon or not. You'll only get one shot at it. If he won't allow himself to be directed by you, it will become an endless battle for control. You fought the archetype of domination, but its shadow aspect also lives within the dragon. Don't get tricked."

"I had no idea. Grandma didn't tell me about any of this."

"No, and she wouldn't because she probably trusted me to give you the message. That may also be the reason she agreed for us to meet."

"I see. So what happened to you? Did your inner dragon rise three times?"

"Yes, it did, and I am still battling with it. Maybe he's more willing to be ridden by a woman," Diego laughs. "I almost died when he rose up the third time, which is when I sought the help of your grandmother. She saved my life, but she had to sever the connection. I wasn't ready for it. I lost control, all the while believing I was fully in control. I became impossible, and hurt a lot of people in the process. That may also be why your grandmother is so cautious about our connection. She doesn't want your inner dragon to revive mine, and vice versa."

"What if our dragons are actually connected and yours couldn't complete its rite of passage because mine had not yet awoken? What if they balance each other?"

"That's a lovely thought, Rose, and very romantic too, but I'd be careful to make that connection. Keep your freedom. Don't give your power away. In any case, I don't deserve it."

"You sound very harsh on yourself. Can't you forgive yourself for what happened?" Rose asks.

"Not yet. I'm not a free man. Not yet."

"Perhaps you had all of those problems with your inner dragon because your feminine side is wounded," Rose suggests. She feels sad and rebellious to hear him speak like that. She's not yet hearing the humility and wisdom behind his words. He is more conscious of his own shadow than she realizes, which is also what attracts her. They continue to walk in silence, playing with their feet in the water and watching the seagulls out at sea. The tide is ebbing, leaving behind an intricate design of wavy puddles and sandy grooves. Clouds are reflected in the tide pools.

Rose feels like she's in a dream, and she loves every minute of it. She notices how their bodies have synchronized naturally, with their feet moving at the same pace and their rhythmic breathing harmonized. She feels a deep and ancient connection with Diego, and so much sadness in him as well. She wants to help, but doesn't know how, and she isn't sure she's even meant to help, or whether he'd allow it.

He senses her mood. "It's okay. Please don't worry about me. I'm fine, truly. It's kind of you to want to help me, but this is my battle with myself. You can't help me. Keep your focus on your process; the world is opening up to you. Embrace it with open arms. I owe my life to your grandmother, and want to make sure I always honor that, starting by not involving you in my battles."

"Thank you, Diego. You're probably right. You're actually a much nicer person than I thought you would be," she grins.

He smiles at her sweetly, then shifts his head to scan the horizon. He looks like a sailor searching for the wind that can take his boat out to sea. He can sense that this wind is coming soon and wants to cherish every moment he can have with Rose, not knowing when or if they'll meet again after he sets sail.

Rose enters a light trance; a liquid state of consciousness through which the waves of her individual consciousness have merged with the ocean of universal consciousness. She recalls her earlier conversation with Olaf about the Cosmic Navel Cord, and feels it tug behind her physical navel. Her vision shifts. She sees into the world from her timeless soul, amplified by the strong resonance between herself and this man.

Diego notices that something profound is happening for her. "Are you okay?"

"Yes, I can't speak right now," she answers softly. "I feel like my whole world is turning upside down or inside out. It's the strangest experience. I'm seeing the Cosmos under my feet, rather than sensing it all around me."

He continues to walk by her side and wonders whether she has spontaneously slipped into the Cosmic mind, the way he sometimes does when his consciousness expands. She's no longer seeing the physical beach on which they're walking. Instead, she sees the beach as a geometric surface; a luminous ocean of light beneath her feet.

Her vision continues. As she looks into this ocean of light, she notices informational patterns and fractal codes that seem to shape and attract the liquid light to the surface. She now walks the Cosmic interface as a surface boundary between two different orders of reality: the Cosmic world of nonlocal informational fields, and the local physical world of space and time. Above the surface, she's still aware of the familiar, local world of people walking their dogs, and seagulls diving for fish in the sea. She even notices the wind that's blowing through the dunes and softly touches her curls. Yet below the surface, and beneath her feet, is a world of fractal information, liquid light, geometric patterns, and the inner substance of our physical sensory world.

Her vision shows her the inverted reality of our physical world, and the more subtle implicate orders of consciousness. She recalls a quote from physicist David Bohm: "This is the implicate or enfolded order in which space and time are no longer the dominant factors determining the relationships of dependence or independence of different elements. Rather, an entirely different sort of basic connection of elements is possible, from which our ordinary notions of space and time, along with those of separately existent material particles, are abstracted as forms derived from the deeper order."[3]

As she looks again into this ocean of liquid light beneath her feet, she notices how the flux and flow of informational patterns appear to be connected to activities in her mind. She experiments with a thought and realizes that she can somehow influence the field dynamics of this ocean of light with her local mind. She wonders whether the liquid light is her Cosmic mind, and the informational patterns and geometrical shapes, the activity of her local mind. Her thoughts shape and in-form the liquid light. She now experiences the Cosmic interface as a surface boundary that regulates and converges Cosmic potencies and unified flow states into the organized patterns of our physical consciousness and world.

In a flash she realizes, *Cosmic mind is the implicate order for the Universe of space-time and energy-matter. And my local mind is the implicate order for my personal universe of my physical world in space and time. My local mind is the fishing net of the Cosmic mind; the means for consciousness to capture the Cosmic potentials, like imaginal fish, and bring those into manifestation as a physical world of consciousness that is continuously in a state of formation.*

She is about to say something to Diego, but another insight washes over her. *When I see into the world through the netted structures and patterns of my local mind and project the maze of the net onto reality, in that moment I create my ego from my own inner matrix by mistaking the net for reality. When I see into the world from the implicate orders of Cosmic mind, I see and experience wholeness everywhere. My local mind is an instrument; an operating system of consciousness for the purpose of manifestation. It is not the source of my reality.*

Rose has now received the wisdom of the Cosmic Navel Cord, which helps us to realize how our local world unfolds and emerges from the more subtle implicate Cosmic orders of consciousness. As her vision completes, she is fully in Cosmic mind and experiences the birth of the Universe as if it's happening in the present moment. She realizes how the data-structures of the Cosmic hologram emerge from more subtle orders of consciousness. She sees how one of these data-structures became what we now know as space-time, precisely tuned to make the physical Universe possible, and for life to be born and evolve.

The World That Opens Between the Lips

Rose continues to walk slowly while her ordinary perception returns. "Diego, I wish you could see what I've just experienced. I have no idea how to even begin to describe it."

Diego smiles, looking deeply into her eyes and soul. Her whole body starts tingling. She opens her mouth to say something, but he stops her by placing his finger over her lips and pulling her into his arms. Their hearts touch. He kisses her softly on her lips. She melts, yet is also caught by surprise, and wonders for a split second whether she should pull back. The attraction between them is too strong for her to resist. She surrenders to the blissful sensations that now flood through her entire being. Her inner world turns into liquid. She kisses him back, passionately. She wants this moment to last forever, as their energies weave and merge together like two serpents coiling upward around the wizard's staff. A new world of love, attraction, and passion emerges from their lips. *But can it last?*

Her mind spins faster and faster. She becomes the kiss, and so does he. Their consciousness becomes one as the alchemy of their souls unite what long ago was set apart. Their energies merge forgotten worlds and powers from the ancient dragon times. For a brief moment, a bridge has formed, and another giant starts to awaken. They are both transported to the new world made possible by their union; a world Rose has only experienced once in her dream. *That's the kiss! That's THE kiss. It's him!* she realizes, as her heart sings with joy. A whole new chapter of her life is about to begin. But unfortunately, it's not yet time for the bridge to last. A glimpse of hope of what can become possible has now been seeded in their hearts and the hearts of the dragons. But with significant promises like these, also come great challenges and responsibilities. Are they ready for this kind of love? A love that is larger than themselves, from reunification that is beyond their personal lives. A bond that does not break. A bond that is not eroded by the sharp edges of time.

The moment arrives when it is time for their lips to slowly part. Though their souls are still within the world of their sweet reunion, the outer world slowly calls them back. Rose tries to speak, but can't find the words. She sighs deeply. Her heart overflows with joy and sadness. Waves of refreshing seawater swirl and foam around their feet. Seagulls call loudly, as if reminding them not to forget what just happened between them. Life continues.

A playful dog runs past them. She shakes her wet body then resumes chasing her ball. "Hi!" says the little girl who runs after her dog. Diego and Rose laugh at the dog and the cheerful girl. It sweetens the bitter realization that their lives are calling them back into different worlds that are not yet fused together to unite as one. Rose tries to push away her sadness.

"Diego, can't you stay in Amsterdam longer?" she asks, finally.

"I don't think so," he replies. "My work here is ending soon and I won't have the means to stay."

"Will you come back?" she sighs.

"I will do my best. But remember what I told you: I'm not a free man right now. Your grandmother is right; I'm not the kind of man you need in your life right now."

"Then why did you kiss me?" she asks, biting back tears.

"How could I not, when I know what you mean to me? And you know it too. The bond between us is not of this world."

"But why can't we make a bond like that in this world, or at least explore what could be possible between us?"

"Because the bond is too strong, Rose. It will overtake everything. Neither of us can control it. Let's just enjoy what we have now." Diego takes her hand and pulls her toward him to continue their walk.

"Don't you think it's unfair that life brought us together like this only to then make it impossible to continue further?" she protests.

"I don't think there's anything fair or unfair about it. This moment is more than many people ever get to experience," he replies. "Let's just cherish it for what it is without trying to construct more around it."

Rose wonders what situation she'll find herself in when her inner dragon rises again. "How did you know when the dragon rose for a third time?" she wants to know.

"I didn't, which was part of the problem." Diego smiles.

"Just like the urge to kiss me came over you?"

He laughs. "Now don't spoil the magical moment we just shared! Let's keep it in that precious place beyond words and thoughts."

She nods reluctantly and forces a smile. "I won't spoil it, but I do feel there's something you can help me with. If I merge my energy with another power, or even you, does that mean I'll lose my autonomy?"

"What does autonomy mean for you?" Diego asks.

"That I am still in control of being able to regulate and adapt myself, and can access and direct my creative powers. If I can't do that anymore, then I'm either addicted or overtaken by something else," Rose continues in a dry, factual tone. "Every living system has these innate capacities. It's called autopoiesis in biology and systems sciences."

"And what exactly do you mean by autopoiesis?"

"What I just said. Living systems can be characterized as complex adaptive systems with innate powers of self-creation and regeneration, as well as self-regulation and adaptation. These powers are intrinsic qualities of the Cosmic architecture of life, and the foundation for our autonomy, which is universally given. This is the miracle of life that makes life possible and thrivable."

"Right. So is it the scientist in you who desires to know what you asked me, or Rose the mystic?" he teases.

"Both."

"I expect you know about the role of the ego in its useful expression?"

"Yes, individuation and personhood," Rose answers, "which also helps us to develop boundaries and protect our personal selves."

"Ego serves a developmental purpose as long as we are conscious of it and not consumed by its directives." Diego pauses for a moment. "For many people this desire for individuation and autonomy arises during puberty when we seek to distance ourselves from our parents and want to give birth to our own lives. During the first ten years of our childhood, the ego plays a constructive and formative role in our development by creating boundaries for our individuation. As we grow older, we need to shift the program and adjust it to new levels. If we don't adjust our ego, it can become destructive and rebellious. For a long time, I believed that in order to keep my freedom in society, as well as my freedom in the spiritual worlds, I needed to keep a contrary element alive in myself. I called it my 'Luciferian' element, which I used to protect myself from being overtaken by the collective."

"What do you mean by 'Luciferian?'" Rose asks.

"Lucifer means 'the light bringer' or 'morning star.' In the Gnostic scriptures he's the fallen angel who goes contrary to God's orders, and although badly named a devil in certain Christian traditions, he's not evil. He forces us to awaken our own divine spark, the god within from the darkness of our own unconscious. Hence, *the morning star*. But in order to liberate us, he often acts contrary to what we may want or expect."

"That's similar to Loki in the Norse mythology, although Loki is mostly portrayed as a trickster."

"Yes, in many religions and philosophies there's an archetype for this role," Diego replies.

"Is that so we won't fall asleep in the lower dimensions of the minds of the unaware giants?"

"Precisely," Diego says with a smile. "For a long time, I believed that this contrary part of myself was my lifeline to protect me from the hypnosis of the collective, so as not to be consumed by the oversoul or integrated into the collective matrix. I wanted desperately to keep my autonomy, and thus felt I needed to guard my inner divinity through this Luciferian aspect of myself. This aspect became my most cherished, rebel self. Over time, however, this aspect grew rather destructive, and eventually, also self-destructive."

"How did you feel when you acted from this Luciferian energy?"

"As if I was onto the plot and could hack the codes of the puppet masters. Like I'd found a secret domain that had not yet been cultivated and shaped by human minds. I felt an exhilarating sense of freedom and triumph, which later grew into a sense of superiority and power. As if everyone around me was asleep, except for me."

"Oh, help! I feel like that sometimes," Rose admits honestly. "But is that bad?"

"I believe that inner freedom is a good thing, and that it's actually the true essence of the Cosmic Dragon. Our untamed, primordial consciousness! Yet if we use this freedom for power over others or for ego games, we slip down into shadow dynamics that will eventually undermine the very freedom we thought we had gained. The thing is, you can't claim or own this freedom. You either are it, or you're not."

"Interesting. And in order to be free, do we need to be contrary to life or contrary to conditioning?"

"I think you know the answer to that," Diego grins.

Rose chuckles. "Yes, I do. But, please continue. How did you become destructive?"

"My inner rebel coupled with my ego started to dominate, always seeking more power for more battles to fight and win; more challenges to overcome. I got addicted to danger; to living on the razor's edge. Sometimes I escaped into alcohol and drugs. All the while telling myself I was doing it to be a free man who couldn't be controlled or commanded by anyone. My Luciferian aspect was no longer the liberator, it now became the dominator and the persecutor by telling others about their shortcomings. I believed I was in control of the powers, and feeling invincible made me feel like a god. I started to gain the reputation of being an invincible magus, like the risen dragon, following in the footsteps of my teacher at that time. She was a powerful female sorceress of the dark arts. What I didn't know, or refused to see, was how she used my magical skills to maintain and advance her own influence in our community.

She kept feeding and encouraging this contrary part of myself by elevating it. I was caught up in a huge power trip."

"Grandma said something in passing about that. And then? Didn't you have some kind of inkling that something was off? That you were losing yourself?"

Diego looks up at the sky. "Yes, looking back, I did. But I ignored the signs. My sister was the first to warn me that I was on a power trip, but I wouldn't listen, and then I blocked her communications. When the dragon rose for a third time, I demanded its obedience, as I was its master. Or so I believed..." He shakes his head. "We got into a terrible fight during which I developed a very high fever that no doctor could treat. I was burning to death and getting weaker and weaker, but still I believed that I was on top. I had just enough strength left to go and see your grandmother. She placed me in one of those cabins on their land and started to perform a healing ceremony on me. I can't remember much; I was passed out for many days. She kept my body alive. After one week, while still feeling terribly weak, my cabin became filled with light. As I looked into the light, I saw the most beautiful angelic being: a woman with lush flowing hair draped all around her body like waterfalls. She gave me a cup filled with the healing water of life to drink. When this water entered me, I heard the water sing softly. It was singing me back to life! The most beautiful melodies and sounds I'd ever heard! The woman then showed me how the universal consciousness I had feared would never take away my selfhood, my persona, or my autonomy."

Rose smiles. "Ah, Grandma must have given you the water from her chalice to restore your connection with the Divine Mother. Then what happened?"

"A deep peace entered my heart, and the fever broke. Verdandi told me later how she had to push my inner dragon back into the hidden world because I was not yet ready for its powers. She told me to first resolve my fight with my shadow and my desire for power. For so long I believed I needed to protect myself from the light; from entering that ocean of consciousness that you experienced earlier. I wasn't interested in unity, oneness, or any kind of merging. I wanted to develop my own powers, and most of all, I wanted to keep my mind free from all the brainwashing and manipulation I saw around me. But I didn't see how I was becoming what I was fighting against."

"Wow, that's quite something." Rose squeezes Diego's hand as they continue their walk. "Thank you for sharing this. You've given me a lot to think about." Rose knows that she too has been enjoying this feeling of power and secretly craves more.

Diego holds her hand firmly and places it over his heart. "Don't become like me, Rose. Be careful of who or what you merge or unify with. Make sure it's a real unity, which never asks you to give yourself up. Get to know the *morning star* in you, and the light that rises from the darkness. There are so many false unity movements, false prophets, and globalizing technologies and sciences that promise a transcended humanity; a humanity that is 'so-called' awakened from the sleeping giants. Meanwhile, they become the next giant to induce yet another hypnotic sleep over the masses they seek to control. Awakening is a serious business. It's not for the faint-hearted."

"I agree."

"It's like those dreams within dreams. Just when you think you've woken up, you realize you've only woken up in one dream and are still asleep in another."

"I know those dreams," Rose says. "I used to find them very disturbing. I'd wonder when I'd finally wake up in my own bed, rather than my dream bed. I understand better now why unity consciousness was not something you desired."

"Unity with myself yes, but not with the hypnotized collective or the puppet masters. I didn't want to be used and turned into a tool. Not even a tool of the magi. And I didn't want to lose my individuality or my own divine spark. Yet I almost did."

"It's rather sneaky and ironic that while you attempted to fight this archetype of domination, it still managed to win its influence over you through the one place you didn't look for it."

"Myself. You're right," Diego sighs. "I fell for the classic shadow projection trap. I fought *it* as if I was free and separate from it. But I didn't face my own desire for domination and control, which is what it sought to awaken, so it could sprout inside me like a virus."

"Yes, and by doing so, you also undermined or suppressed the capacities life gave you for your autonomy, and the very foundation of your individuality."

Diego nods. He feels he has said more than enough now. They continue their walk in silence, enjoying each other's presence while they still can. They are both keenly aware that this may be their last time together. For now, anyway. Their futures are uncertain.

"Are you hungry?" Rose asks Diego. "There's a beach café. We could grab something to eat."

"Good idea," he says. "My treat."

Fishing with Our Local Mind in the Ocean of Consciousness

They find a quiet spot that's out of the wind with an expansive view of the sea. Rose sips her iced tea with mint while they wait for their lunch. Diego enjoys a freshly squeezed orange juice.

"Would you like to hear some ideas I have from my earlier vision?" she asks while stirring the leaves of fresh mint in her cup.

"Sure."

She now feels ready to tell him the many details of her vision and the revelations it sparked. He listens attentively.

"So, this vision got me thinking," she says as their lunch arrives, "that our local minds are like the operating systems of our local consciousness; whereas Cosmic mind is like the operating system of nonlocal Cosmic consciousness. What we call 'space-time' in our local reality is really like a holographic data-structure in the Cosmic mind of nonlocal reality, and is part of that operating system. Like an invisible Cosmic interface composed of information; a digital alphabet of sorts, out of which emerges the appearance of our physical universe. Even leading physicists are now postulating that space-time is not the fundamental reality; that it seems to emerge from something deeper that we do not yet understand. Physicist Nima Arkani-Hamed said in one of his lectures that 'space-time is doomed.'[4] This saying has become rather popular since, and hints to a future science that may reveal how both space-time and quantum mechanics emerge from a unified understanding based on new principles about the fundamentals of physics. He mentioned that one of the greatest challenges of our time is to understand what these informational building blocks are, out of which space-time emerges, if indeed space-time is not the fundamental reality."[5]

Diego moves a slice of cucumber around on his plate. "Are you suggesting that Cosmic mind is the operating system of this Cosmic, nonlocal information? And would that imply that mind creates matter?"

"It could," Rose says, straightening her back, "but I would rather suggest that matter is an informational structure or building block of subtle orders of mind, and thus not separate from mind or created by mind. If the structure of space-time does not originate from space-time, but rather from something that precedes it that we do not yet understand, this mysterious 'something' may well be consciousness itself."

"Okay, let's assume it's true," Diego says. "It's then also possible that this holographic data-structure called space-time is only one of many other data-structures. There may be whole other worlds and universes that we have no idea of, as yet. At least not via the known laws of physics, or as long as we only use our local human minds."

"Right." Rose takes another sip of her iced tea. "So if 'mind' is indeed the operating system of consciousness, and not its source, then we'd better learn how to set our personal human mind to the settings of *Cosmic mind*. Our ego doesn't know how to do that, even though it presumes it does. Ego is a local program of the human mind for functioning in *local human* contexts, even though it believes to be so all-powerful that it can direct Cosmic mind and bend the Universe to its will. Ego's instructions for nonlocal consciousness simply don't work."

Diego laughs. "You're very witty. I can see why your grandmother always speaks of you as a 'smart cookie.'"

Rose smiles. "I have other thoughts on my mind that I'd like to explore with you."

"Please do."

"Maybe we're so terrible at manifesting these expanded Cosmic realities because we don't know how to use our local mind as a fishing net of the Cosmic mind."

"You're right," Diego laughs. "Not as long as our local mind is on ego-setting, instead of on Cosmic-setting."

"Yep. Our personal consciousness is always part of the larger universal consciousness. Consider this for a moment: an ocean of consciousness brimming with creative possibilities." Rose stretches her arms out toward the sea. "Let's say that all these Cosmic potentials in this ocean of consciousness are like imaginal fish that we only get flashing glimpses of. *Imagine that.* Just tiny, little glimpses of all that's possible! Within us, we may experience these glimpses as desires and ambitions, especially when these imaginal fish are attracted to the surface by the activities of our local minds." She lowers her arms and looks intently at Diego. "And yet most of us are like a *cat* staring at the elusive and slippery fish in the pond, fearing the water and using the wrong tools to catch them. And when we fall into the pond, we panic and try to get the hell out of that slippery realm, afraid we'll drown as we lose our sense of solid concreteness."

"So we're soggy, frustrated cats. That's quite an image, Rose." Diego laughs loudly. "How would you suggest we learn to fish in this ocean of consciousness?"

"Well, for starters, we should stop fighting our inner dragon," she says. "We need to learn how the local mind operates within the Cosmic mind, and how to put the Cosmic mind in the driver's seat to reprogram our local human minds, which are currently set to ego-control. I believe that the local mind, when properly trained, can actually serve as a meaningful fishing net of the Cosmic mind. Its structures for local embodiment may be the perfect means for Cosmic manifestation, if there weren't all of those interference patterns from the constant chatter of the local radio host called Ego and Shadow that get in the way."

"This is great. Please continue. Oh, and before you do, would you like some dessert?"

"I'd love to try their homemade raspberry frozen yogurt."

"That sounds delicious. I'll have one too." Diego orders their desserts from the waiter, and gestures for Rose to continue sharing her thoughts.

"Okay, here's another image for you. Imagine consciousness as the dancer, the dance, and the danced. Our local minds are like the axes or local portals through which the superposition of the Cosmic dance pops into the local concreteness of our ordinary daily lives. When it pops, an imaginal fish—a Cosmic potential—gets caught in the net of our local minds. As soon as this fish moves through our Cosmic interface—there where Cosmic mind becomes our local mind—we experience this as an idea or inspiration, and our mind gets fired up. Yet most people don't realize that we're now consuming the imaginal fish that we caught in our nets. Energized with Cosmic nourishment, we get busy and start taking action and creating. The problem is that most people don't know how to fish or what to fish for. They act on impulses as soon as they become mentally aroused and stimulated."

"And that's when they need to hire the help of Rose," Diego laughs.

"Let me finish! There's more."

"Okay, but please leave a little something for me to discover. Don't tell me the whole plot," Diego grins.

"I'm sure you'd like to hear this because it seems that's where your Luciferian aspect put you to sleep last time!"

"Go ahead. I'm all ears."

"Imagine again that moment when we catch this imaginal fish filled with Cosmic goodies and meta potentials that previously only existed in a superposition state of possibility. It finally has the chance to become concrete, were it not for a tragic Cosmic comedy. Unfortunately, the ego soon catches the news of what's happened and starts acting like a customs control agent by marching in and taking control of the fish. It declares itself to be in charge and starts to decide what needs to be done with that fish. But the fish gasps for air. It can't breathe in the egoic world, and many die before being able to deliver their promise. Ego gets upset. Surely it can't be blamed for all this misfortune. Especially not when it's in power! So it starts to *fake* the promised success and act as if the desired potentials have manifested. Some even go as far as suggesting that they have mastered the law of attraction, not realizing the mighty dragon they're attracting instead."

Diego sits motionless and listens, mesmerized. Rose's words hit home with the force of truth.

Rose continues, "The Cosmic Dragon knows the laws of the Cosmic Ocean, and it comes to reclaim the captive fish; to return the local mind to the deeper orders of reality from which it attempted to escape, so the domains of egoic control end finally. Unfortunately, in some people this also requires the destruction of their egoic world with its false border controls and fractured operating systems. The Dragon expels its fiery breath and ignites the egoic world with flames. The ego fights back, assisted by the shadow and every power it can conjure up. It jumps on the Dragon and yells, 'You are mine! You'll listen to me, and me only. I command you!'

"The Dragon roars and expels more flames. It will not be controlled, owned, or tamed. It knows how to avoid the captive nets of the local human mind. The ego begins to lose control. The internal fever is rising. The world is burning. This is a fight to the death. The ego won't let go even if it means the death of its host.

"Now everything comes undone: all of the walls it built around itself; all of the false castles and ivory towers. 'Look! It's the Dragon's fault!' the ego shouts. 'He is the monster that needs to be slain! He is the one who tries to kill you and inflict more pain! He is the one I must put in chains, or else he will devour and destroy you, and all you've built will be in vain.'"

Rose feels she's becoming larger than herself and can feel the presence of the Cosmic Dragon within her. She speaks directly to Diego. "Confusion increases, violent nightmares of internal battlefields take over your ordinary mind. The ego jumps in front of your primordial wound; the first wound, the first memory of pain. It says, 'Remember, I am the one who protected you. I am the one who will keep you safe from more pain.' You know very well that this wound has never healed. It couldn't heal, as it provided the energy for your shadow who kept it alive under layers of shame, guilt, doubt, and revenge.

"The Cosmic Dragon returns and rises again through your inner dragon, desperately trying to help you. 'Give up the wound!' he roars. 'Give it to the flames! Don't let this pain consume you! Give it to the higher heart so it can finally heal!' But you can no longer hear the words of your inner dragon. Blinded by fear and consumed by the pain you couldn't or wouldn't release, you cry for all this suffering and anguish to stop.

"The Cosmic Dragon recedes. It doesn't want to harm you or inflict more pain. It promises to return when you're ready to trust the Flame of Love that heals all wounds and liberates the mind. And, like you've experienced yourself, the human realms are still under the tight control of the puppet masters and their egoic operators with their shadow bounty hunters. They believe themselves shielded from the oversight of Cosmic mind by keeping the pain alive, again and again. They don't know that each human being has a Cosmic bypass: a Cosmic Navel Cord, which is our umbilical connection with our Cosmic origins and an innate Cosmic interface. Once this awakens…it changes everything. Yet until that time, the dreams of a better future and a more loving world will continue to crash on the shores of the human mind and scatter the hopes of the possible promises that our hearts know as truth.

"More and more humans are rising and awakening as the Cosmic Dragon awakens our collective heart. The egoic worlds are coming undone. Will you press the reset button and turn your local mind to its original and innate Cosmic settings?"

Diego sighs deeply. "Yes, Rose. I will press the reset button. But how do you know all this about me? It's like you were there when I went through this nightmare. You just gave me the other parts of the puzzle that I was blinded from seeing."

"It came to me when you kissed me and our minds temporarily merged as one. I also know that this is the human tragedy, and the story that has to end.

I've seen it over and over. And somehow, in ways I do not yet understand, the reset code to stop it is alive in me."

"Thank you, Rose. Truly. Thank you." Diego takes her hand in his hand. "I've tried to stay out of this story by keeping away from the fishing nets of the local mind and its limited settings, but it seems that's exactly how I got trapped. Believing I didn't operate in local mind, I couldn't recognize that my own shadow had started to run the show. I know what to do now."

Rose smiles. "My pleasure. And thank you for letting me see all of this, so I don't have to learn this lesson the hard way, like you did."

Becoming the Operating Systems of the New World

All has been said. The silence that follows is sweet. They finish their frozen yogurt while watching the playful dogs on the beach and the seagulls out at sea who are joining the fishing frenzy with the local boats. The sun's rays finally make it through the thick blanket of clouds.

On their walk back, Rose breaks the silence. "Maybe it's a good thing you won't be around much longer," she says.

"How so?"

She kicks and splashes the water with her feet. "I'm not sure I can commit to anyone right now."

"Why?" He looks at her, surprised.

"Because I'm scared to get hurt again. I don't want to be overtaken by a person I have strong feelings for. I'm in a really good place with myself right now, and don't want to wait for phone calls or messages. Or have my mind filled with feelings for another person who then becomes the center of my world. I don't want that anymore."

"Are you admitting to having feelings for me?" Diego stops and looks at her intensely.

"I don't want to talk about it," she says abruptly. "I think you know the answer after all we've experienced today. And you?"

"I think you know the answer, too." Diego smiles.

"Okay, let's shift the topic. Do you know about the Jewish Kabbalah, the mystical teaching about the cosmology of life?" she asks. "My grandfather and dad are really into it."

"Yes, I remember Verdandi telling me. Go on, what would you like to know?"

"I want to learn more about the hidden codes and data-structures that form part of the operating systems of the Cosmic mind. The Kabbalah, as well as the Mayan, Dogon, Hindu, Buddhist, Chinese, Egyptian, and Hopi cosmologies are all giving guidance and instructions about the larger Cosmic mind and how to be aware of the limitations of our local minds."

Diego pauses for a moment. "I suppose you already know about the Kabbalistic Tree of Life with its ten sefirot and—"

Rose interrupts, "Yes, with the twenty-two interdependent paths for the unfolding of four worlds, or five if you include the primordial world of pure infinite consciousness. My grandfather taught me. But I want to know how to find the Cosmic operating systems of this new era inside my body. He did say that according to his friend, Rabbi Joel Bakst, the pineal gland is like the Adamic data center or 'da'at'; the hidden tenth sefirah. Unfortunately, Rabbi Bakst recently passed away. I would have loved to speak with him myself. Apparently, he wrote a lot about da'at as the 'Metatron Operating System' that acts like a superposition of the Cosmic mind."

Diego laughs. "You don't have to look for that in those complex, yet fascinating teachings. Isn't it obvious?"

"What?" she says.

"You are a Cosmic operating system for this new era, Rose. Why else would the Cosmos be sharing all these visions and downloads with you? I'm sure there are others like you, but it seems to me that you are a major Cosmic operating system for the co-creation of these new worlds. You even have the new world architecture coded inside you. You don't see it because you *are* it."

"Ohh. Wow. Okay." Rose suddenly realizes the extent to which Diego really does see her. She feels even more attracted to him.

He looks at her affectionately. "Just make sure you're not letting yourself be overtaken by this mission. Keep a space inside yourself for simply being, Rose. Don't let this path consume you. Don't burn out, like I did."

He notices the faint presence of his own inner dragon after a very long time. It's as if he's letting him know that he's glad to have been understood at last. Diego knows this to be a sign that his inner dragon will return, and he promises him that when that time comes, he'll be ready and won't fight him.

They near the car park. She offers him a lift home, but he has other plans and doesn't want to get closer than they've already become. "Please tell your grandmother that I look forward to joining you both for lunch on Saturday. Thank you for helping me find my heart again, Rose." He kisses her tenderly on her lips before she gets into the car.

"Thank you too, Diego, for all you've given me today. Please do send me a little message once in a while. You have my number," she reminds him as she drives off. She feels happy and sad at the same time. She's glad that Sophia will be joining them for dinner tonight so they can do the healing ceremony for Sam. She doesn't want to get lost in her tidal waves of feelings or over analyze what she's just been through.

On the drive home she thinks about the Cosmic interface and the seven Architect Tools, and how it all seems to form part of a new operating system for the future humans, serving as a new kind of covenant or agreement between the Cosmic and local minds of humanity. She wonders if there's also an equivalent of that process in our technological developments, like the new developments of web3 with blockchain protocols and the ways people can now code their agreements digitally in real time. Rose has always recognized how the human mind is not limited to the brain, or even our experiences, but she feels there's more to discover about this Cosmic interface *as* an operating system for consciousness and the evolution of our human civilizations. Especially for manifesting the higher potentials and higher moral codes of this emerging new era; the new paradigm.

Our Birth Connection to the Three Mothers

Later that evening, Sophia helps herself to a second serving of lasagna. "This is so delicious, Auntie," she tells Verdandi. "I understand you need to go back to your husband, but it's been so good to have you here. Rose and I are going to miss you very much."

"The pleasure's been all mine, Sophia," Verdandi smiles. "I'm happy to know that Rose has such a good friend here who's like a true sister to her. Why don't you join us later this year in Iceland?"

"I'd love that! What do you think, Rose?"

"I think it's a great idea. The winter solstice and Christmas are so special in Iceland, and it's not that much colder than what you're used to here in the

Netherlands," Rose says dreamily, while her mind wanders back to Diego and their passionate kiss.

"Alright then, I'll do it," Sophia rejoices. "I can put in for some time off at the hospital. It'll be so nice to be with your family for the holidays, since I won't be able to travel to Australia to be with my own family this year."

Verdandi squeezes the young woman's hand gently, and says, "Remember to come back over here this Sunday after lunch for your ceremony with the architect tools. Li will be here too. I'll teach you both how to make your own Avatar pouches."

"I can't wait. Thank you so much," Sophia says with a bright smile.

Rose and Verdandi have already gathered the miniature architect tools for Sophia and Li. They're small enough for them to take with them when traveling. On Sunday, Verdandi will transmit the blessings from the mother pouch to these tools. She's been hand-sewing little Avatar pouches for all three of them.

"Rose, please prepare the living room and bring the mother pouch from my room. It's time to give you both the practice for the Cosmic Navel Cord. When we've finished, we'll do a brief healing ceremony for Sam. I spoke with his mother earlier today and she told me she'd appreciate any help they can get for her son. He's still traumatized by the whole incident and is suffering from violent nightmares."

Sophia is grateful that Verdandi agreed to step in and assist the boy in this way. Her heart goes out to him. "Auntie, could you tell us a little more about this Cosmic Navel Cord? My mom dried my physical navel cord after birth and kept it for me in a little medicine pouch, which I wear during ceremonies. Is the Cosmic Navel Cord similar?"

Rose returns from the bedroom and hands Verdandi her pouch. Her grandmother takes the braided cord from the pouch and moves it gently between her fingers as if it is a living snake. "This cord is very old," she says. "If you look closely, you can see that it's braided with three cords. It's been used many times in our ceremonies. My grandmother told me that long ago the colors of these three cords were silver, white, and blue. This cord also exists in an archetypal and symbolic form. That way you can always call upon its powers, whether you physically have a cord like this or not.

"The three interwoven cords serve to remind you of your direct connection with three primary sources of life, three sources of consciousness, and the three primordial Mothers: Mother Cosmos who birthed the Universe... Mother Universe who birthed the physical world of space-time and energy-matter, including our Earth, and all the galaxies, planets, and stars...and our Mother Earth who gave birth to our planet and humanity so that your life in this physical form became possible."

"Like those Russian matryoshka dolls," Sophia laughs. "Each time you open one mother figure, you find another mother figure within it."

"Yes," Rose pipes in, "with the Cosmic Mother as the largest doll who carries within her the Universe Mother, who carries within her all the planetary mothers, as well as all the moons and stars, and all expressions of life, including each of us."

Sophia asks Verdandi, "Will we make our own cords like that on Sunday?"

"Yes, Sophia. That's the plan. I've already gathered all of the required materials for each of you. Now let me continue, so I can start your practice." Verdandi smiles at the young women. "Even the sun is about to go to bed. The silver cord represents your birth connection with the Cosmic Mother, who is also the Cosmic Tree of Life. She is actually an androgynous archetype who carries within Her the Mother and Father aspect as one unity. Just like the Cosmic Serpent is androgynous and self-conceiving, though outwardly feminine, and the Cosmic Dragon is androgynous and self-conceiving, but outwardly masculine. When referring to Her birth-giving powers we'll refer to this Mother archetype as a She, but never at the exclusion of the Father or masculine qualities."

"Does that mean that men also have a Cosmic Mother aspect in them, and even a Cosmic womb?" Rose asks.

"Of course, love, which is why some men feel more feminine on the inside, and may even feel confused about this or scared to tell others about their feminine qualities. Especially those men with strong creative and artistic powers who often act in the role of a receptive life-giving womb for others and see themselves as birthers of new ways."

"I never thought about that before," Sophia says with sparkling eyes. "Please continue, Auntie."

"Mother Cosmos gave birth to your soul and the soul of the Universe, who became Mother Universe so each of our souls could have a physical place to live, grow, and evolve together. Through your navel cord connection with the Cosmic Mother, you also come to understand the Cosmic laws of creation and manifestation, and how to apply your Cosmic powers to become an architect of worlds and realities. Her divine essence and creative powers are always within you as your own soul, in which lay dormant the Cosmic seeds of your lives and the unique potentials of consciousness that are yours to bring into being and co-create with. This cord can thus remind you of your unique essence and soulful tapestry, as well the Cosmic purpose for your life and being. You'll be able to experience more of this soon when I guide you both through the practice for this Architect Tool."

Rose and Sophia sit next to each other on the couch, surrounded by pillows. They place their hands over their belly buttons. Verdandi sits opposite them in a comfortable chair surrounded by flickering candles that illuminate the room with a beautiful, warm glow.

She continues, "The white cord represents your birth connection with Mother Universe who birthed the physical dimensions of life. She helps you understand the universal laws of creation and manifestation, and how to work with the universal powers and conditions of the physical Universe, and how these are precisely tuned for actualizing consciousness through the process of evolution. The white cord also represents the underlying unity in all the diversity and splendor that emerges and manifests from the womb of the Universe. And within the color white are represented all the colors of the rainbow."

"This reminds me of the Rainbow Serpent," Sophia exclaims, "which in our culture is sometimes painted white as well. My mother told me that the Rainbow Serpent is an ancestral Creator Being who shapes and forms our physical world each time she moves her dreamtime body, creating mountains, valleys, rivers, and waterholes in our physical world here."

Verdandi looks at Sophia with great affection. "Thank you for bringing your mother into our conversation. She must be missing you so much. I know my daughter Tara misses Rose tremendously. Let's bring them both here into our conversation by making a place for them in our hearts."

"Yes, I miss Mom a lot," Rose sighs. "That's another thing we have in common, Sophia. We're both far away from our physical mothers. I really wish this pandemic would come to an end, so we can see our parents more often."

Sophia nods quietly. Verdandi hands Rose the cord. "Here, love. After you've been able to receive its transmission, please give it to Sophia." She continues, "Now the blue cord. This one represents your birth connection with Mother Earth, who birthed our physical planet as our common home. She helps you understand the planetary laws of creation and manifestation, and how to work with the unique conditions of life as an evolving planetary being. This blue cord can remind you of all the evolutionary potentials, powers, and capacities that our planet affords us to grow and evolve in consciousness. Through your planetary navel cord connection, you're also reminded that you're always wanted and welcome here on Earth. This is your planetary home that nobody can take away from you. It is your planetary birthright. The color blue also serves to remind you of the importance of water, and how your physical life began in the life-giving waters of your mother's womb, and before that, in the life-giving blue waters of the planetary womb."

Rose carefully hands the cord to Sophia who beams with delight. She places the cord on her belly button. She closes her eyes and experiences how her Cosmic Navel Cord awakens. The energy within and around her navel starts pulsating and throbbing gently. She remembers how she felt as a baby in the womb of her mother, and realizes the importance of the umbilical cord connection and all it represents on so many more levels than just the physical.

"Thank you, Auntie. This is so profound." Sophia carefully hands the cord back to Verdandi. "Now I know that I have three more Mothers in addition to my physical birth mother. We're all grown by four Mothers of four worlds."

"That's right, and the fifth is your own motherhood, which lives in women as well as in men when we become like a mother for the life we bring forth, whether physically in the form of a child, or in the world of ideas, art, projects, and new inventions. Let's take a little pause and have our fruit salad, and then I'll guide you both through this process as a practice."

Practice with the Cosmic Navel Cord

"Take a deep breath in, hold it for a few seconds, then breathe out and relax. Do this a few more times. Each time, relax more deeply and bring your energy and awareness back to yourself. Breathe in again. This time, bring your breath all the way to your navel. As you breathe out, release any tensions that may live around your navel. Relax some more.

"Now place one hand over your belly button and connect with the energy and feelings that live within or around your belly button. Long ago, your umbilical cord formed in the area that is now your navel. It connected your body to the placenta of your mother's womb and provided you with all the nourishment you needed to come into life. If there were any nutrients you felt you lacked or were unable to receive, please know that this can be balanced and corrected right now. Receive energetically, and in wisdom, all the nutrients you need. Receive from the abundance of life all of this precious and infinite nourishment for growing in wholeness, beauty, and health.

"Now become aware of another kind of umbilical cord connection: your Cosmic Navel Cord. This represents your direct Source connection with the Mother wisdom of our Earth, the Mother wisdom of the Universe, and the Mother wisdom of the Cosmos, woven and braided together as a unity that forms an unbreakable bond. In this unity, the silver cord represents your direct connection with Mother Cosmos; the white cord represents your direct connection with Mother Universe; the blue cord represents your direct connection with Mother Earth. Each of these three Mothers gave aspects, powers, and qualities of themselves to you, including the fertilizing and activating Father aspects of Cosmos, Universe, and Earth. These universal Mother and Father qualities of consciousness have now become you. They are yours to further shape, evolve, and carry forth to future worlds and generations.

"Take a moment to become aware of how these qualities of consciousness live in you and in your life. If there are any imbalances in how this has manifested in or through you, you may now form the intention for each of these qualities to balance in wholeness. Become aware of how you too, whether woman or man, have within you the wisdom of the womb; the life-giving wisdom of the archetypal Mother.

"Imagine how the Cosmic womb surrounds the Universe's womb, which surrounds the planetary womb that surrounds our world and your life to help you birth who you are meant to be and become. Allow this sacred womb wisdom to support your life in whatever way support is required for you to live a greater quality of the gift of life that you are.

"Now imagine how this womb wisdom of the three Mothers and these life-giving powers live in you. To what extent have you been able to bring this forth, and perhaps even pass it on in the form of life-giving possibilities, ideas, projects, art, inventions, or any other forms that open possibilities for life and our world to thrive and flourish?

"If you feel any restrictions or blockages around your creative powers, ask the Cosmic Navel Cord to reset your direct connections to the three Mothers and their wisdoms. Ask it to awaken in you the knowledge, understanding, and experience of your essence, your unique purpose, and your unique being of the wholeness we are.

"Ask for this activation, awakening, and actualization to occur gently, in health, and for the greater goodness of your life, and life as a whole. Rest for a few moments in this process as any projections, limitations, or interferences fall away from your direct Source connections. Enjoy how the Divine Mother and Father aspects of your soul essence are restored within and around you.

"Appreciate the wholeness you are and continue to receive from your Cosmic Navel Cord the nourishment, protection, and support for living your life with joy, grace, and wisdom. Allow this process to come to a natural completion, knowing you may always call upon these innate connections whenever required, and continue to receive the nourishment that is there for you. When you're ready, you may open your eyes and move your body. Be fully present here and now."

Healing Our World with the Cosmic Navel Cord

Rose and Sophia slowly open their eyes. They've each had a profound and unique experience. Verdandi has gone to the kitchen to make hot chocolate to go with the ginger cookies she made earlier. When she returns, the sun has set and a soft gentle breeze has entered the living room. The silver rays of the moon look like a luminous umbilical cord connected to the dreamtime. The birds have gone to bed. In the far distance, a dog is barking, as if awakening humanity's unconscious and standing guard for us when we slip into the state of forgetting.

Rose has put on Celtic music. Sophia takes the tray with drinks and cookies from Verdandi and sets it on the table in front of them. After a little pause and some cheerful sharing of each of their experiences, Verdandi asks if they feel ready to do a brief process for Sam. The friends nod their heads eagerly.

"Okay, ladies. I'd like you to call upon the three Mothers with the help of your Cosmic Navel Cord: Mother Cosmos, Mother Universe, and Mother Earth. You may even imagine this Cord as your direct telephone line to each of these three Mothers, or a robe that gently tugs them and brings their wisdom and support into our time and place."

Verdandi continues, "Now think of Sam. Bring forth a memory of him into your mind. See him from the essence of who he is. Ask the three Mothers to place their arms and loving support around Sam to help him heal in himself and in his world what became violated, broken, threatened, or harmed. Intend for the love, support, and protection of the three Mothers and their sacred Father aspects to manifest around Sam. Notice how this creates a powerful healing field around him. Now speak to Sam from your soul, as if you are with him. Remember, you have the nonlocal connection. Let him know that he can freely choose what to receive and draw from this field, as it is for his highest good. Let him know that he has support; he's not alone.

"Form the intention that this pattern of violence, domination, and any other forms of harm leave his life for good, and also clear away from his future path. See his present and future path clear, safe, and supported. Now ask the three Mothers and their Father aspects—the sacred partnership of the divine feminine and masculine qualities that are within all life—to bless his life physically, emotionally, mentally, spiritually, and energetically. Trust the process and release your thoughts and energetic connection with him.

"Now apply the same intention for humanity as a whole. Hold the intention that humanity resolves and heals the roots of all forms of violence, within and around us. Ask the three Mothers and their Father aspects—the sacred partnership of the divine feminine and masculine qualities that are within all of life—to bless our world with the wisdom, love, and consciousness that we need for co-creating and growing our world from wholeness by the power of love. Include yourself in the receiving of the support you've called for. Complete the process with gratitude for all the support that's been given. Bring your own energy and awareness back to yourself. Become fully present here and now. Open your eyes when you feel ready."

Sophia is the first to open her eyes. "This is so powerful. I feel so much better about Sam and his family. I even saw how this bully situation ceased. I don't know what it means, but I simply didn't see those awful men around him anymore. It was like he was shielded from it all. Not only that, but those men were receiving their own wake-up call from the three Mothers!"

Verdandi interjects, "Well, one certainly wouldn't want to go up against three fierce and all-powerful Mothers of that caliber."

Rose adds, "Let's put them in command of the design of the new operating systems for humanity, too."

All three laugh at the thought of that: three archetypal Mothers who work together to put order in our lost worlds and who teach us how to birth a divine union that our world has never seen before. The beginning of the new era is coming closer.

Integration -
The Cosmic Navel Cord

Through this chapter, Rose experiences the workings of the Cosmic Navel Cord and the power of her first tantric kiss at a soul level of her being with Diego. She first learns about the Navel Cord in a fun way from Olaf, who explains how this tool in the game can also serve as a navel reset button or Cosmic bypass to free our consciousness from the hypnotic dreams of the awakening giants. Rose later receives a powerful vision through which she comes to understand how the mind also serves as a Cosmic interface and operating system of consciousness. She also learns about our umbilical Source connection with the three Mothers: Mother Cosmos, Mother Universe, and Mother Earth, and their innate Father aspects.

> *The Cosmic Navel Cord reconnects you with your Avatar consciousness; the realization of who you truly are beyond this time and place. You can call upon the Cosmic Navel Cord to activate and strengthen your umbilical Source connection with Mother Cosmos, Mother Universe, and Mother Earth through which you received the Cosmic, universal, and planetary Mother and Father qualities of consciousness to continue the evolution of life.*

The summary and questions below will help you to integrate and apply the essential teachings of this chapter:

- ◉ During her walk on the beach, Rose entered into the consciousness state of Cosmic mind through which she experienced the world in a nonlocal flow state. In her vision she saw the beach on which she walked as a Cosmic interface, or surface boundary, which regulates and converges Cosmic potencies and unified flow states into the organized patterns of our physical world.

- Cosmic mind can also be seen as the nonlocal implicate orders of space-time and energy-matter, and local mind as the implicate orders of your embodied human reality. Experiment with your local mind as *a fishing net* of your Cosmic mind for manifesting and shaping the imaginal potencies of consciousness that are continuously in a flow state of formation.

- See into the world from the implicate orders of your nonlocal Cosmic mind to experience wholeness everywhere. And remember, your local mind serves as an operating system within your Cosmic mind for the purpose of manifestation. It is, however, not the source of your reality.

- Connect with the Luciferian aspect of yourself that often operates in a contrary manner in an attempt to keep you safe from the hypnotic influence of group thinking and unaware collective consciousness. Explore how you express this aspect and your inner freedom. Remember, freedom is not something you can own or claim; it is who and what you essentially are. *What does Diego's journey of liberation mean for you? Are you in touch with the true essence of the Cosmic Dragon within you? How does your inner dragon express itself?*

- Your personal consciousness is always part of the larger universal consciousness. Your Cosmic interface and the seven Cosmic Architect Tools form part of the new operating systems of the future humans, serving as a new kind of covenant between the larger Cosmic versions of ourselves and our local human realities. The Cosmic interface plays a key role in the evolution of human civilizations by enabling the manifestation of higher order potentials and moral codes.

- The Cosmic Navel Cord as an archetypal Tool represents your umbilical Source connection with Mother Cosmos (silver), Mother Universe (white), and Mother Earth (blue). The three cords are woven and braided together as a unity that forms an unbreakable bond. Within the Mother wisdom is also the Father wisdom and power of creation and manifestation. These universal Mother and Father qualities of consciousness have now become you, and are yours to further shape and carry forth.

- Imagine how the womb wisdom of the three Mothers and their life-giving powers live in you. *To what extent have you been able to bring this forth, and perhaps even pass it on, in the form of life-giving possibilities, ideas, projects, art, inventions, or any other forms that open possibilities for life and our world to thrive and flourish?*

- Mother Cosmos gave birth to your soul and the soul of the Universe, who became Mother Universe so each of our souls could have a physical place to live, grow, and evolve together. She helps you understand the Cosmic laws of creation and manifestation and how to apply your Cosmic powers to become an architect of worlds and realities. Her divine essence and creative powers are always within you as your own soul, in which lie dormant the Cosmic seeds of your lives and the unique potentials of consciousness that are for you to bring into being and co-create with.

- Mother Universe gave birth to the physical dimensions of life. She helps you understand the universal laws of creation and manifestation, and how to work with the unique conditions of our physical universe and how these are precisely tuned for actualizing consciousness through the process of evolution.

- Mother Earth gave birth to our physical planet as our common home. She helps you to understand the planetary laws of creation and manifestation, and how to work with the unique conditions of life as an evolving planetary being.

- If you feel any restrictions or blockages around your creative powers, ask the Cosmic Navel Cord to reset your direct connection to the three Mothers and their wisdoms. Ask it to awaken in you the wisdom, understanding, and experience of your essence, purpose, and unique being.

- You can also call upon the Cosmic Navel Cord to restore within you the Divine Mother and Father aspects of your soul essence, and to receive the Cosmic nourishment, protection, and support for living your life with joy, grace, and wisdom.

- Intend for the love, support, and protection of the three Mothers and their sacred Father aspects to manifest within and around your life and in our world. You can also apply this intention in support of other people who may require healing support or protection during challenging times.

CHAPTER 11

The Future Hack for Evolving Humanity

The Cosmic Mirror

Rose wipes away her tears as she slowly walks home along the same canal where she and her grandmother walked a few weeks ago—the morning that Anna, Verdandi's twin sister, was attacked. A purring, fluffy cat watches her from the roof of the closest houseboat as she passes by, as if sensing her sadness. Rose turns around one last time to catch a final glimpse of Diego as he disappears into the crowd on the other side of the bridge.

Why does he need to go? Life can be so unfair. The tingle of their goodbye kiss still lingers on her lips. "Trust the Grand Architect," he'd whispered into her ear as he stroked her hair. "What's meant to be will be. I'll stay in touch, my beautiful Rose."

She's glad that at least they'd enjoyed a wonderful lunch together. Her grandmother had made a delicious summer soup and Diego had brought a fruit salad with fresh mango. Verdandi's comical stories brought relief to them both. She seemed pleased with his progress over the past few months, and urged him to keep at it. He promised her he would, and that he may come to visit her for another ceremony. Rose blurted out, "Yes! You must come to Iceland! The best time for a ceremony is the winter solstice. I'll be there as well. Promise you'll come then!"

The Cosmic Mirror for the Future Humans Quest

Rose opens the door of her apartment, her cheeks wet with tears. Verdandi walks up to her and embraces her in a loving hug. "Come here, my butterfly girl. You'll see him again. Trust. Give him the space he needs to complete this phase of his journey. And don't get too focused on thinking he is Mr. Right. You have so many more adventures ahead of you."

"I don't want to meet anyone else," Rose tells her. "I want to get to know Diego. I've never felt this way about anyone. When I'm with him, I feel complete. I can't explain it. I just wish I could jump to the future right now, and to the exact time that I'll be seeing him again."

"Patience, darling. You've only seen his best side. He's still a wounded man who's not ready for a relationship just yet. Stay open to what the Universe is bringing into your life. You have an amazing time with Li and his parents in Hong Kong to look forward to. When you see Diego again in the future, your feelings may have changed. Live in the now! Remember, he's a catalyst for awakening feelings that you've never experienced before, but he's not the source of those feelings."

"Okay..." Rose says reluctantly. "But I'm not willing to give up on him that quickly."

"Don't give up on him. I'm just suggesting that you live in the moment and keep yourself open to new possibilities. Alright?"

"Alright."

"There's one more architect tool that I'll need to guide you through, and this may be the perfect time."

"Does it have anything to do with that little mirror that's in the pouch?"

"Yes," Verdandi says mysteriously. "But it's not just any kind of mirror. It's a Cosmic mirror."

"Oh!" Rose perks up. "Could it show me my future? Things about my life that I can't see yet?"

"Let me guess what you want to use it for," Verdandi laughs. "Yes, it can show you many things about yourself, but don't degrade it to a crystal ball for fortune telling."

"I'd love to learn more about this Cosmic mirror."

"Good. And I know just the right person for you to explore this with."

"Who?"

"Olaf! Ask him how he would include a Cosmic mirror in the game you two have been developing."

"Great idea. I'll call him right now," Rose says excitedly.

Olaf lives with his parents, Lucas and Denise, a few hours from Verdandi's sister Anna in Norway. His parents recently decided to divorce, but haven't told Olaf yet. They came to this decision after a process of "conscious uncoupling." Together they realized that their relationship had come to a natural completion, and they both wanted to explore other avenues with different people. They had stayed together for Olaf, and now that he is older, they're planning to tell him of their decision. They also agreed to find separate houses close to one another so they can continue to co-parent him to the best of their abilities.

Rose is worried about her brother and the impact their decision will have on Olaf. She hopes that his work as a marine engineer and his project for developing renewable energy solutions will keep his mind occupied as the family goes through this process. Separations are always hard, especially for children who have no say in the decision. Lucas intends to travel with Olaf to Iceland at the end of the year for their long-awaited family reunion.

When Rose calls, Lucas answers the phone. "Hi, bro. How are you doing these days? I know you have a lot going on," she says.

"Managing. It's not easy, but we're moving forward. How about you?"

"I'm having a great time with Grandma here. Learning a lot. And her cooking…"

"Stop! She's the best cook in the family. You're making me jealous!" Lucas laughs. "Well, have fun. I'm glad she was able to visit you in person."

"Me, too. Hey, I'd love to speak with Olaf. Is he around?"

"He's with Denise in the kitchen. She's teaching him to cook an egg with the sunny side up. Quite an adventure. He insists on frying the *perfect* egg, meaning he doesn't want the yolk to break. We've gone through four eggs already."

"Only four?" Rose laughs. "Well, he knows what he likes."

"Ha. I suppose. I'm glad you phoned, though. It gives me an excuse to stop him before the whole carton of eggs gets scrambled."

"I miss you," she tells her brother.

"You, too, Rose. Here's Olaf."

Olaf takes the phone. His cheeks are flushed and his eyes sparkle with excitement.

"Auntie, I did it!" he exclaims. "I finally did it! I can bake an egg now with the sunny side up!"

"Well done, Olaf. You can make me one next time we meet."

"I will. How are you? Been in any more fights?"

"Not lately," Rose laughs. "I called to ask for your creative input regarding a possible new element we can add to our game."

"Cool. What is it?"

"A Cosmic mirror."

"Sounds interesting," he says. "Tell me more."

"Remember how last time we talked, you introduced the Cosmic cord as a Cosmic bypass tool?"

Olaf nods. "Yeah. For activating our inner Source codes and restoring us to our original selves."

"Exactly."

"So we can receive guidance from our Avatar self without interference from the awakening giants."

"Yes."

"The navel reset button!" Olaf grins. "It really works, you know. Every night I imagine pulling that cord from my belly button before I go to sleep. Ever since I started doing that, I've had much better dreams."

"That's wonderful. Well, the Cosmic mirror is another tool you might enjoy. Do you have a few minutes to talk about it now?"

"Sure."

"Good. Please sit down and get comfortable."

"I'm comfortable."

"Close your eyes and imagine yourself in the Cosmic Compass game again, playing the Future Humans Quest. Remember the game challenges: we play to thrive, not just to survive. We want to evolve and upgrade how the game of life is played on planet Earth. Now imagine going through some of the most difficult game challenges. The giant is awakening and trying to destroy you. She doesn't realize you're there to help her. People are still acting out from their degraded lower selves. They're resisting their need to evolve and upgrade as they desperately try to maintain their hold over the planetary game resources. Our planet is in peril. Species are dying everywhere. Fires, floods, superstorms, earthquakes, and extreme weather events are increasing around the world. Scientists have sent out another urgent alert. They call it 'Code Red for humanity.' World leaders have met for the latest Climate Summit, and have again proven that they lack the vision, courage, and moral leadership to do what is necessary. Small islands, like the Maldives, have been given the death sentence; the world is not prepared to save them from drowning as the seas rise. Our world is a mess, and your team is urgently needed to solve these multiple crises at the same time."

Rose pauses for a moment to give him the time to enter more deeply into this imaginal process with all the real-life world elements that are happening right now. His face looks tense, but he nods his head for her to keep going.

"You're wearing your avatar suit, which is your Cosmic interface for interacting directly with the Cosmic Avatars who've come to help us. As part of your avatar suit you have your Cosmic compass and all the other architect tools for taking on the game challenges. In order to complete the quest, there's one more challenge that you and your team need to complete. You'll need to find a backdoor entrance into the giant's mind to regain the access points over the operating systems of collective consciousness. You've already managed to see through the illusions of the giants in your own mind, and you're now able to enter into your own Avatar consciousness by activating your Cosmic navel cord. Together with your teams, you've activated the upgrade codes of the sleeping giants who are now awakening around the world. By taking on these game challenges, you've also started to upgrade and evolve your own version of the game, as you regain your Cosmic powers and your Avatar consciousness. But there are still many illusions in which you and your team can get caught. The nightmare of the giants is still a living reality for billions of humans on Earth, and many humans are resisting the end of their version of the game of life."

Olaf shuffles his feet and clenches his hands. Rose continues, "The Avatars know how difficult this stage of the quest is, so they've activated another tool in your avatar suit: the Cosmic mirror. As part of the challenge, you'll have to discover how to use this mirror for facing the giants and yourself. How would you use it?"

"I would hold the mirror up to the giants to show them all the bad things they've done!" Olaf declares. "So they have to face how they're destroying our earth and our future, and also how they can make things better."

"And what if the minds of the giants reject this truth?"

"Then I would activate the Cosmic mirror in each of our avatar suits," Olaf replies with a determined voice. "That way all of us who are working to save the planet become like a mirror that forces the giants to wake up by reflecting and sending back their harmful and dominant ways. This will also protect our minds from their influence. The mirror in all of us will feed their stuff back to their giant minds so they have to come face-to-face with themselves. That'll give us the opportunity to reset and upgrade our own versions of who we want to be in the game of life."

"Very smart," Rose replies. "Using the Cosmic mirror to create a collective eclipse point that temporarily blocks out the influence of the giants. And how would you use the mirror for yourself, so you also wake up further?"

Olaf thinks for a moment, then says, "The Cosmic mirror has three time-settings. You can set it to show you your past so you can see all the things you've done. Good stuff *and* bad stuff. You can also set it to the present to see who you are now and the impacts you're creating now. And it can also be set to the future to show you who you *are* becoming and who you *can* become."

"Interesting."

"Yeah! The future setting of the Cosmic mirror is the most interesting. It shows who you'll be if you continue on as you are now, who you can become if you evolve further, and how you could slide back to lower versions of yourself by not completing the challenges of the quest."

"Can you put it in future mode right now?" Rose asks. "Have a look in the Cosmic mirror, and tell me what you see."

"Okay, I'm doing it." He pauses. "It's showing me things I might be doing in the future. I have abilities and powers I didn't know I had."

"What do you see of yourself?"

"I see myself happy. I'm doing well in college and having a good time with my friends and parents," Olaf says with a huge smile. "I see I've sculpted lots of clay figures that look even more amazing than my current ones. Clay giants that are friendly and helpful. I don't need to make clay monsters anymore to scare away the bad giants and their nightmares. I'm a good person. I'm helping the earth to heal from all the damage we've caused. I'm very creative. Hey! I'm playing my drums in a band!"

"That's wonderful, Olaf. How does this knowledge help you to take up the final challenges of the quest?"

"It gives me confidence in myself that I can do it. And it lets me know that I can trust in myself and my future. It also guides me to do things better in the present. It helps me use my creative powers in a way I hadn't thought of yet; especially by sculpting the upgraded, awakened giants out of clay. I can make future versions of our better and restored original selves, too. It's showing me that I don't need to play out the lower, degraded versions of the giants and humanity in my dreams, games, and art."

"What about the Avatars? Do you need to show them the mirror as well?"

"No, they don't need it because they already see into the future. They know who they are and who we are. When we wake up and the giants wake up, we realize how we are the Avatars who have returned!"

"Brilliant. Thanks so much, Olaf."

Olaf bursts out laughing. "Luna stop licking my face. She dropped her slobbery ball right into my lap. I think she wants me to play with her."

Rose laughs too. "Well, give that sweet dog a cuddle from me and let's talk again soon, okay?"

"Okay. Luna, stop! No! You have dog breath! I better go. Bye, Auntie Rose. Kiss Grandma for me."

After the call with her nephew, Rose retreats to the balcony. She watches the swans glide through the waters of the canal, and her thoughts drift to Diego. She recalls the first time they met; the way her body felt when he touched her soul with his intense eyes. Weeks feel like lifetimes.

She calls Sophia for support. The minute Sophia hears Rose speak she can tell from her tone how tender her best friend must be feeling right now.

"How are you doing, sister? You sound so sad."

"I miss him, Sophia."

"I can only imagine your heartache with having to say goodbye so soon."

"We have such a deep, soulful connection."

"I know. It's a blessing that you get to experience that, even though it's so hard right now." Sophia sighs. "I'd love to meet someone I could fall madly in love with. But realistically, when would I have time? I'm so focused on becoming a doctor. Nearly every minute is full of work."

"All of your long hours of study and internship can't last forever. And just think, at the end of it all, you'll be a doctor. You'll be able to help so many people."

"You're right. I'm grateful. It's what I've always wanted to do." Sophia decides to shift the topic. "Are you excited about going to Hong Kong with Li?"

"Oh, yes. What a great opportunity."

"How's your family doing?"

"They're all doing well. I just finished talking with Olaf about the game we're co-creating." Rose tells Sophia the high points of her conversation with her nephew and adds, "The best part was when Olaf looked into the Cosmic mirror and saw himself sculpting the upgraded and awakened giants in the future out of clay. He said it with such innocence. He doesn't realize how profound that really is."

"I'm glad you brought this up," Sophia replies. "There's something I've been meaning to tell you for a while, but never quite knew how to bring up the subject. Those giants you speak of...I hope you realize that they aren't just symbolic or metaphysical as collective archetypes. The giants are also the modern multinational corporations, the political and financial elite, and the world icons and social influencers that everyone looks up to. I'm worried about you, Rose."

"Okay, I'm listening. Why are you worried?"

"I had an awful dream a couple of weeks ago. You were getting squashed by the giants. Especially the American giants in the form of celebrities and influencers who learned about your story and what you're working on. In the dream, the giants were world icons who presented themselves as wanting to help you to reach the world stage as a young woman with powerful ideas. But what they didn't tell you is how they were, in fact, claiming your ideas as their own! Knowing they couldn't stop you, they tried to claim the credit and offspring of all your hard work by bringing this out through their own brands." Rose listens quietly as Sophia continues. "You already had your first encounter with a corporate giant when you presented your project to Mike's company for funding. You're going up against formidable forces, and you have no idea yet of the extent and impact of your own powers. You also saw this in the forest when we intervened to save Sam's life. This world game you've been coming up with is going to be hugely influential; I can feel that with every fiber of my being. Many people are going to want to associate themselves with you. Please be careful of their intentions. Once money and popularity get behind it, the dynamics are going to change, and I don't want you to get hurt or squashed."

"Thank you, sister. I'm glad you told me. Here you are, warning me once again. But this time, I'm listening—truly. Not like that time in the forest when I foolishly ignored your intuition. Some say that it takes three times to complete a lesson…Well, here you go. This is the third time, and I'm listening with my whole heart. I just don't know what to do about it, yet…"

"At least you're more awake to what's going on now. I have a ton of work to do, so I'd better get back to it. I'll see you tomorrow. I'm really looking forward to the ceremony with your grandmother."

"Me, too. Bye, Sophia, and thanks again."

The Call with Hazel Henderson and Mariana Bozesan

Later that evening Rose and her grandmother return from a lovely stroll just in time to set up the computer for their call with Hazel Henderson and Mariana Bozesan. Rose still feels sad, but she's also looking forward to this long-awaited conversation, so she decides to focus on that instead of Diego. She and Verdandi are having a quick preparation call with Li via FaceTime first. Verdandi reminds them of the incredible opportunity they have to learn from these two conscious and impactful businesswomen who are leading international change agents in the ways they use economics, finance, and technology to drive world transformation.

Li has been following the work of Hazel for a long time. He explains to Rose, "I can't believe I finally get to talk with Hazel Henderson *in person*. I'm nervous, actually. I've read so many of her books and articles. She's such an international icon."

"Yep," Rose pipes in. "She's also the founder of Ethical Markets Media, which is a Certified Benefit Corporation. A new way of chartering globally responsible companies!"

"And she's a world-renowned futurist with her evolutionary analyses of economics. I resonate with the way she operates systemically, beyond economics, in ways I'm eager to apply to our business."

"Apparently, she's also famous for finding the blind spots of conventional economists," Rose laughs. "I wonder how your old university professors felt about that?"

Verdandi chuckles. "Sounds like you three will have a lot to talk about. I'm sure Hazel will appreciate your enthusiasm."

"I hope so," Rose says. "I'm excited to meet her friend Mariana, too. I've been digging into her work to prepare for our call, and I'm impressed with how she combines her knowledge of computer science, technology, artificial intelligence, business, psychology, impact investment, and integral theory. She sounds as diverse as I am. And she really knows what it means to transform your life from the most difficult life circumstances. I can't wait to meet them both."

Li adds, "I read that she's also a world-renowned investor and serial entrepreneur who knows how to leverage exponentially growing technologies and ethical AI to accelerate how we can solve our sustainability crisis. That's an important focus. Maybe we should even include that in the compass game. Let's bring that up during our meeting with my dad in Hong Kong."

"Great idea," Rose nods. "Grandma, do you think I could ask them to mentor me?"

"And me too!" Li adds.

"Slow down, you two. Let's have our call with them first," Verdandi laughs. "If that goes well, you can ask them. Now let's get online; we don't want to keep them waiting."

After some brief introductions, Rose addresses the first question to Hazel with a pounding heart. "Um, when I listened to one of your talks recently, you spoke of the importance of applying 'the golden rule' to economics and finance. You warned that corporations have become puppets of what you call 'predatory economics.' You've also mentioned that there's a far greater economy than the market economy, which you call the 'love and caring economy.' Can you tell us more about this?"

"Yes, Rose. The golden rule is about doing as you would be done by. Although money and markets are useful tools that human beings have been using for thousands of years, they didn't get weaponized and modernized until they became linked with the technological, fossil-fueled industrial era. And then it became really easy to use this one single metric, the price system, and money. The price system is a function of human ignorance, because it's always historic. You're always looking back through the rear-view mirror. And the accounting system in economic theory allows for a kind of 'Freudian slip' called 'externalities.' What's an externality, for heaven's sake?

Well, it's whatever I don't want to pay attention to in my business. And if I'm creating impacts that are affecting innocent bystanders, or pollution in the environment, I'm just going to externalize them from my balance sheet and move right ahead and claim profits. When you actually do a correct full spectrum accounting by internalizing these external costs, you'll find that all of the posted profits of every multinational corporation in the world are false. Meaning, none of them made any profit, so it's like a gigantic fraud. And please remember that the role of advertising and marketing, which tries to hook in young people like yourself, evolved out of this market sector and the use of the price system. Many psychologists had been recruited to sharpen our powers of persuasion, as a way to manipulate human beings and their value systems."

Li feels a knot in his stomach as Hazel's words start to sink in. Rose asks him gently if he'd like to ask her a question. He nods and clears his throat. "Thank you profoundly for what you just shared, I just wish it wasn't true. I don't even know how to persuade my own father to change our business model. My dad runs a big financial wealth management fund, as our family comes from a long line of Asian bankers and financial investors. I'm supposed to follow in his footsteps, but I can't. I don't want that kind of predatory economics, as you call it. I don't want to perpetuate the false monetary pricing that we all know is a ticking time bomb, and the primary reason our world is in a crisis. So many people and species are sentenced to death because of our insane pursuit of unlimited economic growth. How can I help change this?"

"Begin by understanding that money is simply information that we happen to believe in; a kind of social protocol, which, just like any other social protocol, is a set of rules that we decide to use as a proxy token of our intentions—and to express what we value. The problem is that we got locked into economic and financial algorithms that only incentivize the seven deadly sins, and are also enormously out of date because they don't take in any externalities. These algorithms don't look at the cost of big market failures, like climate change. You studied economics in college, right? Go back to the first principles in the old economic textbooks, like Adam Smith and his book 'The Theory of Moral Sentiments,' which recognizes the golden rule. Smith says that there are conditions under which you can use markets to efficiently allocate your resources and your intentions. And those conditions are that the buyers and sellers must meet each other in marketplaces with equal power and equal information. And they must *not* inflict any harm on any innocent bystanders. This tells you why, for example, the US health system can never be a free market. Because the buyers—the patients—have almost no power and almost no information. And the sellers—the providers, practitioners, and insurance companies—have all the power *and* all the information. They inflict not only harm on the patients, but also on the general public in society. There are hardly any public health systems that are truly focused on wellness and ecological services, such as clean air and water that we actually need, and which our planet provides for free."

Mariana interjects, "Thank you, Hazel, for reminding us of nature's abundance, which is also free of charge. Humans are part of nature, of course, but through social conditioning, we start believing in scarcity and become fearful and greedy. The fear that there is not enough to go around is now dominating our emotions, our thinking, and our actions. This fear makes us continuously accumulate more and more things at the expense of people and the planet, believing that they give us the security that we seek. But the time has come to realize that fear is a good servant, but a terrible teacher. And so, if you're asking me what each of us can do to get out of our current crisis, I would start with something we can influence, namely our own mind shift. We are the only person thinking in our head, and we must see that scarcity is a lie, and that the human spirit has the ingenuity needed to overcome most challenges. We have proven that many times since the dawn of civilization. This human quality has never been more obvious than now when the collective intelligence of billions of people is converging online through technological evolution showing us how we can provide the solutions to the global grand challenges."

"I'm really curious to learn more about this transformative role of technology, Mariana," Rose says. "Are you saying that technological developments can actually help us to resolve our sustainability crisis *and* help us to evolve? Does this also include the use of AI—artificial intelligence?"

"Yes," Mariana smiles. "As a computer scientist, I'm a huge fan of technology and its extraordinary ability to create abundance to help the people and the planet. It always has because it reflects human innovation, creativity, and consciousness evolution. How we use technology is, however, a direct reflection of our mindset. You can use a knife to feed people or to kill them. Everything we create on the outside is a direct reflection of who we are on the inside. This truth becomes more obvious than ever before through AI algorithms by programmers who, without ethical education, are building their own biases into AIs. Or to stick to Hazel's previous example, how biased views on gender or racial biases can be built in healthcare algorithms. For this kind of transformation to happen, we must continue to create a society that supports high moral and ethical norms, at later stages of consciousness. That's a leadership issue, which means that we need awakened leaders in all parts of society, from education, to business, to politics. We have a long way to go, but it can be done."

Verdandi nods her head in agreement, and turns to speak to Rose and Li. "That's why our previous conversation about entering into higher states of consciousness is so important. As Mariana explained, the world you create around you mirrors your inner states of consciousness. Rose, this may also give you another perspective about the role and purpose of the seven Cosmic Architect Tools I've shared with you this past month. Each of these are Tools of consciousness for developing, attuning, aligning, refining, and manifesting your Cosmic powers and awareness. Mariana, you seem hopeful about the future despite our worsening global crisis and the lack of moral leadership and ethical businesses. What is the source of your hope?"

"I am hopeful because I know that the next 'miracle' is coming," Mariana answers with tears in her eyes. "When Carl Jung was asked whether he believes in God or not, he said, 'I don't have to believe, I know.' Like Jung, who did not believe in a personal God either, I have scientific evidence to prove how the miracle of human consciousness produced the most astounding progress in all areas of life, from modern medicine to the space shuttle. This gives me the certainty that consciousness will survive, but we must act now to ensure the safety of planetary boundaries, without which, our species cannot exist. So, the fact that we still exist shows me that the next evolutionary step in consciousness is emerging. We can do it. I know this in my heart."

"That's so profound," Rose blurts out. "'If we're not meant to go the next step, we wouldn't exist.' That's what I realized when I was dying in the hospital last year—that my future life is born from that next step, and that I can access this next step now already. Thank you so much."

"Thank you," Mariana smiles warmly. "I'm just mirroring you, my dear friends. Thank you, and many blessings to you."

"Hazel, is there anything else you'd like to add?" Verdandi asks lovingly.

"Yes," Hazel says. "The planet is teaching us directly and says, 'Okay, kids, no more time; this is graduation time. And you're going to have to expand your consciousness now to understand the actual, real circumstances of your survival on this planet from our mother star, the sun, who provides us with all those free photons every day. We have to go back and learn from the plant kingdom, which discovered our first technology on this planet, called photosynthesis. Plants take the photons in their leaves and turn them into carbohydrates, which is the basis of our food supply, and all of our worlds, and everything we need for happy lives. At the moment it's all about incentivizing behavior with money, and *that* game is over. How do you go back to incentivizing the golden rule? We can do it. But you have to change the algorithms."

"You sound a great deal like Rose, my friend," Verdandi tells Hazel with a laugh.

"Yes, yes!" Rose exclaims. "And that's what Li and I are going to do, right, Li? Change the algorithms of the game." She's so happy to discover more future humans.

Li nods his head in full agreement. Rose continues, "Li is flying to Hong Kong to meet his parents next week, and I'll be joining him the following week. We're going to propose a plan to financial investors for a very different way of playing the game of life on planet Earth. We've called it the Future Humans Quest, played through the Cosmic Compass game, where we play to thrive, and not just to survive. We play to consciously evolve ourselves and our collective consciousness by using the Cosmic powers of consciousness that are already within us. Through the game, people will discover seven Cosmic Architect Tools for accessing, activating, and developing those powers. The Tools form part of our innate Cosmic architecture and…"

"We need to let them go, love," Verdandi interrupts. "They've been very kind to give us over an hour of their time already."

"Ohh…uhm, sure…Of course. Thank you so much, Hazel and Mariana, I can't wait to talk to you again. I'm so grateful for this conversation."

"You're most welcome, my dear." Hazel smiles while looking at the shining faces of her new, young friends. "Rose, your grandmother shared with me a piece of your writing about five new archetypes you came up with. I just want you to know that I love them all, and can see myself in each one of those five future archetypes. They're wonderful."

"Really? That makes me so happy to know that! Yes, they're the Wholeness Coder, Future Creative, Evolutionary Catalyst, Pattern Weaver, and New Paradigm Storyteller. It is from those archetype patterns that I've been developing all these wild, new ideas. I believe they also represent the archetypal structure of the next step that Mariana spoke of earlier. That's what I know in *my* heart."

"Thank you very much, dear Hazel and Mariana. It's been delightful and most enlightening to speak with you both," Verdandi says in closing.

They complete their call with more happy smiles and the promise to connect again soon. Li feels strengthened and assured from this conversation that the time is ripe for what he feels most passionate about: new, regenerative economics and ethical finance. He's glad that Rose initiated many of the questions since he felt shy expressing his thoughts with those impressive women, and was more interested in listening to what Hazel and Mariana had to say. He feels that a whole new chapter of his life is about to begin with his upcoming trip to Hong Kong, and he's grateful that Rose is at the center of it all. He can't imagine a life and future without her; they complement and motivate each other so well. Their long friendship has strong roots.

He thanks Rose and Verdandi for including him in the call, and says goodnight, his mind loaded with exciting ideas for his future.

Before going to bed, Verdandi calls her granddaughter to come and sit next to her on the couch. "My sweet girl, do you still have energy for the practice I promised you?"

"Yes, I do. Anytime. But how about you? Is it too late for you?"

"No, it's fine," Verdandi smiles. "This will be the perfect time to do this practice so you can integrate it during your sleep. It will also help you to integrate the powerful conversation we just had. Make yourself comfortable and close your eyes."

Practice with the Cosmic Mirror

"Take a deep breath in and out, and relax…Now relax some more. Bring your awareness here and now, relaxing into yourself and the beautiful consciousness you are. Trust in your consciousness; it's wise and infinite, and knows who you are. The Cosmos is the inner architecture, the subtle orders of wholeness, of your life and consciousness. This architecture enables powers and capacities for you to thrive in partnership with life. The Cosmos is the universal intelligence and timeless wisdom that you can call upon, like a trusted friend, whenever you require its support. The Cosmos is also like the Great Architect of the Universe, who can show and teach you so much about the ways things work.

"Take a moment to honor your direct relationship with the Cosmos and the subtle orders of wholeness within you. Imagine how the Cosmos surrounds you as a universal field that is responsive to your touch and presence; an invisible field which lovingly surrounds you like a blanket of love. You can even reach out to this field by lifting and extending your arms and touching it with your hands, your mind, your heart, and your presence. As you do so, feel the streaming of light, energy, and strength flow toward you; empowering you to take on the Avatar tasks in this world through which your own humanity is upgraded to evolve.

"Imagine how the Cosmos hands you a special Architect Tool for gaining further insight into yourself, your life, and your future: the Cosmic Mirror. Open your hands and allow yourself to receive this Cosmic Mirror in a shape and form that is exactly what you need right now. Feel the presence of this Mirror. Position it so you can look directly into it.

"As you look into the Cosmic Mirror you are looking into the reflective power of your Cosmic consciousness. This Cosmic Mirror can vastly expand your awareness of yourself beyond your personal mind. Ask the mirror to show you whatever it is that you need to be aware of for your inner development. Feel how this expands, deepens, and refines your awareness of yourself, your life, and the realities and worlds of which you are a part.

"You can also ask the Cosmic Mirror to show you hidden or dormant powers, talents, and abilities that you didn't even know you had, and yet can support you greatly. There may be forgotten dreams and possibilities, which can also further your path.

"The Cosmic Mirror can also be set to different modes of time: past, present, and future. Intend for the Cosmic Mirror to enter into future mode. Ask it to reveal to you the possibilities of your future human potentials. Allow yourself to become aware of these possible futures of higher orders of reality. Explore this for a few moments...

"The Cosmic Mirror can also help you to become more aware of humanity's future potentials. Intend now for the Cosmic Mirror to reveal to you who we as a species can become, and the world we can co-create if we answer the call of our future becoming of this emerging new era. Receive this information, and become aware of what you need to act upon to more effectively support this future world that works for all.

"Now imagine yourself walking in the blossoming, abundant field of life in this future world. In this world the children are happy and thriving; the elders are cared for and honored for their lifetime contributions. In this world humanity behaves as a wise and caring partner with all of life, with cultures rooted in compassion and acting as responsible future ancestors. It is a world with cities, villages, and communities that bio mimic the incredible intelligence and wisdom of nature. It is a thriving home for all; a world in which our societal systems and technologies honor and work with the life-giving capacities of our Earth to regenerate the multiple dimensions of life we share.

"Experience how our societies have become fertile gardens of abundance that are overflowing with art, song, music, dance, and joy. It is a world with healthy air, drinkable rivers, and oceans that teem with life. The cities and habitats mimic the living Cosmic architecture of nature. Buildings and bio digital materials and objects are now designed to be biodegradable—restoring the biodiversity of our planet and serving as collaborative ecological niches for cohabitation with other species. The buildings and houses in which we live serve as living solar cells that harvest the abundant energy of our sun, and all of our societies are designed to operate as a continual lifecycle in partnership with nature, and without waste.

"This is a world where animals are no longer slaughtered for food production. Humanity grows and shares its food in regenerative and compassionate ways. Each person is living the exquisite genius of their personal and collective potentials. Human beings have become the future humans of a whole new era in consciousness as Cosmic architects of a thrivable world that works for all. Animals, insects, forests, rivers, oceans, soils, skies, and Nature herself are celebrated and safe. It is a world formed through collaborative and inclusive agreements based on living constitutions and covenants that enact and steward the eternal bonds of our unity. Life's abundance is fairly distributed.

"This is a world that you helped to form as its future ancestor, as a Cosmic architect and evolutionary catalyst born from the future potentials that you brought to life. Take your time to enjoy and explore this possible world with all of its marvelous qualities, features, and ways…

"When you feel ready, you may gently complete this process, being fully present, here and now. Open your eyes and move your body. Allow the integration of this future world to happen naturally within your future becoming, and through the actualization of your future human potentials."

Reclaiming the Access Points of the Giants

The following morning Rose wakes up to the smell of freshly baked bread. She's had the most amazing night, filled with vivid thoughts of the new world. Meanwhile, Verdandi has been up for several hours already, baking bread and preparing everything for their lunch and ceremony with Li and Sophia. This is her last Sunday here with Rose. She feels happy and relieved with the turnout of events, even though she knows that her granddaughter still has a lot to learn and realize about herself. Tomorrow she'll fly to Norway to visit her sister Anna to further support her in her recovery from the attack on her life.

Rose shuffles into the kitchen in her pajamas. She rubs her eyes and unties her Viking curls. Verdandi laughs. "What happened to you, my girl? You look like one of those cartoons where the character gets electrified."

"I feel like it too. I just couldn't stop my mind after that incredible conversation we had last night, and then the practice with the Cosmic Mirror. I can see why Hazel and Mariana are your friends; they're so cool. I have a million more questions for them. Remember what Hazel said about money simply being information that we happen to believe in? Like a kind of social protocol? Imagine creating money algorithms as the information of the Cosmic architecture of life. I mean, that creates a totally different world. It would also take care of the ethical AI and algorithms that Mariana spoke of. The key is in understanding the Cosmic architecture of life. Nature already knows this, as it's constantly trading, exchanging, and collaborating for resources, and coming up with the most inventive strategies for thriving together."

"Oh dear, you don't want to have your breakfast first? I see your mind hasn't stopped at all!" Verdandi chuckles.

"I'd love some breakfast. Thanks, Grandma. Your bread is making my mouth water."

"It's almost ready to come out of the oven."

"I wish you didn't have to go. I understand that you have to, though. You're right about my mind this morning. It's full of ideas. We could create new constitutions and new covenants for the new social protocols for a world that works for all. Covenants where nature has a voice by design. And we can explicitly, and by those new agreements, express how much we value life and want all beings to thrive together with Gaia. We can even digitalize those agreements on blockchain, or in other ways we haven't even thought of yet. I just feel it all coming together. You know, I sincerely believe that our lack of understanding of the Cosmic architecture of life is driving the present scarcity mindset of greed and harmful competition. And those ridiculous sacrificial blood contracts."

"Blood contracts?"

"Yes, you know. Those social protocols that people formed long ago as the first forms of trading, believing it was necessary to sacrifice lives and spill blood in order to receive the benevolence of gods, goddesses, and deities."

"Ah, yes…" Verdandi grabs two potholders and moves to the oven to remove the bread she baked.

Rose rattles on, "Our current economic and financial systems are built on slave money and blood sacrifices. Many people still believe in the old mantra—no pain, no gain."

"Love, you do realize it's only eight o'clock in the morning? Don't forget to put the marmalade on the tray."

"I am in timeless consciousness," Rose says cheekily.

"Yes, it shows. So much so that you don't even allow me any time to catch my breath between your waterfall of thoughts."

"But, Grandma, don't you think it's bizarre that we've created a world with so much poverty when the nature of reality is so rich and abundant? Perhaps therein lies the most essential key to understanding how to resolve our world crisis. Think about it. The information of the Cosmic hologram constantly transforms, converges, cycles, and flows through the web of life. The implicate orders of the Universe are also the subtle orders of our mind, which forms the basis for our individuated self aware consciousness. The Universe truly is a sentient being, a Cosmic giant, within which other giants came to be. And some of those giants need a serious upgrade."

"Goodness, you really are on fire. No wonder you couldn't sleep."

"But that's it, Grandma! Olaf was right. We need to use the Cosmic Mirror to shield ourselves from the influence of the collective giants who are not with the future programs, and then hack their access points to us."

"That sounds somewhat violent, love. Are you sure?"

"Yes, I'm sure."

"Would you mind getting our tea and bringing it with you to the living room?"

Rose sets the tea tray onto the table in the living room and sits down on the couch. "We have all the keys and tools we need," she continues, "and if we don't do it, many will die and suffer. Knowing we can prevent all this suffering, don't you think we have a moral obligation to hack the operating systems that cause so much harm, including those that exist in the mental planes?"

"You want to become a hacker now?" Verdandi laughs.

"Well, yes. An ethical hacker. Did you know that you can actually get a university degree to become a certified ethical hacker? How about that! I can see why Mariana loves technology. She understands how technology can be made to express higher levels of consciousness, and how this can accelerate the collective realization of our higher consciousness potentials."

"And how do you plan on hacking these operating systems?" Verdandi asks somewhat hesitantly, knowing that this may open the door for yet another hour of talking.

"Remember that conversation we had with Li a few weeks ago? About the puppet masters who design algorithms to get us hooked and addicted to keep using their social media tools and platforms? When we're trapped in addiction, we don't have full access to our powers. If anything, addiction bootstraps the power of our consciousness against us, like the way a virus uses the intelligence of our body against us. If we can somehow hack those harmful programs by seeding life-based ethical algorithms in our technologies, we can bootstrap collective consciousness to awaken much faster. You said a little while back that evil and shadow are like a reversed kind of intelligence. So, let's use our intelligence to reverse what's reversed. That's what hackers do. They're natural Wholeness Coders and Future Creatives."

"Okay, go on then, as you're in an unstoppable flow." Verdandi hands Rose a thick slice of the freshly baked bread slathered with marmalade.

"Ohh, this is so delicious. I love it when the bread is still warm. I haven't had your homemade bread for such a long time. I wish you had time to bake some more before you go."

"Already done, love."

"You're the best." Rose enjoys her breakfast for a moment before continuing. "I believe that the first step in hacking a system is to scan and collect as much information as possible to know the strengths and weaknesses of the system, and how and where you can gain entrance into it. After that, it's about getting and maintaining access by installing backdoors for maintaining future access, after which, hackers usually clear their tracks. If they're ethical hackers, they may create a report that reveals the weaknesses and vulnerabilities of the system."

"You know a frightening lot about hacking. Where did you come up with all of this?" Verdandi asks.

"Let's just say I've been studying how we can upgrade those harmful operating systems for a while now, knowing that the puppet masters won't let people like me into their game. I'm not a computer scientist or technologist, so my hack will need to be at a different level. I believe that my own rebirth is a future hack, and a very smart *backdoor* through which the Cosmos sent me back with codes and information that would otherwise not have entered humanity's collective consciousness for many more decades."

"Okay, now I understand your fascination." Verdandi gently squeezes her hand.

"I'm like one of those imaginal cells of the operating systems of the new era. What many people don't know is that the imaginal space of our own consciousness is the 'free zone' where algorithmic programs, including AI, break down. That's our free, inner space, which is why it's so important that children are encouraged to dream and trust their imaginal powers. Sadly, it's precisely this inner space and our imaginal powers that people have lost touch with because their minds are so caught up in the madness of the modern world. That's why I believe it's urgent to hack the access points and unplug ourselves from the operating systems of the degraded giants. We must regain the inner bridge to the collective unconscious, just like you showed me how to do with the Key of Darkness last year."

"I'm glad you remember that training," Verdandi smiles. "Go on, darling."

"Through the imaginal realm of consciousness, we can upgrade the dreams of the giants and evolve our own versions of the game, but this requires that we learn how to enter our future human potential consciously. Once we start doing this strategically and together, we can vastly accelerate the evolutionary development of our species. This imaginal state is also the unmanifest future state of our consciousness, which, as you may recall, is also the nonlocal superposition state of information that I told you about before."

"Yes, I remember."

"In short, our future potential is our *free* access into the operating systems of the giants who have hijacked our access to the vast resources of the collective unconscious. Once we regain our access from deep inside—by not buying into the patterns, behaviors, projections, and games of the degraded giants and puppet masters—we can activate the upgrade codes for evolving how we as humans *choose* to play the game of life on planet Earth. Once we learn how to localize, manifest, and embody the future codings of our future human potential, we become the new operating systems for the new era. And here's something else that many people do not realize: our future human potential is our immunization from the lower consciousness programs that are still influencing human consciousness. The butterfly is the future of the caterpillar. When the caterpillar weakens from its overconsumption, viruses start to catalyze the death of its system. This simultaneously activates the butterfly codes, which are not harmed by these viruses. The butterfly consciousness, which is the future coding of the caterpillar, then starts to create the operating systems that become the new butterfly body. The caterpillar body and the viral codes all become part of the butterfly body, decomposed and repurposed by the manifest future consciousness. Nature gives us all the clues we need for a perfect future hack."

"Does this mean that you use the future to hack the codes and programs of the present?"

"Yes! And since we are nature too, we can use our future consciousness to direct viruses and other intelligences in service of our metamorphic transformation. Namely, by directing those to break down the systems that are not or are no longer in service of life. Viruses catalyze the metamorphosis of the caterpillar during its cocooning phase. Our future intelligence is immune from being hacked by the viral programs of the degraded sleeping giants, just like the imaginal cells of the butterfly codes are immune from being harmed by the viruses that are decomposing the caterpillar body and its systems."

"I'm not sure if you realize this," Verdandi smiles, "but you're fully in the flow of the Cosmic Mirror. Keep going, love."

"Thanks, Grandma," Rose grins. "Olaf said that the Cosmic Mirror, in its future mode, showed him how he was making clay figures of the evolved future giants, rather than monsters and harmful giants. What if the Cosmic Mirror can reflect to us the higher order intelligence of our future consciousness, so we can access and incorporate this now? Remember how Mariana mentioned that AI programs require huge amounts of data? How about feeding the operating systems of humanity the information of our more evolved future consciousness by using our future consciousness as a Cosmic Mirror? That way the information and data of the future world of the new era can be directed *to* the collective consciousness of our current world in trouble. All this requires is that we access and align our inner Cosmic Mirror, set it to future mode, and then intend for it to feed our minds with the data of our more evolved future consciousness. That's it! Wow, this Cosmic Mirror is really one of the most powerful Architect Tools, and it completes all the other Tools you've given me."

Verdandi leans back in her chair and sighs deeply. "That's clever. Why don't you tell Mariana about your idea for how to create these future hacks? I'm sure she'd love to hear more about this. You could even explore together how to mimic this future hack technologically to bootstrap collective consciousness to the future of this next step that you both know so fundamentally as the purpose of your existence."

"I'll do that. I'd love to explore this with Sophia, too. I think she'd find it interesting since these future hacks may also offer important keys for how to reverse aging and heal our bodies. Our future consciousness enables our internal systems to experience the more subtle and unified orders of consciousness that are Cosmically coherent, and fundamental to our health and wellbeing. During my near-death experience I entered into the deepest imaginal state of my future potential. I became the imaginal cell of my future human self. I have a sense that our immune system works best when it can also function as an imaginal system, and not just a defense system. Perhaps cancers are actually caused by viral codes of information that we're not able to integrate in our body-mind system, which then create random leftover pieces of codes that start to create a life of their own. Like a genetic malfunction of the body at the immune level of learning."

Verdandi agrees, "Sadly, many humans have also become like a cancer to nature, which is also why we create this enormous amount of waste from our degraded mental programs. Look around and see what we've been doing to our world—discarding and dumping whatever we're not able to integrate into our households, economies, or lives. We dispose of it 'elsewhere,' not realizing how this 'elsewhere' is still part of the same nature that we all breathe and live in. Do you remember that quote from environmental activist, Julia Butterfly Hill? 'When you throw something away, where is 'away?'"

"That's a powerful image, Grandma. Let's continue our exploration when Sophia arrives. I'm sure she'll have a lot more to say about this, which reminds me, I'd better take a quick shower."

"Please do, my darling, and then tidy the living room and help me prepare the altar with your architect tools and pouches."

"I'm so excited. We'll all get to have our own little miniature tools."

"Go take a shower and relax your mind!" Verdandi urges, "I need some silence as well."

Future Hacks for Creating Subconscious Programs of Health

Sophia has been preparing herself quietly for today's ceremony by going for an early walk in nature and connecting with her ancestors. Her parents taught her from an early age what it means to become a custodian of the powers entrusted to us, and how this comes with responsibility for the wellbeing of all life. In her Australian Aboriginal tradition, they refer to this as "Kanyini," which means taking responsibility through unconditional love and enormous caring for all of creation. Sophia lives this relational understanding of Kanyini through her commitment of becoming a medical doctor. She wants to be a doctor of health and wellness, supporting personal, collective, and planetary healing through the enormous and timeless caring capacities of life. She understands deeply that the health and wellbeing of Mother Earth is the foundation for our human health and happiness.

Rose arranged for Sophia to arrive before Li so she could brief her first about her farewell meeting with Diego. Verdandi understands that it's best to give the young women their space so they can have their sister talk before Li joins them. It also provides her with the opportunity to continue packing her suitcase. After some time, Rose calls her grandmother to join their conversation.

"Auntie Verdandi, Rose told me all about the fabulous afternoon you both had with Diego. I hope to meet this interesting man next time he's in town!" Sophia says.

Verdandi smiles. "Who knows when that will be? But right now, let's make sure that our butterfly girl is putting her mind on this upcoming trip with Li. An opportunity like that doesn't come around often. I trust she can count on you, Sophia, to keep her focused on what her priorities are?"

"I'll do my best," Sophia grins, "but you know all too well that Rose can be as stubborn as a goat."

"Oh, you two!" Rose protests with a big smile. "Grandma, I called you in so we could finish the conversation we had earlier about the future hacks. I just explained it to Sophia and she's very interested in applying this future hack to curing illnesses. I was telling her how our immune systems are super learning systems, and that perhaps the hidden power of our immune system is our imaginal power."

Sophia says, "There's some fascinating research from the field of epigenetics, which is at the forefront of modern medicine right now. The research looks at the factors that influence gene activity that is not related to a person's DNA sequence. What this research reveals is how our epigenome responds to how we live our life, including how we interact, what we eat, what we believe, and what we think. This matters because epigenetic changes can influence which proteins are transcribed in our body. Our genes are not deterministic at all, and this imaginal capacity that you're both talking about may also be operative at the level of our epigenome functions."

"It sounds like this research could possibly reveal the biology of our subconscious beliefs and lifestyle habits," Verdandi replies.

"I believe it could. Rose, do you remember that time when your dad put us both in a light hypnotic trance and our eyes stayed closed, even when we wanted to open them? Your dad explained afterward how the invisible power we experienced during hypnosis, in this case to keep our eyelids closed, is not the power of the hypnotist, but the power of our own mind. Your dad said that hypnosis uses suggestions at the level of our subconscious, and it is by the power of our own subconscious mind that the suggestions become empowered."

"I remember that," Rose grins. "He said, 'Your eyelids are getting heavier and heavier. So heavy that even if you try, you cannot open your eyes. You may also experience a beautiful smile on your face.' My eyelids felt so heavy. I wanted to open them, but couldn't. If my mind can have that kind of physical effect on my body, imagine using the subconscious power of suggestion to heal ourselves and our world!"

Sophia laughs. "You should try that technique when you meet with Li's father and his investors. 'Your eyelids are getting heavier and heavier! You now recognize that by funding the Future Humans Quest game, you'll achieve the true purpose that money is supposed to serve. And you and your companies can play the leading role in resolving our world crisis!'"

"Great idea," Rose chuckles. "Maybe I can add something like 'Your mind is now free from the control and influence of egoic programs and shadow games. Your local mind now naturally resets to Cosmic mind. You now recognize the fundamental unity of life, your own autonomy within the universal mind, and your true evolutionary role and purpose for evolving how the game of life is played on planet Earth. You are now able to directly access the powers by which you can evolve yourself and our world to bring forth the promised era of enlightenment.' I'd prefer that kind of subconscious suggestion to flow through all of the corporate offices around the world and the metaworld of the new virtual reality designers. I'm not interested in manipulating people's minds to get them hooked on another program. I'd much prefer to show people the access points of their own minds, and how to regain autonomy and authentic, unscripted self awareness within the universal mind."

"That's why I love you, my sister," Sophia smiles. "Your whole focus is always on liberating people out of the matrix and not on creating another matrix to get people hooked. I know that this is the sole focus of the game you've been developing with your nephew. But whether you like it or not, it's good to realize how humans mostly operate from subconscious programs. Perhaps one step toward the liberation you seek is to create better and more enlightening subconscious programs and suggestions. Your future hack might be the way to finally get through the backdoor so we can shift the destructive and egocentric operating systems of our collective consciousness."

"Excuse me, ladies," Verdandi interjects, "But I'd like to shift the topic now. I know that you two can keep going like this for hours. Sophia, have you had a chance to talk to Sam since we last met? I spoke to his mother the other day, and she mentioned that the healing we performed a few days ago has been helping him sleep much better. I wonder if you have any further details for us?"

"I do. Thanks for reminding me, Auntie. I spoke with him yesterday. He told me he had an unusual dream on Thursday. He explained how the dream started out as one of his usual nightmares that involve getting chased by monsters and being beaten up. But this time, just before the monsters closed in on him, he discovered how he could protect himself. He said, 'As the monsters came closer, I felt a strength well up inside me and all around me. I realized that the monsters can't control me, and that I could change the dream. I turned around to face them, and then did what Rose did: I pushed them back with this invisible force field that I somehow had access to. Like in one of the games I play on my computer, but much better. And it worked! The monsters started to disintegrate in front of my eyes. Then I saw a path open up in front of me where I could walk safely. In the distance was a place in my dreams I've wanted to visit for a long time, but I never managed to arrive there because I always got chased. Now for the first time, the path was clear for me to get there. When I woke up, I felt like I could finally relax. My appetite returned as well.'"

"That's just great," Rose says. "It sounds like the session we did is working. Thanks, Grandma, for all you've been doing for Sam. I'm so glad he's discovering his inner shield."

"That's a very good development," Verdandi adds. "He's on the right track. Let's all keep supporting him for a little while longer until he can internalize this newfound inner strength. And, Rose, please suggest to his parents that he learns some form of martial arts for self-defense."

"I thought that same thing, Grandma. I've already sent his mother a brochure for classes in their area," Rose tells her. She hears a knock at the door. "That must be Li. Just in time." Rose jumps up from the couch and rushes to open the door for their friend, who carefully shakes the rain from his coat before entering the apartment.

Verdandi walks toward him with outstretched arms. "Welcome back, Li. How did you sleep last night after our call with Hazel and Mariana?"

Before he has a chance to answer, Rose interrupts, "I couldn't sleep at all. I was so fired up I couldn't stop thinking about all the things we can and must do."

"Darling, let him answer, please," Verdandi replies.

"I slept well, thanks for asking, Auntie," Li says politely. "I had a long, relaxing meditation before going to bed to prepare myself for our ceremony with you today. My grandfather always reminded me how important it is to embrace the unknown with a quiet mind."

"You're a good influence on Rose," Verdandi chuckles. "See what you can do to quiet her mind; she's been a non-stop chatterbox all morning."

"I'm not sure my methods work on her." Li winks at Rose.

"I know what works well," Sophia pipes up. "Rose, why don't you play your violin for us?"

"Good idea. I've been practicing a new piece called 'Méditation' from the opera *Thaïs* by the French composer Jules Massenet. It's so beautiful. I'll be right back with my violin."

"Okay, love, while you're doing that, let me get our guests something to drink. Li, Sophia, would you like homemade iced tea? Juice? Or something else?"

The two friends both choose iced tea and Verdandi sets off for the kitchen to get their beverages. Rose returns to the living room and begins to tune her violin. After a few minutes she declares her readiness and begins to play "Méditation." The room fills with a heavenly melody that transports them all on a timeless wave of enchantment. Outside, the sun breaks through the heavy clouds, and the cawing of a nearby crow reminds Rose that her beloved Diego is always near in her heart.

"That was so beautiful, Rose," Sophia says with tears in her eyes. "You play with a very different emotional intensity now. Much different than before."

Li adds, "You're very talented. I wish I could play an instrument like that. Thanks for playing for us. How do you feel now?"

"Calmer," Rose says. "More peaceful and centered. Music is my medicine." She pauses. "Hey, is anybody else hungry? I am seriously hungry. Grandma, shall we have lunch?"

Creating the Avatar Medicine Pouches

Verdandi laughs as they gather around the dining table to enjoy a delightful lunch with freshly baked bread and a gorgeous beetroot salad with toasted walnuts and chevre. After they finish their lunch and clear the table, Verdandi shows them the Avatar pouches she's been sewing for them. Sophia and Li beam with anticipation. They're excited about having their own Avatar pouches and embarking on this apprenticeship for learning the ways of the Cosmic Architect Tools: the Ring of Unity, Infinity Hourglass, Cosmic Compass, Fire Stones of Darkness and Light, Cosmic Navel Cord, Singing Chalice, and the Cosmic Mirror.

Rose is thrilled that Verdandi accepted her idea of making these new pouches and architect tools that can pass on the transmissions of the mother pouch and the original tools. Now people like Sophia and Li, and many others too, can also learn how to further actualize and develop their future human powers with the help of the Cosmic Architect Tools. Her grandmother agreed to take the original mother pouch and ring of unity and the other tools back home with her to Iceland because Rose has received all of the transmissions from the seven tools and knows now how to connect directly with the Cosmic Architect Tools.

They had a lot of fun gathering and creating these new miniature tools, especially while scouting for the three compasses. When Rose asked if these new tools have to look exactly the same as the original ones, Verdandi answered, "That won't be necessary, love. As long as they carry the transmissions of the original tools, that's all that's required. Even a shell can be made to carry the connection with the archetypal Singing Chalice once it's been ceremonially prepared for this purpose. What matters is the intention and the energetic connection with the realms beyond this physical world so we may finally regain our Avatar consciousness. The whole avatar concept is about understanding how our inner Cosmic architecture acts as an interface—an avatar—for the higher dimensional realities that humans have grown more and more disconnected from."

Verdandi has hand-sewn each of their pouches with the fabrics that the trio selected and brought to her for this purpose. Li wanted his Avatar pouch to be made from a dark purple satin cloth that has a white dragon embroidered onto it. Sophia chose a handmade cloth from her home country that has an Aboriginal dot painting of the Rainbow Serpent on it. And Rose chose a dark blue velvet cloth, which she received from her grandmother many years ago, with a golden Grail Cup and a blue rose embroidered on it.

"Thank you, Auntie," Sophia says. "I really love how you've made these pouches from the materials we gave you. They look beautiful."

"You're welcome, dear. Now to complete your pouch with your own creative touch, please select a cord from this bundle." Verdandi places the colorful cords on the table. "Rose will show you how to do this last step. The idea is to weave the cord through the rim of your pouch so it can tighten and close. Then when you've finished with that, please select three cords from the other bundle over there, which is for making your own Cosmic navel cord. I'll show you how to weave it together."

"Auntie Verdandi? What exactly does the pouch do?" Li wonders. "It's more than just a bag for our tools, right?"

"Yes, dear. When the architect tools are placed inside the pouch this will shield them from the grosser energies of the outer worlds and keep them safe from any harmful or intrusive dynamics. The pouch also harmonizes and revitalizes the powers and energies of the architect tools, when required."

Sophia and Li smile happily. Their hearts feel full and grateful. While the young friends get into their tasks, Verdandi continues with the preparations for their ceremony. Rose received her initiation with the mother pouch and the ring of unity over a month ago, which activated the transmissions of the Cosmic Architect Tools. Rose's training is somewhat unique because of the ways her deeper powers have been rapidly developing and awakening ever since her near-death experience. In many ways, the Cosmos is initiating Rose directly. The Avatar seeds of consciousness are already active within her. She has been spontaneously entering into profound states of Cosmic consciousness for over a year now. This has also catalyzed her creativity. She's received many startling new insights about the nature of reality and the Cosmic architecture of life.

Verdandi is very conscious of the unique path that her granddaughter is on, which is why her primary focus has been on ways she can best support Rose to integrate all that's been happening. The higher orders of Cosmic realities are always present, yet for most people, their minds filter and block out the reception from those higher orders of consciousness. In Rose's mind, many of the veils and filters have fallen away, as she experiences more and more the reality from her Cosmic mind that knows how to interface between the multi-worlds.

"Auntie, I'm sorry to interrupt you again, but may I ask one more thing?" Li looks at her while trying to push the cord through the rim of his pouch.

"Go ahead," Verdandi smiles.

"I've been reading about mystery schools and the indigenous and Gnostic traditions of initiations in Europe. Many of those systems are very elaborate, and secretive, too. It seems like the system that you're introducing us to is slightly different though. I'm sure it has similar roots, but you're not as secretive about it all, and there's more recognition of the spontaneous ways in which people are now awakening. Am I right?"

"Yes, you are, Li. That's very perceptive of you. Rose's journey has shown me that the ways in which the future humans are to be initiated into these higher orders of consciousness should not be the same as the systems of the ancient mystery schools. Even though I'm an initiate in several of those traditions and hold them all in high regard. The future consciousness of the new era is coming in coded differently. It already contains within it the understanding of the next four Yugas, or major Cosmic cycles. We need to meet consciousness where it's at and not force it through another loop of the old evolutionary pathways. Many future humans who are born now —people like you, Sophia, Rose, and many others—require a new and different approach. What you all have in common is that you naturally have a far more expanded understanding of the nature of reality. Your nervous systems are more easily wired to enter into and integrate these higher consciousness states."

"I appreciate how you have this deep respect for tradition, and at the same time you're not dogmatic," Li tells her. "You really are in touch with the changing times, and you encourage the spiritual traditions to continue evolving. I wish you could explain this to my parents. It would sure make my talk with them a lot easier."

"You can do this, Li. You're more ready and prepared than you realize, and they may be more receptive to you than you think they'll be. Bridging work such as this is part of the role of the future humans for this transition time. The architect tools from the Avatar pouch have been part of my family for a very long time. Traditionally, we've never shared them with anyone outside of the inner circle of initiates. But the seers in our own tradition also spoke of the time of the return of the Avatars. We each knew that this would be the time that humanity had to be trained again in the workings of the Cosmic Architect Tools. We've been waiting for this time when humanity would be ready to regain its direct connection with our Avatar consciousness. Our seers also spoke of this as the time when humanity is awakening from the influence of the giants of domination, and how some of this may lead to new waves of violence and conflict."

Sophia chimes in, "It's interesting how people are already drawn to the avatar concept in science fiction movies, gaming, and now this whole new social media metaverse and the new digital technologies. It's like we've been unconsciously tapping into this for quite some time."

"That's often how it happens," Verdandi answers. "The creatives and inventors are usually the ones who stand at the edge of new waves. The paradigm shifts often become visible through them."

"Yes," Rose adds. "They are the Future Creatives and New Paradigm Storytellers of the future archetypes."

"Now to come back to your question, Li..." Verdandi looks tenderly at Rose. "My wonderful granddaughter over here has given me a truly precious understanding about the spiritual development of the future humans. In many ways, Rose is also initiating me in my next role. We're always learning from each other and growing each other into our future becoming. I've worked with the Cosmic Keys and Cosmic Architect Tools for a long, long time, but the way they've come alive in Rose is quite unique. She's provided me with whole new insights. I'm hoping that this new emerging system will also help you and Sophia, and many others."

"Does that mean we're the first people to receive our own Avatar pouches and architect tools?" Sophia asks.

"You're the first ones to receive these in a way that will now become energetically linked to our Avatar pouch and architect tools, which carry the blessings and transmissions of our long line of druids, seers, magi, wizards, and alchemists. And not just from our human traditions, but from the multi-worlds as well."

"I hadn't considered all of that," Rose says. "Thanks for sharing that, Grandma. I'm starting to understand now why you came. It wasn't just for me; it was for Sophia and Li as well, and the rest of the world. The Avatar portal that opened is so much more than only our entrance into higher orders of reality. It also represents the convergence you just spoke of. Will you give me another initiation today, too?"

Verdandi chuckles. "Don't you worry. You won't be missing out on anything. As we talked about, you already received your initiation with the Avatar mother pouch, as well as the transmissions of the Cosmic Architect Tools. Yes, I will share with you a transmission of the Grail codes of the higher heart through the Singing Chalice."

"Thank you, Grandma." Rose smiles.

Verdandi continues, "Sophia and Li, let's begin with your apprentice initiation, which includes the transmission from the Avatar mother pouch and the ring of unity. Then later, when you feel ready for it, you can ask me for the other transmissions."

"Thanks very much, Auntie," Sophia answers. Li nods his head in agreement.

"You're welcome. Have you all finished weaving your Cosmic navel cords? We need to get started on the ceremony for your initiations soon."

"Like this?" Li answers while showing her his cord.

"Yes, splendid. Please give me those together with your pouches so I can ready them on the altar. Spend some moments in silence now to prepare yourself. No more talking!" Verdandi looks sternly at her granddaughter while she walks to the altar to place the new pouches inside the Avatar mother pouch.

She quiets her mind, which becomes calm and still as a mirror-like lake that captures the Cosmic reflections from the deep wisdom of the unknowable. She surrenders to unity with the Goddess of High Wisdom, the one who initiates us into the mysteries that live beyond the veil of our ordinary minds; the one in whom God and Goddess are united as One.

She looks at the trio and feels profound love for each of them well up from her heart. She feels humbled and grateful that she can support their growth in this way, and thanks the Goddess for bringing them together. She sighs deeply, and smiles.

The Avatar Apprentice Initiation

Verdandi now surrenders fully into her role as Magus and High Priestess, the one who initiates, awakens, and transmits the Avatar powers from the Cosmic Tree of Life and the eternal temple. She wears the ring of unity on her finger and has become the Cosmic interface through which the Divine Mother herself can initiate the apprentice Avatars into the next stage of their development.

The living room has again been transformed into a ceremonial circle with the design of the Cosmic Compass. There are four concentric circles on the floor with the black round stone in the center, surrounded by leaves, flowers, stones, cords, water, fruits, candles, and other sacred objects on the compass coordinates. Candles flicker and illuminate the four directions. Verdandi has burned her special herbs again to purify the space, which has filled the living room with the most wonderful fragrance.

She calls the trio, one by one, to enter the ceremonial circle from the east, and to seat themselves in the center behind the black stone with their eyes closed, facing north to receive the transmissions from the Cosmic Tree of Life. Verdandi starts chanting her ancient invocation. The Avatar portal of the multi-worlds opens. The consciousness of the Cosmic Avatars streams into the room and becomes the pillars of the eternal temple of higher wisdom.

She invokes the Cosmic powers of the mother pouch with otherworldly sounds and invocations of the sacred language of the Cosmic Tree. She then blows three times over it. The mother pouch acts like a sacred womb for the new pouches that are held within it and transmits the blessings and fertilizing powers of the Divine Mother to the new Avatar pouches. She carefully removes the new pouches from the mother pouch and places in them their own architect tools, which she has already ceremonially prepared to carry the vibrations of the Cosmic Architect Tools.

She moves to the trio and places the pouches with their tools into their cupped hands. She asks that they each declare quietly, and by using their power of intention, their readiness and responsibility for receiving their initiation. The powerful vibrations from their Avatar pouches enter their bodies, which each person experiences in a unique way.

Verdandi proceeds by drawing the master symbol over their crowns after which she blows three times over their heads. She then draws the blessing sign with her fingers in the air and over their bodies. Now that their energy bodies are prepared, she opens their pouches one by one.

She first walks to Li and Sophia and fastens the necklaces with their Avatar rings around their necks, so they fall just over their hearts. They will continue to carry these rings around their necks until the time comes that they are ready to wear their ring around their finger. She says softly to them both, "You now have direct connection with the Cosmic Avatars. May the power of the Ring of Unity carry you home to the eternal garden."

As soon as the ring touches Li's chest, he feels a tremendous wave of energy circulate and vibrate through his body, lifting his entire being to a higher plane of existence. With his eyes still closed, he receives a powerful vision. The Ring of Unity manifests in front of him as a portal of flames. Behind the flames, the Cosmic Dragon manifests as the white dragon of his dream and calls him forth to enter. His heart starts beating faster and becomes incredibly hot. He feels an irresistible pull and connection between his own heart and the heart of this dragon. Finally, he surrenders and moves through the ring of fire and enters the immortal land of the Buddhas and the eternal mountains. The white dragon transforms into a wiseman who introduces himself as one of Li's great, great ancestors. The man and the dragon are one. Li receives a profound understanding about the nature and purpose of his own path and the inner nature of his sacred masculine.

Sophia is also going through a profound initiatory experience. The minute the pouch touches her cupped hands, she enters into deep communion with the Divine Mother. The Ring of Unity becomes the body of the Rainbow Serpent who guides her to enter the Dreaming that sources all of creation. She experiences the love of the Divine Mother and becomes aware of the Great Plan and her own role in it. Tears flow over her cheeks in gratitude and awe. She can feel the love of her ancestors and the wisdom of their bones inside her bones, and how these are all part of the bones of the earth. She experiences the unity of life and the healing power that flows forth from the eternal Bond of Unity.

Rose is now ready for her initiation. Verdandi removes Rose's Avatar ring from her pouch and places this onto her finger. This signals her readiness to learn the next lessons of the Ring of Unity through the wisdom of the higher heart, which is part of the Grail path of her ancestry. She can feel the presence of the Cosmic Dragon's heart pulsating strongly within her heart and recalls the many lessons about power and fire that she has gone through over the last several months. The Cosmic Mirror reveals to her what she needs to become aware of in order to deepen her understanding of these challenging experiences.

Verdandi returns from the altar with the singing chalice, which she has filled with the sacred water that carries the vibrations of the eternal Spring of Life, infused by the Grail codes of the higher heart. These codes are essential for the development of our human powers. When the codes of the higher heart are not awakened, the archetypes of domination and disunity will take over human minds. The Grail quest also represents the alchemical transformation that takes place once these sacred codes start to awaken, which enters us onto the path of love.

Verdandi hands the singing chalice to Rose and gently nudges her to drink the blessed water. As soon as the water enters her body, Rose again experiences the codes of the eternal laws. She understands how these laws cannot be understood merely by our minds, for it is the higher heart that knows the truth of what this means. She surrenders to her initiation and closes her eyes. A vision emerges of the Grail as the Singing Chalice, the emerald stone within the Ring of Unity, the codes of the higher heart, and the Cosmic womb, through which eternity is born into the physical world of space and time. As her vision progresses, the Grail transforms into a blue rose, which opens its petals as a Cosmic portal that calls her forth.

She enters the blue rose and is welcomed by a council of beings who emanate profound wisdom and love. The council calls her to take her place and asks if she is ready to embark on the task of the new covenant—the new agreements of the multi-worlds based on the eternal Bond of Unity. They explain to her how this new codex serves to bring humanity together to reconstitute the human world from the codes of the higher heart in order to co-create a thrivable world that is a planetary home for all who live and visit here—the long-awaited, promised new world. Rose is profoundly touched and commits to the task with her whole being. She knows that this is her destiny and understands the higher purpose that the Cosmic Compass game and the Future Humans Quest serve. She then receives the tuition from the council that prepares her for her next tasks.

Verdandi looks around the room and thanks the Cosmic Avatars for all their support and facilitation. It's time to complete the ceremony. She drums softly with the rhythm of Mother Earth's heartbeat to bring the young ones back to the present time and place. Finally, she speaks. "When you feel ready, you may gently open your eyes and stand up. You may now bow toward the seven directions to give your thanks: east, south, west, north, above, below, and the center, and then leave the circle through the east from where you entered. The initiation is now complete. Welcome home, beloved Avatars."

Look for the Dragonfly

The Cosmic Architect Tools are now awakening within you. Through these Tools you can bring forth and develop your Avatar self as a Cosmic interface for the larger realities that are always enveloping and supporting the human world. We'll meet here again soon in our story of the future humans. Look for the dragonfly, and remember to direct the power of fire through the wisdom of your higher heart…

Integration -
The Cosmic Mirror

Through this final chapter, Rose experiences the multidimensional workings of the Cosmic Mirror for developing Cosmic self awareness and shielding the mind from being overtaken by the archetypes of domination and egoic projections. She first explores this Architect Tool with her nephew, Olaf, when they discover how to create a future hack to regain the access points of the operating systems of our collective consciousness. Rose, Sophia, and Li each receive a profound initiation, as well as their own Avatar pouches and architect tools. Rose also receives an activation of the Grail codes and commits to the task of making new covenants. The trio is now ready to gather the teams and start playing the Future Humans Quest in real-life situations.

> *The Cosmic Mirror supports you to become aware of yourself beyond the realities and filters of your local mind. You can call upon the Cosmic Mirror to shield your mind from the interference patterns and projections of the egoic operating systems and shadow dynamics. You can also work with the Cosmic Mirror to receive the information and guidance from your future consciousness and the future humans world of the emerging new era.*

The summary and questions below will help you to integrate and apply the essential teachings of this chapter:

- As Sophia mentioned, the giants are not just symbolic or collective archetypes. They also manifest as the modern multinational corporations, the political and financial elite, and the world icons and social influencers who are followed by so many people. Work with the Cosmic Mirror to become aware of these influences in your life and relationships, and your own influence in the world.

- The Future Humans Quest is the evolutionary call that is awakening in people all over the world. Through this quest we learn how to evolve and upgrade the way we play the game of life on planet Earth, and how to regain our autonomy through the inner guidance of the higher heart.

- During this transition period of the collective awakening, there is a greater potential for escalation, polarization, and violence, as people may act out deeply seated survival patterns. Many of the old paradigm giants are still trying to maintain their influence and investments, resisting the ending of their worlds and influence.

- Your activated future human potential serves as a future hack—a backdoor entrance—into the operating systems and collective dreams of the egoic giants.

- Olaf learns from his future self to create the upgraded and awakened version of the giants and who he chooses to become. *What future version of yourself and collective consciousness are you sculpting into reality?*

- Hazel Henderson and Mariana Bozesan are real people. You can check out our interview with them via our Future Humans website and the endnotes of this book.[6] Hazel and Mariana have entered the book to prepare Rose and Li for taking on the real-world challenges that are part of the Future Humans Quest.

- Become aware of the mental operating systems that live behind the economic, financial, and political systems, and how money and markets have become the weapons and tools of the giants of domination and their single metric price system in the form of money. As Hazel mentioned, apply the golden rule: "Do as you would be done by," also financially.

- Explore what it means for you that money is a kind of social protocol for deciding what we value. *What value and importance do you attribute to money? What is the role of money in your life?*

- Changing the algorithms of the human operating systems is part of the process of changing the rules of the games and co-creating the new covenants.

- Outer change begins with inner change. As Mariana said, open your heart to become aware of the abundance nature provides and how the world you create around you mirrors your inner states of consciousness.

- We've shared with you the ways and powers of seven Cosmic Architect Tools: the Ring of Unity, Infinity Hourglass, Cosmic Compass, Fire Stones of Darkness and Light, Cosmic Navel Cord, Singing Chalice, and the Cosmic Mirror. These are Tools of consciousness for developing, attuning, aligning, refining, and manifesting your Cosmic powers and awareness. Keep practicing and working with these Tools to learn how to access and direct the powers by which you can evolve yourself and our world.

- Through the Cosmic Mirror practice you'll learn to adjust the reflective capacities of your consciousness in various ways and modes. Explore and discover:

- The areas and qualities of yourself that you are not yet conscious of, which is also where the shadow lives, including latent talents, abilities, and powers.

- Your life from a future perspective of the higher orders of reality that form part of your destiny path and soul purpose, including information that your future self is beaming back at you to support your self-actualization.

- The ways and qualities of the worlds of the emerging new era, and what it means for you to become a future ancestor and evolutionary catalyst of the future humans world, including the information from our future humanity to support the birth of this new world.

- Future humans are like the imaginal cells of the operating systems of the new era; a "free zone" where algorithmic programs, including AI, break down and cease to have influence. Whenever you feel trapped, connect with and call upon your innate "free zone," which is also your imaginal space. Dream yourself free and unplug yourself from the hooks of egoic consciousness and shadow realities.

- The avatar concept is about understanding how your inner Cosmic architecture acts as an interface—an Avatar—for the higher dimensional realities that humans have grown more and more disconnected from. These higher and more subtle orders are always present, yet for many people, the mind filters and blocks out the reception from these higher orders of consciousness. Your Cosmic mind knows how to interface between these subtle orders of the multi-worlds.

- The future consciousness of the new era comes in coded differently and requires a new developmental approach and new systems of initiation, like those that form part of the ceremonies and initiations that we share in the *Future Humans Trilogy*. In the reading of these ceremonies and invitations, you also receive the transmissions from these subtle orders of the emerging new era.

- In *The Quest of Rose*, we shared how the Cosmos is like the Holy Grail of communication, guiding us through the information of immortality. We also shared how Rose is part of the bloodlines that connect to the descendants of Jesus Christ and Mary Magdalene, and the mythological understanding of the Grail.

- In this book we have shared the Grail wisdom through the Singing Chalice, the emerald stone within the Ring of Unity, the codes of the higher heart, and the Cosmic womb through which eternity is born into the physical world of space and time.

- After learning from the Cosmic Dragon how to channel her powers through the higher heart, Rose is now ready to take up the tasks of the Grail codes that relate directly to the co-creation of the new covenants of the Bond of Unity of the multi-worlds. She is now empowered and prepared for the tasks that will lead to the gathering of the future human teams, together with Li, Sophia, Diego, Olaf, Verdandi, Dagaz, and others. You'll be able to join their journey in the third book of the *Future Humans Trilogy*.

- The Grail codes of the higher heart are essential for the development of our human powers, cultures, and systems. These codes also serve as the higher upgrade codes for the collective giants and humanity's evolutionary potentials.

- When those codes are not awakened, the archetypes of domination and egoic operating systems will more easily take over human minds. The return of the Avatars also symbolizes the return of these Grail codes in the human worlds for helping us access and manifest the higher orders of reality of our Avatar selves.

- The Grail quest also represents the alchemical transformation that takes place once these sacred codes start to awaken within us, which enters us onto the path of love.

- Rose discovers how the new codex serves to bring humanity together to reconstitute the human world from the codes of the higher heart. Join her now in the co-creation of this promised new world of the future humans.

- *Return of the Avatars* is a journey into the higher heart, through which you learn the fundamental lessons about power, unity, ego, shadow, hope, courage, and love. New choices and possibilities are now awakening within and through you. We will meet again soon to join the future human teams who are gathering.

ENDNOTES

CHAPTER 6

[1] The Cosmic Compass design has been applied by Anneloes Smitsman for the design and architecture of Part 1 of the SEEDS Constitution for the SEEDS ecosystems and to support and guide the Regenerative Renaissance Movements. Website: https://joinseeds.earth/.

CHAPTER 8

[2] This is based on Smitsman, A. (2019). *Love Letters from Mother Earth: The Promise of a New Beginning.* EARTHwise Publications.

CHAPTER 10

[3] Bohm, D. (1980). *Wholeness and the implicate order.* Routledge. P. xviii.

[4] Arkani-Hamed, N. (2017, December 1). *The Doom of Spacetime - Why It Must Dissolve Into More Fundamental Structures* [Video]. PSW Science. https://bit.ly/2SbsI5Y

[5] Arkani-Hamed, N. (2015). *Nima Arkani-Hamed on the Amplituhedron* (Annual Report 2013–2014). Institute for Advanced Study. https://bit.ly/3u5GfJp

CHAPTER 11

[6] To listen to the recordings of our call with Hazel Henderson and Mariana Bozesan, visit the Future Humans YouTube Channel or The Future Humans Podcast via our website: www.futurehumans.world

GLOSSARY

Archetype—A common pattern of behavior that reveals the deeper systemic structures, templates, or codes for the way things form, grow, develop, and evolve. An archetype can also be a psychic or cultural pattern that animates the behavior of a person or a collective of people.

Avatar—From the Sanskrit word "avatāra," which is a concept in Hinduism that refers to the incarnation of divine qualities that descend into human form. In this book we refer to "Avatar" as a quality of our Cosmic self, which acts as a Cosmic interface between the local and nonlocal realities of consciousness.

Complexity—A nonlinear state of connectivity that emerges from the multiple levels of interdependent connections and relationships. Not to be confused with "complicatedness," which refers to a situation or event that is not easy to understand.

Cosmos—From the Greek word "Kosmos," which means "ordered whole" and is also used to refer to the Universe as an orderly, harmonious living system.

Cosmic Architecture—The innate holographic structures, codes, and archetypes of information that shape and influence the way our physical universe forms, grows, and evolves [*see also Implicate Order, and Information*].

Cosmic Hologram—Based on emerging research in physics which suggests that the Universe is a Cosmic hologram because it is informationally unified at all levels and scales of existence [*see also Implicate Order, Information, and Holographic Principle*].

Evolution—An emergent process of learning and development from the tiniest pixels to the larger realities of stars, planets, and each of us, which unfolds via increasing embodied complexity and deepening evolutionary coherence [*see also Complexity, and Evolutionary Coherence*].

Evolutionary Coherence—A dynamic state of harmonic resonance and spontaneous collaboration between the diverse elements and relationships of complex living systems. A natural state of attunement to the innate wholeness and unity of life [*see also Evolution*].

Fractal—Infinitely complex patterns that repeat in a self-creative and self-replicating manner through all dimensions of life. We can discover fractals in the ways flower petals grow and open as unfolding spirals, as well as in the growth patterns of trees and weather patterns. The Cosmic architecture of life is fractal [*see also Cosmic Architecture, and Cosmic Hologram*].

Holographic Principle—A principle in physics that suggests how the appearance of our physical universe as a three-dimensional space originates from a two-dimensional holographic surface or boundary that is mathematically (informationally) encoded at the smallest level of physical reality [*see also Cosmic hologram*].

Imaginal—A future creative state of consciousness that extends beyond the "imaginative" and connects us with the transformative powers of the Universe in the way we think, perceive, and respond.

Implicate Order—A term coined by physicist David Bohm to explain how the physical Universe is part of an undivided holographic wholeness of consciousness, and emerges from more fundamental implicate orders or structures of reality that precede space-time [*see also Holographic Principle*].

Information—The primary entity from which physical reality is constructed, and also the building blocks of consciousness. Life is informationally unified, which suggests that both energy-matter and space-time are complementary expressions of information.

Nonlocality—A principle of quantum physics which Albert Einstein referred to as "spooky action at a distance." Classical physics suggests that physical reality is local, which means that a measurement at one point in space cannot influence what occurs at another point in space, if the distance between the points is large enough. However, quantum physics predicts that physical reality is essentially nonlocal, which means that under certain conditions, a measurement of one particle will correlate instantaneously with the state of another particle, even if the physical distance between the particles is many light-years away. Nonlocality thus suggests that particles at more fundamental levels of reality are informationally correlated. We also use the concept of nonlocality to refer to unity states of consciousness and our creative partnership with the Universe [*see also Holographic Principle*].

Renaissance—A renaissance is a period of significant rebirth, regeneration, and transformation that is often preceded by periods of collapse and crises.

Superposition State—A quantum realm of potentiality where all possible states simultaneously co-exist prior to being observed.

Thrivability—Our innate ability to develop our capacities and actualize our potentials in ways that are generative, life-affirming, and future creative.

Acknowledgements

W e are tremendously grateful for the enormous support we've been receiving for the *Future Humans Trilogy* since its launch in July 2021. We are humbled and grateful for the role we've somehow been entrusted to play in bringing this wisdom forth—now in the form of this book. We, thus, begin our acknowledgments by thanking Gaia, the Cosmos, and consciousness itself for partnering with us in this fascinating co-creation.

Our profound thanks also to all who have walked this path before us—including the brave visionary scientists, rebel misfits, futurists, mystics, magi, storytellers, innovators, and all who stayed true to the higher dream of who we're called to become.

Future Humans communities have been spontaneously forming around the world, initiated by our readers and students who are taking this work further in the most incredible ways. Thank you so much to all of you who are catalyzing this movement and demonstrating how awesome it is to live and grow from our future human potential.

We are also most grateful to our superb publishing team for supporting our choice to publish the *Future Humans Trilogy* independently. Starting with our genius editor, Diane Nichols, for continuing to act as the fairy godmother of this trilogy, and for your unwavering support and editorial genius.

To Ariane Barnes for your marvelous narration of the audiobook versions of *The Quest of Rose* and *Return of the Avatars*, and Jordan Brown for your great audiobook editing. To Dagmar Wolff for your wonderful German translation of *The Quest of Rose,* and for all of your loving support. To Phillippe Laventure for your amazing French translation of *The Quest of Rose.*

To our wonderful team at Oxygen Publishing, including: Carolyn Flower, CEO and Founder; Steve Walters, book designer; Philip Ridgers, proofreader; and Linda Erskine.

To Patrice Offman, for your continual artistry in converging our initial illustrations into attuned masterpieces of originality. To Sam Brown, for your inspiring painting that is part of the cover artwork, which really tells the story of this book.

To Stephen Aizenstat, for being the wizard godfather of the trilogy and the *Future Humans Education* programs and for all of your essential support, as well as your amazing team at Dream Tending and their support for this work.

To Hazel Henderson and Mariana Bozesan for our enlightening and hopeful conversations, which inspired the final chapter of this book, and for your co-creative partnership in the next steps of the *Future Humans* game.

To all the many friends and colleagues who have been supporting us throughout and have gifted us with the most astonishing endorsements and valuable feedback: Deepak Chopra, Jude Currivan, Lynne McTaggart, Donna Eden, David Feinstein, Julie Krull, Bruce Lipton, Dagmar Wolff, Kristie Googin, Hege Forbech Vinje, Caroline Myss, Marianne Williamson, Claire Zammit, Diane Williams, Deborah Moldow, Justine Page, Carolyn Rivers, Jim Garrison, Anne Baring, Wouter van Noort, Ervin Laszlo, Alexander Laszlo, Rama Mani, Alexander Schieffer, Mitchell Rabin, Phil Lane Jr., Chloë Goodchild, Ralph Thurm, Ron van Es, Kees Klomp, Penny Joy, Anita Sanchez, Robynne Nelson, Tomas Björkman, Sasha Siem, Janice Hall, Shani Lehrer, Marci Shimoff, Ben Bowler. And to all of you who are not mentioned here by name, we trust you know who you are and we thank you wholeheartedly!

We also send enormous gratitude to the thousands of students we have had the honor of teaching for so many years, and to their startling insights and ideas that have added so much to our own. In addition, we would also like to extend the following personal acknowledgements:

• • •

From Anneloes

My gratitude and profound thanks to: my children, Manu and Akash, for all your wonderful inputs, questions, cuddles, and patience, and Manu for continuing to build the character of Olaf with your genius ideas that now form part of the Cosmic Compass game. To Mom and Dad, for being the arms of love during the many challenges of my unusual life, and for always believing in me.

To dearest Kurt Barnes, for all the ways you continue to support me and this work from behind the scenes, and for contributing your wisdom of the Gnostic traditions through the character Karl, the father of Rose.

To my sister, Nienke Smitsman, and her partner, Anton Busselman, for your loving support through all those years. And to everyone else who has touched my life and supported me—thank you for walking this path together.

And finally, to my ancestors and the Cosmic Avatars of our greater selves, my deepest gratitude for your trust and timeless support, and for all you've shared that now forms part of this book.

From Jean

My gratitude and profound thanks: to my Shakespearean working partner of so many years, Peggy Rubin. To Kelsey Hill, for taking care of all the office logistics and reminders. To Elizabeth Austin, for your rigorous support. To Michael Korzinski and family, for your wealth of ideas and new thinking. To Drs. Aftab Omer and Melissa Schwartz for your ingenious creation of Meridian University, where I serve as Chancellor, as well as for your support for the trilogy. To Bishop Heather Shea for our long friendship and many adventures in developing a theater and spiritual center on Broadway that helps humanity renew Herself.

To my ancestors, I continue to gather inspiration from the fey wisdom of my mother, Mary Houston (born Maria Annunciata Serafina Fiorina Todaro), and the rich, comic genius of my father, Jack Houston.

To my mentor, Margaret Mead, I remain forever grateful for your rigor and inspiration, and for not suffering fools gladly. My enormous thanks and gratitude to Serafina, my wonderful four-legged companion, for all the joy, playfulness, and wisdom you brought.

To Constance Buffalo, my business partner, whose precise mind and indigenous-spawned deep intelligence keep our enterprises going. To all of my other friends, for your many years of encouragement.

And finally, my undying love and gratitude to my late husband, Robert Masters, whose genius and encouragement was, for me, "the boat of a million years."

• • •

Our warmest thanks, finally, to you, dearest reader, for being part of the reason why we wrote this trilogy, and for joining us on the *quest of the future humans*!

About the Authors

Anneloes Smitsman

Dr. Anneloes Smitsman, Ph.D., LLM, is a futurist, systems scientist, and award-winning pioneer in human development and systems change. She is the Founder and CEO of EARTHwise Centre. Her programs, practices, and strategies are sought after around the world for actualizing our future human potential, and catalyzing the next steps in human consciousness and systemic design for thrivability. She was awarded the Visioneers Lifetime Achievement Award in May 2022, and was crowned overall African Winner in the category Human Development of the Africa's Most Respected CEOs Awards in July 2022. She holds a Master's degree in Law and Judicial Political Sciences from Leiden University, the Netherlands, and received a degree of Doctor from the Maastricht Sustainability Institute, Maastricht University, the Netherlands. Her ground-breaking Ph.D. dissertation, *Into the Heart of Systems Change*, addresses how to diagnose and transform key systemic barriers of our world crisis through its proposed *Transition Plan for a Thrivable Civilization*. Anneloes is the co-author of the *Future Humans Trilogy* with Dr. Jean Houston, and the co-editor and co-author with Dr. Alexander Laszlo of *The New Paradigm in Politics*, and author of *Love Letters from Mother Earth* and the narrated version *Messages from Mother Earth* with soundtracks by Alan Howarth, as well as many other publications. Anneloes is the lead architect of the SEEDS Constitution where she implemented her Cosmic Compass design, and serves as Steward for Hypha, SEEDS, and the EARTHwise Earth Song project. She is a member of the Evolutionary Leaders Circle of The Source of Synergy Foundation.

⊙ To connect with Anneloes Smitsman: anneloessmitsman.com

About the Authors

Jean Houston

Prof. Dr. Jean Houston, Ph.D. is a world-renowned scholar, futurist, and researcher in human capacities, social change, and systemic transformation. She is one of the principal founders of the Human Potential Movement and one of the foremost visionary thinkers and doers of our time. She is also a founder of the field of Social Artistry, "Human development in the light of social change," which has taken her work all over the world. Dr. Houston was awarded the Synergy Superstar Award 2020 by the Source of Synergy Foundation for her exemplary work inspiring us to source our highest human capacities, and received the Visioneers Heros and Heroines of Humanity Award in May 2022. Dr. Houston holds conferences, seminars, and mentoring programs with leaders and change agents worldwide. She has worked intensively in over forty cultures, lectured in over one hundred countries, and worked with major organizations such as UNICEF, UNDP, and NASA, as well as helping global state leaders, leading educational institutions, business organizations, and millions of people to enhance and deepen their own uniqueness. She is the co-author of the *Future Humans Trilogy* with Dr. Anneloes Smitsman, and has authored over thirty-six published books, and a great many unpublished books, plays, articles, and manuscripts. Dr. Houston is Chancellor of Meridian University and has served on the faculties of Hunter College, Marymount College, The New School for Social Research, and the University of California. Dr. Houston was also President of the American Association of Humanistic Psychology, and is the former Chair of the United Palace of Spiritual Arts in New York City.

To connect with Jean Houston: jeanhouston.com

FUTURE HUMANS
PUBLICATIONS & PROGRAMS

Join the Future Humans courses, masterclasses, and coaching classes with Anneloes Smitsman and Jean Houston to further explore and develop your future human potentials and powers. For latest offerings, the Future Humans Podcast, and to stay in touch, visit: **www.futurehumans.world**

Published Books in the Future Humans Trilogy Series

- Book 1—*The Quest of Rose: The Cosmic Keys of Our Future Becoming.*
- German edition of Book 1—*Die Reise der Rose: Die Kosmischen Schlüssel für unser Zukünftiges Werden.*
- Book 2—*Return of the Avatars: The Cosmic Architect Tools of Our Future Becoming.*

Recommended Courses via the Future Humans Website

- The Catalyst Course—for working with *The Quest of Rose.*
- The Future Humans Quest—for working with *Return of the Avatars.*

Other Publications by the Authors

Selected Books by Jean Houston

- The Wizard of Us: Transformational Lessons from Oz.
- The Possible Human: A Course in Enhancing Your Physical, Mental & Creative Abilities.
- Mystical Dogs: Animals as Guides to Our Inner Life.
- A Mythic Life: Learning to Live Our Greater Story.
- Jump Time: Shaping Your Future in a World of Radical Change.
- Mind Games: The Guide to Inner Space (with Robert Masters).

Selected Books by Anneloes Smitsman

- Love Letters from Mother Earth: The Promise of a New Beginning.
- Into the Heart of Systems Change (Ph.D. Dissertation).
- The New Paradigm in Politics (with Alexander Laszlo).

MORE PRAISE FOR
RETURN OF THE AVATARS

"Since the launch of the *Future Human Trilogy*, hundreds of people have been gathering from around the world to work with the powerful content, keys, tools, and practices this series offers. This has strengthened our trust in a new kind of humanity as we learn how to support each other in becoming the required people for this time, and have been developing our imaginal capacities. Our senses have opened toward becoming the 'great unity,' as seekers of the yet unknown. *Return of the Avatars* trains us further by giving us seven Cosmic Architect Tools for developing our future human powers. We now join Rose, Sophia, Li, and Olaf, wisely guided by the magus Verdandi, to discover how to confront the sleeping giants and puppet masters of our social, economic, and political divisions to stop the reckless exploitations of our planet. *Return of the Avatars* shows us how to counteract these developments, starting within oneself, by becoming receptive of capacities we did not even fathom to exist. It follows the great spiritual teachings of the Gnostic and indigenous traditions, and deepens our insights from the new paradigm research, systems change research, and quantum sciences. This book gives hope that humanity will indeed be able to turn around, and become aware and capable of bringing on a brighter future. Using this knowledge in day-to-day contexts enhances the capabilities of consciously responding to daily challenges; in interactions with our family and community, in treatment situations, in artistic expressions, and so much more. Getting in touch with our fuller potential is the greatest gift. In a time of painful separations and social rifts, learning about our fundamental unity is essential for healing ourselves, society, and the planet. This book endows you with the essential tools and abilities for becoming conscious of yourself and the nature of the Universe, returning you to our Original Home."

~ **Dr. Dagmar Wolff**, Ph.D., M.D., Pianist, Educator, Medical Doctor, Founding member of the Future Humans Course Community

"*Return of the Avatars* is an essential guidebook for a world in the midst of radical transformation. As you join the future humans on their quest, you'll find yourself thinking, feeling, acting, and creating in ways you may never have thought possible. Read this book carefully, get immersed in the powerful stories, and bring its wisdom into your life by doing the practices and applying the Cosmic Architect Tools. Enjoy the rising new intelligence it activates in your mind and soul. This spell-breaking adventure will stir awake the deep realization that you are more, far more, than you ever thought to be. You are a future human of the emerging new era; a miracle maker in becoming."

~ **Marci Shimoff**, Author, *Happy for No Reason,*
featured teacher in *The Secret*

"We as humanity are going through an unprecedented transformation—now, at this moment, and in the years to come. Not only are we waking up, but it's happening at a tremendous speed right now. Understanding a larger story in which we are a part, and above all, an understanding of that larger story that goes far beyond the visible world around us. It is the world within us that this book by Anneloes Smitsman and Jean Houston offers us. Who are we, and who are we really? To make the outer world and the inner world coincide, a deep healing is needed. Do we have to leave old, entrenched ideas about ourselves behind us? Is there an alignment needed from our past via the present to another future? This book gives us all the keys to that huge adventure. The adventure of meeting our capacity and full self, and with it, the other, because only in the other do we see ourselves, and that we are not alone in the deepest sense, serving together the three Mothers—Mother Cosmos, Mother Universe, and Mother Earth."

~ **Ron van Es**, Founder of the School for Purpose Leadership

"In their brilliant partnership Dr. Jean Houston and Dr. Anneloes Smitsman bridge the evolving frontier of science with the new understandings from the Awakening and New Spirituality movements as well as the wisdom traditions, and so much more. It's a holy union between them, in their co-authorship of the *Future Humans Trilogy*, one destined to help those on the journey of actualizing their own self-hood and participating in the advancement of a consciousness of wholeness, so needed now to address the changes we are facing and find transformative breakthrough solutions for a renaissance in new, sustainable ways of living and being on the earth."

~ **Carolyn Rivers**, Founder and Director of The Sophia Institute

"*Return of the Avatars* is a well of wisdom, integrating the insights of the new paradigm sciences with the wisdom of ancient mystics. Dr. Anneloes Smitsman and Dr. Jean Houston are astounding evolutionary leaders. Their brilliant storytelling gives an unpolished account of the need for change, with visions, hopes, and practical guidance for awakening, evolving, and upgrading how we live our lives on planet Earth. The reader is assisted in becoming the required one to co-create together a thriving and sustainable world that works for all beings. *Return of the Avatars* speaks on many levels and can profoundly transform your life by catalyzing you into becoming a future human. As soon as I moved into a mode of wonder, openness, deep listening, and receptivity, I experienced how this book responded by gently and lovingly guiding me through each chapter. Then the wisdom started to sink in, fertilize, and vibrate through my bones and tissues, moving me toward increasingly higher levels of alignment, coherence, and wholeness. As the authors remind us, 'A subtle difference in focus makes all the difference.' This book invites you to enter into a deep love for the unknown and let the transformative power of the words move you way beyond your mind—into the depths of your heart, where every inner journey begins."

~ **Dr. Hege Forbech Vinje**, Ph.D. Founder of The Forbech Vinje Academy

"*Return of the Avatars* is an enormous gift for consciously evolving our human capacities, by giving us the tools needed to go deeper within ourselves and find the path forward. It has felt like a deep homecoming to myself, stirring awake a profound innate knowing from a deep slumber. By working with this guidebook and the powerful tools and practices it offers, I feel more settled in myself now, and enhanced in my ability to navigate the challenges of this time. *Return of the Avatars* enables us to actively participate in and catalyze the needed transformation on Earth, so we may be able to thrive together and move forward on the path!"

~ **Kristie Googin**, *Future Humans* Course Community

"You can enjoy *Return of the Avatars* as a lively adventure story or you can amplify your experience by following the creative exercises and visualizations to access the Cosmic Architect Tools that will bring out the Future Human inside of you. This novel is a juicy, entertaining manual for transformation—of ourselves and our world. May the *Future Humans Trilogy* illumine minds and warm hearts across an awakening humanity!"

~ **Rev. Deborah Moldow**, Founder of Garden of Light, Director of the Evolutionary Leaders Circle of The Source of Synergy Foundation

"*The Future Humans Trilogy* is based on the fundamental understanding that at the core and foundation of all cultures of our human family are universal archetypes guiding the dynamic unfolding of our evolutionary development. While our cultural garments may appear different, at the heart of hearts exists the fundamental spiritual reality and understanding of the prior unity and Oneness of our human family and all Life. From this spiritual realization, it becomes crystal clear that 'the Hurt of One is the Hurt of All,' and 'the Healing and Restoration of One is the Healing and Restoration of All.' *Return of the Avatars*, book 2 of the trilogy, prepares us for our spiritual adulthood by helping us remember how despite our culturally diverse pathways—individually and collectively, and from infancy to the dynamic awakening of our spiritual adulthood—life moves us to Oneness and unitary consciousness. *Return of the Avatars* empowers us to walk the mystical path with practical feet, as the seeker is drawn deeper and deeper into the understanding of our collective consciousness, as well as how to address our collective shadow. With a spiritual hunger for the conclusion of what is yet to unfold in book 3, this is a trilogy not to be missed. Inviting us to experience and understand what it means that each of us is 'a Sovereignty, Ancient, Imperishable, and Everlasting!'"

> ~ **Hereditary Chief Phil Lane Jr.**, Ihanktonwan and Chickasaw Nations, Union of the Condor, Quetzal, and Eagle, Founder of Four Worlds International Institute

"In the world of today something more and different than mere willpower and the familiar is being asked of each of us. Cast in breathtaking storytelling, *Return of the Avatars* offers teachings, practices, and tools that open and awaken the wisdom of your higher heart. The journey continues as you follow Rose and her young nephew Olaf through the cultural trance to the hidden place of the Cosmic reset button. This book is a thrilling ride, a deeply meaningful and generative read."

> ~ **Dr. Stephen Aizenstat**, Ph.D. Founder of Pacifica Graduate Institute, The Academy of Imaginal Arts and Sciences, and Dream Tending

"*Return of the Avatars* is where the *Future Humans Trilogy* creates traction toward transformation. It offers practical steps all of us can take that empower our capacity to navigate an increasingly dark world and thrive. The Cosmic Architect Practices and transformational tools are the yellow brick road to the future we all seek for our children unto the seventh generation."

> ~ **Dr. Jim Garrison**, Ph.D. Founder & President of Ubiquity University

"DELICIOUS! Exactly the evolutionary food we now need, cooked to the finest! *Return of the Avatars* provides a profound initiation journey, magnificently crafted for this moment of planetary awakening—deep and accessible, scientific and playful, grounded and imaginative, courageous and irresistible. A Jump-Time book, oozing with the 'lure of becoming' that can propel us into the era of the Future Human. A transformative—and beautifully transgenerational—guide to the New Story that we cannot afford to miss."

~ **Prof. Dr. Alexander Schieffer**, Ph.D. Co-Founder of Home for Humanity, Adjunct Professor, Da Vinci Institute, South Africa

"Be ready for an upgrade! *Return of the Avatars* is much more than a book, it's a sacred initiation that takes us by the hand and leads us through a portal into the world of the Avatars where we can fully access and activate the multidimensional nature of our Cosmic selves and call into being a heart-based future powered by love. This book is a gift to be shared with anyone who deeply loves our Earth and all of the precious beings that call it home."

~ **Diane Williams**, Founder of The Source of Synergy Foundation

"A book written from the cosmic heart—deeply engaging our own heart, as well as our mind. It informs, enlightens, and transforms with a light touch, and more than a touch of magic, to delight us as we journey through it, discovering treasures of insight as we go."

~ **Dr. Anne Baring**, Ph.D. Author, *The Dream of the Cosmos: A Quest for the Soul*

"We need to gather all our forces to meet the challenges that now face us, and will face us in the next future. These forces include that of imagination—in fiction as well as in the interpretation of non-fiction. The authors of this book provide essential tools and ideas to help us gather these forces. Their book is one to savor and to treasure, both for the reading pleasure it offers and for the essential tools it places at the disposal of our rational intellect, as well as of our inherent, and today largely neglected, power of imagination."

~ **Dr. Ervin Laszlo**, Ph.D. Author, *The Upshift: Responsible Living on Planet Earth*, Founder & President of The Laszlo Institute of New Paradigm Research